# Residential Real Estate Transactions

## FOURTH EDITION

**JoAnn Kurtz**

**Joan Emmans**

**Arlene Blatt**

**Judith M. Wolf**

emond ▪ Toronto, Canada ▪ 2016

Emond Montgomery Publications Limited
60 Shaftesbury Avenue
Toronto ON  M4T 1A3
http://www.emond.ca/highered

Printed in Canada.

Emond Montgomery Publications has no responsibility for the persistence or accuracy of URLs for external or third-party Internet websites referred to in this publication, and does not guarantee that any content on such websites is, or will remain, accurate or appropriate.

We acknowledge the financial support of the Government of Canada. *Nous reconnaissons l'appui financier du gouvernement du Canada.*  Canadä

Vice-president, publishing: Anthony Rezek
Acquisitions editor: Lindsay Sutherland
Managing editor, development: Kelly Dickson
Developmental editors: Jamie Bush, David Handelsman
Director, editorial and production: Jim Lyons
Production editor and coordinator: Laura Bast

Copy editor: David Handelsman
Proofreader: Lila Campbell
Typesetters: Tara Wells, Shani Sohn
Indexer: Michael Bunn
Cover design: Tara Wells
Cover image: alexmisu/Shutterstock

**Library and Archives Canada Cataloguing in Publication**

Kurtz, JoAnn, 1951-, author
    Residential real estate transactions / JoAnn Kurtz, Joan Emmans, Arlene Blatt, Judith M. Wolf. — Fourth edition.

Includes index.
ISBN 978-1-55239-670-4 (paperback)

    1. Vendors and purchasers—Ontario—Textbooks.    I. Emmans, Joan, author    II. Blatt, Arlene, author    III. Wolf, Judith M., 1962-, author    IV. Title.

KEO271.K87 2016        346.71304'36        C2015-906306-X
KF665.K87 2016

*To Ely, Max, Jacob, and Danny. —JK*

*To Andrew, Karyn, Kaitryn, and Rudy. —JE*

*To Jeffrey, Jordan, and Matthew. —AB*

*To my Dad—my hero, my greatest supporter,
and my forever inspiration. —JW*

# Contents

## PART I

## INTRODUCTION

### 1 Overview of the Residential Real Estate Transaction

### 2 The Role of the Law Clerk

## PART II

## OVERVIEW OF REAL ESTATE LAW

### 3 Estates and Interests in Land

### 4 Legal Descriptions

# 8 Liens Against Land

# 9 Government Controls over the Use and Subdivision of Land

# 10 Legal Status of the Owner

# 11 Condominiums

## 12 Residential Rental Properties

## 13 Environmental Issues

## 14 Title Searching

# PART III

# THE STANDARD RESIDENTIAL REAL ESTATE TRANSACTION

## 15 Opening and Organizing a Real Estate File

## 16 Reviewing the Agreement of Purchase and Sale

## 17 Title Insurance

## 18 Preliminary Matters

## 19 Requisitions: An Overview

## 23 Buyer's Post-Closing Procedure

## 24 Acting for the Seller

## PART IV
# OTHER RESIDENTIAL REAL ESTATE TRANSACTIONS

## 25 Purchase of a New Home

# List of Figures

# Preface

Residential real estate purchases and sales form a big part of the business of many law firms. Real estate is an area of practice in which lawyers rely heavily on the help of law clerks, legal assistants, and legal secretaries. This book begins by giving students and law clerks an overview of the legal concepts and principles of residential real estate law. It then proceeds to take them step by step through a standard residential real estate transaction. Included are the forms and precedents that they need to perform the routine tasks involved in the purchase and sale of a residential property.

The book ends with discussions about more complex transactions—namely, the purchase of a new home, a condominium, a rural property, or a property being sold under power of sale.

The book deals primarily with the procedures to be followed by a law clerk working for a law firm that is acting for the buyer, although there is a chapter that summarizes the real estate transaction from the perspective of a law firm acting for the seller (Chapter 24) and another chapter that summarizes the real estate transaction from the perspective of the law firm acting for the mortgagee (Chapter 29).

The procedures and precedents provided in this book are meant to be a guide only. Every lawyer or law firm has a certain way of doing things. As a law clerk, you must always follow your firm's practices and procedures.

The fourth edition improves upon the third in several significant respects. The entire text has been revised to reflect the major changes that Ontario's land registration system has recently undergone. We have added a discussion of the electronic registration system and illustrate how to use real estate software to create, share, and submit title documents for registration; to search for property-related information; and to generate legal correspondence and documents required in a standard purchase and sale transaction.

Updated screenshots and completed precedents are included in abundance to help students navigate the practice and procedure in a routine purchase and sale transaction (see the List of Figures on page xiii).

Following is a chapter-by-chapter account of the text's contents and new features

## Chapter 1: Overview of the Residential Real Estate Transaction
This chapter describes the various stages of a standard real estate transaction. Starting with the offer to purchase a particular property, the chapter takes the reader through all the necessary stages up to and including post-closing requirements, and identifies the purpose of each stage.

## Chapter 2: The Role of the Law Clerk
This chapter examines the professional obligations of law clerks working on a real estate transaction. In addition to explaining errors and omissions considerations, we

discuss the Law Society of Upper Canada's *Rules of Professional Conduct* and By-Laws that are relevant to the role of law clerks assisting on a real estate file.

### Chapter 3: Estates and Interests in Land

This chapter explains the meaning of real property and discusses the principles underlying land ownership, including how co-owners of land hold title. We describe the various estates in land and examine other interests in land.

### Chapter 4: Legal Descriptions

This chapter explains how land in Ontario was originally divided and teaches the reader how to identify and describe land using the various types of legal descriptions. We have added a detailed chart that provides an explanation, an example, and a clear illustration of each type of legal description.

### Chapter 5: Land Registration Systems

This chapter explains the concept of land registration and discusses the features of Ontario's current land registration system. It describes the key aspects of the Province of Ontario Land Registration Information System (POLARIS) and includes a discussion of electronic land registration.

### Chapter 6: Charges/Mortgages

This chapter discusses basic mortgage concepts and terminology. It describes the different types of mortgages and explains how mortgages are created, using clear illustrations and examples. The chapter includes a discussion of the rights and obligations of both the mortgagor and mortgagee, and the default remedies available to a mortgagee when the mortgagor breaches an obligation contained in the charge.

### Chapter 7: Electronic Registration and Teraview

This chapter explains the electronic registration system that is currently used in Ontario. It describes how to create a file, search title, and prepare electronic documents. The chapter discusses the requirement for digital signatures, and how to message documents between law firms.

### Chapter 8: Liens Against Land

This chapter defines a lien and explains how a lien against real property is created pursuant to various statutes. It contains a detailed discussion of construction liens and how those liens are created, registered, and discharged. The chapter concludes by explaining the importance of title searching in order to ensure that no liens are registered against real property that is being purchased.

### Chapter 9: Government Controls over the Use and Subdivision of Land

This chapter explains the various controls by the government over the use of land, including zoning by-laws and the need for building permits. It further describes the subdivision control provisions of the *Planning Act* and the importance of conducting an adjoining land search whenever it is relevant.

## Chapter 10: Legal Status of the Owner

This chapter examines various issues with respect to the legal status of the owner of real property. These issues include age and spousal status of an individual owner, what happens when an owner dies, as well as the need for a corporation to be in good standing in order to convey an interest in land.

## Chapter 11: Condominiums

This chapter expands the previous edition's discussion of condominiums. In addition to explaining how a condominium is created, the operation of the condominium corporation, and the aspects of condominium ownership, we have added a discussion of the common-elements condominium.

## Chapter 12: Residential Rental Properties

This chapter provides an overview of residential tenancy law. It explains how residential tenancies are created, and discusses the rights and responsibilities of residential landlords and tenants, including rules about rent and rent increases. It describes how residential tenancies are terminated, by both the landlord and the tenant. The chapter ends with a discussion of the implications for the buyer of a residential rental complex.

## Chapter 13: Environmental Issues

This chapter describes types of environmental issues that might arise in a real estate transaction, and how those issues are dealt with in a real estate transaction. It also explains what steps a buyer should take in order to ensure that the property being purchased is not contaminated.

## Chapter 14: Title Searching

This chapter explains how to conduct a title search in both the Registry and the Land Titles systems. It illustrates the process of title searching in both systems as well as other searches that are relevant to searches in both systems. The chapter includes a sample of both a Registry search and a Land Titles search.

## Chapter 15: Opening and Organizing a Real Estate File

This chapter describes how to open and organize a real estate file, including the creation of a docket in the electronic system. It explains the importance of diarizing various dates in a transaction, as well as the importance of having a checklist to ensure that all steps in a real estate transaction are completed.

## Chapter 16: Reviewing the Agreement of Purchase and Sale

This chapter reviews the agreement of purchase and sale from the perspective of a law clerk who has received a fully executed agreement. It contains a clause-by-clause examination of the standard form of agreement and sale, and discusses particular items of importance, together with the steps a law clerk should take as he or she goes through the agreement.

### Chapter 17: Title Insurance

This chapter discusses the difference between a lawyer's title opinion and title insurance, and explains why title insurance is important. It also discusses what title insurance covers and what is exempt, a lawyer's duty regarding title insurance advice to a client, and the implications of title insurance on buying property.

### Chapter 18: Preliminary Matters

This chapter describes the tasks a law clerk must perform after opening the file and reviewing the agreement of purchase in order to obtain the information needed before the transaction can close, including the information the law clerk must get from the client before preparing the documents required for a real estate purchase, and preliminary letters a law clerk must write. The chapter also discusses the effect that title insurance has on these preliminary steps.

### Chapter 19: Requisitions: An Overview

This chapter deals with the steps a law clerk must take arising from the search of title and the responses to preliminary letters discussed in Chapter 18. The chapter covers the importance of requisitions in a real estate transaction, the different categories of requisitions, and how to determine what requisitions to make. It also discusses the various sources of requisitions, including the title search, and explains how to review a title search to determine what requisitions to make.

### Chapter 20: The Requisition Letter

This chapter examines the standard form of requisition letter and provides examples of specific requisitions for both a Registry system property and a Land Titles property. The chapter explains how to draft a requisition letter, including both the standard requisitions that apply to all purchase transactions, and the specific requisitions arising from a title search and the responses to the preliminary letters discussed in Chapter 18.

### Chapter 21: Document Preparation

This chapter deals with the documents that will be required for the closing by both the buyer's lawyer and the seller's lawyer. The chapter explains the reasons why each document is necessary and how to prepare the documents. The chapter also examines the differences between Land Titles (electronic) documents and Registry (paper) documents. The chapter includes an in-depth discussion of the preparation of the statement of adjustments, including how to calculate the entries in a statement of adjustments.

### Chapter 22: Closing the Transaction

This chapter deals with the closing of the transaction from the perspective of both the buyer and the seller. The chapter covers both preparation for the closing and the closing itself. The chapter includes a discussion of the taxes payable on closing, as well as the calculation of those taxes. The steps in both Registry system closings and electronic closings are discussed.

### Chapter 23: Buyer's Post-Closing Procedure

This chapter covers the steps that a law clerk must take after a purchase transaction has closed, before the file can be closed. It includes a discussion of reporting letters for properties with and without title insurance, and provides a sample for the transaction used in prior chapters. It also provides a sample trust ledger statement.

### Chapter 24: Acting for the Seller

This chapter discusses a transaction from the seller's viewpoint. It outlines the steps that a law clerk must take on a sale; what information is required from the seller; how a law clerk for the seller's lawyer must prepare for closing; and what the law clerk must do after the transaction closes. It includes a sample reporting letter for the seller in the transaction used in prior chapters.

### Chapter 25: Purchase of a New Home

This chapter discusses how the purchase of a new home differs from the purchase of a resale home. It provides information about the warranties that are available for new homes, and the obligations that a builder owes to a buyer if construction of the home is delayed. It also discusses additional adjustments that may be found in the statement of adjustments for the purchase of a new home.

### Chapter 26: Purchase of a Condominium

This chapter provides information about the purchase of a resale condominium, and how it differs from the purchase of other resale residential property. It also discusses the purchase of a new condominium, and outlines how it differs from the purchase of a resale condominium, including the two-stage closing.

### Chapter 27: Purchase of a Rural Property

This chapter discusses the additional issues that may arise in the purchase of a rural property (that would not occur in the purchase of an urban property). These include water supply and sewage, access to the property, issues unique to waterfront properties, and rural zoning.

### Chapter 28: Purchase of a Property
### Under Power of Sale

This chapter provides information about buying property when the owner of the property has defaulted under the terms of his or her mortgage, and the mortgagee is selling under power of sale. It includes samples of the documents required. New to this edition are instructions for creating the documents with Teraview software, and a sample of a Teraview-generated transfer.

### Chapter 29: Acting for the Mortgagee

This chapter discusses how to prepare a mortgage in both the Land Titles and Registry systems. It includes information on the different requirements for new mortgages, and mortgages to refinance a property (both when the law firm acted for the owner and when the firm did not act for the owner, when the property was purchased). It also discusses what amounts the mortgagee may deduct from the money that will be advanced to the client under the mortgage.

## Acknowledgments

We would like to thank the following people for their help in updating the text: Sarah Cook of Collingwood, and Ken Goodbrand of Stouffville, who answered our questions.

Thank you also to the instructors who reviewed the text: Jacqueline Asselin, Algonquin College; Richard Desrocher, George Brown College; Kirk Rintoul, Humber College; and Shane Ellis, Georgian College.

# About the Authors

**JoAnn Kurtz** carried on a general practice with an emphasis on family law and real estate before joining Seneca College, where she is the program coordinator for the Law Clerk Diploma program of the School of Legal and Public Administration. She has taught various topics, including contract law, family law, residential tenancy law, and advocacy, and is the author or co-author of many general interest and academic texts. She attended New York University and holds a JD from Osgoode Hall Law School.

**Joan Emmans** is a retired college professor and lawyer. Prior to retirement, she taught in the School of Legal and Public Administration at Seneca College—mainly in the areas of real estate and family law. She obtained her law degree from Queen's University. A member of the Law Society of Upper Canada, she practised law for 12 years, and taught real estate law to real estate agents for the Ontario Real Estate Association, prior to joining the faculty at Seneca. As well as co-authoring *Residential Real Estate Transactions*, she contributed a chapter on real estate law to an introductory legal textbook.

**Arlene Blatt** is a full-time professor in the School of Legal and Public Administration at Seneca College and teaches a variety of legal subjects to paralegal and law clerk students. She obtained her JD from Osgoode Hall Law School and is a member of the Ontario Bar. She has co-authored four Emond publications: *Advocacy for Paralegals*, *Residential Real Estate Transactions*, *Legal Entities and Relationships*, and *Legal Research: Step by Step*. She has also contributed a chapter on residential landlord and tenant law to an introductory legal textbook. Her areas of academic interest include landlord and tenant law, real estate law, and legal research.

**Judith M. Wolf** is a professor at Seneca College in the School of Legal and Public Administration. She teaches a variety of courses, including real estate law, employment law, debtor–creditor law, ethics, and legal entities. As a sole practitioner since 1990, she acts as counsel to financial institutions and private investors in all areas of mortgage work and mortgage remedy work and acts on behalf of individuals with respect to the purchase, sale, and refinancing of property. She is the author of *A Practical Guide to Mortgage Remedies in Ontario* and co-author of *Legal Entities and Relationships*. She has also contributed a chapter on real estate law to an introductory legal textbook. She has her JD from Osgoode Hall Law School.

# PART I

# Introduction

# Overview of the Residential Real Estate Transaction

1

## LEARNING OUTCOMES

After reading this chapter, you will understand:

- The stages of a residential real estate transaction

- How the agreement of purchase and sale affects the residential real estate transaction

- What a survey is and why it is important when you are purchasing residential real property

- What searches are required to ensure that good title is delivered to a buyer of residential real property

- How a residential real estate transaction is completed

# Introduction

A legal professional's responsibilities in a residential real estate purchase are to

- open and organize a file;
- review the agreement of purchase and sale;
- review the plan of survey of the property (if one is available);
- search the title to the property;
- conduct other relevant searches, known as off-title searches;
- arrange to have the client set up new utility accounts;
- discuss with the client the advantages of obtaining title insurance;
- advise the client on how to take title to the property;
- prepare or review all of the necessary documents;
- prepare for the closing, including the execution of documents by the client;
- close the transaction and register the documents;
- notify the realty tax department of the change in ownership; and
- provide the client with a reporting letter and opinion as to title or title insurance.

Some of these tasks are performed by a law clerk; others may be done only by a lawyer. These tasks have changed a great deal in recent years because the province of Ontario has essentially completed the process of automating its land registration system. At this time, the title records of 99.9% of all properties in the province are stored electronically in databases that are part of the Province of Ontario Land Registration Information System (POLARIS). The conversion from a paper system to the electronic one, which started back in 1985, has been implemented gradually across the province. Law firms are able to access POLARIS online from their office computers, which enables legal professionals to conduct searches and register documents by using software known as "Teraview."

Before learning about these tasks—the steps and procedures, within a residential real estate transaction, for which a legal professional is specifically responsible—you must understand the general stages of the transaction and the purpose of each stage.

## The Stages of a Real Estate Transaction

Let's take a closer look at the stages of a real estate transaction, which comprises

- the offer;
- the agreement of purchase and sale;
- the survey;
- the title search;
- other searches, considerations, and inquiries;

- obtaining title insurance;
- taking title;
- preparing and reviewing the documents;
- preparing for closing;
- the closing; and
- meeting the post-closing requirements.

## The Offer

A real estate purchase starts with an **offer**—usually an offer by the buyer to purchase a particular property. A lawyer should review an offer to purchase before the buyer signs it, but usually this doesn't happen. Instead, the offer is usually prepared by a real estate agent, signed by the buyer as the **offeror**, and presented by the agent to the seller as the **offeree**. The standard form of offer is meant to allow the offeree to accept the offer by signing it. Instead of accepting the offer, the offeree may reject it or "sign it back"—that is, amend it in some way and present it back to the original offeror as a **counteroffer**. If there is a **sign-back**, the original offeror may accept it, reject it, or sign it back to the offeree in turn. Once the offer is accepted, it becomes a contract that is referred to as the **agreement of purchase and sale**.

## The Agreement of Purchase and Sale

The work of the law firm usually starts when it receives a copy of the signed agreement of purchase and sale.

The parties to the agreement of purchase and sale are the seller and the buyer. The seller agrees to transfer title to the property to the buyer on the **closing date** in return for the payment of a specified amount. The buyer agrees to accept title and to pay that sum of money. The agreement sets out the terms on which and the manner in which title is to be transferred. *The agreement does not transfer title.*

The residential real estate transaction covers the time from the **execution** or signing of the agreement of purchase and sale to, and in fact beyond, the actual transfer of title on closing. During this time, it is the role of the buyer's lawyer to make sure that the title transferred on the closing date is exactly the same as the title the seller promised to deliver. It is the role of the seller's lawyer to make sure that the seller is in a position to transfer title.

The buyer's lawyer makes sure that proper title is transferred by conducting a number of searches and by making various inquiries. The seller's lawyer must anticipate and respond to questions raised by the buyer's lawyer and clear up, where possible, any matters that are contrary to the agreement of purchase and sale.

## The Survey

When clients buy "a house," what they are actually buying is the land and the buildings that happen to be located on it. It is therefore important to make sure that

**offer**
proposal from one person to another that, when accepted, becomes a contract

**offeror**
person who makes an offer

**offeree**
person to whom an offer is made

**counteroffer**
offer tendered by the original offeree as an alternative to the original offer; also known as a sign-back

**sign-back**
offer whereby the original offeree changes some of the terms in the original offer, initials the changes, and then submits it to the original offeror

**agreement of purchase and sale**
contract created once an offer of purchase and sale has been accepted

**closing date**
day on which a real estate transaction is completed and title is transferred

**execution**
signing of a document; also a short name for a writ of execution or a writ of seizure and sale

- the house and other structures are located wholly within the property lines of the land being purchased;
- neighbours' buildings are not located on the land;
- the parcel of land is as big as the client has been led to believe;
- any fences are located on the lot lines; and
- the size and location of the house and other buildings satisfy zoning requirements.

**plan of survey**
schematic sketch showing the boundaries of a property and the location of all fences, structures, and rights of way

You can be sure of these matters only if a **plan of survey** exists for the property being purchased. A plan of survey is prepared by an Ontario land surveyor and is based on a physical examination of the property. That is, the surveyor examines the property and prepares a schematic sketch showing its boundaries and the location of fences, structures, and rights of way.

Often, no up-to-date plan of survey is available, because earlier surveys have been lost or become obsolete. However, title insurance (discussed in detail in Chapter 17) will usually protect the buyer against problems that the plan of survey might have revealed.

## The Title Search

**encumbrances**
charges, claims, liens, or liabilities attached to a property

The agreement of purchase and sale usually states that the property's title is to be transferred to the buyer free of **encumbrances** except those specified in the agreement. One such exception might be a mortgage that the buyer has agreed to assume.

It is up to the buyer's lawyer to satisfy himself or herself that the title to the property delivered on closing is the title that was promised to the buyer. The buyer's lawyer will search the title to the property to confirm that the seller is the owner of the land and to identify any encumbrances against the property. If the search of title reveals any encumbrances that are not supposed to be there, the buyer's lawyer will require the seller's lawyer to correct these title defects by the time of closing. For example, if there is a mortgage registered on title that the buyer has not agreed to assume, the buyer's lawyer will require the seller's lawyer to have the mortgage *discharged* (in other words, paid off and removed from title). If there are any title problems that the seller cannot clear up, the buyer may be entitled to end the deal and get his or her **deposit** back.

**deposit**
part of the purchase price prepaid when the contract is entered into and applied against the purchase price

The seller's lawyer must make sure that title to the property conforms to the agreement. If it does not, it is the lawyer's job to "fix" the title by the time of closing. For example, the lawyer may have to arrange to discharge any outstanding mortgage that the buyer did not agree to assume.

## Other Searches and Inquiries

A number of other matters that affect title to the land are dealt with in the agreement of purchase and sale and must be confirmed through various searches and inquiries.

These are known as off-title searches, and the extent to which they are required depends on whether or not title insurance is being obtained.

### Building and Zoning Considerations

Is the property zoned to allow the buyer's intended use? Do the size and location of the buildings on the property conform with relevant bylaws? Are there outstanding work orders against the property? You must contact the municipal building and zoning departments for the answers to these questions, which can be answered fully only if you provide these departments with a copy of the survey. If there is no survey to provide, title insurance will protect the buyer against potential building and zoning problems.

### Public Utility Accounts

Certain unpaid utility accounts, such as water, can be added to the municipal tax bill and become a lien on the land. Therefore, you must contact any public utilities provided by the municipality to find out the status of the accounts. The seller must pay any outstanding balances by closing. These utility searches will probably not be required if the buyer is obtaining title insurance.

### Realty Taxes

Realty tax arrears also constitute a lien on the land. Accordingly, you must contact the municipality to ensure that the seller has paid all taxes owing up to the closing date. You do this by requesting a tax certificate from the municipality. Again, if title insurance is being obtained, a tax certificate may not be necessary.

### Writs of Execution

You must contact the sheriff of the relevant judicial district to ensure that there are no outstanding writs of execution, also called writs of seizure and sale (outstanding judgments). Such writs constitute a lien against the land.

### Other Inquiries

Depending on the nature of the property, you may have to make additional inquiries of municipal, provincial, or federal government departments. For example, if the property is rural, you will need to inquire about whether the well water and the septic system meet government standards.

### Mortgages

In most real estate transactions, the buyer will arrange a charge or mortgage in order to pay for the property. Because the mortgagee (lender) is receiving an interest in the land, the mortgagee (just like the buyer) must be sure that the title to the property is good. The mortgagee will need a lawyer to check the title and to prepare the mortgage documents. The mortgagor (borrower) pays the mortgagee's legal fees. In order to keep the fees as low as possible, the mortgagee will usually agree to use the mortgagor's (the buyer's) lawyer to do the work. As a result, when your firm is acting for a buyer, you will often be doing the legal work for the mortgagee too.

The interests of the mortgagee and the buyer are similar. As a result, much, although not all, of the work that you will be doing for the mortgagee will also be for the buyer.

Mortgages are discussed in more detail in Chapter 6.

## Title Insurance

In Ontario, in recent years, title insurance has become an increasingly popular option for buyers of property and for the lawyers representing them. A buyer may purchase title insurance for the property instead of relying on a lawyer's opinion that the buyer has good title to the property. Without a title insurance policy, it is up to the lawyer to ensure that there are no problems with the title, and he or she will do so by conducting searches and making letter inquiries, all of which cost money— sometimes a significant amount.

Under a title insurance policy, the insurer "insures over" certain problems that might arise on title. Title insurers assume the risk of some of the problems that searches or letters of inquiry might disclose, thus saving the buyer the cost of the searches. Some policies protect the buyers from problems that an up-to-date survey might disclose, such as an encroachment by a neighbouring property. A buyer may save several hundred or even several thousand dollars by not having to pay for a new survey. Title insurance also protects a buyer against post-closing events, such as a fraudulent mortgage being placed on the property.

Every title insurance policy has exceptions to its coverage and specific requirements that the lawyer acting for the buyer must meet. It is up to the lawyer to discuss with the client whether he or she wishes to purchase title insurance and what policies are available. Under rule 6.1-6.1 of chapter 6 of the *Rules of Professional Conduct* governing lawyers (see Chapter 2, The Role of the Law Clerk), this task cannot be delegated to a law clerk.

## Taking Title

The lawyer will also talk to the client about how ownership of the property will be taken—whether in one name alone or with another person, either as tenants in common or as joint tenants. Again, this is something only a lawyer should do. Taking title is discussed in Chapter 3.

## Document Preparation and Review

**statement of adjustments**
statement that outlines the various credits and debits against the purchase price and specifies the exact amount to be paid on closing

The seller's lawyer prepares the transfer, which the buyer's lawyer reviews before closing. The seller's lawyer also prepares a **statement of adjustments**. This statement determines the exact amount to be paid on closing, and the lawyer prepares it by calculating various credits and debits against the purchase price as set out in the agreement of purchase and sale. Adjustments are made for expenses such as taxes, utilities, and mortgage payments that the seller paid in advance. If the seller has paid more than his or her share of the expense, the buyer will have to compensate the seller for that overpayment. If the seller has not paid enough, the unpaid portion will be subtracted from the purchase price on the grounds that the buyer will ultimately have to pay the expense.

For example, suppose a purchase is closing on September 15 and the seller has paid the realty taxes for the entire year. The seller is responsible for the payment of taxes only until the date of closing. Taxes will therefore be prorated to the date of closing, and the buyer, in addition to the purchase price, will have to reimburse the seller for that overpayment.

Although the seller's lawyer prepares the statement of adjustments, the buyer's lawyer reviews it. You must have the information required to verify all amounts that appear. You must also know how to calculate the various adjustments.

In addition to the transfer and statement of adjustments, other documents must be prepared in order to close the deal. These documents include directions, undertakings, supplementary agreements, declarations of possession, and affidavits.

## Preparation for Closing

In preparation for closing, some documents must be signed by the buyer and others by the seller. Conveyancing documents that are registered electronically are not actually signed by the parties. Instead, the parties sign an acknowledgment and direction, authorizing their respective lawyers to sign and release the documents electronically on their behalf using e-reg™. The lawyers must explain to their respective clients the conveyancing documents that are covered by the acknowledgment and direction, before having the clients sign the form. E-reg and the electronic signing process are explained in detail in Chapter 7.

Pursuant to rule 6.1-6.2, lawyers assume complete professional responsibility for documents signed electronically. They have an obligation both to ensure that documents registered electronically are completed properly and to certify that fact by signing for "completeness" (to be discussed in more detail in Chapter 7). A law clerk cannot sign for completeness.

The seller's lawyer will (1) calculate how much money is required to complete the transaction (the **balance due on closing**), (2) decide to whom the money should be paid, and (3) give that information to the buyer's lawyer. The buyer's lawyer will tell the buyer how much money is needed in order to close. The buyer's lawyer will receive the closing funds from the buyer and any lenders involved, and ensure that they are payable as the seller directs. Both lawyers must finalize arrangements for the actual closing of the transaction.

## The Closing

The lawyers do not physically meet for electronic closings. Rather, they follow an **escrow closing** procedure set out in the **document registration agreement (DRA)**, which the lawyers sign prior to the closing. They courier to each other any materials

**balance due on closing**
exact amount the buyer pays to the seller when the real estate deal closes

**escrow closing**
exchange and holding of documents, keys, and money by the lawyers pending registration of the electronic documents

**document registration agreement (DRA)**
agreement entered into by the lawyers for the parties in a purchase and sale transaction that deals with the procedures for electronic registration and the escrow closing arrangement

required for closing, such as documents, keys, and money. When the seller's lawyer is satisfied that he or she has received all that is required, he or she releases, through Teraview, the transfer for registration. When the buyer's lawyer is satisfied that he or she has received all that is required, he or she signs in to Teraview, checks to make sure that title to the property has not changed since the title search was done (known as a **subsearch**), and then registers the transfer and mortgage, if any.

If the closing is not done electronically, the lawyers for the parties (or their agents) meet, usually at the appropriate land registry office. At that time, the seller's lawyer gives a key and all the necessary documents, including the transfer, to the buyer's lawyer. The buyer's lawyer gives the seller's lawyer the closing funds. The buyer's lawyer does a subsearch of title to make sure that the state of the title has not changed since the search of title was completed. If satisfied that there have been no changes, the buyer's lawyer registers the transfer/deed of land and mortgage, if any.

**subsearch**
brief examination of title records, undertaken on closing, that covers the period from the date of the title search up to the date of closing, to make sure that nothing has been registered on title since the title search was done

## Post-Closing Requirements

After the closing, the lawyers notify the relevant offices, such as the municipal assessment department, of the change in title. The seller's lawyer pays any outstanding real estate commission and pays off any liens, expenses, or mortgages that still need to be discharged. The balance of the proceeds will be paid to the seller. Both lawyers must follow up on any undertakings given on closing, prepare reporting letters to their clients, and submit their statements of account.

## KEY TERMS

agreement of purchase and sale, 5

balance due on closing, 9

closing date, 5

counteroffer, 5

deposit, 6

document registration agreement (DRA), 9

encumbrances, 6

escrow closing, 9

execution, 5

offer, 5

offeree, 5

offeror, 5

plan of survey, 6

sign-back, 5

statement of adjustments, 8

subsearch, 10

## REFERENCES

Law Society of Upper Canada, *Rules of Professional Conduct* (Toronto: LSUC, 2000), online: <http://www.lsuc.on.ca/WorkArea/DownloadAsset.aspx?id=2147486159>.

## REVIEW QUESTIONS

1. How does a real estate purchase start?

2. Who are the parties to the agreement of purchase and sale?

3. What do the parties to the agreement of purchase and sale agree to do?

4. Does the agreement of purchase and sale transfer title?

5. What is the role of the buyer's lawyer in a residential real estate transaction?

6. What is the role of the seller's lawyer?

7. How can a buyer of real property confirm the boundaries of the property and the location of fences, structures, and rights of way, if any?

8. Why does the buyer's lawyer search the title to the property?

9. What are some of the other searches or inquiries that the buyer's lawyer might conduct?

10. How does title insurance save a buyer money?

11. What is a statement of adjustments, and who prepares it?

12. What is the procedure for an electronic closing?

# The Role of the Law Clerk

# 2

## LEARNING OUTCOMES

After reading this chapter, you will understand:

- What errors and omissions insurance is and why it is necessary in a real estate transaction

- How the Law Society regulates the conduct of lawyers and law clerks in a real estate transaction

- What the confidentiality obligations of lawyers and law clerks are in a real estate transaction

- Which tasks lawyers may assign to a law clerk in a real estate transaction

- What constitutes conflict of interest in a real estate transaction

# Introduction

In the previous chapter, you learned the various stages of a real estate transaction. Now, let's look at your role—the law clerk's role—in this process. You are expected to know the routine procedures in a real estate transaction. If a routine question arises in the course of the file, you should know the answer or be able to find it. At the same time, if anything out of the ordinary arises, you must notify the lawyer handling the file.

Your job will include opening and organizing a real estate file. All files have critical deadlines, such as the requisition date and the closing date, and you must be able to determine what those deadlines are and to make sure you meet them. The law firm will expect you to obtain routine documents from third parties and to extract the information you need from these documents.

Certain standard elements and principles apply to all real estate transactions, and you are expected to be familiar with them. At the same time, each law firm or individual lawyer will have a certain way of doing things. Therefore, in addition to knowing the standard procedures, you must know the procedures and forms used by the firm you work for. For example, many law firms use a software program called Conveyancer, while other firms use different software or even, in some cases, their own precedents instead of software.

# Errors and Omissions Considerations

All lawyers have errors and omissions insurance to protect themselves and their clients in case they are negligent in performing their clients' work. This insurance coverage is required by the **Law Society of Upper Canada (LSUC)**, the professional body that governs lawyers in Ontario, and it is provided by the **Lawyers' Professional Indemnity Company (LAWPRO)**.

When you work as a law clerk, the law firm is responsible for all the tasks that you perform. If you make a mistake that results in a loss to the client, the law firm is responsible to the client for that loss, and the firm's errors and omissions insurance will probably cover any claim. Despite this coverage, lawyers are still concerned about mistakes and negligence claims. Errors are very expensive to a lawyer, for several reasons. First, a mistake may cost the lawyer the client and whatever future fees that client would pay. Second, a mistake takes time to correct, and since lawyers base their fees on time, the time they spend correcting a mistake represents lost revenue. Third, although lawyers are insured, they must pay the deductible portion of the claim. The deductible portion is typically $5,000 per claim, though the amount will vary depending on the law firm's insurance coverage. Another financial factor to consider, where insurance claims are concerned, is that the law firm's insurance premiums will increase if claims are made.

It is therefore very important that you avoid making mistakes that could give rise to an insurance claim. You can do so by following standard office procedures and by not overstepping the bounds of your assigned responsibilities. You should follow all instructions exactly as given and document all steps you take and conversations you

**Law Society of Upper Canada (LSUC)** professional body governing the activities of lawyers in Ontario

**Lawyers' Professional Indemnity Company (LAWPRO)** insurance company controlled by the Law Society of Upper Canada that insures lawyers against errors and omissions and administers TitlePLUS, a title insurance product

have—especially conversations with clients. You should not make decisions that are not yours to make, and you should try to avoid situations in which you may be called upon to do so. When questioned about matters that lie outside your authority, refer these questions to the lawyer handling the file. If you know that the lawyer will be away from the office during important times, you should make sure that another lawyer is available in the event of an emergency. You should also keep an eye out for mistakes made by others. If you notice something questionable in the file, bring it to the lawyer's attention. You may save the lawyer from a possible negligence claim.

# Professional Conduct Limitations

The legal profession is governed by statute, and statute law determines, among other things, the educational and other qualifications that a person must meet in order to practise law in Ontario. The *Law Society Act* also establishes the Law Society of Upper Canada as the professional body that governs the conduct of lawyers (and paralegals) in Ontario.[1]

Lawyers in Ontario are required to follow the Law Society of Upper Canada's *Rules of Professional Conduct* (the Rules) and its By-Laws. Failure to follow the rules set out in these two codes may result in disciplinary proceedings being brought against the lawyer. A lawyer who is found guilty of a breach may face a range of penalties, including disbarment. Although you, as a law clerk, will not be subject to disciplinary proceedings, you nonetheless need to know and follow the rules set out in the *Rules of Professional Conduct* and By-Laws. Two rules in particular are relevant to the role of law clerks in real estate transactions. These rules concern

- confidentiality, and
- supervision of assigned tasks and functions.

## Confidentiality

Rule 3.3-1 of chapter 3 of the *Rules of Professional Conduct*, entitled "Relationship to Clients," requires lawyers to keep all information from and about a client strictly confidential:

> A lawyer at all times shall hold in strict confidence all information concerning the business and affairs of the client acquired in the course of the professional relationship and shall not divulge any such information unless
>
> (a) expressly or impliedly authorized by the client;
> (b) required by law or by order of a tribunal of competent jurisdiction to do so;
> (c) required to provide the information to the Law Society; or
> (d) otherwise permitted by rules 3.3-2 to 3.3-6.

---

1 However, since only lawyers are permitted to handle real estate transactions, we limit our discussion to lawyers only.

The commentary to the rule sets out the rationale for the rule as follows:

> A lawyer cannot render effective professional services to the client unless there is full and unreserved communication between them. At the same time, the client must feel completely secure and entitled to proceed on the basis that, without any express request or stipulation on the client's part, matters disclosed to or discussed with the lawyer will be held in strict confidence.

The following excerpt from the commentary to the rule clarifies the level of care that lawyers are expected to take in protecting client confidentiality:

> A lawyer should avoid indiscreet conversations, even with the lawyer's spouse or family, about a client's affairs and should shun any gossip about such things even though the client is not named or otherwise identified. Similarly, a lawyer should not repeat any gossip or information about the client's business or affairs that is overheard or recounted to the lawyer. Apart altogether from ethical considerations or questions of good taste, indiscreet shop-talk between lawyers, if overheard by third parties able to identify the matter being discussed, could result in prejudice to the client. Moreover, the respect of the listener for lawyers and the legal profession will probably be lessened.

Law firms expect the same level of behaviour from their law clerks.

## Supervision of Assigned Tasks and Functions

Chapter 6 of the *Rules of Professional Conduct* and By-Law 7.1 deal with the relationship between lawyers and their students, employees, and others. Section 6.1 of the Rules, entitled "Supervision," discusses the responsibilities of a lawyer who assigns tasks and functions to a non-lawyer. It also sets out what tasks and functions a lawyer may and may not assign.

Rule 6.1-1 of the Rules provides that direct supervision of a non-lawyer by a lawyer is required:

> A lawyer shall in accordance with the by-laws
> (a) assume complete professional responsibility for their practice of law, and
> (b) shall directly supervise non-lawyers to whom particular tasks and functions are assigned.

The commentary to this rule makes it clear that a lawyer may assign certain tasks and functions to a non-lawyer, such as a law clerk, who "is competent to do work under the supervision of a lawyer." The lawyer must, however, directly supervise the work and maintain a direct relationship with the client. The extent of supervision required will depend on the type of legal matter involved and the law clerk's level of experience. The lawyer is responsible for educating the law clerk concerning the duties assigned to him or her and for supervising the manner in which the duties are carried out. The lawyer must review the law clerk's work at sufficiently frequent intervals to ensure that it is completed properly and on time.

The commentary to rule 6.1-1 specifically addresses real estate transactions. It provides that a lawyer may permit a non-lawyer to attend to all matters of routine administration, to assist in more complex transactions, to draft statements of account and routine documents and correspondence, and to attend at registrations.

A lawyer may not, however, assign to a non-lawyer ultimate responsibility for

- the review of a title search report;
- the review of documents before signing;
- the review and signing of a letter of requisition;
- the review and signing of a title opinion; or
- the review and signing of a reporting letter to the client.

In addition, in transactions for which electronic registration is used, only a lawyer may sign for completeness of any document, and a lawyer must sign any "compliance with law" statements. (See Chapter 7, Electronic Registration and Teraview.)

Rule 6.1-6.1 covers the assignment of tasks with respect to title insurance in real estate matters. A lawyer shall not permit a non-lawyer to

- provide advice to a client with respect to any insurance, including title insurance, without supervision;
- present insurance options or information regarding premiums to a client without supervision;
- recommend one insurance product over another without supervision; or
- give legal opinions regarding the insurance coverage obtained.

Rules 6.1-5 and 6.1-6 deal with the electronic registration of title documents. Under the e-reg™ system, every user, including lawyers and non-lawyers, is issued a specially encrypted diskette and pass phrase. The combination of the diskette and pass phrase identifies the user and controls access to the system. In order to maintain and ensure the security of the diskette, rule 6.1-5 provides that a lawyer shall not disclose his or her pass phrase to anyone else or permit anyone else, including a non-lawyer employee, to use the lawyer's diskette. Rule 6.1-6 requires the lawyer to ensure that any non-lawyer employed by the lawyer does not disclose his or her pass phrase to anyone else or permit anyone else to use the non-lawyer's diskette.

The By-Laws apply to both lawyers and paralegals and therefore use the term "licensees" rather than "lawyers." By-Law 7.1 sets out the requirements for licensees with respect to tasks done by non-licensees, such as law clerks.

Section 4(1) of By-Law 7.1 indicates that licensees must assume complete professional responsibility for the practice of law with respect to clients' affairs, and must directly supervise all non-licensees who are assigned work relating to those clients' affairs.

Section 4(2) of By-Law 7.1 sets out the licensee's specific responsibilities, including the ones that apply to law clerks. These responsibilities are as follows:

- the licensee shall not permit a non-licensee to accept a client on the licensee's behalf;
- the licensee shall assign to a non-licensee only tasks and functions that the non-licensee is competent to perform;

- the licensee shall ensure that a non-licensee does not act without the licensee's instruction;
- the licensee shall review a non-licensee's performance of the tasks and functions assigned to him or her at frequent intervals;
- the licensee shall ensure that the tasks and functions assigned to a non-licensee are performed properly and in a timely manner;
- the licensee shall assume responsibility for all tasks and functions performed by a non-licensee, including the preparation of all documents; and
- the licensee shall ensure that a non-licensee does not act finally in respect of a client's affairs.

Section 5 of By-Law 7.1 indicates that a non-licensee cannot, *without prior express authorization from the licensee,*

- give or accept an undertaking on behalf of the licensee,
- act on behalf of the licensee in routine administrative matters before an adjudicative body, or
- take clients' instructions.

A non-licensee cannot negotiate with a third party on behalf of a client without the client's consent (and permission from the licensee), and the licensee must approve the results of any such negotiations.

Section 6 of By-Law 7.1 sets out tasks that cannot be performed by a non-licensee. These tasks include

- giving legal advice;
- appearing before an adjudicative body, except as provided in section 5, unless the non-licensee is authorized under the *Law Society Act* to do so;
- negotiating with third parties, except as provided in section 5;
- signing correspondence, other than that of a routine administrative nature;
- forwarding documents (other than routine ones) to clients, without prior review by the licensee; and
- using the licensee's personalized, specially encrypted diskette to access the system for the electronic registration of title documents.

If the rules concerning the assignment of tasks are contravened, the instructing lawyer, not the law clerk, is subject to disciplinary proceedings. Even so, it is important for you to understand and follow these provisions. You should never unilaterally, without the knowledge of the instructing lawyer, undertake work contrary to the provisions of chapter 6 of the *Rules of Professional Conduct*. Rule 6.1-1(a) states that the lawyers handling the files are responsible for their practice of law, and their practice of law includes all the work that you perform. Your contravening the Rules could lead to disciplinary proceedings being brought against the lawyer. If this were to happen, your future at the law firm would not be very bright.

What about a situation in which the lawyer handling the file contravenes By-Law 7.1 by assigning work to you that only a lawyer should undertake? This puts you in an awkward and uncomfortable situation. On the one hand, it is very difficult, if not impossible, to refuse to follow your employer's instructions. On the other hand, even though it will be the lawyer and not you whom the Law Society of Upper Canada will discipline if it discovers that you did the work, you may still be blamed. Your best approach in such a situation is (1) to carry out the assigned tasks while always referring the work back to the instructing lawyer for review, and (2) to document this referral by memo. For example, if the lawyer handling the file directs you to review a title search, to decide on the appropriate requisitions to be made on title, and to draft a requisition letter, you should return the title search and draft requisition letter to the lawyer with a memo stating that the material is being returned to the lawyer for review. And you should place a copy of the memo in the file.

If the lawyer tries to assign a task to you that "lawyers themselves may not do"—in other words, something that neither law clerk nor lawyer should undertake—serious misconduct may well be involved. In these circumstances, depending on the particular situation, you should probably refuse to perform the task.

To summarize:

- a law clerk should be aware of the provisions of chapter 6 of the *Rules of Professional Conduct* and of By-Law 7.1;
- a law clerk should never unilaterally, without the instructing lawyer's knowledge, undertake work in contravention of the provisions of chapter 6 of the *Rules of Professional Conduct* or of By-Law 7.1;
- if the law clerk is assigned work that a lawyer is required to undertake, he or she should perform the work but should refer it back to the instructing lawyer for review and should document the referral by memo; and
- if assigned work that would be improper for a lawyer to undertake, the law clerk should in most circumstances refuse to perform the work.

## Conflict of Interest

The Law Society of Upper Canada's *Rules of Professional Conduct* also address the issue of conflict of interest in the real estate area. Pursuant to rule 3.4-1 of chapter 3, a lawyer is required to avoid conflicts of interest. Rules 3.4-12 through 3.4-16 deal with the situation where a lawyer is representing both the lender and the borrower in a mortgage transaction. The rules generally prohibit a lawyer from acting for both the borrower and the lender unless

- the lawyer practises in a remote location where there are no other lawyers who could conveniently be retained by either party;
- the borrower is buying property from the lender and the mortgage represents part of the purchase price;
- the lender is a bank, trust company, insurance company, credit union, or finance company that lends money in the ordinary course of its business;
- the amount of the mortgage does not exceed $50,000; or
- the borrower and the lender are not at "arm's length" as defined in the *Income Tax Act*.

# KEY TERMS

Law Society of Upper Canada (LSUC), 14

Lawyers' Professional Indemnity Company (LAWPRO), 14

# REFERENCES

*Law Society Act*, RSO 1990, c L.8.

Law Society of Upper Canada, "By-Laws," online: <https://www.lsuc.on.ca/by-laws>.

Law Society of Upper Canada, *Rules of Professional Conduct* (Toronto: LSUC, 2000), online: <http://www.lsuc.on.ca/WorkArea/DownloadAsset.aspx?id=2147486159>.

# REVIEW QUESTIONS

1. Why do lawyers have errors and omissions insurance, and who provides it?

2. Who is responsible for the mistakes made by a law clerk?

3. What are the *Rules of Professional Conduct*?

4. What do the *Rules of Professional Conduct* provide with respect to confidentiality?

5. Under what conditions, pursuant to the *Rules of Professional Conduct* and the By-Laws, may a lawyer assign work to a non-lawyer, and what qualifications must such a non-lawyer have?

6. Under the *Rules of Professional Conduct* and the By-Laws, what may a lawyer permit a law clerk to do in a real estate transaction?

7. Under the *Rules of Professional Conduct* and the By-Laws, what may a lawyer not delegate to a law clerk in a real estate transaction?

8. What may a lawyer not permit a law clerk to do with respect to title insurance?

9. What are the main points for a law clerk to keep in mind, in light of what the *Rules of Professional Conduct* and the By-Laws provide with respect to the supervision and assignment of tasks and functions?

10. Summarize the provisions of the *Rules of Professional Conduct* regarding conflicts of interest in real estate transactions.

# PART II

# Overview of Real Estate Law

# Estates and Interests in Land

3

## LEARNING OUTCOMES

After reading this chapter, you will understand:

- The meaning of real property and the principles underlying land ownership

- The various estates in land

- Other interests in land that are not estates in land

- How co-owners of land hold title

# Introduction

The legal term for land is **real property**. This term is used to describe land and everything attached to it, including

- minerals below the surface of the land;
- airspace above the land;
- buildings placed on the land; and
- **fixtures** on the land—immovable posessions attached to the real property, or **personal property** that has become attached or affixed to the land.

The law that deals with real property dates back to feudal times in England, and much of the terminology still in use today also dates from that time. In feudal times, the King of England owned all land and granted some of his subjects **estates** in land in return for their service and allegiance. The king had the right to take back the land if a subject **forfeited** it—for example, by committing treason.

The English law of real property was brought to Ontario, and today the Crown remains the ultimate owner of all land. Therefore, the government controls the use, disposition, and development of all land in Ontario.

Because the Crown is the ultimate owner of all land, and because land is permanent and immovable, owning land is different from owning other kinds of property. Land ownership is more like "possession," together with rights and obligations that are recognized and enforced by law. Indeed, individuals don't own *land*; rather, they own estates or **interests** in land. The rights that people have with respect to their land depend on the estate or interest they have.

In this chapter we will look at

- estates in land,
- other interests in land,
- possessory interests in land,
- fixtures, and
- title to land.

# Estates in Land

An estate in land is an interest in land that gives the owner the right to **exclusive possession** of the land. There are three types of estates in land:

- the fee simple estate;
- the life estate; and
- the leasehold estate.

# Fee Simple Estate

The **fee simple estate** (also called a **freehold estate**) is the greatest interest in land that an individual can have. The Crown (the government) grants the fee simple estate to the first "owner" by way of **Crown patent**. The Crown is still the ultimate owner of the land, but the "owner" has all of the rights to the land, subject only to the Crown.

In theory, the fee simple estate extends physically upward into the sky and downward to the centre of the earth. In fact, there are limitations in both directions. A landowner cannot sue for trespass the owner of an airplane flying overhead. However, the owner could sue the owner of a neighbouring property who makes permanent use of the first owner's airspace—for example, by building a structure that hangs over the property. With respect to rights below the surface, most Crown patents do not include oil and mineral rights, which are reserved for the Crown.

A person who has the fee simple estate (called "the owner in fee simple") has the right to exclusive possession of the land and the right to dispose of the land for an infinite period of time. That person is considered to be the true owner of the land and has all the rights associated with land ownership, including the right to

- grant the fee simple estate to someone else (by sale or gift);
- grant a life estate in the property;
- grant a leasehold estate in the property (rent the property); and
- convey the property by inheritance (with or without a will).

The Crown may reacquire the land by way of **expropriation**. This must be done for public purposes (for example, a road widening or new highway), and the owner must be compensated for the value of the land. If the owner in fee simple dies without leaving a will and has no surviving heirs or relatives, the land will **escheat**, or revert to the Crown. See Figure 3.1 for an illustration.

> **fee simple (or freehold) estate**
> the right to exclusive possession and the right to dispose of the land for an indefinite period of time
>
> **Crown patent**
> grant of land by the Crown (the government) to the first owner
>
> **expropriation**
> reacquisition of land, with compensation, by the Crown for public purposes
>
> **escheat**
> reversion of property to the Crown

**Figure 3.1   How Escheat Works**

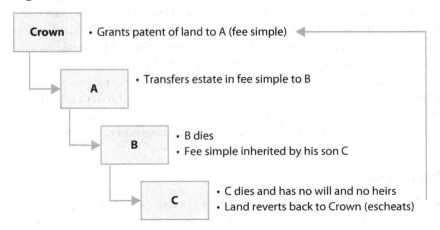

## Life Estate

**life estate**
right to exclusive possession of the property for the length of a particular lifetime

A **life estate** grants to the owner (called the "life tenant") the right to exclusive possession of the property for the length of a particular lifetime (usually, but not always, that of the owner of the life estate). A life estate runs for an indefinite period of time—we know it will end, but we don't know when. On the death of the person to whose life the life estate is tied, the life estate ends and the property reverts to the person who holds the estate in fee simple (called the "remainderman").

The owner of the fee simple estate can convey the fee simple to another person and reserve a life estate to himself or herself, keeping the use of the property until death. Also, the owner in fee simple can convey a life estate to one person and the fee simple estate to yet another. For example, in a will, a husband can leave a life estate in his home to his wife and the fee simple estate to his son upon the wife's death. Life estates are most commonly conveyed to family members.

Once a life estate is created, the owners of the life estate and the fee simple estate both have legal, though different, rights to the same property. For example, assume that, in his will, Guillermo leaves the fee simple estate in his property to his son Antonio, subject to a life estate in the property to his wife June. As the life estate holder or life tenant, June is entitled to exclusive possession of the property during her lifetime. As soon as June dies, the life estate ends, and Antonio (the remainderman) obtains full rights to the property. Even though Antonio holds the fee simple estate, his estate is limited by June's life estate. In other words, Antonio is entitled to possession of the property only when June dies and the life estate ends. Note that June must use the land in a reasonable manner, is responsible for maintaining the property (for example, paying property taxes and paying interest on any mortgage), and must not **commit waste** on the land—that is, she must not tear down buildings or destroy trees.

**commit waste**
destroy, abuse, or make permanent undesirable changes to a property

The person with the fee simple estate in land may grant successive life estates in that same parcel of land. For example, assume that David owns the fee simple estate in land and grants a life estate first to Bob, then to Chuck, and then to Don. When Bob dies, Chuck gets a life estate in the property. When Chuck dies, Don gets a life estate in the property. When Don dies, David will regain full ownership and possession of the property, assuming he is still alive. If he is dead, David's heirs will inherit the property. If David has no heirs and no will, the property will escheat to the Crown.

The owner of a life estate (life tenant) in land may grant the right to possession of the land to someone else, but that right to possession will end when the life tenant dies. For example, assume that Ben is the owner in fee simple of a property that has a townhouse. He grants Sam a life estate in the property. Sam, who does not wish to live there, in turn grants Alice the right to exclusive possession of the townhouse. As soon as Sam dies, the life estate ends, and the right to possession reverts to Ben.

## Leasehold Estate

**leasehold estate**
right to exclusive possession of property for a specified period of time in return for the payment of rent

A **leasehold estate** grants the right to exclusive possession of the property for a specified period of time in return for the payment of rent. This estate creates a landlord–tenant relationship between the parties.

For example, assume that Ben has the fee simple estate in a townhouse property and grants a leasehold estate to Sam. Both Sam and Ben will have legal rights to the same property. Sam is entitled to exclusive possession of the property during the term of the leasehold agreement and must pay rent to Ben. Ben is entitled to regain possession of the property only when the lease terminates.

See Figure 3.2 for an illustration of the relationship among a fee simple estate, a life estate, and a leasehold estate.

**Figure 3.2    Relationship Among a Fee Simple Estate, a Life Estate, and a Leasehold Estate**

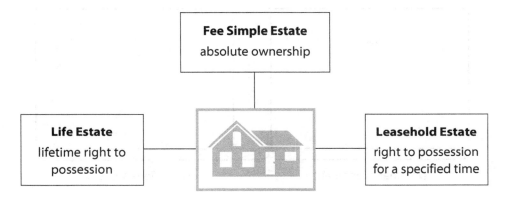

## Other Interests in Land

As stated above, all estates in land confer on the owner of the estate the right to exclusive possession of the land. There are interests in land that are not estates in land. These interests do not confer on their owners a right of exclusive possession to the land. Instead, they confer the right to use the land, without changing the landowner's estate in land.

### Easements

An **easement** is the right to use a portion of someone else's land for a specific purpose, without requiring the owner's permission each time. An easement is often referred to as a **right of way**.

For example, assume that Sam has a garage at the back of his townhouse but does not own the driveway. The land on which the driveway is situated is owned by his neighbour, Bob. Sam would need an easement interest in Bob's land to be able to use the driveway to get to his garage. If Bob grants Sam an easement, Sam will be entitled to use the easement only for access to the garage. He is not entitled to park his car in the driveway and thereby obstruct the easement.

The land that supplies the easement is called the **servient tenement**, and the land that benefits from the easement is called the **dominant tenement**. The servient

**easement**
right to use a portion of someone else's land for a specific purpose, without requiring the owner's permission

**right of way**
right to use a portion of another's land for access purposes

**servient tenement**
land over which an easement runs

**dominant tenement**
land that benefits from an easement

tenement and the dominant tenement must each be owned by different people for an easement to exist. In the previous example, Bob's land is the servient tenement and Sam's townhouse property is the dominant tenement. See Figure 3.3 for an illustration.

### Figure 3.3   Composition of an Easement

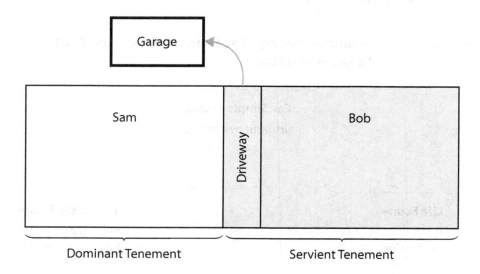

In the case of a mutual driveway (not uncommon in older urban residential areas), each landowner owns the part of the driveway that is situated on his or her own land. In addition, each has an easement interest over the other's land—that is, the right to use the other's part of the driveway in order to access his or her own garage.

For example, assume that Keith and Adam are neighbours and share a single driveway that leads to a garage behind each home. Figure 3.4 illustrates this easement situation.

Adam owns property A, subject to easement #1 in favour of Keith, and he owns easement #2 over Keith's property. Keith owns property B, subject to easement #2 in favour of Adam, and he owns easement #1 over Adam's property. Property A is the servient tenement for easement #1, and property B is the dominant tenement. Property B is the servient tenement for easement #2, and property A is the dominant tenement. In this example, each property is both a dominant tenement and a servient tenement.

The owner of a servient tenement cannot do anything to obstruct an easement. For example, Adam cannot park his car on the mutual driveway and thereby prevent Keith from using the driveway to get to his garage.

An easement interest attaches to the land, not the owner. If Keith sells his property to Susie, she will acquire the easement over Adam's land, giving her the right to use the driveway to gain access to the garage. Similarly, if Adam sells his land to Betty, she gets the land subject to the easement in favour of Keith and cannot block the driveway.

## Figure 3.4   Easements: Mutual Easements

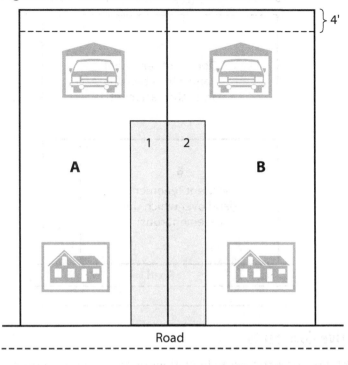

Easements are usually created when the owner of the servient tenement grants an easement to the owner of the dominant tenement in writing. This is called an **express grant**. They can also be created by **prescription**—if the easement is used over a period of 20 years. For a more complete discussion of easements by prescription, see below under the heading "Possessory Interests in Land." An **easement implied by law** is created when the only way to get access to a property or a main road is by crossing over another person's property.

Figure 3.5 illustrates a situation in which an easement will be implied by law. As you can see, the only way the owner of parcel A can get access to the road is by crossing over B's land.

Utility companies commonly have easement rights over landowners' property so that they can service and maintain their utility lines. Return to Figure 3.4: assume that Bell Canada has an easement over the rear four feet of the property, behind the two owners' garages. Bell Canada is entitled to have access to that part of Adam's and Keith's land without their permission. Adam and Keith cannot obstruct Bell Canada's easement—for example, by building a permanent shed on the rear four feet of their property.

Neighbours whose houses are very close together may have the right to enter upon the neighbouring property to facilitate maintenance and repair work. For example, an owner may need to place a ladder on a neighbour's property to get access to a roof.

**express grant**
creation of an easement by written document from the owner of the servient tenement to the owner of the dominant tenement

**prescription**
means by which an interest is acquired in another's land after a period of 20 years of open and uninterrupted use

**easement implied by law**
easement that is created when the only way to gain access to a property is by crossing over another property

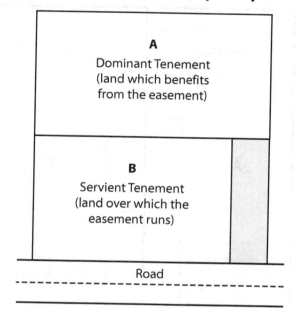

**Figure 3.5   An Easement Implied by Law**

## Restrictive Covenants

A **restrictive covenant** imposes limitations on the use of the property. It is typically a promise by an owner to refrain from doing something on the property—for example, parking a boat in a driveway. A restrictive covenant attaches to the land and therefore will bind subsequent owners of the property. In order to be enforceable, the restriction must be reasonable in nature and cannot be contrary to public interest. The restriction must also be negative in nature, which means that it is a promise *not* to do something, as opposed to a promise to do something. For example, "all front doors must be painted red" is not a valid restrictive covenant because it is stating what must be done, as opposed to what must not be done. "Front doors must not be painted green," on the other hand, is a valid restrictive covenant.

Builders often use restrictive covenants in subdivision developments to maintain control over the appearance of homes. Builders also use restrictive covenants to make sure that homeowners do not change the grading of the land, because such changes could affect drainage and cause flooding.

These types of restrictions will either be included in a deed or registered as a separate document on title to property. Like easements, they run with the land and will be binding on subsequent buyers of the property. Sometimes, restrictive covenants exist for a certain period of time, at the end of which they expire. Expired restrictive covenants will not bind subsequent buyers.

## Mineral Rights

Most Crown patents do not convey mineral rights but retain them for the benefit of the Crown. The Crown can transfer the mineral rights to a person other than the owner of the fee simple estate. When a person acquires mineral rights in the land of another person, that interest is called a **profit à prendre**.

## Riparian Rights

**Riparian rights** are the rights of an owner of land to a watercourse that runs through, or is adjacent to, the property. The owner of the land has the right to the use and flow of the water but cannot interfere with the flow of the water to downstream users.

# Possessory Interests in Land

The various interests in land are generally acquired when the owner of the interest expressly grants it to another person. It is possible, however, for a person to acquire an interest in someone else's land by simply using the land over an extended period of time. In such a case, the interest is said to have been acquired by **possession**, by **adverse possession**, or by prescription. It is possible to acquire, by possession,

- the fee simple estate in a property,
- an easement over a property, or
- the right to an encroachment over a property.

Possessory interests can be acquired only in the Registry system, and not in the Land Titles system. (We will discuss these systems further in Chapter 5, Land Registration Systems.) Since most property in Ontario is now in the Land Titles system, possessory interests are not as relevant as they once were.

## Fee Simple Estate

A person who does not own land can acquire the owner's fee simple estate by treating the land as his or her own over a period of time. If a person exercises exclusive possession over another person's property **adversely** (without the owner's permission), openly, and continuously, the original owner's interest in the land will be **extinguished** after 10 years of uninterrupted use, and the person who has used the land will obtain the fee simple estate.

For example, assume that Ellen and Brenda own adjacent properties. Ellen maintains a vegetable garden on part of the land owned by Brenda. Ellen takes care of the garden for many years. Brenda never tends to the garden and never uses the property. Brenda knows about the garden on her land, but neither consents to it nor does anything to stop it. After 10 years, Ellen will acquire by adverse possession a valid claim to the land, and Brenda will lose the right to regain possession of the land.

For this to be the case, the period of Ellen's possession must be continuous and undisputed. If the true owner of the land regains possession at any time during the 10 years, the time period stops running. For example, Brenda can stop the 10 years from running by simply using the property herself, even for a short period of time, or by telling Ellen she can no longer use it.

---

**profit à prendre**
interest created when mineral rights are acquired in the land of another person

**riparian rights**
rights to the use of a watercourse running through or adjacent to the property

**possession**
control or occupancy of land regardless of ownership

**adverse possession**
valid title to land through open, visible, and uninterrupted possession of that property, without the owner's permission, for a period of at least 10 years

**adversely**
without the owner's permission

**extinguish**
bring to an end

Adverse possession claims attach to the land, not to the owner. For example, if Ellen sells her property to Nancy after using the garden on Brenda's land for six years, and Nancy continues to use the garden, uninterrupted, without consent, and exclusively, for four more years, she will acquire the right to that piece of Brenda's land.

## Easements

It is possible to acquire an easement interest by prescription if the following conditions are met:

- The easement has been used openly and continuously for at least 20 years (there can be different owners during this period).
- The owner of the servient tenement knows that the easement is being used.
- The owner of the servient tenement has not consented to the use of the easement.
- The owner of the servient tenement has not received any payment for the use of the easement.

In the case of an easement by prescription, the easement is imposed by law on the owner of the servient tenement. At any time during the 20-year period, the owner of the servient tenement is entitled to prevent the use of the property and thus prevent the creation of the easement, in which case the time period could start to run again. But if the owner of the servient tenement does not stop the owner of the dominant tenement from using the easement during the 20-year period, the owner of the dominant tenement has the right to use the easement forever.

Refer to Figure 3.6, and assume that Erin owns lot A and Jeffrey owns lot B. Lots A, B, C, and D are very large lots. Jeffrey works at a school that is near the corner of lots A and C. It's faster for Jeffrey to get to work if he cuts across lot A. If Jeffrey starts to use this shortcut and does so regularly for 20 years, he will acquire an easement interest in Erin's property, by prescription. If Erin wants to stop this from happening, all she has to do is tell Jeffrey to stop using her land at any time during the 20-year period. Afterward, it will be too late to prevent him from acquiring an easement interest in her land. If, after 12 years of using the shortcut, Jeffrey sells lot B to Jake, and Jake continues to use the shortcut, the 20-year period continues to run, and Jake will be able to claim an easement interest in Erin's land, by prescription, after 8 more years of using the shortcut.

## Encroachments

**encroachment**
building or structure intruding upon someone else's land

An **encroachment** is any building or structure that intrudes upon someone else's property. A common example is the overhang of a roof or the eaves of a building that is situated too close to the property line. In this situation, an easement by prescription may be created after 20 years, after which the owner of the adjoining property will no longer be able to force the removal of the overhang. Another example is a shed or fence that ends up being partly or wholly built on the land of a

**Figure 3.6   Easement Interest by Prescription**

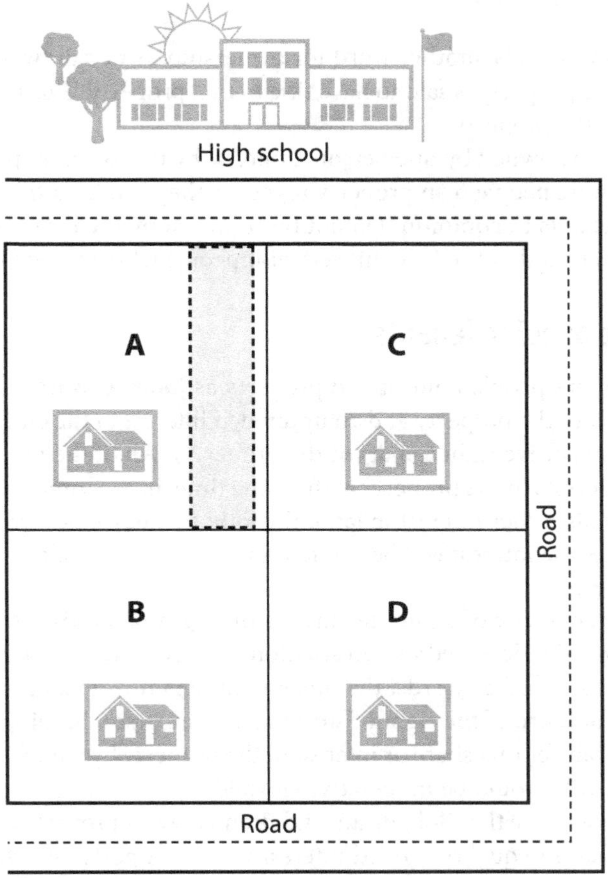

neighbour. This second example will give rise to a claim for adverse possession if the structure remains for a period of 10 years. In other words, the original owner of the land will no longer be able to demand the removal of the encroaching structure.

# Fixtures

Fixtures are items of personal property that are permanently or constructively attached to real property and become part of it. Unless specifically excluded from the sale of the property, fixtures must be left behind by sellers when they move out. The rules for determining whether or not certain items have become attached to the land or to the building are very confusing. Some of the factors are

- the degree of **annexation** (attachment) to the land;
- the ability to remove the fixture without causing serious damage to it or to the land or building to which it is attached; and
- the use of the fixture.

**annexation**
attachment

# Title to Land

**title**
legal right to the owner-
ship and possession
of property; evidence
showing such a right

In real estate law, **title** is another word for ownership. A person who holds the fee simple estate in a property is said to have title to that property. This person is known as the owner of the property.

Property can be owned by one person alone, or by two or more people together. When two or more people own property together, they can hold title either as joint tenants or as tenants in common. Do not be confused by the term "tenants." These people are owners and not to be confused with people who pay rent to landlords.

## Holding Title as Joint Tenants

**joint tenants**
two or more people owning
property where on the
death of one, the survivors
inherit the deceased's share

When two or more people hold title to property as **joint tenants**, each person has an equal interest in the property and an undivided interest in the entire property (as opposed to an exclusive right to part of the property). All of the joint tenants must receive their interests in the property at the same time, in the same deed. If one joint tenant conveys his or her interest in land, the joint tenancy is severed, and the person who receives the interest will be a tenant in common (see below) with the other owner or owners.

**right of survivorship**
automatic vesting of an
interest in the surviving
joint tenant or tenants
when one joint tenant dies

The key characteristic of a joint tenancy is the **right of survivorship**. When one joint tenant dies, the deceased's interest automatically **vests** in the surviving joint tenant or tenants. In other words, the other joint tenant or tenants receive the deceased's share. Because of the right of survivorship, a person holding title as a joint tenant cannot transfer that share or interest in the property by will. Such a provision, if included in a will, would be inoperative (invalid).

**vest**
provide an immediate
right to present or future
ownership or possession

For example, assume that Bob, Brian, and Brenda own a property as joint tenants. Each of them has an equal one-third interest in the property, which gives each of them rights to the entire property. If Bob dies, his interest automatically vests in Brian and Brenda, as joint tenants, who now each have an equal one-half interest in the property. If Brian dies, his interest vests in Brenda, who becomes the sole owner of the property.

## Holding Title as Tenants in Common

**tenants in common**
two or more people owning
property where on the
death of one, the deceased
person's share passes to
his or her heirs rather
than the other owners;
no right of survivorship

When two or more people hold title as **tenants in common**, there is no right of survivorship, and the interests do not have to be equal. For example, one tenant in common can own three-quarters of the property while the other tenant in common owns one-quarter. Although the interests of each tenant may not be equal, each tenant still has an undivided interest in the entire property (as opposed to an exclusive right to part of the property). Each tenant in common may transfer the individual interest in the property to a third party or dispose of it by will.

For example, assume that Bob and Brian own a property as tenants in common. They can each have a 50 percent interest in the property, or Bob may have a 75 percent interest and Brian a 25 percent interest. If Bob dies, his interest in the property becomes part of his estate and passes to his heirs by will or intestacy. If Bob sells his interest to David, Brian and David will own the property as tenants in common.

## The Partition Act

When two people own property, one owner may want to sell the property while the other may not. While it is legally possible for a part owner of property to sell only that person's interest in the land, in practice it is difficult to find a buyer who wants to own land as a tenant in common with a stranger. If the owners can't agree whether to sell the property, one owner can seek a court order under the *Partition Act* to force the sale of the entire property.

## KEY TERMS

| | | | |
|---|---|---|---|
| adversely, 31 | escheat, 25 | interests, 24 | right of survivorship, 34 |
| adverse possession, 31 | estate, 24 | joint tenants, 34 | right of way, 27 |
| annexation, 33 | exclusive possession, 24 | leasehold estate, 26 | riparian rights, 31 |
| commit waste, 26 | express grant, 29 | life estate, 26 | servient tenement, 27 |
| Crown patent, 25 | expropriation, 25 | personal property, 24 | tenants in common, 34 |
| dominant tenement, 27 | extinguish, 31 | possession, 31 | title, 34 |
| easement, 27 | fee simple (or freehold) | prescription, 29 | vest, 34 |
| easement implied by | estate, 25 | profit à prendre, 31 | |
| law, 29 | fixtures, 24 | real property, 24 | |
| encroachment, 32 | forfeit, 24 | restrictive covenant, 30 | |

## REFERENCES

*Partition Act*, RSO 1990, c P.4.

## REVIEW QUESTIONS

1. What does real property include?

2. What is a fixture?

3. Ariel owns a house in Ontario and has no relatives whatsoever. If he dies without leaving a will, what will happen to the house he owned?

4. Jose has the fee simple estate in land. Jose wants to move to California for a year and would like to sell the land or, alternatively, rent it to someone while he is away. Is he allowed to do this? Explain your answer.

5. Sam lived in a home with his wife, Susan. In Sam's will, he left the fee simple estate to his son, Jonas, subject to a life estate to Susan. Sam recently died, and Jonas would like to move into the home right away. Can Jonas force Susan to leave and move into the home?

6. Referring to the facts in question 5, assume that Susan grants a leasehold estate to Bruno. If Susan dies, does Jonas have to continue renting the house to Bruno? Explain your answer.

7. Jake and Judy are neighbours who share a mutual driveway. Neither owns the entire driveway. What type of interest do Jake and Judy have in each other's property?

8. For an easement to exist, there must be a dominant tenement and a servient tenement. Explain the meaning of these two terms.

9. How is an easement created?

10. Which of the following is a valid restrictive covenant? Explain your answer.

    a. You must not install a satellite dish on the property.

    b. You must install a satellite dish on the property.

11. What are riparian rights?

12. What happens if a person exercises exclusive possession of another person's property openly and continuously, without the owner's permission, for over 10 years?

13. Provide an example of an encroachment.

14. In real estate law, what does the term "title" mean?

15. Michelle and Sylvia own property together as joint tenants. Michelle's will leaves all her property to her son Noel. What will happen to the property if Michelle dies?

16. Referring to the facts in question 15, assume instead that Michelle and Sylvia own the property as tenants in common. What will happen to the property if Michelle dies?

# Legal Descriptions 4

## LEARNING OUTCOMES

After reading this chapter, you will understand:

- How land in Ontario was originally divided

- How to identify land using its "legal description"

- How to describe land using a metes and bounds description

- What a reference plan is and when it is required

- What a plan of subdivision is and when it is required

# Introduction

Documents that create an interest in land describe the property by using a **legal description**, not the property's municipal address. Rather than using the street number and name, the legal description describes the property with reference to recorded maps, surveys, or plans of the land. All land in Ontario has a legal description. Land registration systems record the documents that create an interest in land by using the legal description of the property.

# Original Division of Land in Ontario

Knowing how land in Ontario was originally divided can help you understand legal descriptions and Ontario's land registration system.

In the 18th century, the Crown hired land surveyors to identify and record all the land in the province. The surveyors divided the province first into counties and then into townships. They then created east–west road allowances in each township to provide access to the main roads. The surveyors used a measuring tool called a "Gunter's chain," which is the equivalent of 66 feet (approximately 20.1 metres). Each road allowance was 1 chain wide, and the distance between road allowances was 100 chains, or 6,600 feet (1¼ miles, or approximately 2 kilometres). The creation

of the road allowances resulted in the formation of areas of land called **concessions**. By this method, the townships were laid out into a grid pattern as illustrated in Figure 4.1. (Note: The illustrations in Figures 4.1 to 4.7 are not to scale.)

**Figure 4.1   Division of Land into Concessions**

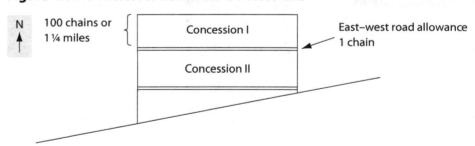

This kind of layout made it possible to identify a parcel of land by referring to its location in a particular county, township, and concession. For example, a property is located in Concession I, in the Township of Nottawasaga, in the County of Simcoe.

Next, the surveyors mapped out north–south road allowances within the concessions. These road allowances were surveyed in a similar manner to the east–west road allowances: the distance between them was 100 chains (1¼ miles, or approximately 2 kilometres), and each road allowance was 1 chain wide. The intersection of the north–south road allowances with the east–west road allowances created squares of 1,000 acres each—enormous parcels of land. (See Figure 4.2.)

**Figure 4.2   Division of Concessions by Road Allowances**

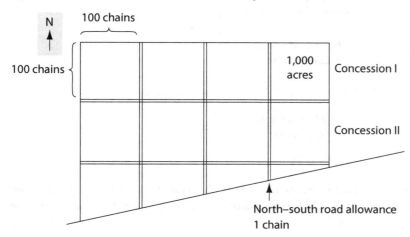

The 1,000-acre squares were divided into **lots** by surveying additional boundary lines. Each lot was 20 chains × 100 chains, or 200 acres, and was assigned a concession lot number. Most original Crown patents were grants of either the whole or half of one of these concession lots. Figure 4.3 illustrates this further division.

**lot**
200-acre parcel of land created during the original division of land into concessions; also, a parcel of land created by a plan of subdivision

**Figure 4.3   Division of Concessions into Lots**

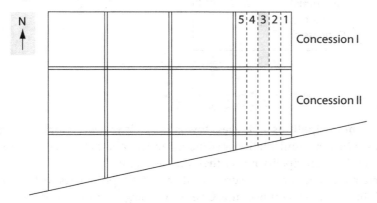

As a result, it became possible to describe a parcel of land even more precisely by referring to the county, township, concession number, *and* lot number. For example, the shaded area in Figure 4.3 can now be described as Lot 3, Concession I, Township of Nottawasaga, County of Simcoe.

In time, lots were further divided into even smaller parcels of land. The most common division was to halve them between the east–west road allowances, so that each half would have access to a road. This created a 100-acre parcel of land. Reference to the north or south half of the lot could now be added to the description of land situated within the lot, as illustrated in Figure 4.4.

**Figure 4.4    Division of Concession Lot into Half Lots**

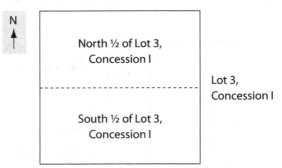

A further division could be made between the west and the east half of each part of the lot, which, again, would further narrow the description of land within that lot, as illustrated in Figure 4.5.

**Figure 4.5    Division of Concession Half Lot into Quarter Lots**

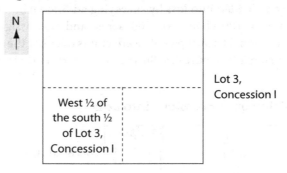

## Modifications to the Original System

**municipality**
form of urban organization including cities, towns, and villages

Over time, **municipalities**—villages, towns, and cities—were formed within the townships. Once a municipality was incorporated, the land was described with reference to the municipality rather than the township.

As certain areas became more urbanized, large farm properties within them were divided into smaller lots for housing. Over time, the government instituted controls over the division of land by requiring a **plan of subdivision** whenever a concession lot was divided into smaller lots. Once a plan of subdivision is registered, the land is described with reference to the plan, rather than the concession lot.

**plan of subdivision**
registered plan illustrating the measurements and boundaries of all lots and streets created by the division of concession lots into many smaller lots

## Legal Descriptions

Legal descriptions have changed over time as Ontario has evolved from primarily a farming culture to an urban and suburban culture. Large parcels of farmland are divided into smaller parcels for housing. Today, land in Ontario, depending on its size and location, may be described

- by reference to lot and concession;
- by reference to a registered plan of subdivision; or
- by reference to a reference plan.

## By Reference to Lot and Concession

The original division of land into concessions and lots made it possible to describe all land with reference to something permanent. All land could be described by identifying the lot, concession, township, and county within which the land was situated.

It becomes more difficult to describe a parcel of land that is not exactly a whole, half, or quarter of a concession lot, such as the land represented by the shaded area in Figure 4.6. One starts by describing the part of the concession lot within which the parcel of land is situated—part of the east half of the south half of Lot 3, Concession I—but a further description is needed to clarify the boundaries of the shaded area.

**Figure 4.6    Division of Concession Quarter Lots into Smaller Parcels**

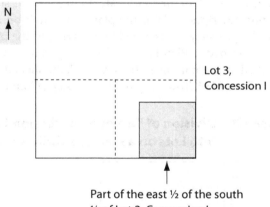

Lot 3, Concession I

Part of the east ½ of the south ½ of Lot 3, Concession I

This further description is called a **metes and bounds description**. It describes, in words, the boundaries and dimensions of a parcel of land in relation to lot lines. By following this written description, it is possible to sketch the outlines of the parcel to provide a picture of the area of land.

The legal description of the shaded area in Figure 4.6 would read as follows:

> Part of the east ½ of the south ½ of Lot 3, Concession I, Township of Nottawasaga, County of Simcoe, more particularly described as follows:
>
> Commencing at the southeast corner of Lot 3, Concession I;
> Thence north 200 feet along the easterly boundary line to a point;
> Thence west 200 feet, parallel to the southerly boundary line to a point;
> Thence south 200 feet, parallel to the easterly boundary line to a point.

**metes and bounds description**
written description of the boundaries and dimensions of a parcel of land in relation to lot lines; enables a sketch of the parcel to provide a picture of the area of land

Thence east 200 feet, along the southerly boundary line to the point of commencement.

All land in Ontario was originally described by reference to concessions and lots, together with a metes and bounds description, if necessary.

## By Reference to a Registered Plan of Subdivision

As described above, large farm properties were divided into smaller lots as certain areas became more urbanized. Developers subdivided whole concession lots or portions of them into many smaller residential or commercial lots for sale. In order to control how this development took place, the government of Ontario began to require developers to register a plan of subdivision showing the measurements and boundaries of all lots and streets created. For a discussion of the role of plans of subdivision in controlling the development of land, see Chapter 9, Government Controls over the Use and Subdivision of Land. When a plan of subdivision is registered, it is assigned a number. Each lot on the plan is assigned a number as well.

The registration of the plan affects the legal description of the property. Suppose a developer purchases the parcel of land shown in Figure 4.6 for the purpose of creating a subdivision. Before the plan of subdivision is registered, the property is described as part of the east half of the south half of Lot 3, Concession I, followed by the metes and bounds description. After the plan of subdivision is registered and assigned a number, the property is described by referring to the plan number. The entire parcel is now described as Plan 1234, and each separate lot within the plan of subdivision is described by its lot number. In Figure 4.7, the shaded part of Plan 1234 is described as Lot 5, Plan 1234, Township of Nottawasaga, County of Simcoe.

### Figure 4.7    Division of Part of a Concession Lot into Lots on a Plan of Subdivision

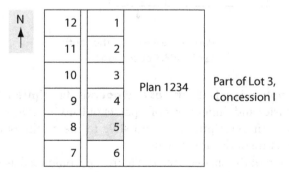

## By Reference to a Reference Plan

A surveyor prepares a reference plan in order to illustrate, in pictorial form, boundaries of land that were previously described in words using a metes and bounds description. The three reasons for creating and registering a reference plan are

1. to replace a complicated metes and bounds description;
2. to illustrate the severance of a lot; and
3. to illustrate a parcel of land where an easement has been granted (often to municipalities).

## Replacing a Metes and Bounds Description

A reference plan may be required to replace a metes and bounds description if the latter is so complex that there is a likelihood of error. In that case, a survey is prepared to clearly illustrate and mark the boundaries of the land in question. That survey is then registered as a **reference plan**. The reference plan is given a plan number preceded by the letter "R," which stands for "Reference Plan." Reference plans are often referred to as "R-Plans."

**reference plan**
registered survey prepared to illustrate the boundaries of a parcel of land

Once a reference plan is registered, one may describe the land by simply identifying its part or parts on the reference plan. The complex metes and bounds description is no longer required. For example, if a reference plan is registered on Lot 3, Concession I, Township of Nottawasaga, County of Simcoe, and if the land being conveyed is the east half of the south half of Lot 3, and if that land is described as Part 1 on R-Plan 4646, the legal description would be as follows: "Part of Lot 3, Concession I, Township of Nottawasaga, County of Simcoe, designated as Part 1 on R-Plan 4646." In this example, "Part 1 on R-Plan 4646" replaces the lengthy metes and bounds description.

## Severing a Lot

A reference plan may be required when an owner severs and sells part of a parcel of land (without using a plan of subdivision). Severances often create irregular and complicated boundaries of land. The reference plan clearly illustrates what part of the land is being severed and removes the need to create a new metes and bounds description.

## Creating an Easement

A reference plan may be required when an easement is created over property. The location of the easement on the original parcel of land can be easily depicted on a reference plan, and the land, together with the easement, can be more easily described by parts identified on the reference plan than by a metes and bounds description.

Figure 4.8 reproduces Reference Plan 65R-3541, which is a reference plan of Lots 88, 89, and 90 on Subdivision Plan 65M-1879 (reproduced in Figure 4.9). The plan was prepared to illustrate the severance of each of these lots as well as the creation of two easements affecting Lots 89 and 90.

As the plan illustrates, the three lots were severed into two parcels each, with each parcel identified by part numbers. Take a look at Lot 89. The northerly parcel comprises Parts 3 and 4, and the southerly parcel comprises Parts 5 and 6 on the reference plan. The plan also illustrates an easement affecting Lots 89 and 90, in the form of a mutual driveway shared by the two parcels.

**Figure 4.8   Reference Plan**

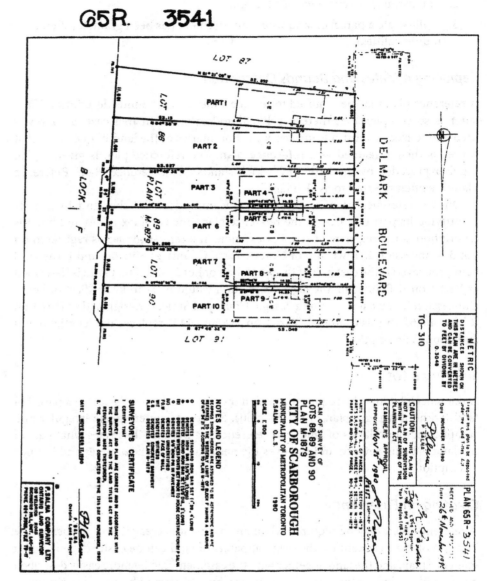

**Figure 4.9   Plan of Subdivision**

The legal description of the north half of Lot 89 reads as follows:

> In the City of Scarborough, in the Municipality of Metropolitan Toronto and being composed of part of Lot 89, Plan 65M-1879, designated as Parts 3 and 4 on Reference Plan 65R-3541 TOGETHER WITH an easement over Part 5 of the said plan and SUBJECT TO an easement over Part 4 on said plan in favour of the owner of Parts 5 and 6 of said plan.

The exact location and boundaries of the parcels and the easement are more easily described by a "picture" than by words. Also, metes and bounds descriptions are very problematic because of the typographical errors that have crept into deeds over time. These errors have in some cases created a lot of confusion as to the actual legal descriptions. For this reason, the land registrar generally no longer allows property to be conveyed with a metes and bounds description. Today, the land registrar typically insists that the owner register an R-Plan before transferring title, so that the legal description will be much clearer.

Figure 4.10 summarizes the different types of legal descriptions.

## Figure 4.10   Summary of Legal Descriptions

| Type of Description | Explanation | Example | Illustration |
|---|---|---|---|
| Whole concession lot | Parcel of land is described identifying the lot number and concession number | Lot 3, Concession I, Township of Nottawasaga, County of Simcoe | |
| Part (half or quarter) of a concession lot | Parcel of land is described by identifying the part of the concession lot | North ½ of Lot 3, Concession I, Township of Nottawasaga, County of Simcoe | |
| | | West ½ of the south ½ of Lot 3, Concession I, Township of Nottawasaga, County of Simcoe | |

(Figure 4.10 is continued on the next page.)

| Type of Description | Explanation | Example | Illustration |
|---|---|---|---|
| Metes and bounds description | Parcel of land is described using a written description of the land's boundaries and dimensions | Part of the north ½ of Lot 3, Concession I, Township of Nottawasaga, County of Simcoe, more particularly described as follows:<br><br>• Commencing at the northeast corner of Lot 3<br>• Thence south along the easterly border of Lot 3 a distance of 50'<br>• Thence west in a straight line running parallel with the northerly border of Lot 3 a distance of 150'<br>• Thence north in a straight line running parallel with the westerly border of Lot 3 a distance of 50' to a point in the northerly border of Lot 3<br>• Thence east along the northerly border of Lot 3 a distance of 150' to the point of commencement | Point of Commencement<br><br>Lot 3, Concession I |
| Reference plan | Parcel of land is described by identifying part(s) on the reference plan | Part of Lot 3, Concession I, Township of Nottawasaga, County of Simcoe, designated as Part 1 on R-Plan 63R-373 | Part 1 |
| Whole lot on a plan of subdivision | Parcel of land is described by identifying the lot and plan number | Lot 5, Plan 1234, Township of Nottawasaga, County of Simcoe | 14  1<br>13  2<br>12  3  Plan 1234<br>11  4<br>10  5<br>9  6<br>8  7 |

| Type of Description | Explanation | Example | Illustration |
|---|---|---|---|
| Reference plan (part of a lot on a plan of subdivision) | Parcel of land is described by identifying the lot and plan number on the plan of subdivision, followed by the part(s) on the reference plan (required when lot is severed) | Part of Lot 5, Plan 1234, Township of Nottawasaga, County of Simcoe, designated as Part 1 on Plan 63R-1234 | |

# KEY TERMS

concession, 38

legal description, 38

lot, 39

metes and bounds description, 41

municipality, 40

plan of subdivision, 40

reference plan, 43

# REVIEW QUESTIONS

1. How was land in Ontario originally divided?

2. What is a metes and bounds description?

3. What does a plan of subdivision illustrate?

4. When a plan of subdivision is registered, how is the property legally described?

5. When is a reference plan required?

6. Provide the legal description for the following parcels of land:

   a. the entire Lot 4, situated in Concession III, Township of Cavan

   b. the northwest quarter of Lot 2, Concession V, Township of Cavan

   c. the east half of Lot 7, Plan 1245, which was severed by Reference Plan R-6789. (In that plan, the west half of Lot 7 is designated as Part 1 and the east half as Part 2.)

# Land Registration Systems

# 5

## LEARNING OUTCOMES

After reading this chapter, you will understand:

- The concept of land registration

- The difference between the Land Titles system and the Registry system

- What a legal description is, and how it is derived

- How property in Ontario was mapped for the electronic land registration system, and how property identifier numbers (PINs) were created

- How electronic land registration differs from the paper-based system

# Introduction

Land registry systems record the consecutive ownership of land and other interests in land. These systems evolved over time, and registration of interests in land is mandatory. If an interest in land is not registered, a person who does not have actual notice of the unregistered interest may acquire an interest in the land that has priority over the unregistered interest.

# An Overview

A land registration system provides an orderly and detailed system of recording all interests affecting land. Documents that create or dispose of an interest in land or otherwise affect the use of land are filed and assigned a registration number. Information about the registered document and the interest it has created is summarized and entered into books and records to which the public has easy access.

The purpose of a land registration system is to provide protection for subsequent transactions with respect to the same land. It does so by

- establishing priority between competing claims against land; and
- providing public notice of interests in land.

Registration of a document merely provides notice of the existence of the document. It does not make the document legally effective.

## Priority Between Competing Claims

Priority of claims is based on the date and time of the document's registration, not the date on which the document was signed. If two people claim to have an interest in the same land, the interest with the earlier registration date will prevail, regardless of the date on which the transaction was completed.

For example, assume that John Smith needs a loan. On Thursday morning, he gets a loan from his bank and provides a signed charge/mortgage on his property in favour of the bank. The bank doesn't register the mortgage until Friday morning. In the meantime, on Thursday afternoon, John gets another loan from his Uncle Sam and also provides a signed mortgage on his property in favour of his uncle. His uncle registers his mortgage that same day. Uncle Sam's mortgage will have priority over the bank's even though it was signed *after* the bank's mortgage.

## Public Notice of Interests in Land

**deemed**
accepted as conclusive of a certain state or condition in the absence of evidence or facts usually required to prove that state or condition

Registration also offers protection for subsequent dealings with the same land by providing notice to the public of existing interests in the land. Any person who deals with land is **deemed** to have notice of interests that are already registered against the land and takes the land subject to those interests. This is true even if in fact the person has no personal or actual knowledge of the earlier interest in the land.

An interest in land that is not registered does not get the same protection. An unregistered claim against land may be defeated by a subsequent registered interest in the same land if the person registering the subsequent interest had no actual notice of the prior claim.

For example, assume that Mr. Singh agrees to sell to Mr. Jones a parcel of land in five years in exchange for five yearly payments in the amount of $50,000 each. Mr. Jones does not register a notice of this agreement on title to the land. Three years later, Mr. Singh dies and his executor, not knowing of the agreement, transfers the land to Mr. and Mrs. Greenwald, who also have no knowledge of the agreement. Mr. and Mrs. Greenwald search the title records prior to the sale. According to the title records, Mr. Singh had title free and clear of any other claims. Once Mr. and Mrs. Greenwald register their deed, Mr. Jones's claim on the land will be extinguished, unless Mr. and Mrs. Greenwald *actually* knew of the existence of Mr. Jones's prior agreement (had actual notice of his interest). In the absence of actual notice to Mr. and Mrs. Greenwald, Mr. Jones's unregistered interest will be void as against Mr. and Mrs. Greenwald's interest in the property.

# The Registry System

There are two systems of land registration in Ontario: the Registry system and the Land Titles system. All land in Ontario has been assigned to one of these two systems.

The **Registry system** was the first land registration system in Ontario. It was established in 1795 and is governed by the *Registry Act*. Under this system, all documents affecting title to a property are filed for registration in the appropriate registry office, and all registered documents are recorded in an index book called an abstract book. On being registered, a document is assigned a registration number, which is noted on the document along with the date of registration and the registrar's certificate as evidence of the registration.

**Registry system**
land registration system in Ontario governed by the *Registry Act*

## Abstract Books

**Abstract books** are organized by township. When land was first transferred by Crown patent, the land registrar in the geographic area where the land was situated opened a new page in the abstract book for each concession lot that had been patented. All registrations relating to that piece of land, starting with the Crown patent, are recorded on the appropriate page in the abstract book in order of registration, together with a brief summary of the document. The actual documents are filed in the office and are available for the public to examine (originally in paper form and later either in paper form or on microfilm). For example, there is an abstract book for the Township of Cavan, Concession III. Inside the abstract book, there are separate pages for each of Lots 1, 2, 3, and so on. If the concession is later subdivided by a registered plan of subdivision, the registrar creates a new abstract book for the plan of subdivision, with a separate page for each lot within the plan.

If a lot has been severed into two or more parcels, information relating to all the different parts of the lot continues to be entered on the same page for that lot. For

**abstract book**
book in the Registry system that records registered interests in land

example, assume that Lot 7, Plan 1234 has been severed into a west half and an east half. There will be an abstract book for Plan 1234 that contains a page for Lot 7. That page contains entries for registered documents that deal with either half of the lot. People searching the title to Lot 7 have to sort through the various entries and determine which entries are relevant to the half of the lot they are interested in.

As discussed below under the heading "POLARIS," the print abstract books have been replaced by computer-generated title indexes. However, print abstract books are still used occasionally for title searching in the Registry system, and are discussed in Chapter 14.

## Legal Descriptions

A document that is to be registered in the Registry system must contain a legal description of the property. The legal description will refer first to the lot number and then to the number of the concession or plan of subdivision in which the lot is located. An example for a plan of subdivision would be Lot 5, Plan 1234, Township of Nottawasaga, County of Simcoe.

## Effect of Registration

**grant**
document that transfers ownership of land

Section 74 of the *Registry Act* provides that registration of a document constitutes notice of the document to all persons claiming an interest in the land subsequent to registration. Registration, however, does *not* guarantee that a document is valid or legally effective. Under the Registry system, an individual acquiring an interest in land must both review the abstract book *and* examine all documents noted on title, to ensure that all the documents have the legal effect they purport to have.

**deed**
document that transfers ownership of land

## Types of Documents

**transfer**
document that transfers ownership of land

Many different kinds of documents have been registered over the years under the Registry system. These include

**power of attorney**
document authorizing someone to deal with land or other property on the owner's behalf

- documents that transfer ownership of land—called, at different times, **grants**, **deeds**, or **transfers**;
- documents that create a mortgage against land—called, at different times, mortgages or charges;

**bylaw**
law that is passed by a municipality

- documents related to mortgages—discharges of mortgage (or discharges of charge), agreements amending mortgage (or charge), and assignments of mortgage (or charge);
- **powers of attorney**—documents that authorize someone to deal with land on the owner's behalf;

**subdivision agreement**
agreement between a municipality and a builder setting out the terms under which the builder is allowed to subdivide the land

- **bylaws**—laws passed by a municipality that affect land;
- **subdivision agreements**—agreements between a municipality and a builder setting out the terms under which the builder is allowed to subdivide the land;

- documents dealing with the estates of owners—**wills** and certificates proving payment of inheritance taxes; and
- **deposits**—documents that verify or clarify facts related to the title to the property.

These documents are discussed in more detail in Chapter 14, Title Searching, and in Chapter 20, The Requisition Letter.

# The Land Titles System

The **Land Titles system** is the other system of land registration in Ontario, and it is now the main system. It was established in 1885 and is governed by the *Land Titles Act*. Unlike the Registry system, which simply provides a record of documents affecting title, this system provides a statement of title as a fact; the government guarantees the accuracy of title to land registered in the Land Titles system. The parcel register (discussed below) always reflects the current state of title. There are, however, a number of qualifications to the government's certification of title. For example, land in the Land Titles system is subject to

- provincial taxes, succession duties, and municipal taxes;
- rights of the Crown by authority of any statute; and
- *Planning Act* considerations.

Under the Land Titles system, the land registrar assumes responsibility for stating whether the title of the current registered owner is valid. If there is an error regarding title, a person wrongfully deprived of some estate or interest in land can request compensation from the **Land Titles Assurance Fund**, a fund established under the *Land Titles Act*.

## Parcel Register

In the original Land Titles system, registrations were recorded in a book called the **parcel register**. Parcel registers were organized differently than were abstract books under the Registry system. Each separately owned parcel of land, whether a whole lot or a part of a lot, was assigned its own page, and all entries on that page related only to that parcel of land. As each new registration was certified by the land registrar, the registrar either cancelled earlier registrations by ruling them off or modified them. Documents in the Land Titles system, as it developed, were stored in a computer index and were available for public viewing on microfilm. Today, as discussed below under the heading "POLARIS," the parcel registers are all computerized.

## Legal Descriptions

A document that is to be registered in the Land Titles system must, as in the Registry system, contain a legal description of the property, but legal descriptions in the Land Titles system are different from those in the Registry system. In the Land Titles

**will**
document stating how a person's property will be dealt with upon the person's death

**deposit**
document registered on title that verifies or clarifies facts related to the title

**Land Titles system**
land registration system in Ontario governed by the *Land Titles Act*

**Land Titles Assurance Fund**
fund established under the *Land Titles Act* to compensate a person wrongfully deprived of an estate or interest in land as a result of an error regarding title

**parcel register**
book in the Land Titles system that records all registered interests in land

system, the legal description will refer to the parcel number and then the section number, in addition to the lot and plan number. If the parcel is the whole of a lot, the parcel number will be followed by "–1." If the parcel is a part of a lot, the parcel number will be followed by "–2," "–3," and so on. Plan of subdivision numbers start with the number of the Land Titles office in which the plan is registered, followed by the letter "M" for "Master of Land Titles." Two examples of legal descriptions in the style of the Land Titles system are as follows:

- Parcel 4–1, Section 66M3456, being Lot 4, Plan 66M3456, City of Toronto; and
- Parcel 2–3, Section 66M3456 (part of Lot 2, Plan 66M3456), City of Toronto.

In both of these examples, 66 is the number of the Toronto Land Titles Office. The first example is the description of the whole of a lot, a fact that is indicated by the "–1" in the parcel number. The second example is the description of part of a lot, as indicated by "–3" in the parcel number.

# POLARIS

**POLARIS**
Province of Ontario Land Registration Information System; computerized land information system

The province has almost completed a major revision to land registration in Ontario. The project, called **POLARIS** (Province of Ontario Land Registration Information System), began in 1985 with the overall objective of simplifying registration of documents and title searching.

The *Land Registration Reform Act*, which was originally enacted in 1984 and came into effect on April 1, 1985, authorized the implementation of the POLARIS initiatives, which include

1. computerizing title records for each property in Ontario;
2. developing a property mapping system;
3. standardizing forms and procedures;
4. converting Registry system properties to the Land Titles system;
5. converting all paper documents to microfilm;
6. providing for electronic title searching and writ searching;
7. providing for the electronic registration of documents; and
8. integrating all land-related information and databases into one centralized, online land information system.

As of March 2011, 99.9 percent of all land in Ontario was registered under the Land Titles system, and since then the Registry system has been used only for properties that could not be converted to the Land Titles system because of an outstanding title issue. In the Land Titles system, land records have now been computerized in one centralized system, and searches and registrations can be done online using Teraview software, discussed below and in Chapter 7. The POLARIS initiatives have effectively all been implemented, and almost all searches and registrations are now completed electronically.

Below, we will look at the following key aspects of POLARIS:

- computerization of land records;
- documents used under POLARIS;
- property mapping under POLARIS; and
- electronic land registration.

## Computerization of Land Records

POLARIS consists of three databases:

1. *Title Index database.* This database replaces the paper abstract book (in the Registry system) and the parcel register (in the Land Titles system) with computer-generated title indexes.
2. *Property Index database.* This database provides a visual index map to all properties and illustrates the property's position in relationship to adjoining properties. Each property is assigned a property identifier number (PIN). The PIN links the information in this database to the information in the Title Index database.
3. *Central Image Storage database.* This database contains images of all documents that have been registered, and allows online access to all registered documents.

## POLARIS Documents

Prior to 1985, documents used to convey an interest in land were often extremely lengthy. Also, different documents were used, depending on whether the property was registered in the Land Titles system or the Registry system. POLARIS created five document forms, to be used in both systems. These forms were standardized, shortened, and designed to accommodate any registered interest in land. The five forms are

- Form 1, Transfer/Deed of Land, used to register an ownership interest in the land (reproduced in Figure 5.1—see end of chapter);
- Form 2, Charge/Mortgage of Land, used to register a charge (mortgage) interest in the land (reproduced in Figure 5.2—see end of chapter);
- Form 3, Discharge of Charge/Mortgage, used to register a discharge of a charge interest in the land (reproduced in Figure 5.3—see end of chapter);
- Form 4, Document General, used to register any other type of instrument or interest that affects the use of the land (reproduced in Figure 5.4—see end of chapter); and
- Form 5, Schedule, used to register additional information that will not fit on any of the other forms (reproduced in Figure 5.5—see end of chapter).

These forms eliminated the requirement for personal and corporate seals, and the need for the lengthy affidavits that previously accompanied documents affecting land. The truth of statements set out in each form is acknowledged when the form is signed.

Initially, these five forms were used in both systems. Now, the forms are used only in the Registry system, since the Land Titles system is entirely electronic and no longer uses paper documents. Samples of the electronic forms are found in Chapter 7.

## Property Mapping Under POLARIS

Under POLARIS, all properties in Ontario are mapped. Property mapping allows for

- the determination of the number of properties in a given area;
- the creation of a unique identifying number for each property, a number that provides access to title records; and
- the visual identification of properties, of their location, and of the location of adjoining properties.

**block**
area of land created during the mapping of property under POLARIS

The province has been divided into **blocks**, with each block identified by a five-digit **block number**. Block index maps illustrate the location of numbered blocks within a municipality. Blocks have been further divided into **properties**, each identified by a unique four-digit **property number**. The combination of the block number and the property number creates a unique nine-digit **property identifier number (PIN)** for every property.

**block number**
five-digit number assigned to a block; the first part of the PIN

When a property was entered into POLARIS, the page in the abstract book or parcel register was stamped with a notation indicating the date of automation. Registrations that take place after that date are recorded on the computerized abstract only and can be accessed using the PIN.

**property**
term used to describe area of land created by the division of blocks during the mapping of land under POLARIS

Once a property has been entered into POLARIS, title information is indexed according to the PIN and not according to the legal description of land. The legal description of the land remains unchanged, but title-related information can be accessed only by using the PIN, not by the legal description.

**property number**
four-digit number assigned to a property; the second part of the PIN

## Electronic Land Registration

The final stage of POLARIS, after land registration records were automated and Registry system properties were converted to the Land Titles system, was electronic registration (or **e-reg**). It is a fully electronic and paperless registration system for properties in the Land Titles system.

**property identifier number (PIN)**
unique nine-digit number for each property created by combining the block number and property number for that property

Electronic registration is provided for in part III of the *Land Registration Reform Act*. Section 21 of the Act provides that an electronic document that creates, transfers, or otherwise disposes of an estate in land need not be in writing or signed. Electronic registration enables documents to be created, signed, exchanged between law offices, maintained, and registered, all in an electronic format. Documents are no longer registered by personally attending at the land registry office. They are registered electronically from a personal computer in a lawyer's office or from kiosks at the land registry office.

**e-reg**
an electronic registration system under POLARIS

In addition, e-reg software allows lawyers and the public to conduct database searches and to view and print title indexes.

### Using the Electronic Land Registration System Through Teraview

The Ontario government licensed Teranet Inc. to create the Electronic Land Registration System (ELRS) for the government of Ontario. In order to use the ELRS, a person (lawyer or law firm) must purchase the **Teraview** software and a licence, and must be authorized by the Director of Land Registration, which requires applying to be a Teraview Account Holder. Other people in the Teraview Account Holder's office can obtain Personal Security Licences (PSLs) that allow them to access the system to look at documents, to change or create documents, and to register documents, all under the supervision of the Teraview Account Holder.

Certain functions, such as making **compliance with law statements** (statements in which a lawyer states that all necessary requirements have been met), can be performed only by qualified lawyers. This is discussed further in Chapter 7.

### Documents for Electronic Registration

Under the *Land Registration Reform Act*, the format of electronically registered documents is different from the paper forms. Special templates containing substantially the same information as POLARIS forms have been created for e-reg use.

The documents are prepared by means of the Teraview software, which provides an onscreen menu from which the user selects the form required. Once the user enters the PIN of the property into the form, the system automatically loads into the new document the name of the present owner, the municipal address, and the legal description. If the user needs to include statements in the document, such as statements under the *Planning Act* or *Family Law Act*, he or she selects them from a drop-down list of all possible statements. This process of carrying forward information and entering it into the document is called **pre-population**. It removes the need to enter basic information already contained in the register. The system prompts the user to enter the names of new owners and any other new title information. The program automatically warns the user if he or she has left something out of a draft registration, such as a required statement. The system allows for the registration of a document only after all mandatory information has been submitted.

Since e-reg documents are electronic, there is no paper document for a lawyer or client to sign. As a result, the system uses **digital signatures**. Participating lawyers are assigned a unique digital identifier comparable to a password or bank PIN, which serves as a signature.

**Teraview**
software used to access the Electronic Land Registration System in Ontario

**compliance with law statement**
a lawyer's statement that the applicable legal requirements have been met

**pre-population**
electronic process of copying information from a database into a document

**digital signatures**
unique digital identifiers used by lawyers when documents are registered electronically, comparable to a password or bank PIN

## KEY TERMS

## REFERENCES

*Condominium Act, 1998*, SO 1998, c 19.

*Family Law Act*, RSO 1990, c F.3.

*Land Registration Reform Act*, RSO 1990, c L.4.

*Land Titles Act*, RSO 1990, c L.5.

*Planning Act*, RSO 1990, c P.13.

*Registry Act*, RSO 1990, c R.20.

## REVIEW QUESTIONS

1. What are two important features of a land registration system?

2. Shondra is buying a property and is told that the property is in the Land Titles system. What is the advantage of the property being in the Land Titles system?

3. What information is recorded in the abstract book and the parcel register?

4. What is the effect of registration of a document?

5. How is priority determined between two competing interests in land?

6. List three initiatives of the POLARIS project.

7. What information do you require to access the computerized land records?

8. What is e-reg?

9. How are documents submitted if they are going to be registered electronically?

10. What is a digital signature?

**Figure 5.1   Transfer/Deed of Land**

### Figure 5.2 Charge/Mortgage of Land

**Charge/Mortgage of Land**

Form 2 — Land Registration Reform Act

Province of Ontario

DYE & DURHAM CFS POLARIS 1995

**B**

**(1) Registry** ☐ **Land Titles** ☐ **(2)** Page 1 of ____ pages

**(3) Property Identifier(s)** Block ____ Property ____ Additional: See Schedule ☐

**(4) Principal Amount** ____ Dollars $

**(5) Description**

FOR OFFICE USE ONLY

**New Property Identifiers** Additional: See Schedule ☐

**Executions** Additional: See Schedule ☐

**(6) This Document Contains** (a) Redescription New Easement Plan/Sketch ☐ (b) Schedule for: Description ☐ Additional Parties ☐ Other ☐ **(7) Interest/Estate Charged**

**(8) Standard Charge Terms** — The parties agree to be bound by the provisions in Standard Charge Terms filed as number ____ and the Chargor(s) hereby acknowledge(s) receipt of a copy of these terms.

**(9) Payment Provisions**
(a) Principal Amount $ ____ (b) Interest Rate ____ % per annum (c) Calculation Period ____
(d) Interest Adjustment Date Y M D (e) Payment Date and Period ____ (f) First Payment Date Y M D
(g) Last Payment Date ____ (h) Amount of Each Payment ____ Dollars $
(i) Balance Due Date ____ (j) Insurance ____ Dollars $

**(10) Additional Provisions**

Continued on Schedule ☐

**(11) Chargor(s)** The chargor hereby charges the land to the chargee and certifies that the chargor is at least eighteen years old and that

The chargor(s) acknowledge(s) receipt of a true copy of this charge.
Name(s) ____ Signature(s) ____ Date of Signature Y M D

**(12) Spouse(s) of Chargor(s)** I hereby consent to this transaction.
Name(s) ____ Signature(s) ____ Date of Signature Y M D

**(13) Chargor(s) Address for Service**

**(14) Chargee(s)**

**(15) Chargee(s) Address for Service**

**(16) Assessment Roll Number of Property** Cty. Mun. Map Sub. Par.

**(17) Municipal Address of Property** **(18) Document Prepared by:**

FOR OFFICE USE ONLY

Fees

Registration Fee ____

Total ____

**Figure 5.3   Discharge of Charge/Mortgage**

**Figure 5.4    Document General**

**Figure 5.5 Schedule**

Province
of
Ontario

DYE & DURHAM CO. INC.—Form No. 990
Amended NOV. 1992

# Schedule

Form 5 — Land Registration Reform Act

**S**

Page_____

Additional Property Identifier(s) and /or Other Information

FOR OFFICE
USE ONLY

# Charges/Mortgages 6

## LEARNING OUTCOMES

After reading this chapter, you will understand:

- Basic mortgage concepts and terminology
- How to create a mortgage
- What the obligations of a mortgagor are
- How to determine priority of mortgages
- What mortgage remedies are available to a mortgagee

# Introduction

Most people need to borrow money to finance the purchase of real property, and sometimes people who already own a property may need to borrow money to renovate or pay off other debts. When people use real property as security for a loan, a mortgage or charge is created. Today, the terms "mortgage" and "charge" mean the same thing and are used interchangeably; there is no legal distinction between them. Historically, however, the terms had different meanings.

"Mortgage" is a much older term than "charge," dating back to the 12th or 13th century. In Ontario, until the late 20th century, the term was used to mean a loan secured against land registered in the Registry system. A mortgage actually transferred the legal estate in land to the lender (called the **mortgagee**). The landowner/borrower (called the **mortgagor**) was entitled to remain in possession and have title restored when the debt was paid in full. The term "charge" was used to describe a loan secured against land registered in the Land Titles system. A charge did not transfer the legal estate to the lender (called the **chargee**), but, instead, created only an encumbrance on the legal estate of the landowner/borrower (called the **chargor**).

The *Land Registration Reform Act* eliminated the distinction between the Registry system and the Land Titles system and created a document—the charge/mortgage of land form—to be used in both. The charge/mortgage of land has the same legal effect as a charge under the Land Titles system. When a charge/mortgage of land is registered, it conveys an interest (but not an ownership interest) in the land secured by the charge to the lender (chargee). The document also contains details of the loan, including all the provisions for its repayment. If the chargor doesn't pay or breaches other terms of the charge, the chargee can sell the property and use the proceeds to pay off the money owing.

**mortgagee**
lender

**mortgagor**
borrower and owner

**chargee**
lender

**chargor**
borrower and owner

# The Parties to a Charge/Mortgage

The terminology concerning a charge/mortgage can be confusing to anyone who is not familiar with this area of law. The *chargor/mortgagor* is the landowner who is borrowing the money, also referred to as the *debtor*. The *chargee/mortgagee* is the financial institution (such as a bank), company, or individual who lends the money, also referred to as the *creditor*. The chargor/mortgagor gives the charge/mortgage (the security interest in the land) to the chargee/mortgagee.

For example, assume that Alice borrows $100,000 from Best Bank and gives a charge on her property as security for the loan. Alice is the chargor, and Best Bank is the chargee. A search of title to Alice's property will show Alice as the owner and Best Bank as the holder of a charge interest in the amount of $100,000. Both Alice and Best Bank will have a registered interest in the property.

Most borrowers and lenders and many lawyers still use the term "mortgage" and related terms in describing these transactions. For the remainder of this chapter, when discussing charges and mortgages, we use the terms *mortgagor* and *mortgagee* interchangeably with *chargor* and *chargee*. We also refer to the mortgagor/chargor as the borrower, and the mortgagee/chargee as the lender. It is common to hear all of these terms being used when you are arranging a mortgage.

# Priorities Between Charges

It is possible for the owner of real property to grant successive charges to different lenders. If multiple charges are registered against title, the order of registration determines the order of **priority** between (or among) the charges. The charge with the earlier registration date (or the earlier registration time on the same date) will have priority. In the event of default, the charge with priority will be paid out first.

For example, Steven arranges a new charge for $350,000 with Best Bank to help pay for his $500,000 house. Six months later, Steven arranges to borrow $100,000 from Generous Bank to help pay for renovations to the house. Steven can give another charge to Generous Bank as security for the loan. The charge in favour of Best Bank is called a **first charge**, and the charge in favour of Generous Bank is called a **second charge**. Best Bank's charge is said to have priority over Generous Bank's charge. Steven will have to make the loan payments on both charges in accordance with the payment schedules in the loan agreements. The priority of registration does not mean that Best Bank gets its loan paid off before payments begin to Generous Bank. However, if Steven ever defaults on the loan, the priority of registration determines the rights to **realize on the security** by selling the land. The proceeds of any sale under the power of sale (discussed below) will be used to pay Best Bank's charge first. Any money that is left over will be used to pay Generous Bank. Therefore, if the property sells for $400,000, Best Bank will receive the first $350,000, and Generous Bank will receive only the balance of $50,000 because it is second in priority.

# How a Charge Is Created

Charges most commonly arise in the context of a purchase of real property. The possible circumstances including the following:

- The buyer can arrange a **new charge** with a bank or other lender and use the borrowed money to pay for the property. If there is already a charge registered against the title to the property, the buyer will agree with the seller, in the agreement of purchase and sale, that the existing charge will be discharged prior to closing. A new charge can also be created by a person who is already the owner of the property. For example, if Alan owns a cottage, and he wants to borrow $35,000 to buy a new car, he can mortgage the cottage to secure the loan.

- The buyer can agree to assume (take over) an existing charge already registered on title and pay the seller the purchase price less the amount of this charge (called an **assumed charge**).

- The buyer can agree to borrow money for the purchase price from the seller and give back to the seller a charge on the property as security for the loan (called a **vendor-take-back charge** or **charge taken back**).

**priority**
rank or status of a registered interest in land as determined by the date of registration of that interest

**first charge**
charge registered first and thus taking priority over subsequently registered charges

**second charge**
charge registered after the first charge and thus having subsequent priority to the first

**realize on the security**
seize and/or sell the charged property

**new charge**
arrangement by the buyer for a new loan by way of a charge for the purchase of property

**assumed charge**
existing charge taken over by the buyer, who pays the seller the purchase price of the property minus the outstanding balance of the charge

**vendor-take-back charge (or charge taken back)**
charge created when the seller of a property agrees to lend the buyer money toward the purchase price and the buyer gives the seller a charge on the property as security for the loan

Usually a buyer will require only one charge when buying a home. However, a buyer can obtain more than one if it is needed. For example, a buyer can assume an existing charge and also arrange a new one as a second charge; or a buyer can arrange two new charges—a first charge and a second charge.

## New Charge

A new charge (also referred to as an *arranged charge*) is used when the buyer makes arrangements with a lender to borrow money by way of a charge for the purchase of property. For example, assume that Sam is selling his home for $300,000. Bao wants to buy the home but he only has $200,000. Bao will have to borrow the additional funds needed from his bank and use the property as security for the loan. The bank will give Bao $100,000, and Bao will give the bank a charge on the property. Bao will have $300,000 to pay to Sam, and Sam will transfer title to Bao. Title to the real property will show (1) Bao as the owner of the property and (2) a charge in the amount of $100,000 in favour of the bank. Preparation of a new charge is discussed in Chapter 29, Acting for the Mortgagee.

Figure 6.1 illustrates the flow of money and property interests in a new charge transaction.

### Figure 6.1    New Charge Transaction

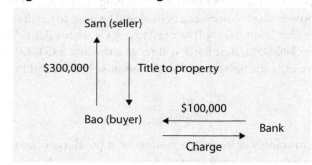

## Assumed Charge

Instead of arranging a new charge, a buyer may agree to assume an existing charge previously registered against title to the property being purchased. The buyer will pay the seller the purchase price minus the outstanding balance owing on the charge. The buyer will take over the charge and make the future loan payments.

A buyer may choose this option if (1) the balance outstanding on the existing charge is close to the amount the buyer needs to borrow and (2) the existing charge has favourable terms. For example, the interest rate payable on the charge may be lower than the interest rate the buyer would get if arranging a new charge. In addition, assuming a charge may eliminate the legal costs that are involved in arranging a new charge.

The seller may also benefit if the charge is assumed, because a lender generally charges a **prepayment penalty** if a borrower pays off the charge before the end of the term. The seller will not have to pay off the charge early (or the penalty) if the

**prepayment penalty**
penalty charged by the lender if the borrower pays off the charge before the end of the term

buyer assumes the charge. It should be noted that the consent of the lender is generally required for a charge to be assumed by a buyer.

For example, assume that Sam is selling his home to Bao for $300,000. There is an outstanding charge in favour of Best Bank in the amount of $100,000; that is, Sam owes Best Bank $100,000. Bao has only $200,000 and needs to borrow $100,000. If the interest rate of Sam's charge is 3 percent, and the best interest rate that Bao can obtain from a lender is 5 percent, then Bao is better off assuming Sam's charge. If Best Bank agrees, Bao assumes this charge and pays Sam $200,000 (the amount of the purchase price less Sam's debt). In effect, Bao will replace Sam in the relationship with Best Bank and assume all of Sam's obligations under the charge.

Figure 6.2 illustrates the flow of money and property interests in an assumed charge transaction.

**Figure 6.2   Assumed Charge Transaction**

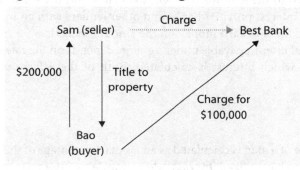

## Vendor-Take-Back Charge

Sometimes a buyer is unable to borrow money from traditional sources or to borrow enough money to purchase the property. In this situation, a buyer may ask the seller to lend the buyer money, and, if the seller has no other attractive offers for the property, the seller may agree to do so and take back a charge on the property. This type of charge is referred to as a vendor-take-back charge, or charge taken back. It may be a first charge or a second or subsequent charge.

For example, assume that Sam is selling his property for $300,000. Bao is willing to pay $300,000 for the property but can come up with only $250,000. Sam can agree to accept payment of $250,000 at the time of the sale and, effectively, loan Bao the difference by taking back a charge on the property in the amount of $50,000.

Figure 6.3 illustrates this type of charge transaction.

**Figure 6.3   Vendor-Take-Back Charge Transaction**

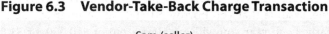

# Charge Terminology

Discussing charges involves a number of specialized terms. The most important ones are discussed below.

## Principal

**principal**
amount of money borrowed under a loan

The **principal** is the amount of money borrowed by the chargor (or loaned by the chargee) under the charge, which the chargor must repay.

## Interest

**interest**
amount added to the principal amount of the loan in return for the right to obtain and use the money advanced

In addition to repaying the principal over time, the chargor must also pay **interest**, an amount added to the loan for the right to borrow and use the money advanced under the loan. Interest provides banks and other lenders with an incentive to lend money, allowing them to earn money on the amount loaned.

The amount of interest payable under a charge depends on the rate of interest and the intervals at which interest is calculated. Both of these factors are discussed below.

## Interest Rate

**interest rate**
rate charged for the use of borrowed money, calculated as a percentage of the amount of the loan

**fixed interest rate**
rate of interest that remains the same for the term of the charge

**variable interest rate**
rate of interest that fluctuates with changing market conditions during the term of the loan

**prime lending rate**
interest rate, based on the Bank of Canada rate, at which banks lend to most credit-worthy customers

The **interest rate** of a loan is calculated as an annual percentage of the amount of the loan. A charge can have a **fixed interest rate** or a **variable interest rate**. A fixed interest rate remains at the same percentage for the entire term of the charge. A variable interest rate changes during the term of the charge as the **prime lending rate**—based on the Bank of Canada rate—fluctuates. A variable rate will typically be expressed as "prime plus X percent." As the prime lending rate goes up and down, so does the interest rate on the charge.

## Calculation of Interest

The frequency at which interest is calculated under a charge is another factor in how much interest is payable under the charge. Usually, interest is not calculated as frequently as charge payments are made. Interest is often calculated annually (yearly) or semi-annually (twice per year), while charge payments are made at more frequent intervals—weekly, biweekly, or, most commonly, monthly. The frequency of the calculation affects the dollar amount of the interest payable: the more frequently interest is calculated, the more interest the mortgagor ends up paying.

For example, assume that you borrow $10,000 at an interest rate of 10 percent calculated yearly. Each year you will pay 10 percent of $10,000, or $1,000. The following illustrates an interest calculation for the same loan, but calculated (or compounded) half-yearly rather than yearly:

- After six months, you will owe interest of $500 (yearly interest at 10 percent on $10,000, or $1,000 divided by 2).

- If the interest is not paid at that time, interest for the next six months is calculated on the new total owing of $10,500 (that is, the original principal of $10,000 plus the interest for the first six months of $500). The interest for this six-month period is 10 percent of $10,500 divided by 2, or $525.

- The total interest payable for the year is $1,025, as compared to $1,000 in the previous example.

Most institutional charges calculate interest semi-annually. However, it is always important to pay attention to both the rate of interest in a charge and the frequency at which interest is calculated. A lower rate of interest can be offset by frequent calculation of the interest at that rate. This is known as **compounding the interest**.

All of the examples in this chapter assume that mortgage payments are made monthly.

## Term

The **term** of the charge is the period of time within which the chargor has agreed to repay the loan in full. It is usually between one and five years. At the end of the specified term (also known as the **maturity date**), the chargor must either pay back the outstanding balance of the loan or renew the charge for another term. For example, assume that Alan borrows money from Best Bank on December 1, 2015. If the mortgage is for a two-year term, Alan will have to repay Best Bank on December 1, 2017 or renew the charge for another term. If the charge is renewed for another term, which is most often the case, the interest rate may change, depending on current market rates.

## Amortization Period

The **amortization period** of a charge is the total length of time it will take to pay off the charge in full following the monthly payment amounts in the charge. Most people borrow hundreds of thousands of dollars, and the term of most charges is 5 years or less. The monthly payments on such a large principal amount would be too much for most people to afford if they were expected to repay the loan in full over such a short term. As a result, most charges are amortized over a much longer period of time than the term of the charge (usually 25 years).

If a charge has a 5-year term and a 25-year amortization period, the monthly payments of the charge are calculated as if there were 25 years to pay off the loan. At the end of the 5-year term, a very large amount of the principal will remain unpaid. This large final payment is called a **balloon payment**.

For example, assume that Alice has arranged a charge with Best Bank in the amount of $100,000 at a fixed interest rate of 5 percent. The term of the charge is 2 years, and the loan has an amortization period of 25 years. The monthly payments are $581.61. If Alice were to make monthly payments of $581.61 for 25 years, the loan would be paid in full. Because the term is a much shorter period of time than the amortization period, at the expiration of the 2-year term, the balance outstanding on the loan will be $95,740.20. At this point in time, Alice will either have to make

**compounding interest**
adding interest to the principal and then calculating future interest on that amount

**term**
length of time that the borrower and lender are bound by the charge contract

**maturity date**
date on which any outstanding balance of a charge is to be paid

**amortization period**
length of time it takes to repay a loan in full following the schedule of monthly payments in the charge

**balloon payment**
final payment for the amount of principal that remains unpaid at the end of the term of a charge

this balloon payment or, more likely, have to renew the charge for another term. Below, we discuss in more detail how these payments are calculated and applied.

## Charge Payments

Principal and interest payable under a charge are paid in arrears, not in advance. If a loan is **advanced** (in other words, the loan money is given to the chargor) on the 1st day of a month, charge payments are not due until the 1st day of the following month. The interest paid at that time is for the use of the money during the preceding month. This contrasts with residential rental payments, which are usually payable in advance—on the 1st day of each month—for the use of the rented premises for that month.

*advanced*
given or provided

## Blended Payments

*blended payment*
charge payment combining principal and interest into equal monthly payments

**Blended payments** combine principal and interest into one monthly payment that remains equal throughout the term of the mortgage. In other words, the payment amount remains the same each month; part of each payment is applied toward the interest that has accumulated on the loan, and the remaining part is applied toward repaying the principal. Initially, although the payment is the same each month, a greater portion of it is applied toward interest than toward principal. Gradually, over the term of the loan, as more of the principal is repaid, the interest portion of each payment decreases (because interest is paid only on the outstanding principal) while the portion applied toward repayment of the principal increases.

## Non-Blended Payments

*non-blended payment*
charge payment that does not blend or combine principal and interest into equal payments; the amount of principal repaid each month is a fixed amount and the amount of interest is calculated on the outstanding principal at the time

**Non-blended payments** do not combine principal and interest into equal monthly payments. The amount of principal repaid each month is a fixed amount, and interest is paid on the outstanding principal at the time. The amount of interest payable decreases as the loan is paid off, and so the total monthly payment decreases each month.

## Interest-Only Payments

In some charges—most commonly, private charges as opposed to institutional charges—the borrower is required to pay only the interest on the principal, with nothing paid toward the principal itself until the end of the charge term, at which time the full principal is due.

## Amortization Schedule

*amortization schedule*
schedule setting out the breakdown of each monthly blended payment between principal and interest, and the remaining principal balance after each payment

An **amortization schedule** illustrates how blended payments are applied each month. It shows what part of each monthly payment is applied toward principal, what part is applied toward interest, and the principal balance outstanding on the charge after each payment is made. Figure 6.4 shows the amortization schedule for

Alice's charge with Best Bank, discussed above—that is, a charge of $100,000 that has a fixed interest rate of 5 percent, a 2-year term, and a 25-year amortization period. Each monthly payment of $581.61 combines principal and interest. Note how the interest portion of each payment decreases while the principal portion increases. Note also how little of the principal amount will be repaid after the first two years. In fact, after 24 months of payments, the principal owing (the balloon payment) is $95,740.20. Alice can either pay this amount in full (if she has the money), renew the term of the charge at the current interest rate, or refinance the charge. Renewing the term of the charge and/or refinancing the amount outstanding requires the chargor to negotiate with the existing chargee or with a different chargee to obtain the best interest rate possible. If Alice (the chargor) refinances with a different bank, she will use the money advanced by that bank to pay off the remaining balance.

**Figure 6.4   Amortization Schedule—Principal $100,000, Interest 5%, 2-Year Term, 25-Year Amortization**

| Payment number | Principal outstanding | Payment | Interest portion | Principal portion | Principal balance after payment |
|---|---|---|---|---|---|
| 1 | $100,000.00 | $581.61 | $412.39 | $169.22 | $99,830.78 |
| 2 | $99,830.78 | $581.61 | $411.69 | $169.92 | $99,660.87 |
| 3 | $99,660.87 | $581.61 | $410.99 | $170.62 | $99,490.25 |
| 4 | $99,490.25 | $581.61 | $410.29 | $171.32 | $99,318.93 |
| 5 | $99,318.93 | $581.61 | $409.58 | $172.03 | $99,146.90 |
| 6 | $99,146.90 | $581.61 | $408.87 | $172.74 | $98,974.16 |
| 7 | $98,974.16 | $581.61 | $408.16 | $173.45 | $98,800.72 |
| 8 | $98,800.72 | $581.61 | $407.45 | $174.16 | $98,626.55 |
| 9 | $98,626.55 | $581.61 | $406.73 | $174.88 | $98,451.67 |
| 10 | $98,451.67 | $581.61 | $406.01 | $175.60 | $98,276.06 |
| 11 | $98,276.06 | $581.61 | $405.28 | $176.33 | $98,099.74 |
| 12 | $98,099.74 | $581.61 | $404.57 | $177.06 | $97,922.68 |
| 13 | $97,922.68 | $581.61 | $403.82 | $177.79 | $97,744.90 |
| 14 | $97,744.90 | $581.61 | $403.09 | $178.52 | $97,566.38 |
| 15 | $97,566.38 | $581.61 | $402.36 | $179.25 | $97,387.12 |
| 16 | $97,387.12 | $581.61 | $401.62 | $179.99 | $97,207.13 |
| 17 | $97,207.13 | $581.61 | $400.87 | $180.74 | $97,026.39 |

(Figure 6.4 is concluded on the following page.)

| Payment number | Principal outstanding | Payment | Interest portion | Principal portion | Principal balance after payment |
|---|---|---|---|---|---|
| 18 | $97,026.39 | $581.61 | $400.13 | $181.48 | $96,844.91 |
| 19 | $96,844.91 | $581.61 | $399.38 | $182.23 | $96,662.68 |
| 20 | $96,662.68 | $581.61 | $398.63 | $182.98 | $96,479.70 |
| 21 | $96,479.70 | $581.61 | $397.87 | $183.74 | $96,295.97 |
| 22 | $96,295.97 | $581.61 | $397.12 | $184.49 | $96,111.47 |
| 23 | $96,111.47 | $581.61 | $396.36 | $185.25 | $95,926.22 |
| 24 | $95,926.22 | $581.61 | $395.59 | $186.02 | $95,740.20 |

## Interest Adjustment Date

**interest adjustment date** date on which an adjustment is made for interest that accumulates between the date the loan was advanced and the charge payment date for the following month; assuming that charge payments are being made monthly, this date will be one month before the date of the first regular payment

Charge payments are sometimes arranged to be payable on the 1st or 15th day of each month. Often the loan is advanced on a different day of the month. If all of the monthly payments are going to be equal, an adjustment must be made for interest that accumulates between the date the loan was advanced and the charge payment date for the following month. The interest adjustment date is the date from which interest is calculated. Assuming that charge payments are being made monthly, the **interest adjustment date** will be one month before the date of the first regular payment.

For example, assume that Ahmed borrows money on March 5 and arranges for monthly payments to be made on the 1st day of each month. The first monthly payment from Ahmed will be due not on April 1 but on May 1. April 1 will be the interest adjustment date, and a separate payment will be made for interest accrued between March 5 and April 1. This interest amount may be deducted from the amount advanced under the charge or may be paid by the chargor on April 1.

## Closed Charge

**closed charge** charge that prohibits repayment of the loan before the expiry of the term

**interest differential** difference between the lender's current interest rate and the interest rate of the charge

A **closed charge** prohibits repayment of the loan before the expiry of the specified term. For example, assume that Bao borrows money from Best Bank, to be paid back in three years. Two years later, Bao wins the lottery and wants to pay off the charge. If the charge is closed, Best Bank can refuse early repayment. Best Bank does not want to lose the interest that it will receive during the last year of the loan. Best Bank might permit early repayment if Bao pays a prepayment penalty. A prepayment penalty is typically calculated as the greater of three months' interest or the **interest differential** for the balance of the term. The interest differential is the difference between the lender's current interest rate and the interest rate of the charge. There will be an interest differential if the current rate is lower than the rate of the charge.

In the case of Bao's loan, for example, assume that one year remains in the charge term and that the charge rate is 5 percent while the current interest rate is 4 percent. Best Bank will charge Bao the greater of either three months' interest or 1 percent (the interest differential) of the remaining balance. There is no interest differential if the current rate is higher than the interest rate of the charge, in which case the prepayment penalty will be three months' interest. So, if the current interest rate is 5 percent while the interest rate of the charge is 4 percent, Best Bank will charge Bao three months' interest.

Closed charges typically have lower interest rates and longer terms than open charges.

## Open Charge

An **open charge** permits repayment of the loan before the expiry of the specified term. If the charge is fully open, the chargor can prepay the principal in any amount and at any time. Often, the charge will be partially open, permitting repayment, but only for a specified amount and only on certain dates. For example, the charge may permit the chargor to pay up to 15 percent of the principal on the anniversary date of the charge in each year. If the charge is fully open, the chargor is not required to pay a prepayment penalty. If the charge is partially open, the chargor is not required to pay a prepayment penalty on that open portion.

**open charge**
charge that permits repayment of the loan before the expiry of the term

Open charges typically have higher interest rates and shorter terms than closed charges.

# Rights and Obligations of the Parties

As previously discussed, a charge is a loan transaction in which the loan is secured by the transfer of an interest in the land. Both the chargor and the chargee have rights and obligations.

## Chargor

The chargor's rights include the following:

- to remain in possession of the property during the term of the charge, as long as the chargor complies with the terms of the charge; and
- to have the charge discharged when the principal amount and interest are paid in full.

The chargor's obligations include the following:

- to make all charge payments in full and on time, both under the current charge and under any other prior charges;
- to maintain adequate insurance on the charged property;
- to pay all realty taxes;
- to comply with all laws affecting the property (for example, if the property is zoned for office use only, the chargor cannot open a restaurant); and
- to keep the charged property in good condition so that its value does not decrease.

## Chargee

The chargee's rights include the following:

- to have a charge interest in the property;

**covenant**
promise

- to receive the chargor's personal **covenant** (promise) to repay the loan; and
- to receive principal and interest payments in accordance with the terms of the charge.

The chargee's obligations include the following:

- to leave the chargor in exclusive possession of the property, so long as there is no breach of the terms of the charge; and
- to provide a **discharge of charge** when the charge is paid in full.

**discharge of charge**
a document given by the chargee to the chargor confirming that the loan has been paid in full and extinguishing the chargee's interest in the property

# Charge Form

The charge form sets out all of the payment provisions of the loan agreement. In addition, the charge (whether paper or electronic) contains the following information:

- the name(s) of the chargor(s);
- the name(s) of the chargee(s);
- certification that the chargor(s) is (are) at least 18 years old;
- the spousal status of the chargor(s) and statements ensuring compliance with the *Family Law Act* (if a chargor is married and the property being charged is the matrimonial home, the chargor's spouse must consent to the charge, even if the spouse is not an owner);
- acknowledgment by the chargor(s) of receipt of a true copy of the charge;
- the filing number of the standard charge terms deemed to be included with the charge, if applicable (see below);
- the amount of insurance on the property being charged (coverage is usually for the full replacement value of the property—also known as the guaranteed replacement cost—or, at the very least, for the amount of the loan [the chargee will be entitled to the insurance proceeds in the event that the property is destroyed]); and
- any additional provisions (such as prepayment provisions).

An electronic charge must also contain a statement as to whether the charge is being signed under a power of attorney. This is discussed further in Chapter 7, Electronic Registration and Teraview. A blank paper charge form can be found in Figure 5.2 in Chapter 5. An electronic charge form can be found in Figure 7.2 in Chapter 7.

# Standard Charge Terms

Standard charge terms set out, in detail, the rights and obligations of the chargor and the chargee. The *Land Registration Reform Act* permits a chargee to file its own set of charge terms in the land registry office and incorporate those terms into every charge to which it is a party, instead of having to attach the terms to each one. Standard charge terms are assigned a number when filed, and the chargee, by identifying the filing number in a charge, can ensure that the provisions of the previously filed standard charge terms are incorporated into the new charge. Figure 6.5, at the end of the chapter, is an example of a set of standard charge terms.

# Implied Covenants in a Charge

Pursuant to section 7(1) of the *Land Registration Reform Act*, every charge is deemed to include the covenants contained in that Act, unless the charge incorporates a set of standard charge terms filed by the chargee. In that case, the implied covenants are excluded. The covenants contained in the Act deal primarily with the obligations of the chargor and are more limited in scope than the typical set of standard charge terms. It is very rare for a charge not to incorporate standard charge terms.

# Transfers by Chargee and Chargor

Chargees have the right to transfer their rights under the charge to a third party, and chargors have the right to sell the property notwithstanding the existence of the charge. A transfer by either party has an effect on the rights and obligations of the other.

## Transfer by Chargee

A chargee may sell or assign the right to repayment of the loan to a third party. For example, assume that Sam mortgaged his property to Charlie. If Charlie needs the money prior to the end of the term, he can transfer the charge to Alice, who will pay Charlie the principal amount outstanding (or some discounted amount). Sam will then make the monthly payments to Alice, and not to Charlie. Charlie does not need Sam's consent to the transfer, but Sam must be notified before he is required to make the payments to Alice.

Alice will take the charge subject to the state of accounts existing between Sam and Charlie at the time of the transfer. Alice should request that Sam sign an acknowledgment confirming the amount of principal and interest outstanding at the time of the transfer. This prevents Sam from later claiming that a lesser amount is due under the charge.

## Transfer by Chargor

An owner of property that has a charge registered against it may sell or transfer the property without the consent of the chargee. If the buyer does not ask to have the charge discharged, he or she will assume the charge subject to the state of accounts that exists between the seller/chargor and the chargee at the time of the transfer. (See the discussion earlier in this chapter under the heading "Assumed Charge.")

The chargee cannot prevent the chargor from selling the property, but the charge is likely to contain a clause (called a **due-on-sale clause**) that permits the chargee to **accelerate** (demand immediate) full payment of the loan in the event that the chargee does not approve the new buyer. In such a case, an owner who wants to sell the property subject to a charge will require the consent of the chargee.

A buyer who is assuming a charge should get an assumption statement from the chargee confirming the state of accounts between the original chargor and the chargee as of the date of the assumption. This prevents the chargee from later claiming that a greater amount is due under the charge.

A chargor who transfers the property remains responsible, under the covenant, to repay the amount of the charge and may be sued by the chargee if the new owner defaults on the payments. The seller/chargor can escape future liability only by obtaining a specific release from the chargee.

**due-on-sale clause**
provision in a charge permitting the chargee to accelerate full payment of the loan in the event that the chargor sells the property and the chargee does not approve the buyer

**accelerate**
demand immediate payment

## Discharge of Charge

When a charge has been paid in full, the chargor is entitled to receive a discharge of charge/mortgage. Registration of a discharge on title extinguishes the chargee's interest in the property. Prior to making the final payment, the chargor should obtain a discharge statement from the chargee confirming the exact amount owing on the charge as of the anticipated payment date. (See Figure 5.3 in Chapter 5 and Figure 24.2 in Chapter 24.)

## Default Remedies

**Default** occurs when the chargor breaches one or more of the obligations contained in the charge. The most obvious and most common form of default is the failure to make principal and interest payments when due.

Other breaches that can be classified as default include

- failure to arrange adequate insurance on the property;
- failure to pay property taxes;
- failure to make payments to any prior charges; and
- failure to maintain the premises in a reasonable state of repair.

Most charges contain an **acceleration clause** that permits the chargee to demand immediate payment of the full amount of the loan in the event of default. In most

**default**
breach of one or more of the obligations contained in the charge; most commonly, the failure to remit principal and interest payments when due

**acceleration clause**
clause permitting the chargee to demand immediate payment of the full amount of the loan in the event of default

cases, the chargor will be unable to pay the amount owing, and the chargee can then choose from one of the available default remedies.

The chargee can simply sue the chargor for payment of the debt secured by the charge and hope to recover on the judgment. Typically, however, the chargee will choose a remedy that involves "realizing on" (that is, seizing) the secured property. The chargee may either

- sell the property through power-of-sale provisions contained in the charge;
- obtain title to the charged property by means of a foreclosure action; or
- sell the property pursuant to a judicial sale action.

In all cases, the chargee will want vacant possession of the property. Unless the chargor moves out voluntarily, the chargee will require an order for possession of the charged property.

There are many business matters and legal issues to consider when choosing the appropriate remedy. The main features of each remedy are discussed below.

## Power of Sale

The **power of sale** (the power to exercise the remedy of sale) is generally contained in every charge and permits the chargee to sell the charged property and use the proceeds of the sale to repay the charge debt. The person buying from a chargee who is exercising the power of sale acquires good title, free and clear of the chargor's interest in the property. Power of sale is the most commonly used remedy because it is relatively quick, inexpensive, and simple to implement.

Except in very rare circumstances, the charge must be in default for at least 15 days before the chargee can start power-of-sale proceedings. The chargee then serves the chargor with a **notice of sale under mortgage**, which sets out the particulars of the default and the amounts owing under the charge. The notice must also be served on

- the spouse of the chargor;
- all subsequent chargees;
- any execution creditors of the chargor;
- the solicitor for any construction lien claimants; and
- any other person with an interest in the charged property.

The notice must allow the chargor at least 35 days either to put the charge back into good standing (by paying off any arrears that are due) or to pay off the loan completely. During this 35-day period (called the **redemption period**), the chargee cannot take any steps to sell the property. For example, the chargee cannot advertise the property for sale or hire a realtor to sell the property. If the charge is still in default after the 35-day period expires, the chargee can then proceed to sell the property.

The chargor continues to have the right to put the charge back into good standing and **redeem** the property until the property is sold. However, as soon as an agreement of purchase and sale is signed, the chargor loses the right to redeem the property.

**power of sale**
power to exercise the remedy of sale in case of default under a charge

**notice of sale under mortgage**
document used in a power of sale setting out the particulars of the default and the amounts owing under the charge

**redemption period**
period of 35 days, after the chargor is in default, during which (1) the chargor has the opportunity to put the charge back into good standing and redeem the property and (2) the chargee cannot take steps to sell the property

**redeem**
release or free land from a claim against it by paying the amount owing under the charge

Once the property is sold, the chargee is required to apply the proceeds to pay off the outstanding debt, including all costs incurred in the sale. The chargee is accountable to the chargor and the holder of any subsequent encumbrances for any surplus left over after paying the debt and the expenses related to the sale. If the proceeds of sale are insufficient, the chargee can sue the chargor for the deficiency.

The person who buys the property under power of sale acquires good title to the property, provided the sale was properly conducted and all appropriate parties were duly served with the notice of sale.

## Foreclosure

**foreclosure**
court action whereby the chargee obtains legal title to the property after default by the chargor

A judgment for **foreclosure** gives legal title of the property to the chargee and is obtained by court action commenced by the chargee. Once the chargee becomes the registered owner of the property, the chargee has the choice of keeping the property or selling it. The chargee is no longer accountable to the chargor or other subsequent encumbrancers, whose rights will have been extinguished by the final order for foreclosure. If the chargee eventually sells the mortgaged property and the proceeds are more than the amount of the debt, the chargee can keep the surplus and does not have to pay the surplus to any subsequent encumbrancers or to the chargor.

Similarly, the chargee is no longer accountable to the chargor if the proceeds from a subsequent sale of the property are less than the amount of the debt.

The chargor and any subsequent chargee can defend the foreclosure action or request time to bring the charge back into good standing. They can also request that the property be sold instead of foreclosed. By requesting a sale, the chargor converts the foreclosure action into a judicial sale, as discussed below.

A chargor will likely defend a foreclosure action if the property is worth a lot more than the balance outstanding on the charge, thus preventing the chargee from gaining a windfall by selling the property and keeping the entire profit. For example, assume that Best Bank has a mortgage in the amount of $220,000 on a property that is worth $500,000. If Best Bank forecloses on the property and then sells it for $500,000, Best Bank can keep the $280,000 profit it makes on the sale. If, however, the chargor defends the foreclosure action and asks the court to convert the foreclosure action into a sale instead, then Best Bank will receive only the amount owing to it, but not more. Best Bank can keep $220,000, and the remaining $280,000 will be paid to any subsequent mortgagees, if any. If there is anything left after that, it goes to the chargor.

If the chargor requests time to pay but fails to do so within the time permitted by the court (usually six months), then the chargee can apply for a final order of foreclosure.

## Judicial Sale

**judicial sale**
sale of charged property ordered and administered by a court

In a **judicial sale**, a court orders the sale of the property and oversees all matters related to the sale. The sheriff carries out the sale by tender or public auction under the authority of a writ of seizure and sale. A chargee can start an action for a judicial sale. More commonly, however, a judicial sale takes place when a chargor asks that a foreclosure action be converted to a judicial sale.

The proceeds from a judicial sale are applied first against the charge debt and any expenses of the sale. Any surplus will then be applied against the amount outstanding on any subsequent charges, and the balance, if any, will go to the chargor. In this way, the chargor is released from the claims of all other chargees to the extent that the sale money will cover those claims.

## Possession

The remedy of possession does not involve a sale of the property. Rather, it gives the chargee the right to take possession of the property after obtaining a **writ of possession** from the court. While in possession, the chargee is referred to as the **chargee in possession** and is obligated to maintain the property so that it does not deteriorate. If the property is vacant, the chargee can rent out the premises and apply the rental income to the outstanding debt. If there are tenants living on the property, they will be directed to pay their rent to the chargee in possession, not to the chargor. This remedy is used in combination with whichever of the previous remedies the chargee has chosen.

**writ of possession**
court order giving the chargee the right to take possession of the property

**chargee in possession**
chargee who takes possession of the charged property after default by the chargor

## KEY TERMS

accelerate, 80

acceleration clause, 80

advanced, 74

amortization period, 73

amortization schedule, 74

assumed charge, 69

balloon payment, 73

blended payment, 74

chargee, 68

chargee in possession, 83

chargor, 68

closed charge, 76

compounding interest, 73

covenant, 78

default, 80

discharge of charge, 78

due-on-sale clause, 80

first charge, 69

fixed interest rate, 72

foreclosure, 82

interest, 72

interest adjustment date, 76

interest differential, 76

interest rate, 72

judicial sale, 82

maturity date, 73

mortgagee, 68

mortgagor, 68

new charge, 69

non-blended payment, 74

notice of sale under mortgage, 81

open charge, 77

power of sale, 81

prepayment penalty, 70

prime lending rate, 72

principal, 72

priority, 69

realize on the security, 69

redeem, 81

redemption period, 81

second charge, 69

term, 73

variable interest rate, 72

vendor-take-back charge (or charge taken back), 69

writ of possession, 83

## REFERENCES

*Family Law Act*, RSO 1990, c F.3.

*Land Registration Reform Act*, RSO 1990, c L.4.

# REVIEW QUESTIONS

1. What is a mortgage or charge?

2. Stefano borrowed money from Best Bank and gave Best Bank a charge on his property. Who is the chargor and who is the chargee?

3. If there are multiple charges registered against title, how is the order of priority between the charges determined?

4. Lynne sold her house to Bill and lent him $200,000 so that he could complete the sale. How should Lynne secure this loan?

5. What is an assumed charge?

6. Charge payments include both principal and interest. Define each of these terms.

7. What is the difference between the term of the charge and the amortization period?

8. What information does an amortization schedule provide?

9. Assume that a charge payment is made that includes both principal and interest. Is this a blended or a non-blended payment?

10. Peggy arranges a charge on November 15. Her charge payments are due on the 1st day of each month.

    a. What is the interest adjustment date?

    b. When is the first regular monthly mortgage payment due?

11. What are standard charge terms?

12. What happens when a charge has been paid in full?

13. What are the remedies available to the chargee when the chargor breaches one or more of the obligations contained in the charge?

# DISCUSSION QUESTIONS

1. A charge has a 5-year term and a 25-year amortization period. What will happen at the end of the term?

2. Anita has a closed charge with her bank. She has just won the lottery and wants to pay off the charge. Can she do this? Explain your answer.

3. In addition to making regular payments, what obligations does the chargor have?

4. Sheila wants to sell her home. She is concerned because there is an outstanding charge on the property. What are her rights?

## Figure 6.5    Standard Charge Terms

Page 1                                                    Dye & Durham Co. Inc, Form No. 301A

*Land Registration Reform Act*

### SET OF STANDARD CHARGE TERMS

Filed by                                          **Filing Date:  October 14, 2004**

**Dye & Durham Co. Inc.**                          **Filing number:  200434**

---

*The following Set of Standard Charge Terms shall be deemed to be included in every charge in which the set is referred to by its filing number, as provided in section 9 of the Act.*

**Exclusion of Statutory Covenants**    1.   The implied covenants deemed to be included in a charge under subsection 7(1) of the *Land Registration Reform Act* as amended or re-enacted are excluded from the Charge.

**Right to Charge the Land**    2.   The Chargor now has good right, full power and lawful and absolute authority to charge the land and to give the Charge to the Chargee upon the covenants contained in the Charge.

**No Act to Encumber**    3.   The Chargor has not done, committed, executed or wilfully or knowingly suffered any act, deed, matter or thing whatsoever whereby or by means whereof the land, or any part or parcel thereof, is or shall or may be in any way impeached, charged, affected or encumbered in title, estate or otherwise, except as the records of the land registry office disclose.

**Good Title in Fee Simple**    4.   The Chargor, at the time of the execution and delivery of the Charge, is, and stands solely, rightfully and lawfully seized of a good, sure, perfect, absolute and indefeasible estate of inheritance, in fee simple, of and in the land and the premises described in the Charge and in every part and parcel thereof without any manner of trusts, reservations, limitations, provisos, conditions or any other matter or thing to alter, charge, change, encumber or defeat the same, except those contained in the original grant thereof from the Crown.

**Promise to Pay and Perform**    5.   The Chargor will pay or cause to be paid to the Chargee the full principal amount and interest secured by the Charge in the manner of payment provided by the Charge, without any deduction or abatement, and shall do, observe, perform, fulfill and keep all the provisions, covenants, agreements and stipulations contained in the Charge and shall pay as they fall due all taxes, rates, levies, charges, assessments, utility and heating charges, municipal, local, parliamentary and otherwise which now are or may hereafter be imposed, charged or levied upon the land and when required shall produce for the Chargee receipts evidencing payment of the same.

**Interest After Default**    6.   In case default shall be made in payment of any sum to become due for interest at the time provided for payment in the Charge, compound interest shall be payable and the sum in arrears for interest from time to time, as well after as before maturity, and both before and after default and judgement, shall bear interest at the rate provided for in the Charge.  In case the interest and compound interest are not paid within the interest calculation period provided in the Charge from the time of default a rest shall be made, and compound interest at the rate provided for in the Charge shall be payable on the aggregate amount then due, as well after as before maturity, and so on from time to time, and all such interest and compound interest shall be a charge upon the land.

**No Obligation to Advance**    7.   Neither the preparation, execution or registration of the Charge shall bind the Chargee to advance the principal amount secured, nor shall the advance of a part of the principal amount secured bind the Chargee to advance any unadvanced portion thereof, but nevertheless the security in the land shall take effect forthwith upon the execution of the Charge by the Chargor. The expenses of the examination of the title and of the Charge and valuation are to be secured by the Charge in the event of the whole or any balance of the principal amount not being advanced, the same to be charged hereby upon the land, and shall be, without demand therefor, payable forthwith with interest at the rate provided for in the Charge, and in default the Chargee's power of sale hereby given, and all other remedies hereunder, shall be exercisable.

**Costs Added to Principal**    8.   The Chargee may pay all premiums of insurance and all taxes, rates, levies, charges, assessments, utility and heating charges which shall from time to time fall due and be unpaid in respect of the land, and that such payments, together with all costs, charges, legal fees (as between solicitor and client) and expenses which may be incurred in taking, recovering and keeping possession of the land and of negotiating the Charge, investigating title, and registering the Charge and other necessary deeds, and generally in any other proceedings taken in connection with or to realize upon the security given in the Charge (including legal fees and real estate commissions and other costs incurred in leasing or selling the land or in exercising the power of entering, lease and sale contained in the Charge) shall be, with interest at the rate provided for in the Charge, a charge upon the land in favour of the Chargee pursuant to the terms of the Charge and the Chargee may pay or satisfy any lien, charge or encumbrance now existing or hereafter created or claimed upon the land, which payments with interest at the rate provided for in the Charge shall likewise be a charge upon the land in favour of the Chargee. Provided, and it is hereby further agreed, that all amounts paid by the Chargee as aforesaid shall be added to the principal amount secured by the Charge and shall be payable forthwith with interest at the rate provided for in the Charge, and on default all sums secured by the Charge shall immediately become due and payable at the option of the Chargee, and all powers in the Charge conferred shall become exercisable.

**Power of Sale**    9.   The Chargee on default of payment for at least fifteen (15) days may, on at least thirty-five (35) days' notice in writing given to the Chargor, enter on and lease the land or sell the land. Such notice shall be given to such persons and in such manner and form and within such time as provided in the *Mortgages Act*.  In the event that the giving of such notice shall not be required by law or to the extent that such requirements shall not be applicable, it is agreed that notice may be effectually given by leaving it with a grown-up person on the land, if occupied, or by placing it on the land if unoccupied, or at the option of the Chargee, by mailing it in a registered letter addressed to the Chargor at his last known address, or by publishing it once in a newspaper published in the county or district in which the land is situate; and such notice shall be sufficient although not addressed to any person or persons by name or designation; and notwithstanding that any person to be affected thereby may be unknown, unascertained or under disability. Provided further, that in case default be made in the payment of the principal amount or interest or any part thereof and such default continues for two months after any payment of either falls due then the Chargee may exercise the foregoing powers of entering, leasing or selling or any of them without any notice, it being understood and agreed, however, that if the giving of notice by the Chargee shall be required by law then notice shall be given to such persons and in such manner and form and within such time as so required by law. It is hereby further agreed that the whole or any part or parts of the land may be sold by public auction or private contract, or partly

# Figure 6.5   Continued

Page 2 - SET OF STANDARD CHARGE TERMS
Filing Date:
Filing No.

Dye & Durham Co.Inc. Form No. 301A

one or partly the other; and that the proceeds of any sale hereunder may be applied first in payment of any costs, charges and expenses incurred in taking, recovering or keeping possession of the land or by reason of non-payment or procuring payment of monies, secured by the Charge or otherwise, and secondly in payment of all amounts of principal and interest owing under the Charge; and if any surplus shall remain after fully satisfying the claims of the Chargee as aforesaid same shall be paid as required by law. The Chargee may sell any of the land on such terms as to credit and otherwise as shall appear to him most advantageous and for such prices as can reasonably be obtained therefor and may make any stipulations as to title or evidence or commencement of title or otherwise which he shall deem proper, and may buy in or rescind or vary any contract for the sale of the whole or any part of the land and resell without being answerable for loss occasioned thereby, and in the case of a sale on credit the Chargee shall be bound to pay the Chargor only such monies as have been actually received from purchasers after the satisfaction of the claims of the Chargee and for any of said purposes may make and execute all agreements and assurances as he shall think fit.  Any purchaser or lessee shall not be bound to see to the propriety or regularity of any sale or lease or be affected by express notice that any sale or lease is improper and no want of notice or publication when required hereby shall invalidate any sale or lease hereunder.

**Quiet Possession**   10. Upon default in payment of principal and interest under the Charge or in performance of any of the terms or conditions hereof, the Chargee may enter into and take possession of the land hereby charged and where the Chargee so enters on and takes possession or enters on and takes possession of the land on default as described in paragraph 9 herein the Chargee shall enter into, have, hold, use, occupy, possess and enjoy the land without the let, suit, hindrance, interruption or denial of the Chargor or any other person or persons whomsoever.

**Right to Distrain**   11. If the Chargor shall make default in payment of any part of the interest payable under the Charge at any of the dates or times fixed for the payment thereof, it shall be lawful for the Chargee to distrain therefor upon the land or any part thereof, and by distress warrant, to recover by way of rent reserved, as in the case of a demise of the land, so much of such interest as shall, from time to time, be or remain in arrears and unpaid, together with all costs, charges and expenses attending such levy or distress, as in like cases of distress for rent.  Provided that the Chargee may distrain for arrears of principal in the same manner as if the same were arrears of interest.

**Further Assurances**   12. From and after default in the payment of the principal amount secured by the Charge or the interest thereon or any part of such principal or interest or in the doing, observing, performing, fulfilling or keeping of some one or more of the covenants set forth in the Charge then and in every such case the Chargor and all and every other person whosoever having, or lawfully claiming, or who shall have or lawfully claim any estate, right, title, interest or trust of, in, to or out of the land shall, from time to time, and at all times thereafter, at the proper costs and charges of the Chargor make, do, suffer and execute, or cause or procure to be made, done, suffered and executed, all and every such further and other reasonable act or acts, deed or deeds, devises, conveyances and assurances in the law for the further, better and more perfectly and absolutely conveying and assuring the land unto the Chargee as by the Chargee or his solicitor shall or may be lawfully and reasonably devised, advised or required.

**Acceleration of Principal and Interest**   13. In default of the payment of the interest secured by the Charge the principal amount secured by the Charge shall, at the option of the Chargee, immediately become payable, and upon default of payment of instalments of principal promptly as the same mature, the balance of the principal and interest secured by the Charge shall, at the option of the Chargee, immediately become due and payable. The Chargee may in writing at any time or times after default waive such default and any such waiver shall apply only to the particular default waived and shall not operate as a waiver of any other or future default.

**Partial Releases**   14. The Chargee may at his discretion at all times release any part or parts of the land or any other security or any surety for the money secured under the Charge either with or without any sufficient consideration therefor, without responsibility therefor, and without thereby releasing any other part of the land or any person from the Charge or from any of the covenants contained in the Charge and without being accountable to the Chargor for the value thereof, or for any monies except those actually received by the Chargee.  It is agreed that every part or lot into which the land is or may hereafter be divided does and shall stand charged with the whole money secured under the Charge and no person shall have the right to require the mortgage monies to be apportioned.

**Obligation to insure**   15. The Chargor will immediately insure, unless already insured, and during the continuance of the Charge keep insured against loss or damage by fire, in such proportions upon each building as may be required by the Chargee, the buildings on the land to the amount of not less than their full insurable value on a replacement cost basis in dollars of lawful money of Canada. Such insurance shall be placed with a company approved by the Chargee.  Buildings shall include all buildings whether now or hereafter erected on the land, and such insurance shall include not only insurance against loss or damage by fire but also insurance against loss or damage by explosion, tempest, tornado, cyclone, lightning and all other extended perils customarily provided in insurance policies including "all risks" insurance. The covenant to insure shall also include where appropriate or if required by the Chargee, boiler, plate glass, rental and public liability insurance in amounts and on terms satisfactory to the Chargee. Evidence of continuation of all such insurance having been effected shall be produced to the Chargee at least fifteen (15) days before the expiration thereof; otherwise the Chargee may provide therefor and charge the premium paid and interest thereon at the rate provided for in the Charge to the Chargor and the same shall be payable forthwith and shall also be a charge upon the land. It is further agreed that the Chargee may at any time require any insurance of the buildings to be cancelled and new insurance effected in a company to be named by the Chargee and also of his own accord may effect or maintain any insurance herein provided for, and any amount paid by the Chargee therefor shall be payable forthwith by the Chargor with interest at the rate provided for in the Charge and shall also be a charge upon the land. Policies of insurance herein required shall provide that loss, if any, shall be payable to the Chargee as his interest may appear, subject to the standard form of mortgage clause approved by the Insurance Bureau of Canada which shall be attached to the policy of insurance.

**Obligation to Repair**   16. The Chargor will keep the land and the buildings, erections and improvements thereon, in good condition and repair according to the nature and description thereof respectively, and the Chargee may, whenever he deems necessary, by his agent enter upon and inspect the land and make such repairs as he deems necessary, and the reasonable cost of such inspection and repairs with interest at the rate provided for in the Charge shall be added to the principal amount and be payable forthwith and be a charge upon the land prior to all claims thereon subsequent to the Charge. If the Chargor shall neglect to keep the buildings, erections and improvements in good condition and repair, or commits or permits any act of waste on the land (as to which the Chargee shall be sole judge) or makes default as to any of the covenants, provisos, agreements or conditions contained in the Charge or in any charge to which this Charge is subject, all monies secured by the Charge shall, at the option of the Chargee, forthwith become due and payable, and in default of payment of same with interest as in the case of payment

# Figure 6.5    Continued

Page 3 - SET OF STANDARD CHARGE TERMS
Filing Date:
Filing No.

Dye & Durham Co. Inc. Form No. 301A

before maturity the powers of entering upon and leasing or selling hereby given and all other remedies herein contained may be exercised forthwith.

**Building Charge**

17. If any of the principal amount to be advanced under the Charge is to be used to finance an improvement on the land, the Chargor must so inform the Chargee in writing immediately and before any advances are made under the Charge. The Chargor must also provide the Chargee immediately with copies of all contracts and subcontracts relating to the improvement and any amendments to them. The Chargor agrees that any improvement shall be made only according to contracts, plans and specifications approved in writing by the Chargee. The Chargor shall complete all such improvements as quickly as possible and provide the Chargee with proof of payment of all contracts from time to time as the Chargee requires. The Chargee shall make advances (part payments of the principal amount) to the Chargor based on the progress of the improvement, until either completion and occupation or sale of the land. The Chargee shall determine whether or not any advances will be made and when they will be made. Whatever the purpose of the Charge may be, the Chargee may at its option hold back funds from advances until the Chargee is satisfied that the Chargor has complied with the holdback provisions of the *Construction Lien Act* as amended or re-enacted. The Chargor authorizes the Chargee to provide information about the Charge to any person claiming a construction lien on the land.

**Extensions not to Prejudice**

18. No extension of time given by the Chargee to the Chargor or anyone claiming under him, or any other dealing by the Chargee with the owner of the land or of any part thereof, shall in any way affect or prejudice the rights of the Chargee against the Chargor or any other person liable for the payment of the money secured by the Charge, and the Charge may be renewed by an agreement in writing at maturity for any term with or without an increased rate of interest notwithstanding that there may be subsequent encumbrances. It shall not be necessary to register any such agreement in order to retain priority for the Charge so altered over any instrument registered subsequent to the Charge. Provided that nothing contained in this paragraph shall confer any right of renewal upon the Chargor.

**No Merger of Covenants**

19. The taking of a judgment or judgments on any of the covenants herein shall not operate as a merger of the covenants or affect the Chargee's right to interest at the rate and times provided for in the Charge; and further that any judgment shall provide that interest thereon shall be computed at the same rate and in the same manner as provided in the Charge until the judgment shall have been fully paid and satisfied.

**Change in Status**

20. Immediately after any change or happening affecting any of the following, namely: *(a)* the spousal status of the Chargor, *(b)* the qualification of the land as a family residence within the meaning of Part II of the *Family Law Act,* and *(c)* the legal title or beneficial ownership of the land, the Chargor will advise the Chargee accordingly and furnish the Chargee with full particulars thereof, the intention being that the Chargee shall be kept fully informed of the names and addresses of the owner or owners for the time being of the land and of any spouse who is not an owner but who has a right of possession in the land by virtue of Section 19 of the *Family Law Act.* In furtherance of such intention, the Chargor covenants and agrees to furnish the Chargee with such evidence in connection with any of *(a), (b)* and *(c)* above as the Chargee may from time to time request.

**Condominium Provisions**

21. If the Charge is of land within a condominium registered pursuant to the *Condominium Act* (the "Act") the following provisions shall apply. The Chargor will comply with the Act, and with the declaration, by-laws and rules of the condominium corporation (the "corporation") relating to the Chargor's unit (the "unit") and provide the Chargee with proof of compliance from time to time as the Chargee may request. The Chargor will pay the common expenses for the unit to the corporation on the due dates. If the Chargee decides to collect the Chargor's contribution towards the common expenses from the Chargor, the Chargor will pay the same to the Chargee upon being so notified. The Chargee is authorized to accept a statement which appears to be issued by the corporation as conclusive evidence for the purpose of establishing the amounts of the common expenses and the dates those amounts are due. The Chargor, upon notice from the Chargee, will forward to the Chargee any notices, assessments, by-laws, rules and financial statements of the corporation that the Chargor receives or is entitled to receive from the corporation. The Chargor will maintain all improvements made to the unit and repair them after damage. In addition to the insurance which the corporation must obtain, the Chargor shall insure the unit against destruction or damage by fire and other perils usually covered in fire insurance policies and against such other perils as the Chargee requires for its full replacement cost (the maximum amount for which it can be insured). The insurance company and the terms of the policy shall be reasonably satisfactory to the Chargee. This provision supersedes the provisions of paragraph 15 herein. The Chargor irrevocably authorizes the Chargee to exercise the Chargor's rights under the Act to vote, consent and dissent.

**Discharge**

22. The discharge of the Charge shall be prepared by the Chargee and all legal and other expenses for the preparation and execution of such discharge shall be borne by the Chargor.

**Guarantee**

23. Each party named in the Charge as a Guarantor hereby agrees with the Chargee as follows:

   (a) In consideration of the Chargee advancing all or part of the Principal Amount to the Chargor, and in consideration of the sum of TWO DOLLARS ($2.00) of lawful money of Canada now paid by the Chargee to the Guarantor (the receipt and sufficiency whereof are hereby acknowledged), the Guarantor does hereby absolutely and unconditionally guarantee to the Chargee, and its successors, the due and punctual payment of all principal moneys, interest and other moneys owing on the security of the Charge and observance and performance of the covenants, agreements, terms and conditions herein contained by the Chargor, and the Guarantor, for himself and his successors, covenants with the Chargee that, if the Chargor shall at any time make default in the due and punctual payment of any moneys payable hereunder, the Guarantor will pay all such moneys to the Chargee without any demand being required to be made.

   (b) Although as between the Guarantor and the Chargor, the Guarantor is only surety for the payment by the Chargor of the moneys hereby guaranteed, as between the Guarantor and the Chargee, the Guarantor shall be considered as primarily liable therefor and it is hereby further expressly declared that no release or releases of any portion or portions of the land; no indulgence shown by the Chargee in respect of any default by the Chargor or any successor thereof which may arise under the Charge; no extension or extensions granted by the Chargee to the Chargor or any successor thereof for payment of the moneys hereby secured or for the doing, observing or performing of any covenant, agreement, term or condition herein contained to be done, observed or performed by the Chargor or any successor thereof; no variation in or departure from the provisions of the Charge; no release of the Chargor or any other thing whatsoever whereby the Guarantor as surety only would or might have been released shall in any way modify, alter, vary or in any way prejudice the Chargee or affect the liability of the Guarantor in any way under this covenant, which shall continue and be binding on the Guarantor, and as well after as before maturity of the Charge and both before and after default and judgment, until the said moneys are fully paid and satisfied.

   (c) Any payment by the Guarantor of any moneys under this guarantee shall not in any event be taken to affect

# Figure 6.5   Concluded

Filing Date:
Filing No.

the liability of the Chargor for payment thereof but such liability shall remain unimpaired and enforceable by the Guarantor against the Chargor and the Guarantor shall, to the extent of any such payments made by him, in addition to all other remedies, be subrogated as against the Chargor to all the rights, privileges and powers to which the Chargee was entitled prior to payment by the Guarantor; provided, nevertheless, that the Guarantor shall not be entitled in any event to rank for payment against the lands in competition with the Chargee and shall not, unless and until the whole of the principal, interest and other moneys owing on the security of the Charge shall have been paid, be entitled to any rights or remedies whatsoever in subrogation to the Chargee.

(d)   All covenants, liabilities and obligations entered into or imposed hereunder upon the Guarantor shall be equally binding upon his successors.  Where more than one party is named as a Guarantor all such covenants, liabilities and obligations shall be joint and several.

(e)   The Chargee may vary any agreement or arrangement with or release the Guarantor, or any one or more of the Guarantors if more than one party is named as Guarantor, and grant extensions of time or otherwise deal with the Guarantor and his successors without any consent on the part of the Chargor or any other Guarantor or any successor thereof.

*Date of*
*Charge*

**24.**   The date of the Charge unless otherwise provided shall be the earliest date of signature by a Chargor.

*Interpretation*

In construing these covenants the words "Charge", "Chargee", "Chargor", "land" and "successor" shall have the meanings assigned to them in Section 1 of the *Land Registration Reform Act* and the words "Chargor" and "Chargee" and the personal pronouns "he" and "his" relating thereto and used therewith, shall be read and construed as "Chargor" or "Chargors", "Chargee" or "Chargees", and "he", "she", "they" or "it", "his", "her", "their" or "its", respectively, as the number and gender of the parties referred to in each case require, and the number of the verb agreeing therewith shall be construed as agreeing with the said word or pronoun so substituted. And that all rights, advantages, privileges, immunities, powers and things hereby secured to the Chargor or Chargors, Chargee or Chargees, shall be equally secured to and exercisable by his, her, their or its heirs, executors, administrators and assigns, or successors and assigns, as the case may be.  The word "successor" shall also include successors and assigns of corporations including amalgamated and continuing corporations.  And that all covenants, liabilities and obligations entered into or imposed hereunder upon the Chargor or Chargors, Chargee or Chargees, shall be equally binding upon his, her, their or its heirs, executors, administrators and assigns, or successors and assigns, as the case may be, and that all such covenants and liabilities and obligations shall be joint and several.  And the headings beside each paragraph herein are for reference purposes only and do not form part of the covenants herein contained.

<u>**ACKNOWLEDGMENT**</u>

This Set of Standard Charge Terms is included in a Charge dated the          day of
made by

as Chargor(s)

To

as Chargee(s)

as Guarantor(s)

and each Chargor and Guarantor hereby acknowledges receipt of a copy of this Set of Standard Charge Terms before signing the Charge.

| | |
|---|---|
| _____ | _____ |
| *Guarantor(s)* | *Chargor(s)* |
| _____ | _____ |

# Electronic Registration and Teraview

7

## LEARNING OUTCOMES

After reading this chapter, you will understand:

- The role of electronic registration in real estate transactions

- The application of Teraview to electronic registration

- How to create a file in Teraview

- How to choose a land registry office in Teraview

- How to prepare and sign electronic documents in Teraview

- The concept of messaging documents in Teraview

- How to register a document in Teraview

- The importance of the docket summary

# Introduction: An Overview of Electronic Registration

As discussed in Chapter 5, Ontario began a major reform to the land registration systems in 1985, with a project called POLARIS (Province of Ontario Land Registration Information System). The *Land Registration Reform Act* authorized the implementation of the POLARIS initiatives, which include (1) converting all properties to the Land Titles system, (2) providing for electronic registration, and (3) providing for electronic title and execution searching.

Today, the electronic system is used for virtually all property in Ontario. With electronic registration (known as e-reg), documents can be created, signed, exchanged between law offices, and then registered, all in electronic format.

# Working with Teraview

Teraview software is required for the electronic registration system, and most lawyers who practise real estate law have this software. Using Teraview, lawyers conduct real estate closings electronically from their offices rather than in person at a land registry office (LRO). In addition, Teraview makes it possible for titles to be searched outside of regular business hours. (Registration, however, can take place only during business hours.) Teraview has made the process of completing a real estate transaction much simpler and more efficient than it was under the old paper-based system.

**disbursements**
a lawyer's out-of-pocket expenses

The Teraview software is relatively inexpensive. Although a fee is charged each time the software is used, that cost is typically charged to the client as a **disbursement**. The software is also available for the public's use at the LROs, a convenience that allows members of the public (for a fee) to search title or obtain information about the ownership of particular real property.

Every Teraview user in a law firm requires a user name and pass phrase and either a USB or a personal diskette in order to access the system. Users are regularly prompted by the software to change their pass phrases.

## Creating a File

**docket**
file in which all documents pertaining to a particular transaction are located

With the Teraview system, all documents pertaining to a particular transaction are located in a single file, called a **docket**. For example, if a law firm is acting for a buyer who is also arranging a charge, the docket created by Teraview will contain both the transfer and the charge. Creating a docket in Teraview is discussed more fully in Chapter 15, Opening and Organizing a Real Estate File.

## Choosing a Land Registry Office (LRO)

Teraview provides access to all of the 55 LROs in Ontario. This means that a lawyer can conduct searches and close transactions anywhere in Ontario, without having to leave his or her office. Under the old paper-based system, a buyer of out-of-town property would usually hire a law firm in that location. For example, if Joanna lived in Toronto and was buying two properties, one in Toronto and the other in Owen Sound, she would typically have hired two different lawyers. Today, she would not need to do so because one lawyer can do the work on both transactions, regardless of the location of the lawyer's office.

Teraview assigns each user a main, or default, LRO on the basis of the location of the majority of properties that each user in the law firm acts in connection with. For example, if Larry Lawyer does most of his real estate work in Toronto, his default LRO will be Toronto. Each time he logs in to Teraview, that LRO is displayed by default. If Larry acts for a client in connection with a property located outside Toronto, he will need to change his LRO. The fee for using the Teraview software is lower when the user is working on a property within his or her main LRO. For example, if Larry Lawyer, whose main LRO is Toronto, is acting on a property in Toronto and another property in Owen Sound, the fees for the Toronto property will be less than those for the Owen Sound property. For that reason, it is common for multiple Teraview users within a law firm to each have different default or main LROs.

## Title Searching

Title searching in Teraview is simpler and faster than title searching in the old paper-based system. As mentioned above, a lawyer can conduct searches both inside and outside LRO hours without having to leave his or her office. Title searching is discussed in detail in Chapter 14.

# Preparing Documents

Under e-reg, Teraview is used to create all registered documents in electronic rather than paper format. Transfers and charges are the two most commonly required documents. Discharges (required to remove from title charges that have been paid in full) are also frequently required, but they are typically prepared by the chargee. (Discharges are discussed in Chapter 6, Charges/Mortgages.) Although an electronic document looks quite different from the equivalent paper document, it contains all the same information.

Figures 7.1 and 7.2 show, respectively, a sample transfer and charge created electronically by means of Teraview. Compare these documents with their paper equivalents, shown in Chapter 5 as Figures 5.1 and 5.2. Document preparation in Teraview is discussed in detail in Chapter 21.

## Figure 7.1 Transfer Created Electronically

| | |
|---|---|
| LRO # 65 **Transfer** | **In preparation** on 2015 07 02 at 10:21 |
| *This document has not been submitted and may be incomplete.* | yyyy mm dd Page 1 of 2 |

### Properties

*PIN* 12345-6789 LT *Interest/Estate* Fee Simple

*Description* Parcel 170-1, Section 65M-1234

*Address* 166 Valley Road
Newmarket, Ontario

### Consideration

*Consideration* $ 580,000.00

### Transferor(s)

The transferor(s) hereby transfers the land to the transferee(s).

*Name* MERCIER, FRANCOIS
Acting as an individual

*Address for Service* 97 Brook Street
Newmarket, Ontario
L3H 1V2

I am at least 18 years of age.

HUGUETTE MARIE MERCIER and I are spouses of one another and are both parties to this document

This document is not authorized under Power of Attorney by this party.

*Name* MERCIER, HUGUETTE MARIE
Acting as an individual

*Address for Service* 97 Brook Street
Newmarket, Ontario
L3H 1V2

I am at least 18 years of age.

FRANCOIS MERCIER and I are spouses of one another and are both parties to this document

This document is not authorized under Power of Attorney by this party.

| Transferee(s) | | Capacity | Share |
|---|---|---|---|
| *Name* | GRANT, HENRY ALBERT<br>Acting as an individual | Joint tenant | |
| *Date of Birth* | 1952 03 27 | | |
| *Address for Service* | 166 Valley Road<br>Newmarket, Ontario<br>L3H 3B3 | | |
| *Name* | GRANT, WILMA HEATHER<br>Acting as an individual | Joint tenant | |
| *Date of Birth* | 1955 03 18 | | |
| *Address for Service* | 166 Valley Road<br>Newmarket, Ontario<br>L3H 3B3 | | |

# Figure 7.1 Continued

LRO # 65 **Transfer**            **In preparation** on 2015 07 02    at 10:21

*This document has not been submitted and may be incomplete.*        yyyy mm dd     Page 2 of 2

| *Calculated Taxes* |
|---|

*Provincial Land Transfer Tax*            $8,075.00

### Figure 7.1   Concluded

---

**LAND TRANSFER TAX STATEMENTS**

In the matter of the conveyance of:      Parcel 170-1, Section 65M-1234

---

BY:      MERCIER, FRANCOIS
         MERCIER, HUGUETTE MARIE

TO:      GRANT, HENRY ALBERT                                                    %(all PINs)
         GRANT, WILMA HEATHER                                                   %(all PINs)

---

1.  GRANT, HENRY ALBERT AND GRANT, WILMA HEATHER

    I am

    ☐ (a) A person in trust for whom the land conveyed in the above-described conveyance is being conveyed;

    ☐ (b) A trustee named in the above-described conveyance to whom the land is being conveyed;

    ☑ (c) A transferee named in the above-described conveyance;

    ☐ (d) The authorized agent or solicitor acting in this transaction for _____ described in paragraph(s) (_) above.

    ☐ (e) The President, Vice-President, Manager, Secretary, Director, or Treasurer authorized to act for _____ described in paragraph(s) (_) above.

    ☐ (f) A transferee described in paragraph ( ) and am making these statements on my own behalf and on behalf of _____ who is my spouse described in paragraph (_) and as such, I have personal knowledge of the facts herein deposed to.

---

2.  I have read and considered the definition of "single family residence" set out in subsection 1(1) of the Act. The land being conveyed herein:

    contains at least one and not more than two single family residences.

---

3.  **The total consideration for this transaction is allocated as follows:**

    (a) Monies paid or to be paid in cash                                                   580,000.00

    (b) Mortgages   (i) assumed (show principal and interest to be credited against purchase price)     0.00
                    (ii) Given Back to Vendor                                             0.00

    (c) Property transferred in exchange (detail below)                                         0.00

    (d) Fair market value of the land(s)                                                        0.00

    (e) Liens, legacies, annuities and maintenance charges to which transfer is subject          0.00

    (f) Other valuable consideration subject to land transfer tax (detail below)                 0.00

    (g) Value of land, building, fixtures and goodwill subject to land transfer tax (total of (a) to (f))   580,000.00

    (h) VALUE OF ALL CHATTELS - items of tangible personal property                              0.00

    (i) Other considerations for transaction not included in (g) or (h) above                    0.00

    (j) Total consideration                                                                 580,000.00

---

**PROPERTY Information Record**

A. Nature of Instrument:       Transfer

                  LRO  65     Registration No.              Date:

B. Property(s):                PIN           Address              Assessment
                                                Roll No

C. Address for Service:        166 Valley Road
                             Newmarket, Ontario
                             L3H 3B3

D. (i) Last Conveyance(s):     PIN 12345-6789      Registration No.

   (ii) Legal Description for Property Conveyed : Same as in last conveyance?  Yes ☑  No ☐  Not known ☐

## Figure 7.2 Charge Created Electronically

LRO # 65 **Charge/Mortgage** | **In preparation** on 2015 07 02 at 10:26

*This document has not been submitted and may be incomplete.* yyyy mm dd Page 1 of 2

---

**Properties**

*PIN* 12345-6789 LT *Interest/Estate* Fee Simple

*Description* Parcel 170-1, Section 65M-1234

*Address* 166 Valley Road
Newmarket, Ontario

---

**Chargor(s)**

The chargor(s) hereby charges the land to the chargee(s). The chargor(s) acknowledges the receipt of the charge and the standard charge terms, if any.

*Name* GRANT, HENRY ALBERT
Acting as an individual

*Address for Service* 166 Valley Road
Newmarket, Ontario
L3H 1V2

I am at least 18 years of age.

I am not a spouse

This document is not authorized under Power of Attorney by this party.

*Name* GRANT, WILMA HEATHER
Acting as an individual

*Address for Service* 166 Valley Road
Newmarket, Ontario
L3H 1V2

I am at least 18 years of age.

I am not a spouse

This document is not authorized under Power of Attorney by this party.

---

**Chargee(s)** | *Capacity* | *Share*

*Name* DATA BANK OF CANADA
Acting as a company

*Address for Service* 111 Richmond Street
Toronto, Ontario
M1B 1B1

## Figure 7.2   Concluded

LRO # 65   **Charge/Mortgage**         **In preparation** on  2015 07 02  at  10:26

*This document has not been submitted and may be incomplete.*       yyyy mm dd     Page 2 of 2

| *Provisions* |
|---|

| | | | |
|---|---|---|---|
| *Principal* | $ 280,000.00 | *Currency* | CDN |
| *Calculation Period* | semi annually, not in advance | | |
| *Balance Due Date* | 2021/01/01 | | |
| *Interest Rate* | 3.0% | | |
| *Payments* | | | |
| *Interest Adjustment Date* | 2016/01/01 | | |
| *Payment Date* | first day of each month | | |
| *First Payment Date* | 2016/02/01 | | |
| *Last Payment Date* | 2021/01/01 | | |
| *Standard Charge Terms* | 202020 | | |
| *Insurance Amount* | full insurable value | | |
| *Guarantor* | | | |

## Mandatory Statements for Transfers and Charges

It is mandatory that all transfers and charges contain the following three statements concerning the legal status of the owner:

1. *Statement of age.* This statement ("I am at least 18 years of age") confirms that the owner is of legal age to undertake the transaction.

2. *Spousal statement.* The transferor or chargor must state his or her spousal status to ensure that there are no claims of possession against him or her under the *Family Law Act.*

3. *Statement of whether the document is being signed under a **power of attorney**.* The statement typically reads as follows: "This document is not authorized under Power of Attorney by this party." This statement is included because registered documents are rarely signed under a power of attorney. If a power of attorney is being used, however, the lawyer must confirm its validity and select the appropriate statement.

**power of attorney**
document authorizing someone to deal with land or other property on the owner's behalf

It is worth noting that the statement of age and the spousal statement are also required for transfers and charges that are in paper format. However, the power of attorney statement is required for electronic transfers and charges only.

## Compliance with Law Statements

In addition to the mandatory statements, transfers and charges must contain certain **compliance with law statements** (for example, *Planning Act* statements, discussed in Chapter 9), which only a lawyer may complete.

**compliance with law statement**
a lawyer's statement that the applicable legal requirements have been met

The requirement of compliance with law statements replaces the requirement of filing supporting documents with the LRO. Prior to electronic registration, the lawyer acting for the seller of a property under power of sale (in a mortgage) had to attach all of the supporting documents (for example, notice of sale and affidavit of service) to a registered document. Under electronic registration, the lawyer does not have to file the documents. Instead, he or she electronically signs a statement that all of the requirements have been satisfied for the power of sale to be completed and the transfer registered. Although the supporting documentation is not filed, a lawyer acting for the seller must keep copies of the supporting documents in his or her file in case of any future challenge to the transaction's validity. The buyer's lawyer can rely on compliance with law statements and does not have to examine the supporting documents.

# Signing Documents

Documents created by means of Teraview are signed with electronic signatures. All documents require a signature for "completeness." Transfers require, in addition, a second signature for "release."

## Signing for Completeness

Only a lawyer can sign for completeness. By doing so, the lawyer confirms that the document is correct and that he or she has the authority to act for the client.

The seller's lawyer or law clerk uses the information that he or she has in order to prepare the electronic transfer and then "messages" (sends) the document electronically to the buyer's lawyer. Both lawyers sign for completeness when satisfied that the document is complete.

### Unique Lawyer Statement

If the buyer and seller have different lawyers, as is usually the case, each lawyer must check off a "unique lawyer statement" to confirm that he or she is acting for one party only. In the statement, the seller is referred to as the "party from" and the buyer is referred to as the "party to." If one lawyer is acting for both parties, he or she must check off one of the "exemption law statements," confirming that he or she is permitted to act on both sides of the transaction because there is no conflict of interest.

For example, if a father is gifting his property to his daughter, no conflict of interest exists because the transaction is between related people with a common interest. In this case, the lawyer will sign the exemption law statement that says, "I am the solicitor for the transferor(s) and the transferee(s) and this transfer is being completed in accordance with my professional standards."

The person signing the transfer or charge will be prompted if any information is missing, and will be directed to the missing fields. Signing for completeness is possible only after all of the required information has been inserted.

If a change is made to a document after signing, all signatures are removed by the software. This ensures that no changes can be made to a document without the knowledge of both lawyers.

## Signing for Release

A law clerk can sign a document for release (a lawyer's signature is not required) because the document has already been reviewed by the lawyer. The seller's law firm signs the documents for release only after receiving the closing proceeds because a document for release, once it is signed, is, in effect, delivered to the other party for registration.

### Acknowledgment and Direction

**acknowledgment and direction**
document signed by a party to a real estate transaction authorizing his or her lawyer to sign and release a document electronically on his or her behalf

Before a document is released, a lawyer must have the authorization of his or her client in the form of an **acknowledgment and direction**, which is created in Teraview. A sample acknowledgment and direction is found in Figure 7.3.

A separate acknowledgment and direction is required for each document to be registered. For example, if Henry Albert Grant and Wilma Heather Grant are buying a property and financing the purchase by way of a charge, they will sign two acknowledgment and direction forms, one for the transfer and the other for the charge. If a lawyer or law clerk wants to print only a draft of a document, it is possible to do so without the acknowledgment and direction. Preparation of the acknowledgment and direction is discussed in Chapter 21, Document Preparation.

## Figure 7.3 Sample Acknowledgment and Direction

### ACKNOWLEDGEMENT AND DIRECTION

**TO:** Judith M. Wolf
(Insert lawyer's name)

**AND TO:** Kurtz, Emmans, Blatt & Wolf
(Insert firm name)

**RE:** GRANT purchase from MERCIER, 166 Valley Road, Newmarket ('the transaction")
(Insert brief description of transaction)

**This will confirm that:**

● I/We have reviewed the information set out in this Acknowledgement and Direction and in the documents described below (the "Documents"), and that this information is accurate;

● You, your agent or employee are authorized and directed to sign, deliver, and/or register electronically, on my/our behalf the Documents in the form attached.

● You are hereby authorized and directed to enter into an escrow closing arrangement substantially in the form attached hereto being a copy of the version of the Document Registration Agreement, which appears on the website of the Law Society of Upper Canada as of the date of the Agreement of Purchase and sale herein. I/We hereby acknowledge the said Agreement has been reviewed by me/us and that I/We shall be bound by its terms;

● The effect of the Documents has been fully explained to me/us, and I/we understand that I/we are parties to and bound by the terms and provisions of the Documents to the same extent as if I/we had signed them; and

● I/we are in fact the parties named in the Documents and I/we have not misrepresented our identities to you.

● I, _____, am the spouse of _____, the (Transferor/Chargor), and hereby consent to the transaction described in the Acknowledgment and Direction. I authorize you to indicate my consent on all the Documents for which it is required.

### DESCRIPTION OF ELECTRONIC DOCUMENTS

The Document(s) described in the Acknowledgement and Direction are the document(s) selected below which are attached hereto as "Document in Preparation" and are:

☐ A Transfer of the land described above.

☐ A Charge of the land described above.

☐ Other documents set out in Schedule "B" attached hereto.

Dated at _____, this _____ day of _____, 20____ .

**WITNESS**

(As to all signatures, if required)

_____     _____
                                     HENRY ALBERT GRANT

                                     _____
                                     WILMA HEATHER GRANT

                                     _____

# Messaging Documents

Documents are messaged between law firms so that they can be signed by both lawyers. For example, a transfer that is prepared by the seller's lawyer will be messaged to the buyer's lawyer so that the information about the buyer, such as the buyer's title information and land transfer tax information (discussed more fully in Chapter 21), can be added.

To message a document, the user selects "Messages" in the top toolbar, and then "Compose," as shown in Figure 7.4. The recipient's user name is entered if it is known, and the document is sent. If the recipient's user name is not known, it can be found by entering the account (the name of the law firm) and then selecting "Find."

When the buyer's law firm receives the transfer, the user is prompted to find the appropriate docket so that the received transfer will be added to it. This way, all documents relating to one file are located in the same place.

For example, assume that your firm is acting for Henry Albert Grant and Wilma Heather Grant on the purchase of their home. They have arranged mortgage financing with Best Bank, for whom you are also acting. The seller's law firm prepares the transfer to your clients, and meanwhile you prepare the charge in favour of Best Bank in docket 15-3355. When the seller's law firm completes the transfer, it messages the transfer to you. When your firm receives the transfer from the seller's law firm, you are prompted to put it in docket 15-3355.

**Figure 7.4   Messaging a Document**

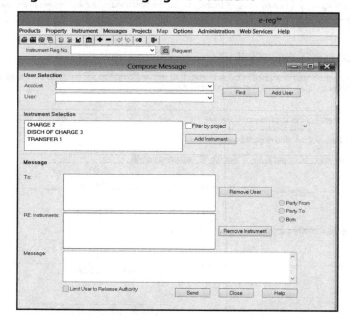

# Electronic Closings

An electronic closing is easier than a paper closing because it takes place in the lawyer's office. There is no need to go to an LRO. The seller's lawyer delivers the key(s) along with the seller's closing documents to the buyer's lawyer, and the buyer's lawyer delivers the money for closing as well as the buyer's closing documents to the seller's lawyer. These deliveries are typically made by courier. Closing documents are discussed in Chapter 21.

Prior to the closing, the law firms for both parties sign (or otherwise agree to the adoption of ) a **document registration agreement (DRA)**, which obligates the lawyers to hold all documents, keys, and money pending completion of the transaction. This is known as an **escrow closing**. The DRA further states that if for any reason the transaction is not completed, the documents, keys, and money will be returned. See Figure 7.5 for a sample DRA.

Once both sides have received their courier packages from the other side, the seller's lawyer releases the transfer (by signing for release), and the buyer's lawyer will then be able to register the transfer and—if the law firm is also acting for the mortgagee—the charge. If the law firm is acting on the purchase and the mortgage, the transfer must be registered first, because the charge cannot be registered until the new owner (the buyer) is actually on title.

Before registration of the documents, Teraview will prompt the user to subsearch title to the property. The purpose of a subsearch is to make sure that nothing un-expected has been registered on title since the title search was completed. Title searching is discussed in Chapter 14, and subsearching is discussed in Chapter 22, Closing the Transaction. As long as nothing unforeseen has been registered, the transfer and the charge (if applicable) will be registered.

**document registration agreement (DRA)** agreement entered into by the lawyers in a purchase and sale transaction that deals with the procedures for electronic registra-tion and the escrow closing arrangement

**escrow closing** exchange and holding of documents, keys, and money by the lawyers pending registration of the electronic documents

# Execution Search

When a transfer is registered, Teraview automatically searches for executions against the transferors (sellers). The buyer's law firm must also search for executions against the buyer if a mortgage is being registered or a mortgage is being assumed. Figure 7.6 illustrates an electronic execution certificate that is clear (that is, it shows no out-standing executions). Executions are discussed in Chapter 14, Title Searching.

## Figure 7.5 Sample Document Registration Agreement

### DOCUMENT REGISTRATION AGREEMENT

BETWEEN:

**JUDITH M. WOLF (KURTZ, EMMANS, BLATT & WOLF)**
(hereinafter referred to as the "**Purchaser's Solicitor**")

AND:

**HARVEY BROOKS (BROOKS & DUNN)**
(hereinafter referred to as the "**Vendor's Solicitor**")

RE: Henry Albert Grant and Wilma Heather Grant (the "**Purchaser**") purchase from Francois Mercier and Hugette Marie Mercier (the "**Vendor**") of (the "**Property**") pursuant to an agreement of purchase and sale dated Decmeber 1, 2015, as amended from time to time (the "**Purchase Agreement**"), scheduled to be completed on December 15, 2015 (the "**Closing Date**")

---

**FOR GOOD AND VALUABLE CONSIDERATION** (the receipt and sufficiency of which is hereby expressly acknowledged), the parties hereto hereby undertake and agree as follows:

Holding Deliveries In Escrow

1.        The Vendor's Solicitor and the Purchaser's Solicitor shall hold all funds, keys and closing documentation exchanged between them (the "Requisite Deliveries") in escrow, and *shall* not release or otherwise deal with same except in accordance with the terms of this Agreement. Both the Vendor's Solicitor and the Purchaser's Solicitor have been authorized by their respective clients to enter into this Agreement. Once the Requisite Deliveries can be released in accordance with the terms of this Agreement, any monies representing payout funds for mortgages to be discharged shall be forwarded promptly to the appropriate mortgage lender. [1]

Advising of Concerns with Deliveries

2.        Each of the parties hereto shall notify the other as soon as reasonably possible following their respective receipt of the Requisite Deliveries (as applicable) of any defect(s) with respect to same.

Selecting Solicitor Responsible for Registration

3.        The Purchaser's Solicitor shall be responsible for the registration of the Electronic Documents (as hereinafter defined) unless the box set out below indicating that the Vendor's Solicitor will be responsible for such registration has been checked. For the purposes of this Agreement, the solicitor responsible for such registration shall be referred to as the "Registering Solicitor" and the other solicitor shall be referred to as the "Non-Registering Solicitor":

Vendor's Solicitor will be registering the Electronic Documents ☐

---

[1] Solicitors should continue to refer to the Law Society of Upper Canada practice guidelines relating to recommended procedures to follow for the discharge of mortgages.

## Figure 7.5   Continued

**Responsibility of Non-Registering Solicitor**

**and**

**Release of Requisite Deliveries by Non-Registering Solicitor**

4.      The Non-Registering Solicitor shall, upon his/her receipt and approval of the Requisite Deliveries (as applicable), electronically release for registration the Electronic Documents and shall thereafter be entitled to release the Requisite Deliveries from escrow forthwith following the earlier of:

a)      the registration of the Electronic Documents;

b)      the closing time specified in the Purchase Agreement unless a specific time has been inserted as follows [_____ a.m./p.m. on the Closing Date] (the **"Release Deadline"**), and provided that notice under paragraph 7 below has not been received; or

c)      receipt of notification from the Registering Solicitor of the registration of the Electronic Documents.

If the Purchase Agreement does not specify a closing time and a Release Deadline has not been specifically inserted the Release Deadline shall be 6.00 p.m. on the Closing Date.

**Responsibility of Registering Solicitor**

5.      The Registering Solicitor shall, subject to paragraph 7 below, on the Closing Date, following his/her receipt and approval of the Requisite Deliveries (as applicable*)*, register the documents listed in Schedule "A" annexed hereto (referred to in this agreement as the **"Electronic Documents"**) in the stated order of priority therein set out, as soon as reasonably possible once same have been released for registration by the Non-Registering Solicitor, and immediately thereafter notify the Non-Registering Solicitor of the registration particulars thereof by telephone or telefax (or other method as agreed between the parties).

**Release of Requisite Deliveries by Registering Solicitor**

6.      Upon registration of the Electronic Documents and notification of the Non-Registering solicitor in accordance with paragraph 5 above, the Registering Solicitor shall be entitled to forthwith release the Requisite Deliveries from escrow.

**Returning Deliveries where Non-registration**

7.      Any of the parties hereto may notify the other party that he/she does not wish to proceed with the registration[2] of the Electronic Documents, and provided that such notice is received by the other party before the release of the Requisite Deliveries pursuant to this Agreement and before the registration of the Electronic Documents, then each of the parties hereto shall forthwith return to the other party their respective Requisite Deliveries.

**Counterparts & Gender**

8.      This Agreement may be signed in counterparts, and shall be read with all changes of gender and/or number as may be required by the context.

**Purchase Agreement Prevails if Conflict or Inconsistency**

9.      Nothing contained in this Agreement shall be read or construed as altering the respective rights and obligations of the Purchaser and the Vendor as more particularly set out in the Purchase Agreement, and in the event of any conflict or inconsistency between the provisions of this Agreement and the Purchase Agreement, then the latter shall prevail.

**Telefaxing Deliveries & Providing Originals if Requested**

10.      This Agreement (or any counterpart hereof), and any of the closing documents hereinbefore contemplated, may be exchanged by telefax or similar system reproducing the original, provided that all such documents have been properly executed by the appropriate parties. The party transmitting any such document(s) shall also provide the original executed version(s) of same to the recipient within 2 business days after the Closing Date, unless the recipient has indicated that he/she does not require such original copies.

---

[2] For the purpose of this Agreement, the term "registration" shall mean the issuance of registration number(s) in respect of the Electronic Documents by the appropriate Land Registry Office.

## Figure 7.5 Concluded

Dated this _____ day of <u>December, 2015</u>.

| | |
|---|---|
| Name/Firm Name of Vendor's Solicitor | Name/Firm Name of Purchaser's Solicitor |
| <u>Harvey Brooks</u> | <u>Judith M. Wolf</u> |
| _____ | _____ |
| _____ | _____ |
| Name of Person Signing | Name of Person Signing |
| _____ | _____ |
| (Signature) | (Signature) |

**Note: This version of the Document Registration Agreement was adopted by the Joint LSUC-CBAO Committee on Electronic Registration of Title Documents on *March 29, 2004* and posted to the web site on *April 8, 2004*.**

<u>**SCHEDULE "A" TO THE DOCUMENT REGISTRATION AGREEMENT**</u>

**Electronic Documents to be registered on closing (in order of priority)**

**Transfer/Deed of the Property from the Vendor in favour of the Purchaser.**

**First Charge/Mortgage against the Property from the Purchaser in favour DATA BANK OF CANADA**

**Figure 7.6 Electronic Execution Certificate That Shows No Outstanding Executions**

 Ontario

### CLEAR CERTIFICATE / CERTIFICAT LIBRE

SHERIFF OF / SHÉRIF DE : REGIONAL MUNICIPALITY OF YORK (NEWMARKET)

CERTIFICATE # /
N° DE CERTIFICAT : 26045040-56773411

DATE OF CERTIFICATE /
DATE DU CERTIFICAT : 2015-JUN-26

**SHERIFF'S STATEMENT**

THIS CERTIFIES THAT THERE ARE NO ACTIVE WRITS OF EXECUTION, ORDERS OR CERTIFICATES OF LIEN FILED WITHIN THE ELECTRONIC DATABASE MAINTAINED BY THIS OFFICE IN ACCORDANCE WITH SECTION 10 OF THE *EXECUTION ACT* AT THE TIME OF SEARCHING AGAINST THE REAL AND PERSONAL PROPERTY OF:

**DÉCLARATION DU SHÉRIF**

CE CERTIFICAT ATTESTE QU'IL N'Y A AUCUNE ORDONNANCE ACTIVE OU AUCUN BREF D'EXÉCUTION FORCÉE OU CERTIFICAT DE PRIVILÈGE ACTIF DANS LA BASE DE DONNÉES ÉLECTRONIQUE MAINTENUE PAR CE BUREAU AUX TERMES DE L'ARTICLE 10 DE LA *LOI SUR L'EXÉCUTION FORCÉE* AU MOMENT DE LA RECHERCHE VISANT LES BIENS MEUBLES ET IMMEUBLES DE :

**NAME SEARCHED / NOM RECHERCHÉ**

| # | PERSON OR COMPANY / PERSONNE OU SOCIÉTÉ | NAME OR SURNAME, GIVEN NAME(S) / NOM OU NOM DE FAMILLE, PRÉNOM(S) |
|---|---|---|
| 1. | PERSON / PERSONNE | MERCIER, FRANCOIS |
| 2. | PERSON / PERSONNE | MERCIER, HUGUETTE MARIE |

**CAUTION TO PARTY REQUESTING SEARCH:**

1. IT IS THE RESPONSIBILITY OF THE REQUESTING PARTY TO ENSURE THAT THE NAME SEARCHED IS CORRECT.

2. BY VIRTUE OF THIS CERTIFICATE, THE SHERIFF IS ASSURING THAT THIS NAME WILL REMAIN CLEAR UNTIL THE END OF CLOSE OF THIS BUSINESS DATE, UNLESS THE SHERIFF IS DIRECTED OTHERWISE UNDER AN ORDER OF THE COURT.

**AVERTISSEMENT À LA PARTIE QUI DEMANDE LA RECHERCHE :**

1. IL INCOMBE À LA PARTIE QUI DEMANDE LA RECHERCHE DE S'ASSURER QUE LE NOM RECHERCHÉ EST EXACT.

2. EN VERTU DU PRÉSENT CERTIFICAT, LE SHÉRIF ASSURE QUE CE NOM DEMEURE LIBRE JUSQU' À LA FIN DE CETTE JOURNÉE DE TRAVAIL, À MOINS DE RECEVOIR DES DIRECTIVES CONTRAIRES AUX TERMES D'UNE ORDONNANCE DU TRIBUNAL.

**CHARGE FOR THIS CERTIFICATE** CDN 22.00
**/ FRAIS POUR CE CERTIFICAT :**

**SEARCHER REFERENCE /
REFERENCE CONCERNANT
L'AUTEUR DE LA DEMANDE :**

CERTIFICATE # / N° DE CERTIFICAT: 26045040-56773411                    Page 1 of 1

# The Docket Summary

The docket summary in Teraview lists all of the disbursements incurred on the real estate transaction. These disbursements include the government's fees for registering documents and obtaining execution certificates and Teraview's fees for electronic title searching. For example, if you are acting for the buyers, who are also getting a mortgage, your disbursements will be the cost of the title search, the fees for the registration of the transfer and charge, and the cost of the execution searches against the buyers and sellers.

The docket summary is very useful in ensuring that the law firm is compensated for all its disbursements. It also provides an itemized list of the disbursements in the event that a client asks for it.

A sample docket summary is shown in Figure 7.7.

# Scenario and Sample Documents

Assume that the firm of Kurtz, Emmans, Blatt & Wolf has just opened a new file for Henry Albert Grant and Wilma Heather Grant, who are buying the property described in the agreement of purchase and sale in Chapter 16. The file number is 15-3355.

The buyers are obtaining a new mortgage in favour of Data Bank of Canada. The principal amount is $280,000, with an interest rate of 3 percent. The term of the mortgage is five years. Below are the steps that will be performed in connection with this transaction:

1. The seller's law firm will prepare the transfer (see Figure 7.1).
2. The seller's lawyer will message the transfer to the buyer's law firm, which completes the document by adding the buyer's information. Once this is done, both lawyers will sign for completeness and sign the unique lawyer statements.
3. Both law firms will print the acknowledgment and direction for their respective clients to sign. See Figure 7.3 for the buyer's acknowledgment and direction.
4. The buyer's lawyer will prepare the charge and the acknowledgment and direction to be signed by the chargor (the buyer). See Figure 7.2 for the charge.
5. When the seller's law firm receives the closing proceeds and the buyer's documents, the lawyer or law clerk will sign for release.
6. When the buyer's law firm receives the seller's documents and the key(s), the lawyer or law clerk will sign for release and register (after subsearching title to ensure that nothing unexpected has been registered).
7. If executions need to be searched against the buyer (that is, if there is a charge being registered or there is a charge being assumed), the buyer's lawyer or law clerk will search executions, if that has not already been done. Even if executions against the buyer have already been searched, they will have to be searched a second time if title insurance is not being obtained.
8. The buyer's lawyer or law clerk will register the transfer and then the charge. Executions against the seller are searched automatically.

## Figure 7.7 Sample Docket Summary

Teraview ® Account: (JUDIWOLF - KURTZ, EMMANS, BLATT & WOLF)

## Deposit Account Charges

## For Docket (15-3355 - GRANT)

Report from Mar 23 2015 12:00AM to Jun 23 2015 11:59PM

| Session Begun: Jun 16 2015 10:16AM | | | User Name: | JWolf001 | |
|---|---|---|---|---|---|
| Description of Charges | Statutory Fee | ELRSA Fee | GST/HST | PST | Total |
| Parcel register, key LRO | $8.00 | $10.00 | $1.30 | $0.00 | $19.30 |
| Parcel register, key LRO, add'l pages | $2.00 | $2.00 | $0.26 | $0.00 | $4.26 |
| Session Total | $10.00 | $12.00 | $1.56 | $0.00 | $23.56 |

| Totals of All Sessions Combined | | | | | |
|---|---|---|---|---|---|
| Description of Charges | Statutory Fee | ELRSA Fee | GST/HST | PST | Total |
| Parcel register, key LRO | $8.00 | $10.00 | $1.30 | $0.00 | $19.30 |
| Parcel register, key LRO, add~'l pages | $2.00 | $2.00 | $0.26 | $0.00 | $4.26 |
| Total | $10.00 | $12.00 | $1.56 | $0.00 | $23.56 |

Courier, handling, and copy charges incurred within the 3 hours immediately
preceding the time of reporting may not be included.

Includes statutory services supplied on behalf of the Ontario Government under exclusive licence
Billing data more than two years old will not appear on this report
Teraview is a registered trademark of Teranet Inc.
123 Front Street West, Suite 700, Toronto. Ontario. M5J 2M2, Telephone: (800) 208-5263 or (416) 360-1190

GST: Goods and Services Tax / HST: Harmonized Sales Tax (BN#130867526)
PST: Provincial Sales Tax (#6234-9979)

Deposit Account Charges for Docket (15-3355 - GRANT)

## KEY TERMS

acknowledgment and direction, 100

compliance with law statement, 99

disbursements, 92

docket, 92

document registration agreement (DRA), 103

escrow closing, 103

power of attorney, 99

## REFERENCES

*Family Law Act*, RSO 1990, c F.3.

*Land Registration Reform Act*, RSO 1990, c L.4.

*Planning Act*, RSO 1990, c P.13.

## REVIEW QUESTIONS

1. Your firm is representing Ernie Jacobs, who is purchasing a property in Toronto.

   a. How will you receive the transfer from the lawyer for the seller?

   b. If you are the law clerk working on the file, can you sign the transfer for completeness? Explain.

   c. Can you sign the transfer for release?

2. In the scenario described above, does Ernie have to sign a DRA? Explain.

3. Assume that Ernie is also getting a mortgage from ABC Bank. How many acknowledgment and direction forms will Ernie have to sign? Explain.

4. What form does Teraview produce in order to assist a lawyer in calculating the total disbursements on a file?

5. What three statements pertaining to the legal status of the owner must be in every electronic document?

6. Erin and Samson Matthews are buying two properties. One is in Toronto, and the other is in northern Ontario. Both are in the Land Titles system. Given the distance between the properties, they are wondering whether they need to retain two separate lawyers, one for each transaction. Will that be necessary? Explain.

# Liens Against Land

8

## LEARNING OUTCOMES

After reading this chapter, you will understand:

- What a lien is
- How a lien arises
- What Ontario statutes provide for liens against real property
- How to determine whether or not there is a lien affecting real property
- How a lien is enforced

# Introduction

A **lien** is a claim against land that acts as security for the payment of a debt owed by the landowner. The enforcement of a lien involves selling the property and applying the sale proceeds to the unpaid debt.

Many statutes affect property owners by providing lien rights to their land. Some statutes provide lien rights to private individuals and businesses, and other statutes give lien rights to the government.

# The Municipal Act, 2001

The *Municipal Act, 2001* requires property owners to pay realty taxes annually. To calculate the amount of tax, multiply the tax rate by the current value at which the property has been assessed. For example, assume that a home has an assessed value of $330,700. If the residential property tax rate for the year is set at 0.8889546 percent, the realty taxes on the property for that year will be $2,939.77 (that is, $330,700 × 0.008889546).

Realty taxes, depending on the municipality, may be paid in several installments or on a monthly basis by automatic withdrawal from the owner's bank account. It is also possible for owners to arrange to have their taxes paid through the bank that holds their mortgages.

The *Municipal Act, 2001* provides that unpaid realty taxes create a lien against land. The lien is automatic; the municipality does not have to register the lien against title to the land. It is a special lien on the land that takes priority over any other claim or lien except the Crown's.

The *Municipal Act, 2001* also permits municipalities to add to a property owner's taxes any unpaid fees and charges relating to the supply of a **public utility**. A public utility is defined in the Act to include a system that provides the public with any of the following supplies or services:

- water;
- sewage;
- fuel, including natural gas;
- energy, excluding electricity;
- heating and cooling; and
- telephone.

These unpaid fees and charges may be collected in the same manner as taxes.

If the owner fails to pay tax arrears, the *Municipal Act, 2001* permits the municipality to sell the property under a tax sale. A municipality may commence this process if taxes remain unpaid on January 1 in the third year following the year in which the taxes became due and owing (section 373(1)). To begin the process, the treasurer of the municipality registers a tax arrears certificate against title to the property, indicating the amount owing for tax arrears, including interest, penalties, and costs (defined in the Act as the "cancellation price"). If the cancellation price is not paid within one year of the date of registration of the tax arrears certificate, the property may be sold by public sale. If the cancellation price is paid within the pre-scribed amount of time, the treasurer registers a tax arrears cancellation certificate against title to the land.

Pursuant to the Act, proceeds received from a tax sale are applied first to pay the tax arrears. Any surplus is paid to others claiming an interest in the land, in order of their respective priorities. Any remaining balance is paid to the owner.

A title search will not reveal a lien for unpaid taxes. To make sure there is no lien against the property, a buyer should get a certificate from the municipal tax depart-ment confirming that all taxes have been paid. If, however, a buyer is getting title insurance, a tax certificate may not be required. Title insurance is discussed in Chapter 17.

## The Corporations Tax Act

Under the *Corporations Tax Act*, corporations with a permanent establishment in Ontario are required to pay taxes to the provincial government. The Act allows the government to register a lien on title to property owned by a corporation for unpaid taxes. A title search will reveal whether such a lien exists.

## The Income Tax Act

Section 116 of the federal *Income Tax Act* imposes taxes on non-residents of Canada who sell real property located in Canada. If these taxes are not paid, the buyer of the property will be liable to pay the tax. The buyer must therefore ensure that the seller is not a non-resident; or, if he or she is a non-resident, that the required taxes have been paid; or that the property is exempt from this tax. Otherwise, the buyer should withhold sufficient funds from the purchase price to cover the potential tax liability.

The standard form of agreement of purchase and sale requires the seller to supply the buyer with either a sworn statement that the seller is not a non-resident of Canada or a certificate from the Canada Revenue Agency confirming that the taxes, if any, have been paid in full and exempting the buyer from liability.

## The Land Transfer Tax Act

Land transfer tax is a provincial tax payable by the buyer of real property in Ontario. The amount is based on the value of the real property alone. Any chattels (movable personal property) included in the sale are not subject to land transfer tax, but they are subject to harmonized sales tax (HST). For example, if the buyer is paying $300,000 for a house that includes chattels valued at $5,000, the buyer will pay land transfer tax on $295,000 and HST on $5,000. There are some conveyances that may be exempt from the payment of land transfer tax, including

- property transferred under a will,
- property transferred between spouses, and
- property transferred by gift.

Section 15.1(1) of the *Land Transfer Tax Act* provides for a lien against real property for any unpaid tax.

Under this Act, a buyer is required to complete a land transfer tax affidavit confirming the purchase price, so that the appropriate land transfer tax can be calculated. In the old paper system, the buyer signed a separate land transfer tax affidavit that was attached to the transfer provided by the seller before registration. In the current electronic system, the buyer signs an acknowledgment and direction (as discussed in Chapter 7) authorizing his or her lawyer to complete the land transfer tax portion of the transfer. This tax and affidavit are further discussed in Chapter 21, Document Preparation and Chapter 22, Closing the Transaction.

## The Execution Act

**judgment creditor**
party to whom a court awards the payment of money

**writ of execution**
judicial order addressed to the sheriff requiring the enforcement of a judgment

**judgment debtor**
party against whom a court awards the payment of money

A **judgment creditor** (someone who is owed money pursuant to a court judgment) may enforce the judgment by filing a **writ of execution** (or writ of seizure and sale) with the sheriff in the jurisdiction where the **judgment debtor** (someone who owes money pursuant to a court judgment) owns real property. The writ of execution is a lien against the land, and the sheriff can execute the writ by seizing and selling the property. A writ of execution expires after six years but can be renewed indefinitely by the judgment creditor for consecutive six-year periods.

If the judgment debtor does not own any real property at the time the writ is filed with the sheriff, but subsequently acquires real property, the writ will bind that property if the following conditions are met:

- the writ has not expired,
- the debt remains unpaid, and
- the property is situated in the jurisdiction where the writ has been filed.

If a writ of execution is on file against a judgment debtor during the period that he or she owns the land, the writ can be enforced against any person who subsequently acquires an interest in the land. As a result, it is necessary for a buyer or lender to search for executions against the current owner (and past owners in the Registry system).

## The Construction Lien Act

**improvement**
changes made to real property, including construction, alteration, repair, installation, erection, and demolition

**construction lien**
lien against land that may be claimed by a person providing labour, services, or materials to a construction project

Tradespeople, labourers, and material suppliers whose efforts contribute to an **improvement** of real property are entitled to a **construction lien** against that land for the value of the services performed. Improvements include construction, alterations, repairs, installations, erections, and demolitions.

### The Construction Process

Many people may be involved in a construction project, each having a different contractual relationship with the property owner. Knowing who these people are and how they are connected to a construction project will help you understand construction lien concepts.

The owner of the land usually hires a general contractor to supervise and complete the entire project. The general contractor then enters into subcontracts with companies or individuals who specialize in a particular trade required for the project, such as carpentry, electrical, mechanical, painting, and so on. These companies or individuals may then enter into subcontracts with workers and suppliers. In a very large construction project, many different tradespeople may be supplying work and materials.

The relationship between these parties is sometimes thought of as a pyramid, referred to as the **construction pyramid**, with the owner at the top, followed by the general contractor and different levels of subcontractors. The construction pyramid is illustrated in Figure 8.1.

**construction pyramid**
illustration of the contractual relationships between parties in a typical large construction project

**Figure 8.1   The Construction Pyramid**

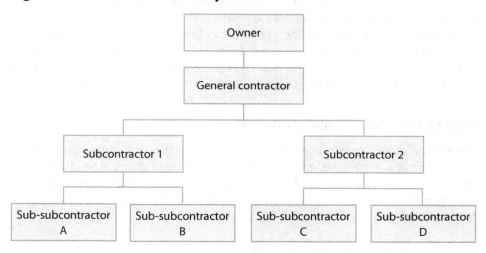

Each contractor shown in the figure has a contractual relationship only with the person directly above or below him or her in the construction pyramid. The general contractor is the only one who has **privity of contract** with the owner.

Each contractor must look to the person directly above him or her for payment. For example, sub-subcontractor A is paid by subcontractor 1; subcontractor 1 is paid by the general contractor; and the general contractor is paid by the owner.

**privity of contract**
doctrine of contract law that prevents a person from seeking enforcement of a contract unless he or she is a party to the contract

## The Need for Construction Lien Legislation

The *Construction Lien Act* is designed to provide financial protection for all subcontractors in the construction pyramid. Without this legislation, subcontractors could not assert a direct claim against the owner—even though they had supplied services or materials to the construction project, thereby enhancing the value of the owner's property—because they lack privity of contract with the owner.

For example, assume that Olive hires George, a general contractor, to supervise the renovation of her kitchen. George hires a company called Kitchens R Us to install the kitchen. George tells Kitchens R Us to bill him, and he bills Olive for the work performed by this company, plus a fee for himself. Assume that Olive pays George, but George does not pay Kitchens R Us. At common law, Kitchens R Us could sue only George, not Olive.

Even though Kitchens R Us has contributed to the improvement of Olive's home and has thereby enhanced its value, Kitchens R Us, without construction lien legislation, would have no direct claim against either Olive or the real property. Kitchens R Us would be forced to wait in line for payment by George, together with all of his other ordinary judgment creditors. Construction lien legislation allows Kitchens R Us to make a claim directly against Olive and her land, even though there is no direct contractual relationship between the parties.

## The Construction Lien

To summarize, a construction lien is a lien against land that may be claimed by a person who provides labour, services, or materials to a construction project. Every subcontractor in the construction pyramid has lien rights regardless of how contractually far removed he or she is from the owner of the land. The lien attaches to the land upon which the construction takes place and is for the value of the work completed or the materials supplied by the subcontractor claiming the lien.

## How to Preserve a Construction Lien

**preserve**
ensure that lien rights are protected and do not expire by registering a claim for lien against title to the property on which work was performed within 45 days of completion of the work

The right to claim a construction lien arises as soon as the work starts or the materials are supplied. No further action is required to acquire the right to claim a lien. The claimant must, however, take steps to **preserve** an existing lien by registering the claim for lien against the property within 45 days of completion of work or delivery of materials.

## The Expiry of Construction Lien Rights

Even though the right to a lien arises as soon as services or materials are supplied to an improvement, most subcontractors and tradespeople will not register a lien immediately. Instead, they will wait for payment for a reasonable period of time after the work has been completed or abandoned. However, they can't wait forever: they must take steps to preserve their lien rights within 45 days of completion of the job. Otherwise, the rights will be deemed to have expired.

If a subcontractor fails to preserve a lien, he or she will lose the right to claim a lien against the owner and the owner's property. However, legal remedies for breach of contract can still be pursued against the person directly above the subcontractor in the construction pyramid (the person with whom there is privity of contract).

The legislation provides for the expiry of unregistered claims to prevent liens from looming over title indefinitely and to allow owners and contractors to finalize construction projects.

## Perfecting a Construction Lien

Once a lien has been preserved, it must be **perfected** within a prescribed time in order to remain enforceable. To perfect the lien, the lien claimant must commence legal proceedings by issuing a statement of claim in the court office of the jurisdiction where the land is located. The lien claimant must also register a **certificate of action** against title to the property.

A preserved lien must be perfected within 45 days of the last day on which the lien could have been preserved—in other words, 90 days after the work has been completed. If it is not perfected by this time, the lien will be deemed to have expired. A perfected lien will also expire if a lien action is not set down for trial within two years of the date the statement of claim was issued.

## The Holdback

A **holdback** is money that a payer is required to deduct from an amount owing to a payee and to hold for a specified period of time. The *Construction Lien Act* requires each level of payer in the construction pyramid to retain a 10 percent holdback when the payer makes a payment to a payee at the next level below in the construction pyramid. The holdback is for the benefit of those tradespeople who are one level below the payee, and two levels below the payer, in the pyramid.

The statutory holdback amount is 10 percent of the value of the work performed or the materials supplied. The holdback is released or paid out when all potential liens have either expired or been resolved.

Assume that Olive and George, from the kitchen renovation example above, have agreed upon a contract price of $10,000. When Olive pays George, she must hold back 10 percent, or $1,000, from this payment. If George does not pay Kitchens R Us, the holdback ensures that these funds will be available for Kitchens R Us to draw from. If George pays Kitchens R Us in full, and no liens are claimed, Olive will be able to release the $1,000 to George.

If an owner receives written notice of a construction lien in addition to the 10 percent statutory holdback, the owner must hold back from future payments an amount equal to the amount being claimed under the lien.

The holdback is mandatory: parties to a construction or renovation contract cannot contract out of the holdback requirement. As long as the owner has fulfilled the statutory requirements and retained the required amount, the owner has no further liability toward the lien claimant. In other words, the owner's personal liability toward the lien claimant does not exceed the amount of the required holdback.

If the owner fails to hold back the required amount, lien claimants may enforce their lien rights by claiming the amount of the holdback. If the owner doesn't pay, the lien claimants can demand that the property be sold to satisfy their claims. In the above example, if George does not pay Kitchens R Us and Olive has failed to hold back the $1,000, Olive will be required to pay $1,000 to Kitchens R Us. If Olive doesn't pay, Kitchens R Us can force the sale of Olive's property to satisfy the debt.

**perfect**
ensure that a preserved lien does not expire by commencing an action to enforce the lien and registering a certificate of action against title to the property

**certificate of action**
certificate of the court verifying that a statement of claim has been filed in a construction lien action

**holdback**
sum of money required to be deducted by the payer and held for a specified period of time from the amount owing to a payee in a construction contract

### Completion Date of the Contract

It is important to determine the completion date of an improvement. On that date, the clock starts running on the limitation periods for preserving and perfecting liens, and the date affects the timing of the release of holdback funds.

It may be difficult to establish the completion date on a very large construction project, so the *Construction Lien Act* contains detailed procedural rules for determining this date. For example, under the Act, a contract will be deemed to be complete when the value of the work remaining to be finished or corrected is not more than $1,000 or 1 percent of the contract price, whichever is less.

The Act also permits release of holdback funds 45 days after "substantial performance" of the project. *Substantial performance* is defined in the Act as the time at which the improvement can be used for its intended purposes and can be completed for a specified percentage amount of the contract price.

## Clearing a Lien from Title

**discharge of lien**
document registered on title that discharges a construction lien

An owner can clear a lien from title by obtaining a release from the lien claimant and registering it on title. The owner can also obtain an order discharging the lien and vacating the certificate of action by paying the full amount of the lien claim plus a prescribed amount of costs into court. The money paid into court takes the place of the land as security for the lien. A **discharge of lien** can be registered or the certificate of action can be **vacated** if a perfected lien has expired, because no action has been taken for two years following perfection of the lien.

**vacated**
removed from title by registration of a court order that vacates or annuls the certificate of action

## Implications for Title Searching

A buyer of real property must ensure that no liens have been registered on title to the property on or before closing. If the search of title discloses a lien, the buyer's lawyer should requisition its discharge. Requisitions are discussed in Chapter 19, Requisitions: An Overview.

If no liens are registered on title at the time of closing, the buyer will obtain title free from any future lien claims provided that (1) he or she has not paid more than 30 percent of the purchase price before closing, and (2) title is not transferred until the home is ready for occupancy, as evidenced by a certificate of completion and possession. In that case, the buyer will not be liable for liens that are preserved or registered after the date of closing.

## KEY TERMS

certificate of action, 117

construction lien, 114

construction pyramid, 115

discharge of lien, 118

holdback, 117

improvement, 114

judgment creditor, 114

judgment debtor, 114

lien, 112

perfect, 117

preserve, 116

privity of contract, 115

public utility, 112

vacated, 118

writ of execution, 114

## REFERENCES

*Construction Lien Act*, RSO 1990, c C.30.

*Corporations Tax Act*, RSO 1990, c C.40.

*Execution Act*, RSO 1990, c E.24.

*Income Tax Act*, RSC 1985, c 1 (5th Supp), as amended.

*Land Transfer Tax Act*, RSO 1990, c L.6.

*Municipal Act, 2001*, SO 2001, c 25.

## REVIEW QUESTIONS

1. How is a lien enforced?

2. Sophia owns a townhouse in Toronto, Ontario and has not paid realty taxes for the past two years. Referring to the appropriate legislation, explain to Sophia what can happen if she doesn't pay the taxes owing.

3. Fernando resides in Rome, Italy but owns real property in Canada. He recently listed the property for sale, and Bruno is interested in purchasing it. Referring to the relevant legislation, explain what tax implications Bruno should be aware of in this situation.

4. George files a writ of execution with the sheriff on February 2 against Sam. Sam does not own any real property. On November 15, Sam buys his first home. Does the writ bind this property?

5. Willy is a subcontractor who has not been paid for the painting services he provided for a renovation. Can he sue the owner of the property? Explain.

6. Dimitre is the owner of a property. He hired Ali as a contractor to renovate his kitchen, and Ali hired Susan to install the kitchen cabinets. Susan completed the work on April 15 and sent Ali a bill for $3,000. It is now May 1 and Susan has not been paid.

   a. What are Dimitre's obligations under the *Construction Lien Act* when he pays Ali?

   b. What steps must Susan take to collect the money owing to her?

   c. What happens if Dimitre fails to hold back the required amount?

# Government Controls over the Use and Subdivision of Land

# 9

## LEARNING OUTCOMES

After reading this chapter, you will understand:

- The need for regulating undesirable uses and division of land

- How zoning bylaws regulate the use of land

- How building permits regulate the development of land and the construction of buildings on land

- How the *Planning Act* regulates the subdivision of land

- The importance of compliance with the *Planning Act*

- How to conduct a *Planning Act* search

# Introduction

An owner of land is not free to do absolutely anything with that land; the rights of the owner are subject to governmental regulation. To protect neighbours from the undesirable uses to which an owner might put his or her land, the government controls the way an owner uses land. The government also controls the subdivision of land, because increased development requires increased government services.

For example, if someone purchases a home on a very large lot in a quiet residential neighbourhood and decides to convert the property into a restaurant, the neighbours will likely object. They expect their neighbourhood to remain both quiet and residential. Consider another example: if the new owner wants to tear down the house and build three townhouses for resale, the neighbours, again, will likely object because the new owner's project will change the character of the neighbourhood. In addition, the city might object because three homes would occupy an area that was intended for only one, creating an increased demand for the provision of city services such as water, sewage, garbage pickup, and schools.

The *Planning Act* is provincial legislation created to prevent owners from using or developing land in ways that are inconsistent with good municipal planning. The *Planning Act* was first passed after the Second World War, when there was a sudden increase in urban growth and development. Though the Act has been amended many times, the methods of control used in the original legislation have not changed substantially.

The Act regulates undesirable uses of land through **zoning** and ensures that land is divided in an orderly way through **subdivision control**.

# Zoning

Zoning regulates undesirable land use in developed areas through the use of an **official plan** and **zoning bylaws**.

## Official Plan

An official plan is a statement of planning principles for a municipality. It is prepared for the municipality by the local planning board and is submitted first to the municipal council for adoption and then to the provincial government for approval. The municipality cannot create or amend bylaws or undertake any public work that does not conform to the official plan.

## Zoning Bylaws

The municipality regulates the use of land by enacting bylaws. These bylaws divide the municipality into zoning areas and define the use to which land and buildings can be put in each zone. For example, property in one zoning area can be used only for single-family dwellings, while property in another area can be used only for commercial or industrial purposes. Every parcel of land is currently in a prescribed

**zoning**
classification of permitted land use that includes categories such as residential, commercial, industrial, and agricultural

**subdivision control**
government control over the division of land into smaller parcels

**official plan**
statement of planning principles prepared for a municipality by the local planning board

**zoning bylaws**
bylaws enacted by a municipality to regulate the use of land

zoning area and cannot be used for any purpose other than the one specified for that area, unless a re-zoning application is successful.

Bylaws also regulate the size, shape, and location of all buildings and structures on a lot by providing specific set-back requirements, yard allowances, and lot sizes. For example, a bylaw may state that a house cannot be situated less than 1.22 metres (four feet) from the side lot line.

Sometimes the use of land or a location's size or structure does not conform to a current bylaw but was legal prior to the enactment of the bylaw. If the use has not been discontinued or the structure has not changed, then both are permitted to continue as a **legal non-conforming use**.

If a property does not conform to a current bylaw and the use is not a legal non-conforming use, then the owner can seek a **consent to variance** from the municipal **committee of adjustment**. A consent will be granted if the failure to conform is minor in nature and the overall intent and purpose of the bylaw and official plan are maintained. Otherwise, it may be necessary to obtain an amendment to the bylaw for the use or structure to continue.

## Building Controls

A form of land-use regulation is found in the *Building Code Act, 1992*, a provincial statute that sets the standard of construction for buildings throughout Ontario. It is enforced by municipalities, which in some cases may also have additional municipal property standard bylaws.

Municipalities also regulate land use by requiring a **building permit** to be issued before construction or renovation of a building. A building permit is a document that grants the applicant legal permission to start construction of a "building," as defined by the *Building Code Act, 1992*. The Act's definition of "building" is quite broad and includes not just houses but additions, garages, porches, and decks, among other things.

The permit ensures that building construction meets the minimum standards set out in the *Building Code Act, 1992* and in any municipal bylaws regulating such features as structures' height, location, floor area, external design, character, parking facilities, and use. An applicant will be granted a building permit only after demonstrating that the plans comply with the *Building Code Act, 1992* and all relevant bylaws.

Some buildings are designated as historic sites under the *Ontario Heritage Act* and cannot be altered or demolished without the consent of the municipality.

## Subdivision Control

The purpose of subdivision control is to restrict the division of land into smaller parcels. When such a **severance** takes place, the population of the area increases, as does the need for municipal services such as roads, street lights, curbs, sewers, schools, and parks. The subdivision control provisions of the *Planning Act* ensure that these additional services are paid for by the developer and not the municipality.

**legal non-conforming use**
status of a building or use of a property that does not conform to the current municipal bylaw but is acceptable because the building or use existed before the passing of the bylaw and has not subsequently been altered or discontinued

**consent to variance**
committee of adjustment approval of a building or use of a property when it does not conform to a current bylaw and is not a legal non-conforming use

**committee of adjustment**
independent body appointed by a municipality with the authority to grant consent to conveyances that result in a severance

**building permit**
document that grants legal permission to start construction of a building, as defined by the *Building Code Act, 1992*

**severance**
division of land into smaller parcels

Landowners must seek government consent to any transfers of land that result in the division of an owner's property into two or more smaller parcels. The Act controls the division of land whether one parcel of land is being divided into 2, 20, or 200 smaller parcels.

## Section 50 of the Planning Act

Section 50 of the *Planning Act* is the main instrument of subdivision control in Ontario. It affects virtually every transaction that involves the creation of an interest in real property. The legislation is designed to ensure that owners cannot, without permission, deal with their land in any way that will result in a division of that land.

## The Basic Prohibition

Section 50(3) of the Act essentially prohibits every "transaction" conveying an interest in land, unless the transaction falls within one of the exceptions specified in the Act. The definition of "transaction" is very broad and covers virtually all common dealings with land, including

- selling land,
- mortgaging or charging land,
- entering into an agreement of purchase and sale of land, and
- leasing land for more than 21 years.

A conveyance contrary to the *Planning Act* does not create or convey any interest in land. In other words, the transaction will be void.

## Exceptions to the Basic Prohibition

There are four exceptions to the basic prohibition in section 50(3). A transaction is *permitted* as long as it falls within one of the exceptions. The exceptions are designed to cover situations in which either land is not being divided, or, if it is, there has already been municipal or governmental consideration of planning issues. Therefore, the exceptions allow a transaction to proceed because, in the case of each exception, the purposes of subdivision control have already been served. The four areas of exception may be characterized as follows:

1. whole lot on a plan of subdivision,
2. no fee in abutting lands,
3. transactions involving the government, and
4. government consent obtained.

### 1. Whole Lot on a Plan of Subdivision

Section 50(3)(a) provides an exception to the basic prohibition if the property being sold is within a registered plan of subdivision. If it is a whole lot, planning and subdivision control issues would already have been considered and approved by the government prior to registration of the plan of subdivision. As a result, the underlying purpose of section 50 has been served, and there is no need to prohibit the conveyance of the lot. If it is part of a lot, it must comply with section 50(5). (See the discussion under the heading "Part Lot Control," below.)

Under section 50(4), a municipality may pass a bylaw deeming an existing plan that is at least eight years old *not* to be a registered plan of subdivision for the purposes of section 50(3) of the Act. A municipality passes this kind of bylaw to regain planning control in a case where it believes that a previously approved plan is outdated or is no longer effective because of changes in development. In such a case, a lot situated on the affected plan will no longer qualify as a lot on a registered plan of subdivision and the protection of this exception will therefore be lost.

Assume that the two subdivision lots in Figure 9.1 are on Plan 2345. John owns Lots 1 and 2 and wants to convey Lot 1 and keep Lot 2. John can rely on the exception provided in section 50(3)(a) and convey Lot 1 without violating the *Planning Act*. If, however, Plan 2345 is deemed by a bylaw *not* to be a registered plan of subdivision, John cannot rely on this exception and must qualify for another exception in order to proceed.

**Figure 9.1    Adjoining Lots on a Plan of Subdivision**

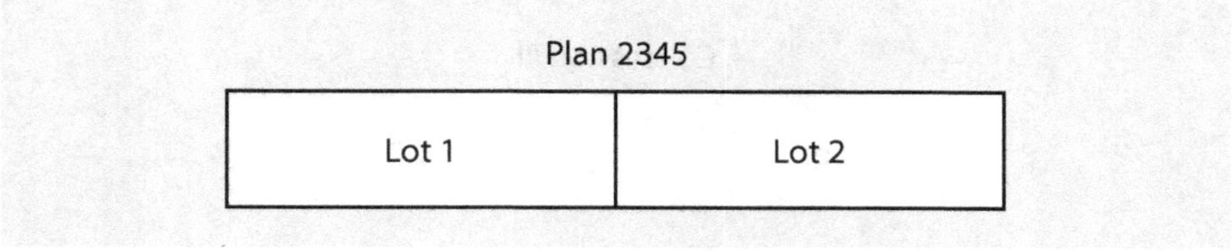

**2.  No Fee in Abutting Lands**

Section 50(3)(b) sets out the major exception to section 50(3)'s basic prohibition against transactions conveying an interest in land. This exception deals with adjoining, or abutting, land. Land is considered to be abutting, or adjoining, when it shares a common boundary. Look at the parcels in Figure 9.2. Parcels 1, 3, and 5 abut parcel 2 because they each share a common boundary with it. However, parcels 2 and 6 are not considered to be adjoining land.

**Figure 9.2    Adjoining, or Abutting, Parcels of Land**

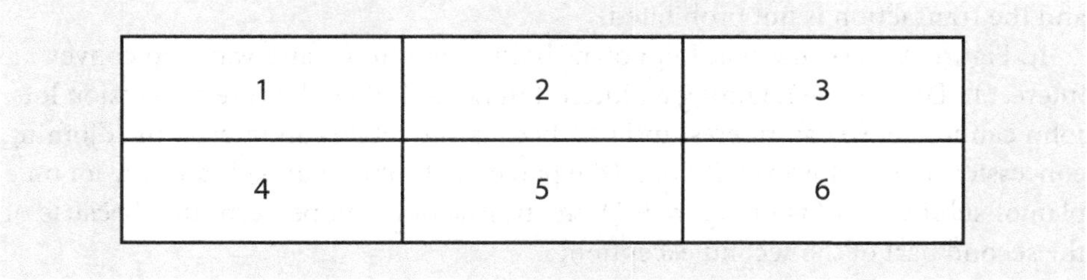

Section 50(3)(b) is easier to understand if broken down into two parts. The first part provides an exception to the basic prohibition, and the second part provides an exception to the first part.

The exception provided by the first part applies to a transaction in which the person dealing with the property does not retain the fee (ownership) or equity of redemption (a mortgagor's interest in mortgaged land) in any land abutting the land that is being dealt with. This type of transaction is permitted because the owner's holding is not being divided into smaller parcels when the owner conveys everything that is owned. If, however, the owner deals with part of the land while retaining ownership of adjoining land, the owner is effectively dividing the land into two parcels. Such a transaction, which is exactly the type that the Act is designed to prevent, is prohibited.

Under the *Planning Act*, it doesn't matter if adjoining properties were originally acquired as separate parcels of land. For example, assume that John acquired concession Lot 1 in 2003 and concession Lot 2 in 2008, illustrated in Figure 9.3. He now wants to convey Lot 1. For *Planning Act* purposes, adjoining lands owned by the same person merge into one parcel. As a result, John cannot sell Lot 1 while retaining an interest in Lot 2, even though, historically, they were two separate properties.

**Figure 9.3   Adjoining Concession Lots**

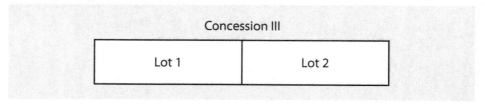

The second part of section 50(3)(b) provides an exception to the first part of the section. This exception applies if the retained land is a whole lot on a plan of subdivision. In other words, if the owner conveys land while retaining an interest in adjoining land, the transaction will not be prohibited as long as the retained land is a whole lot on a plan of subdivision.

Return to Figure 9.1 and assume, this time, that John owns only Lot 1. If Lots 1 and 2 are whole lots on a plan of subdivision, John can convey an interest in Lot 1 and rely on the first exception. If these lots are concession lots, as illustrated in Figure 9.3, John can also convey an interest in Lot 1 and rely on the first part of the second exception. Since he owns only Lot 1, he is not retaining an interest in adjoining land, and the transaction is not prohibited.

In Figure 9.3, assume that John owns both Lots 1 and 2 and wants to convey an interest in Lot 1 while retaining an interest in Lot 2. If these lots are concession lots, John cannot convey an interest in Lot 1 because he retains an interest in adjoining concession Lot 2. However, if Lot 2 (the parcel that John retains) is a whole lot on a plan of subdivision (as in Figure 9.1), the transaction will be permitted because of the second part of the second exception.

Return to Figure 9.2. Assume that John owns parcels 1, 3, and 5 and wants to convey an interest in parcel 5 while retaining an interest in parcels 1 and 3. Since parcels 1, 3, and 5 do not abut, John can convey an interest in parcel 5 and rely on the second exception. When developers acquire land, they often use this "checkerboard" scheme to avoid future *Planning Act* issues: they register alternating parcels of land in the names of different owners to avoid *Planning Act* problems when subsequently selling off parcels of land.

In the past, developers also used **simultaneous conveyances** as a device to get around the prohibition against retaining abutting land. Return to Figure 9.3 and assume that John owns the two abutting concession lots. He could convey the two lots at exactly the same time to two different people and try to rely on the second exception. He would argue that at the time of the conveyance, he did not retain the fee in abutting land. Section 50(15) was enacted to close this loophole. It provides that if two parcels of land are being conveyed at the same time to two different people, the owner is deemed to retain the ownership in abutting land for the purposes of section 50(3).

> **simultaneous conveyance**
> two abutting parcels of land conveyed at the same time to two different people

### 3.  Transactions Involving the Government

Conveyances to and from governmental authorities are permitted. Sections 50(3)(c), (d), and (e) set out the exceptions as follows:

- government acquisitions and dispositions,
- acquisitions for transmission lines (pipelines), and
- acquisitions for conservation purposes.

### 4.  Government Consent Obtained

If a conveyance will result in the division of a larger piece of property into smaller parcels, and the transfer does not fall into any of the previous exceptions, the owner must seek government consent to the transaction. The nature of the consent required depends on the extent of the proposed division. If a parcel is being divided into relatively few parcels, the owner of the land can seek consent of the committee of adjustment under section 50(3)(f). If a parcel is being divided into many parcels, the owner of the land must seek government approval for a registered plan of subdivision.

#### CONSENT OF THE COMMITTEE OF ADJUSTMENT

A committee of adjustment is an independent body appointed by a municipality. It can grant consent to conveyances that result in a severance. A consent lapses after two years if the transaction for which it was granted is not completed. Once the transaction takes place, no further consent is required to deal with that particular parcel of land in the future. The procedure for obtaining consents is described in section 53 of the Act.

### REGISTERED PLAN OF SUBDIVISION

When a large block of undeveloped land is divided into lots for sale, the developer must register a plan of subdivision. Before the province will approve the plan, it will require the developer to enter into agreements with the municipality and public utilities to provide—at the developer's expense—the extra services required by the increased population. Such services might include water mains, sewers, street lights, sidewalks, curbs, schools, and parks.

## Part Lot Control

As discussed above, an exception to the basic prohibition against transactions conveying an interest in land exists for transactions that deal with a whole lot on a registered plan of subdivision. Section 50(3)(a) provides for this exception. The exception does not, however, apply to *part* of a subdivision lot. If an owner wants to convey only part of a subdivision lot while retaining the remainder, the exception provided in section 50(3)(a) will not apply.

**part lot control**
government control over transactions involving part of a subdivision lot

Section 50(5) deals with transactions involving part of a subdivision lot. These provisions (referred to as the **part lot control** provisions) are identical in structure to those contained in section 50(3). A person cannot deal with part of a lot on a registered plan of subdivision unless the transaction falls within one of the specified exceptions. The exceptions mirror those contained in section 50(3). In order to deal with a part of a lot, you must

- not be retaining the fee in abutting land, other than a whole lot on a plan of subdivision;
- be selling to or purchasing from the government; or
- be seeking municipal consent.

Figure 9.4 illustrates the application of the part lot control provisions. Assume that John owns Lots 1 and 2 and divides the lots as shown, in order to convey the west half of Lot 1. He cannot do so because he retains an interest in the abutting east half of Lot 1. The retained land is not a whole lot on a plan of subdivision and therefore the exception does not apply.

### Figure 9.4   Part Lots on a Plan of Subdivision

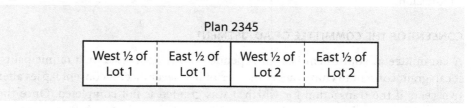

Section 50(5)(e) provides an exception if you are dealing with the part of a parcel of land that remains after the other part was acquired by a body with rights of expropriation. In Figure 9.5, Lots 1 and 2 are whole lots on a plan of subdivision. The owner could therefore convey either lot and not be in breach of the Act. Assume that the municipality acquires an interest by way of expropriation in the front 10 feet of these lots. Without section 50(5)(e), the owner would not be able to convey either lot because it could no longer be described as a whole lot on a plan of subdivision.

**Figure 9.5   Expropriation of Parts of Lots on a Plan of Subdivision**

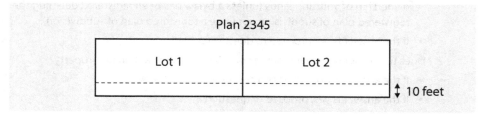

Under section 50(7), a municipality can pass a bylaw exempting land from the part lot control provisions. If such a bylaw is passed, the sale of part of a lot—a sale that would otherwise contravene the Act—can proceed without consent. In some circumstances, it may be less trouble for a developer to get a municipality to pass a part lot exemption bylaw than to obtain consent for each transaction.

For example, assume that a developer has bought the land in Figure 9.5 and intends to divide the two lots in half so that she can build four semi-detached homes. The developer would not be able to sell any of the homes because they are each located on part of a lot and she retains an interest in adjoining land. In these circumstances, the developer can either seek consent from the committee of adjustment for each transfer or ask the municipality to pass a part lot exemption bylaw.

The provisions of the *Planning Act* are complex. See Figure 9.6 for an orderly approach to determining whether the sale of property will comply with the Act.

## Important Dates

Over the years, the *Planning Act* has been amended many times. As loopholes have been discovered, new provisions have been added to close them. What may not have been a contravention of the Act at one point in time may have later become a contravention. As a result, the date of a conveyance is extremely important. The following list includes some of the more significant amendments to consider when reviewing title to determine whether previous transactions have complied with the *Planning Act*:

- *June 15, 1967.* Any contraventions that occurred prior to this date were forgiven. This is as far back in time as you need to search for *Planning Act* compliance.

- *June 27, 1970.* Subdivision control was imposed on all land in Ontario. Prior to this date, subdivision control applied only if the particular municipality had passed a subdivision control bylaw designating land as subject to the Act's subdivision control provisions.

**Figure 9.6   An Approach to Planning Act Issues**

In trying to determine whether there is a *Planning Act* problem, ask yourself the following questions:

1. Is the land being conveyed the whole of a lot on a registered plan of subdivision?
   - If the answer is yes, there is no contravention of the Act and no concern about ownership of abutting lands (unless a bylaw has been registered deeming the registered plan of subdivision *not* to be a registered plan of subdivision).
   - If the answer is no, proceed to question 2.
2. Does the owner of the land being conveyed also own adjoining property?
   - If the answer is no, there is no contravention of the Act.
   - If the answer is yes, proceed to question 3.
3. Is the adjoining land that the owner is retaining a whole lot on a plan of subdivision?
   - If the answer is yes, there is no contravention of the Act.
   - If the answer is no (and the transfer is not to or from a government agency), proceed to question 4.
4. Has there been consent to the conveyance (and therefore consent to the severance into two or more parcels) by either an application to the committee of adjustment or the registration of a plan of subdivision?
   - If the answer is yes, there is no contravention of the Act.
   - If the answer is no, there is a contravention of the Act and the conveyance will be a nullity. It will not create or convey any interest in land.

---

- *March 31, 1979.*  A parcel of land created by a conveyance with consent does not require further consent even though the subsequent grantor owns abutting land.
- *August 1, 1983.*  Consent is not required for a conveyance of a parcel of land if consent has been obtained to convey the abutting parcel.
- *July 26, 1990.*  Severances in wills are prohibited without consent. Prior to this date, the *Planning Act* did not affect such severances. An owner of a parcel of land could convey parts to different beneficiaries, even though such a subdivision was contrary to the intentions of the Act.

## Curing Provisions

As mentioned above, the *Planning Act* was amended on June 15, 1967 to cure all previous contraventions of the Act. An additional curing provision applies if the appropriate *Planning Act* statements are completed in the transfer.

In an electronic transfer (see Figure 7.1 in Chapter 7), there are three *Planning Act* statements for completion by each of the seller, the seller's lawyer, and the buyer's lawyer. The seller states that to the best of his or her knowledge and belief, the transaction does not contravene the *Planning Act*. (The seller does so only after his or her lawyer explains what the *Planning Act* says.) The seller's lawyer and the buyer's lawyer each confirm that to the best of their knowledge and belief, the *Planning Act* has not been contravened. These statements are among the required compliance with law statements discussed in Chapter 7, and they must be signed by a lawyer.

The equivalent statements in the paper system are found in boxes 13 and 14 of the POLARIS transfer/deed of land (see Figure 5.1 in Chapter 5).

After the appropriate statements are signed, the transfer and all previous conveyances affecting the parcel of land are deemed to comply with the *Planning Act*. If a contravention of the Act has previously occurred, it will, in effect, be forgiven. There are serious penalties for anyone who knowingly makes a false statement.

## Implications for Title Searching

The penalty for non-compliance with the *Planning Act* is very serious: the transfer, and any transfer that flows from it, is null and void. Accordingly, a title search must include steps to ensure that the *Planning Act* has been complied with, not only by the current owner, but by past owners as well. Therefore, the search of title will extend to adjoining properties to determine the owners of the land adjoining the land that your client is purchasing.

When conducting a *Planning Act* search, you are checking to determine whether there was ever any common ownership between the subject property and the adjoining properties. If not, there could never have been an illegal division of land or violation of the Act. On the other hand, if at any point during the relevant period the same person owned both the subject property and an adjoining property, you must ensure that any transactions dealing with those properties complied with the provisions of the *Planning Act*.

Through your search, you are determining answers to the following questions and proceeding as the answers dictate:

1. Is the property you are searching a whole lot on a plan of subdivision?

   If yes, there can be no contravention of the *Planning Act* (unless a bylaw has been registered deeming the registered plan of subdivision not to be a registered plan of subdivision), and you do not have to search abutting land.

   If no, you must search the title to adjoining properties.

2. What are you searching for?

   You are checking the registration records to ascertain the names of the current and past owners of all adjoining properties. Determine whether any owners of those adjoining properties simultaneously owned the property being searched.

3. How far back must you search?

   If the property you are searching was previously conveyed with an electronic transfer containing the completed three *Planning Act* statements or a paper transfer/deed of land containing the completed *Planning Act* statements in boxes 13 and 14, you need only search back to the date of that transfer.

You do not need to search beyond that date because all previous conveyances are deemed to comply with the *Planning Act*.

If the property has been converted from the Registry system to the Land Titles system (as a result of POLARIS), then title is guaranteed to be free of *Planning Act* contraventions as of the date of the conversion. You must still do a *Planning Act* search from the date of conversion onward.

If there has been a conveyance or other transaction with consent, the consent cures prior contraventions. Also, sections 50(3) and (5) will not apply to subsequent dealings with the same parcel of land.

In all other cases, you must search back as necessary (40 years, if you are searching in the Registry system). See Chapter 14 for a discussion of title searching.

Figure 9.7 illustrates the sale of part of a lot on a plan of subdivision and the land adjoining that property. Your client is purchasing the east half of Lot 15. In addition to doing a full search of title to the east half of Lot 15, you must also search the title to the adjoining properties—Lot 16, Lot 2, and the west half of Lot 15—to determine the identity of past owners.

**Figure 9.7    Adjoining Land Search**

| Street | | | |
|---|---|---|---|
| Lot 14 | West ½ of Lot 15 | East ½ of Lot 15 | Lot 16 |
| Lot 1 | Lot 2 | | Lot 3 |
| Street | | | |

Assume that the registrar's abstract for each of the properties discloses the following ownership:

| East ½ Lot 15 | West ½ Lot 15 | Lot 2 | Lot 16 |
|---|---|---|---|
| Fred Black | Fred Black | Frank Jones | Ted Long |
| 1970–1982 | 1970–1995 | 1986–present | 1965–1987 |
| Al Green | Stan Smith | | Larry Bird |
| 1982–present | 1995–present | | 1987–present |

In this example, there is a potential *Planning Act* problem because Fred Black owned both the east half and the west half of Lot 15 from 1970 to 1982. At that time, he conveyed the east half (the property your client is now purchasing) to Al Green. The property Fred Black conveyed to Al Green was part of a lot, and Fred Black still retained ownership of the adjoining west half. Unless the deed to Al Green contained a consent from the committee of adjustment, this transaction contravened the *Planning Act*, and the transfer to Al Green is a nullity. If Al Green does not have valid title to the property, your client will not receive good title on completion of this transaction.

Now assume that Al Green, in the above example, conveyed the property to Sara Fotia in 1996. In that transfer, the *Planning Act* statements were properly completed. You do not have to search for *Planning Act* compliance on adjoining land before 1996 because any previous contraventions are forgiven. You do not even have to find out about the earlier possible contravention on the transfer from Fred Black to Al Green. Even if there was no consent to that conveyance, the contravention of the Act is forgiven.

## KEY TERMS

building permit, 123

committee of adjustment, 123

consent to variance, 123

legal non-conforming use, 123

official plan, 122

part lot control, 128

severance, 123

simultaneous conveyance, 127

subdivision control, 122

zoning, 122

zoning bylaws, 122

## REFERENCES

*Building Code Act, 1992*, SO 1992, c 23.

*Ontario Heritage Act*, RSO 1990, c O.18.

*Planning Act*, RSO 1990, c P.13.

## REVIEW QUESTIONS

1. Why was the *Planning Act* established?

2. How does the municipality regulate the use of land?

3. What is a legal non-conforming use?

4. What is the purpose of subdivision control?

5. How does the *Planning Act* ensure control over the subdivision of land?

6. What are the four main exceptions to the basic prohibition under section 50(3) of the *Planning Act*?

7. When title is being searched, what steps must be taken to ensure compliance with the *Planning Act*?

8. Lots 1 to 3 are all within a registered plan of subdivision. Eduardo owns all three lots. Can Eduardo sell Lot 2 and keep Lots 1 and 3 without contravening the *Planning Act*?

| Lot 1 | Lot 2 | Lot 3 |
|-------|-------|-------|

9. Lots 1 to 4 are concession lots.

| Lot 1 | Lot 2 |
|-------|-------|
| Lot 3 | Lot 4 |

a. Assume that Eduardo owns Lots 1 and 2 only. Can Eduardo sell Lot 1?

b. Assume that Eduardo owns Lots 1 and 4 only. Can Eduardo sell Lot 1?

c. Assume that Eduardo owns Lot 1 only. Can Eduardo purchase Lot 2?

10. Lots 1 to 3 are concession lots. Eduardo owns all three lots. Can Eduardo sell Lot 3 only? Explain.

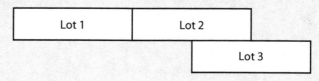

| Lot 1 | Lot 2 |       |
|-------|-------|-------|
|       | Lot 3 |       |

11. You are purchasing the east half only of Lot 3, which is situated within a plan of subdivision. The land is registered in the Registry system.

| Lot 1 | Lot 2 |
|-------|-------|
| Lot 3 | Lot 4 |
| Lot 5 | Lot 6 |

   a. As part of your title search, what properties must you search to ensure *Planning Act* compliance?

   b. How far back must you search?

   c. Assume that in 1990, Ann Jones had owned both the west half and east half of Lot 3 and sold the west half to Bob Smith. Are there any potential *Planning Act* issues? What should you look for?

12. Lots 1 and 2 are within a registered plan of subdivision. Eduardo owns both lots.

| Lot 1 | West ½ of Lot 2 | East ½ of Lot 2 |
|-------|-----------------|-----------------|

   a. Can Eduardo sell Lot 1 only?

   b. Can Eduardo sell only the west half of Lot 2?

   c. Can Eduardo sell only the east half of Lot 2?

13. Assume that Eduardo, from the previous question's scenario, owns Lot 1 and only the west half of Lot 2.

   a. Can Eduardo sell Lot 1?

   b. Can Eduardo sell the west half of Lot 2?

# Legal Status of the Owner

# 10

## LEARNING OUTCOMES

After reading this chapter, you will understand:

- Why it is important to determine the legal status of an owner of real property

- What happens when an owner of real property changes his or her name during the period of time that he or she owns the property

- How family law legislation protects the rights of a married person with respect to property owned by his or her spouse

- What happens to title when an owner of real property dies during the time that he or she owns the property

- What happens to real property owned by a corporation that dissolves during the time that it owns the property

- How to transfer real property owned by a partnership or held by a trustee

# Introduction

The legal status of the owner of real property can have an impact on the owner's title, and it affects the requirements for conveying interests in the land. In this chapter, we look at the impact of the following matters:

- change of name,
- marriage,
- death,
- age,
- corporations,
- partnerships, and
- trustees.

# Change of Name

Owners of real property may change their names. A man or woman may apply for a formal change of name under the *Change of Name Act*, or a spouse may informally change his or her family name upon marriage or divorce. A change of name has an impact on title if it takes place between the time that the owner acquires the property and the time that the owner transfers it. Anyone reviewing the title must be satisfied that the person transferring the property is the same person who acquired the property.

If the property is registered in the Registry system, the transfer from the person must contain information to indicate that the person granting title (with the new name) is the same person as the person who took title (under the old name). The transfer should use the new name when naming the transferor and include the old name, preceded by the word "formerly," in parentheses.

If the property is registered in the Land Titles system, the registered owner must use the exact name currently entered on the parcel register in any future dealings with that parcel of land. A change-of-name application must be registered on the parcel before the owner can convey the parcel using a different name.

# Marriage

Over the years, husbands and wives have had different property rights with respect to each other. These rights can affect a spouse's title to real property.

## Dower

**dower**
entitlement of a widow to a one-third life interest in the total value of any land that her husband owned during their marriage

Before April 1978, a widow was entitled to a one-third life interest in the total value of any land that her husband owned during their marriage. This ancient right, known as **dower**, was designed to protect widows in the days when married women were not legally allowed to own property. Dower not only applied to property owned by the husband at the time of his death, but could also apply to property he had previously transferred. This would affect subsequent owners, unless the wife had barred her dower by signing the deed.

Dower rights did not attach to land

- owned by a man in joint tenancy with any other person;
- owned by a man in partnership with any other person;
- owned by a man in trust for another person;
- in a state of nature (in other words, unimproved land);
- dedicated as streets and public highways;
- in which the man had only the equity of redemption[1] during marriage and which he disposed of during his lifetime; or
- granted to the husband "to uses."[2]

In addition, a wife's dower right ended on her death or if

- the parties divorced,
- the wife committed adultery,
- the parties separated,
- the wife's whereabouts were unknown,
- the wife lived outside Ontario from the time of the marriage, or
- the wife was confined to a mental hospital when the husband acquired the land.

To protect the buyer against potential dower claims, a male grantor was required to disclose his marital status by swearing an affidavit contained in the deed. If the affidavit stated that he was married, the grantee would know that the grantor's wife's consent to the transfer must be obtained.

Dower was abolished on March 31, 1978 by the *Family Law Reform Act*.

## Rights Under the Family Law Act

The *Family Law Reform Act*, enacted in 1978, abolished dower and instead gave both husbands and wives special rights to their matrimonial home. These rights are continued under the current *Family Law Act*, which replaced the *Family Law Reform Act*.

---

1 A mortgage constituted a transfer of the legal estate. If a man bought land subject to a mortgage, he acquired only the equity of redemption or the right to redeem the property after repayment of the loan. If he mortgaged the property before marriage, he would own only the equity of redemption during the marriage.

2 Rather than stating that title was being granted "in fee simple," a deed would state that the title was granted "to such uses as the grantee may permit."

### Definition of Matrimonial Home

matrimonial home
defined under the *Family
Law Act* to include every
property in which a person
has an interest and that
is (if the parties are still
married), or was (if the
parties have separated)
at the time of separation,
occupied by the spouses
as their family residence

A **matrimonial home** is defined under the *Family Law Act* to include every property in which a person has an interest and that is (if the parties are still married), or was (if the parties have separated) at the time of separation, occupied by the spouses as their family residence. Spouses may have more than one matrimonial home. For example, a family may have a city home and a cottage. If they are both used as a family residence, they will both be matrimonial homes.

If spouses have more than one matrimonial home, they can *jointly* choose to designate only one of their properties as their matrimonial home. This designation must be signed by both parties and registered on the title to that property. If the designation is later cancelled, all properties that meet the definition of a matrimonial home are again considered as such.

### Rights of the Spouses

Under the *Family Law Reform Act* previously, and now the *Family Law Act*,

- both spouses have equal rights to possession of a matrimonial home; and
- neither spouse can dispose of or encumber an interest in a matrimonial home without the consent of the other spouse. If a matrimonial home is transferred without the appropriate consent, the transaction may be set aside by a court.

These rights apply even if the matrimonial home is registered in the name of one spouse only. They apply only to legally married spouses and are dependent on the continuation of the marital relationship. If the marriage ends by either death or divorce, the rights end. The rights may also be ended by a separation agreement or court order.

### Implications for Title Searching

These rights have implications for title searching. Since 1978, the marital (or spousal) status of every person, male or female, who conveys or mortgages land is relevant. Every transfer since 1978 should contain evidence of the marital status of the transferors. Before the *Land Registration Reform Act*, this evidence took the form of an **affidavit of spousal status** attached to the transfer. After the *Land Registration Reform Act* eliminated affidavits, the evidence was provided in the statement of age and spousal status in box 8 of the Transfer/Deed of Land. In the electronic system, a spousal statement is required for each transferor.

affidavit of spousal
status
affidavit attached to a
deed (in use after 1978
until the *Land Registration
Reform Act* came into force)
that provided evidence of
the marital status of the
grantors or transferors

If the affidavit or statement discloses that a transferor is married, the consent of the transferor's spouse is required unless

- the property is not a matrimonial home;
- some other property has been designated as the matrimonial home; or
- the spousal rights have been released by a separation agreement or court order.

Specific wording is required in the transfer to satisfy the requirements of the *Family Law Act*. In electronic transfers, the lawyer chooses the appropriate statement from the pre-populated choices. The statements required are covered in Chapter 21, Document Preparation, under the heading "Transfer of Title."

If a transfer contains an affidavit or statement in the correct form indicating that no spousal consent is necessary, a **bona fide purchaser for value** without notice to the contrary may rely upon the statement. Note that "notice" means constructive notice, not actual notice. Accordingly, any evidence indicating that the transferor in question was in fact married and that the property was therefore a matrimonial home could constitute constructive notice. Such evidence would prevent a buyer from being able to rely on the statement.

For example, assume that your title search discloses a transfer containing a statement that the transferor is not a spouse. However, prior to that transfer, the same transferor executed and registered a charge/mortgage in which there is a statement that he is a spouse and that his spouse consented. The prior document gives you notice that the property might be a matrimonial home and the current statement may therefore be false. You would have to find out what happened to the spouse and why she or he didn't sign the transfer.

> **bona fide purchaser for value**
> buyer of property who gives valuable consideration for the property and is acting in good faith

# Death

The death of a registered owner of real property has an effect on the title to real property.

## Joint Tenancy

If land is registered in the names of two or more persons as joint tenants and one of the joint tenants dies, title automatically passes to the surviving joint tenant(s) by right of survivorship. Property owned in joint tenancy cannot be left to a beneficiary in a will by anyone other than the last surviving joint tenant.

### Registry System

If, when a joint tenant dies, jointly owned land is registered under the Registry system, no action is necessary to amend title until the surviving joint tenant(s) wishes to deal with the land. At that time, the transfer, charge, or lease must contain **recitals** or statements indicating what happened to the other joint tenant. The party receiving the interest in land may require proof of death. A subsequent title searcher will likewise want proof of the death. Proof of death may take the form of a death certificate, attached to the document as a schedule or registered separately as a document general. Before the *Land Registration Reform Act*, proof of death could also be found as a sworn statement in one of the affidavits, such as the affidavit of age and spousal status. It should be noted that a recital in a deed or transfer that is more than 20 years old constitutes proof of the fact recited.

> **recital**
> statement that sets out facts on which a document is based

### Land Titles System

Under the Land Titles system, the surviving joint tenant(s) must submit a survivorship application to the Land Titles office to delete the name of the deceased joint tenant from the register and to show the surviving joint tenant(s) as the owner(s). The application must be accompanied by (1) an affidavit and (2) evidence of the death of the joint tenant in the form of a death certificate or a "certificate of appointment of estate trustee" (in the past, called "letters of administration" or "letters probate").

## Estate Conveyancing

If property is not held in joint tenancy, the property will be transferred in accordance with the instructions in the owner's will, if there is one. If the owner dies without a will, the property will be transferred to next of kin as provided by statute.

On the death of the owner, the power to deal with the property passes to the estate trustee (previously called the "executor" if there was a will and the "administrator" if there was not). If there is a will, the estate trustee must deal with the property as directed by the will—either by transferring the property to a named beneficiary or by selling it to a third party.

**transmission application**
document that is registered on title in order to enable an estate trustee to transfer property

In the Land Titles system, the estate trustee must register a **transmission application**. Once the transmission application is registered, the estate trustee can transfer the property by registering a specific type of transfer called a "transfer by personal representative," which must contain specific statements. An estate trustee is a personal representative.

## Succession Duty

From January 1, 1970 until April 10, 1979, the Ontario government collected succession duties with respect to the property of deceased persons. Unpaid succession duties constituted a lien on the property of the deceased. Accordingly, if a Registry system search of title discloses that an owner of land died between January 1, 1970 and April 10, 1979, you must make sure that an Ontario succession duty release has been registered on the title to the property. A release is necessary for jointly owned property as well, unless the property was held jointly with the deceased's spouse.

# Age

Generally, a contract entered into by a minor, other than a contract for necessities, is not enforceable against him or her, and is voidable at the minor's option. Transfers and charges of land made by a minor are void. All transfers contain an affidavit (prior to the *Land Registration Reform Act*) or statement of age confirming that the transferor is at least 18 years of age. In paper transfers, the statement of age is found in box 8 of the Transfer/Deed of Land. In electronic transfers, the lawyer chooses the appropriate statement from the pre-populated choices in the same menu as the *Family Law Act* statements.

**Children's Lawyer**
government official charged with protecting the best interests of children in the province

Land cannot be sold or transferred by a minor without the consent and approval of the **Children's Lawyer**, a government official who has the responsibility of protecting the best interests of children in the province.

# Corporations

A corporation is a legal entity capable of owning land.

## Corporate Status

A corporation may be dissolved voluntarily by its shareholders or involuntarily by the government. If a corporation is dissolved, the ownership of any real property that the corporation has not disposed of escheats, or reverts to the Crown. As a result, it is necessary to make sure that all companies in the chain of title were in existence during the entire period that they were on title.

## Change of Name

Under the Registry system, a corporation that changes its name during the period of ownership of the land must register the articles of amendment by which the name was changed. The transfer must refer to the existence and registration of the articles of amendment. Under the Land Titles system, it is necessary either to apply to amend the register to change the name of the corporate owner or to give evidence of the change of name at the time the land is conveyed.

## Indoor Management Rule

Outsiders dealing with a corporation can assume that the corporation acted properly and in accordance with its bylaws in selling land that it owns. Deeds by corporations registered before the *Land Registration Reform Act* came into effect must have a corporate seal and a signature. Today, a corporate seal is no longer required; instead, a transfer by a corporation must be signed under the words "I have the authority to bind the corporation."

# Partnerships

A partnership is a form of business arrangement. If land is owned as partnership property, all partners must sign the transfer, and it must also contain a statement that

- the land was bought as partnership land,
- the land was held as partnership land, and
- the partners signing the transfer were at all relevant times the only partners.

# Trustees

If property is held by a trustee in trust for someone else, a buyer does not have to question or investigate the trustee's authority to deal with the property.

## KEY TERMS

affidavit of spousal status, 140

bona fide purchaser for value, 141

Children's Lawyer, 142

dower, 138

matrimonial home, 140

recital, 141

transmission application, 142

## REFERENCES

*Change of Name Act*, RSO 1990, c C.7.

*Family Law Act*, RSO 1990, c F.3.

*Family Law Reform Act* (repealed).

*Land Registration Reform Act*, RSO 1990, c L.4.

## REVIEW QUESTIONS

1. Does the change of a property owner's name affect title?

2. What is a matrimonial home?

3. Susan Smith owns real property registered in the Land Titles system. Susan has recently changed her name to Susan Wong. What must Susan do when she sells the property?

4. Betty Buyer receives a transfer from Sammy Seller that contains the following statement: "I am a spouse. The property is not designated under section 20 of the *Family Law Act* as a matrimonial home by me and my spouse, but there is such a designation of another property as our matrimonial home, which has been registered and which has not been cancelled." Is Sammy's spouse required to consent to the transfer? Explain your answer.

5. Phillip and Rosanna live in Kingston, Ontario. When they got married, Phillip moved into the house Rosanna already owned. Title to the house is registered in her name only. Together they purchased a cottage in Muskoka, where they spend most weekends.

   a. Which property is their matrimonial home: the house, the cottage, or both?

   b. Can Rosanna sell or mortgage the Kingston property without Phillip's consent?

6. Pedro and Guillermo owned property as joint tenants. The property is registered in the Land Titles system. Pedro recently died and Guillermo wants to sell the property. What must he do?

7. If a corporation is dissolved, what happens to any real property that has not been disposed of?

8. Who must sign the transfer of property owned by a partnership?

# Condominiums

11

## LEARNING OUTCOMES

After reading this chapter, you will understand:

- How a condominium is created
- How condominium ownership differs from freehold ownership
- What the common elements in a condominium are
- What a common-elements condominium (CEC) is
- How a condominium is administered

# Introduction

Condominium ownership combines individual ownership of a condominium unit with shared ownership of the common elements of the condominium development. This legal structure of ownership can apply to various types of physical structures—high-rise and low-rise multiple-unit buildings, townhouses, and free-standing homes. Condominiums may be residential or commercial. Condominium ownership in Ontario is governed by the *Condominium Act, 1998*.

# The Nature of a Condominium

Condominium ownership involves three elements (with the exception of the CEC, discussed below):

1. the *condominium unit*, which is individually owned in fee simple;
2. the *common elements*, which are owned by all of the individual unit owners as tenants in common; and
3. the *condominium corporation*, of which each unit owner is a voting member.

## Condominium Unit

**condominium unit**
unit that is part of a condominium development

The **condominium unit** may be a residential suite in a multiple-unit building, an office suite in a commercial building, a townhouse, or a free-standing house. The owner of each unit usually has title only to the interior of the unit.

## Common Elements

**common elements**
areas of the condominium development owned by all of the individual unit owners as tenants in common

**exclusive-use common elements**
areas of the condominium development owned by all unit owners but used only by designated unit owners

The **common elements** are generally areas such as the lobby, grounds, parking lot, corridors, and recreational facilities, which are used by all of the unit owners. The common elements also include the exterior structure of the condominium building and all shared mechanical equipment, such as heating, cooling, and water systems. Certain common elements may be **exclusive-use common elements**, to be used only by specific unit owners. These include designated parking spots and lockers, balconies, patios, and back or front yards that are attached to the specific units. Note, however, that in some cases, parking spots and lockers are separate units that are bought and sold apart from the main units.

## Common-Elements Condominium

**common-elements condominium (CEC)**
a condominium composed solely of common elements

**parcels of tied land (POTLs)**
parcels of land whose owners have consented to their property being permanently tied to a common-elements condominium

A relatively new condominium type is the **common-elements condominium (CEC)**, in which the condominium property consists only of common elements. Owners of the CEC are owners of nearby freehold land who have consented to their land being permanently "tied" to the CEC and who hold title to the CEC as tenants in common. Such freehold pieces of land are called "**parcels of tied land**" **(POTLs)**, but are not themselves condominiums. Developers sometimes use the CEC format when building a community of freehold homes with common-elements areas, such as a recreation facility, a community centre, a park, or a parking area, to be used by the nearby freehold owners. The common-elements areas become a CEC, tied to the freehold homes in the community. By using this format, the developer ensures that the property that makes up the CEC will be properly managed and maintained by the nearby landowners who use the property.

## Condominium Corporation

The role of the **condominium corporation** is to manage and administer the condominium property. The duties usually include arranging for maintenance of the property, repairs to the common elements, insurance coverage of the property, administration of common expenses, and administration of the reserve fund (discussed below).

### Common Expenses

As an owner of the common elements and a member of the condominium corporation, each unit owner must pay monthly fees, known as **common expenses**, to meet the corporation's obligations, such as maintenance and repair of the common elements, insurance, snow removal, gardening and landscaping, management, cleaning, and legal and accounting fees. Similarly, in a CEC, the owners of the POTLs pay common expenses to maintain the property included in the CEC.

Common expenses are assessed for each owner on the basis of the size of his or her unit. For example, an owner whose unit occupies one-thirtieth of the total area of all condominium units will pay common expenses equal to one-thirtieth of the total common expenses paid by all the unit owners. If all units are the same size, the share of common expenses will be the same for all unit owners; if some units are bigger, the owners of those units will pay a larger proportion of the common expenses.

If a unit owner or a POTL owner does not pay the common expenses, the condominium corporation has a lien against that owner's property for the amount outstanding. The lien expires three months after the default unless a certificate of lien is registered by the corporation within that time.

### Reserve Fund

Every condominium corporation is required to maintain a **reserve fund**, which is used to cover costs when the common elements need replacement or major repair. Every new condominium corporation carries out a reserve-fund study, which recommends the appropriate amount. A subsequent study is conducted every three years. Part of the monthly common-expense payments are deposited into the reserve fund.

Under the *Condominium Act, 1998*, the amount in the reserve fund should be the greater of

- the amount recommended by the reserve-fund study and
- 10 percent of the total annual common expenses.

In order to start a reserve fund for a new condominium, unit owners are usually required to make an initial lump-sum payment equivalent to between one and three months' common expenses.

**condominium corporation**
corporation that comes into existence upon registration of the condominium plan and whose role is to manage and administer the condominium property

**common expenses**
monthly fees paid by unit owners to cover the condominium corporation's obligations

**reserve fund**
fund that covers costs of major repairs to and replacement of common elements

### Special Assessment

If the funds available from the common expenses or from the reserve fund are insufficient to cover the regular expenses of the corporation or any unforeseen major expense, the unit owners can be required to pay a special assessment to cover the expense.

# Creation of a Condominium

Under the *Condominium Act, 1998*, a condominium is created when a declaration and description are registered in the Land Titles office. At the same time, a corporation without share capital is created. The members of the corporation are the unit owners, who share the assets of the corporation in the same proportion as their proportion of ownership of the common elements.

## Declaration

**declaration**
document that describes the units, setting out their boundaries, the percentage of common elements associated with each unit, and the percentage of common expenses that each unit owner will be required to pay

The **declaration** describes the units, setting out their boundaries. It sets out the percentage of the common elements associated with each unit and the percentage of common expenses each unit owner will be required to pay.

The declaration may also set out any conditions or restrictions regarding the occupation or use of the units or common elements, and it may describe the obligations of unit owners with respect to maintenance and repair of the units and of the common elements.

## Description

**description**
document that includes a survey showing the boundaries of the units, common elements, and exclusive-use common elements

The **description** includes a survey showing the boundaries of the units, the common elements, and the exclusive-use common elements, if any. The condominium plan is given a number upon registration, and each unit is also given a number. For example, the legal description of a unit in a condominium in Aurora that is the 647th condominium registered in York Region might be: Unit 23, York Condominium Plan 647, Town of Aurora, Regional Municipality of York. If the condominium structure is a multi-level, multiple-unit building, the legal description will include a level (floor) number following the unit number.

# Operation of the Condominium Corporation

The duties and functions of the corporation are governed by the *Condominium Act, 1998*, the declaration, and the specific bylaws, rules, and regulations passed by the board of directors of the condominium corporation.

## Bylaws

The **bylaws** are the rules that govern the internal operation of the condominium corporation and cover such matters as

bylaws (condominium)
rules governing the
internal operation of the
condominium corporation

- holding of meetings,
- notice of meetings,
- quorum requirements,
- composition of the board of directors,
- appointment of officers,
- duties and powers of the corporation, and
- banking arrangements.

The board of directors passes bylaws, which must then be confirmed by a majority of the members of the corporation (the unit owners) at a general meeting. Bylaws may be amended by a vote of members holding 51 percent of the common elements. A certified copy of each bylaw must be registered on title for the bylaw to be effective.

## Rules and Regulations

Rules and regulations govern the everyday rights and obligations of the owners regarding the use of units and common elements. For example, rules may prohibit the use of barbeques on balconies and the installation of satellite dishes, and they may impose restrictions on the use of recreational facilities by unit owners and their guests. In order for the rules and regulations to be effective, notice must be given to all unit owners, who have 30 days to register an objection. If 15 percent or more of unit owners object to a rule, a meeting of unit owners must be held to conduct a vote.

# Implications for Buyers

There are special considerations that arise on the purchase of a condominium because of the special nature of condominium ownership. These are discussed in Chapter 26, Purchase of a Condominium.

## KEY TERMS

bylaws (condominium), 149

common elements, 146

common-elements condominium (CEC), 146

common expenses, 147

condominium corporation, 147

condominium unit, 146

declaration, 148

description, 148

exclusive-use common elements, 146

parcels of tied land (POTLs), 146

reserve fund, 147

## REFERENCES

*Condominium Act, 1998*, SO 1998, c 19.

## REVIEW QUESTIONS

1. What are the three elements of condominium ownership?

2. What form may a condominium unit take?

3. What are some examples of a condominium's common elements?

4. What are exclusive-use common elements?

5. What is a CEC, and what does it consist of?

6. What is a POTL, and how does it relate to a condominium?

7. What is the role of the condominium corporation?

8. What are common expenses?

9. How are common expenses assessed?

10. Susan owns a condominium, and has not paid her common expenses for two months. What can be done?

11. Why do condominiums have reserve funds?

12. How is a condominium created?

13. What is the purpose of the bylaws of the condominium corporation, and how can they be amended?

# Residential Rental Properties

# 12

## LEARNING OUTCOMES

After reading this chapter, you will understand:

- The two different types of residential tenancies and how they are created

- The rules regarding rent and rent increases

- The basic rights and responsibilities of residential landlords and tenants in Ontario

- How residential landlords and tenants can terminate a tenancy

- The implications of buying a residential rental property

## Introduction

A residential property that a buyer purchases may be occupied by one or more tenants. The property may be a single-family dwelling that the buyer wishes to occupy personally but that is currently occupied by a tenant, or it may be a residential rental property, such as a duplex, triplex, or small apartment building, that the buyer is purchasing as an investment. Whether the buyer wishes to keep the tenants or have them move out, there are specific concerns that must be addressed. In particular, a buyer who wishes to keep the tenants must be well informed about the legal and financial implications of becoming a landlord.

## Overview of Residential Tenancy Law

All aspects of the residential landlord and tenant relationship are governed by the *Residential Tenancies Act, 2006*. The Act provides specific rules about

- the rights and obligations of the tenant and the landlord;
- the amount of rent that may be charged and permissible rent increases;
- termination of tenancies by the landlord and the tenant; and
- the Landlord and Tenant Board (LTB).

The Act applies to landlords and tenants of all residential units in Ontario, regardless of the type of rental housing. In other words, the Act applies whether the tenant is renting an apartment in a high-rise building, an entire single-family home, or a basement apartment. Each of these is considered a "rental unit" under the Act. The Act also applies regardless of any agreement or waiver to the contrary. If there is any conflict between the terms of a tenancy agreement and the provisions in the *Residential Tenancies Act*, the Act will prevail.

The Act contains special provisions for care homes, mobile home parks, land lease communities, residences in educational institutions, and government housing. These special provisions do not concern the typical buyer of a residential rental property and will not be discussed in this chapter.

The following discussion summarizes some of the aspects of the residential landlord and tenant relationship that may be of particular concern to a prospective buyer of a residential rental property.

### The Landlord and Tenant Board

The Landlord and Tenant Board (LTB) is an independent administrative tribunal established by the *Residential Tenancies Act*. It hears virtually all applications dealing with the rights and obligations of residential landlords and tenants. Applications to the tribunal may be brought by both landlords and tenants. The application process involves very specific rules and procedures, and failure to follow them may jeopardize a party's application.

Landlords who apply to the tribunal are usually seeking to enforce remedies for non-payment of rent or disruptive behaviour. Tenant applications usually deal with maintenance and repair issues. All landlord and tenant applications are resolved through either mediation or adjudication by a tribunal member.

The tribunal's website (<http://www.sjto.gov.on.ca/ltb>) provides free access to detailed information about all matters concerning residential tenancies, including links to

- the *Residential Tenancies Act* and its regulations;
- the rules of practice and procedure that govern the operation of the LTB;
- the required forms; and
- information pamphlets explaining the rights and obligations of landlords and tenants, and applications and hearings before the LTB.

## Creating a New Tenancy

A residential tenancy is created when a landlord and a tenant enter into a **tenancy agreement** or lease. This agreement is usually in writing, but it can also be oral or implied. If it is in writing, the landlord must deliver a signed copy of the agreement to the tenant within 21 days of the date the agreement is entered into. For all new tenancy agreements, the landlord must provide the tenant with written notice of the rental unit's legal name and address for service. A tenant is not obligated to pay rent until the landlord provides this information. However, as soon as the landlord provides it, the tenant must pay any rent that has been withheld.

Before the tenancy begins, the landlord must also provide the tenant with information relating to the rights and responsibilities of landlords and tenants, the role of the LTB, and how to contact the LTB. The board has an information brochure titled "Information for New Tenants" (<http://www.sjto.gov.on.ca/ltb/brochures>) that landlords can download and use for this purpose.

A residential tenant has a **leasehold estate** in the property owned by the landlord. In exchange for the payment of rent, the tenant acquires the right to exclusive possession of the property for a specified period of time.

**tenancy agreement**
written, oral, or implied agreement between a landlord and a tenant that creates the tenancy

**leasehold estate**
right to exclusive possession of property for a specified period of time in return for the payment of rent

## Rules About Rental Payments

The tenancy agreement will specify the amount of rent and when rent payments are due. It should also specify what additional services, if any, are included in the rent, such as heat, parking, cable, or electricity.

When a rental unit becomes vacant and a new tenancy is entered into, the landlord is free to charge any amount of rent the landlord and the new tenant agree to, without any regard to past rents or former tenants. In other words, there is no rent control on a vacant rental unit. As soon as the new tenant takes possession of the rental unit, however, rent control takes effect, and the provisions in the Act regulate future rent increases.

In most cases, rent can be increased only once every 12 months and only by the statutory guideline amount. The guideline amount, which is expressed as a percentage, is the maximum percentage by which a landlord can raise a tenant's rent without obtaining approval from the LTB. The guideline amount is set each August by the Ontario government and applies to rent increases that start on or after January 1 of the following year. The *Residential Tenancies Act* provides that the guideline amount can never be greater than 2.5 percent. For example, assume that the guideline amount for this year is 1.3 percent. As long as it has been at least 12 months since the tenant moved in or since the tenant's rent was last increased, the landlord can increase the rent, but cannot do so by more than 1.3 percent without the approval of the LTB. If the tenant's current rent is $1,000, the maximum the rent can be increased (without requiring LTB approval) is $13, which would make the new rent $1,013.

A landlord must provide the tenant with written notice of the rent increase at least 90 days before the date on which the increase is to take effect, whether or not LTB approval of the rent increase is required. If a tenant does not receive the required notice from his or her landlord, the tenant does not have to pay the increased rent.

A landlord can increase the rent above the guideline amount by applying to and obtaining the approval of the LTB or, in some cases, by agreement with the tenant. The grounds for rent increases that exceed the guideline percentage are

- an extraordinary increase in the cost of taxes or utilities (no limit on the increase);
- capital expenditures; or
- operating costs related to outside security services.

In the latter two cases, the LTB will determine whether the capital expenditures or costs related to outside security services were justified. If so, the increase cannot be more than 3 percent above the statutory guideline amount per year for a maximum of three years.

### Last Month's Rent Deposit

When a new tenancy is created, a landlord can require a deposit equal to one month's rent. The landlord can use the rent deposit only as payment of rent for the last month before the termination of the tenancy. It cannot be used for any other reason. For example, if the tenant causes damage to the rental unit, the landlord cannot use the last month's rent deposit to pay for these losses. If the rent increases during the time the landlord is holding the deposit, the landlord may require the tenant to pay an additional amount to bring the deposit up to the amount of the increased rent. The landlord must pay the tenant annual interest on this deposit in the amount of the guideline percentage increase in effect at the time that the payment becomes due.

The last month's rent deposit is the only type of deposit that the landlord can require a new tenant to pay, with the exception of refundable key or remote-entry-card deposits. The landlord cannot demand any other payment or security deposit from the tenant as a condition of renting the premises.

### Payment of Rent

A tenant is required to pay the rent on the date set out in the tenancy agreement (which is usually the first day of each month). Rent is payable in advance—in other words, at the beginning of a month rather than at the end. If the tenant does not pay the rent in full when it is due, the landlord is entitled to start proceedings to terminate the tenancy and evict the tenant.

Residential landlords do not have the right of **distress** (the right to seize the tenant's personal property) if the tenant fails to pay the rent. A tenant can choose to pay rent by way of postdated cheques or automatic payments (credit card or bank account debits), and a landlord is permitted to ask that payment be made this way, but a landlord cannot require a tenant to do so; a tenant may refuse. A landlord must provide a tenant, free of charge, with a receipt for any rent payments, if such a receipt is requested by the tenant.

**distress**
the right of a commercial landlord to seize and dispose of a tenant's property

## Types of Tenancies

Tenancies are either periodic or for a fixed term. The distinction is important because the Act provides for different notice periods depending on the type of tenancy. A **fixed-term tenancy** has a specified beginning date and end date, and it can be for any period of time. The usual written lease provides for a fixed term of at least one year. A **periodic tenancy** is a tenancy that renews automatically at the end of the relevant period until terminated by either the tenant or the landlord. The period is defined by the frequency of rental payments. The most common form of periodic tenancy is a **monthly tenancy** (also referred to as a month-to-month tenancy).

A fixed-term tenancy that ends and is not terminated or renewed for another fixed term automatically becomes a monthly tenancy. For example, assume that Tina Tenant enters into a one-year lease with her landlord and pays rent monthly. The tenancy is a fixed-term tenancy for one year. At the end of the year, if Tina and her landlord do not terminate the tenancy or sign another one-year lease, the tenancy will become a monthly tenancy. A tenant does not have to agree to a landlord's request to renew the tenancy for another fixed term.

**fixed-term tenancy**
tenancy that has a specified beginning and end date; can be for any period of time, from months to years

**periodic tenancy**
a tenancy that renews automatically at the end of the relevant period until terminated by either the tenant or the landlord, the period being defined by the frequency of rental payments

**monthly tenancy**
a periodic tenancy that renews automatically at the end of each month until terminated by the landlord or the tenant

## Rights of the Residential Tenant

Residential tenants have a number of rights under the *Residential Tenancies Act*.

### Privacy

The Act ensures that tenants have the right to privacy by limiting the landlord's ability to gain access to the unit once it has been rented. A landlord can enter without written notice only

- in the event of an emergency,
- if the tenant consents at the time of entry,
- if the tenancy agreement requires the landlord to clean the rental unit, or

- if the tenancy is ending and the landlord is showing the premises to a prospective tenant.

The landlord can enter the unit with 24 hours' written notice to the tenant only for the reasons specified in section 27 of the Act. These reasons include the following:

- to carry out a repair or do work in the rental unit, or to determine whether repairs are necessary;
- to allow a potential mortgagee or insurer of the residential complex to view the rental unit;
- to allow a potential buyer to view the rental unit; and
- any other reasonable reason for entry specified in the tenancy agreement.

The notice must specify the reason for entering, the date, and the time of day, which must fall between 8 a.m. and 8 p.m. It is illegal for a landlord to enter a tenant's unit without complying with the provisions of the Act. The Act provides specific remedies to a tenant if the landlord enters the unit illegally.

### Maintenance, Repairs, Freedom from Harassment, Etc.

The tenant is responsible for cleaning the rental unit and for repairing any damage caused to the premises by the wilful or negligent conduct of the tenant or his or her guests. If the tenant (or guests) causes damage to the rental unit, the landlord may apply to the LTB for an order requiring the tenant to pay the cost of repairing the damage and to terminate the tenancy and evict the tenant.

The landlord is responsible for maintaining the rental unit (including its appliances) and the common areas of the residential complex in a "good state of repair and fit for habitation" and for complying with all health, safety, and maintenance standards. This obligation exists even if the tenant was aware of the problem or maintenance issue before agreeing to rent the unit. If a landlord does not maintain the unit properly, the tenant may apply to the LTB. If the LTB determines that a landlord has breached his or her repair and maintenance obligations, the LTB may, among other things, order the landlord to make the necessary repairs and/or grant the tenant an abatement (reduction) of rent. In addition, a landlord must not withhold the supply of any vital services, such as heat, gas, and electricity, that the landlord is obligated to provide.

Finally, the Act prohibits landlords from doing any of the following:

- harassing, obstructing, coercing, or threatening a tenant;
- interfering with the reasonable enjoyment of the rental unit or residential complex by a tenant or members of his or her household; and
- changing the locks on any doors in the rental unit or the residential complex without giving the tenant replacement keys.

A tenant can apply to the LTB for relief if his or her landlord breaches any of these obligations.

### Subletting and Assigning a Tenancy

There are very specific provisions dealing with **sublet** and **assignment** of a tenancy. Basically, the Act permits the tenant to sublet or assign the tenancy but only with the consent of the landlord. The landlord cannot unreasonably withhold consent to a request to sublet the rental unit but is entitled to refuse consent to an assignment, in which case the tenant is entitled to terminate the tenancy early.

### Security of Tenure

Residential tenants are protected against unjustified and unlawful evictions. A landlord can terminate a tenancy and evict a tenant only for one of the grounds or reasons specified in the Act and, even then, cannot regain possession of the rental unit without an order from the LTB. Even when a landlord has a reason specified in the Act to evict a tenant, the landlord is not allowed to lock the tenant out of the rental unit or otherwise force the tenant to move out. The only person who is allowed to evict a tenant is the sheriff.

## Rights of the Residential Landlord

The primary right of the landlord is the right to be paid rent by the tenant. The landlord is entitled to receive rental payments when due, as provided for in the tenancy agreement. Non-payment of rent and persistently late payment of rent are both grounds for early termination of the tenancy by the landlord. As stated above, a residential landlord, unlike a commercial landlord, does not have the right of distress (the right to seize the tenant's property) for non-payment of rent.

## Terminating a Tenancy

A tenancy can be terminated by

- agreement between the landlord and the tenant;
- the tenant, with proper notice to the landlord; or
- the landlord, with grounds and proper notice to the tenant.

### Termination by Agreement

A tenant and a landlord can agree to terminate a tenancy at any time.

### Termination by the Tenant

A tenant may terminate a fixed-term or periodic tenancy at the end of the term or period by giving proper notice to the landlord in accordance with section 47 of the Act. The tenant does not need to provide a reason or establish grounds to terminate the tenancy. The length of the notice required depends on the type (periodic or fixed) and term (yearly, monthly, or weekly) of the tenancy.

**sublet**
arrangement whereby a tenant moves out of a rental unit for a period of time and allows another person to reside in the unit until the tenant returns at a specified future date

**assignment**
arrangement whereby a tenant transfers tenancy to another person for the remainder of the tenancy's term

For a monthly tenancy, notice must in most cases be given at least 60 days before the termination date, and that date must be the last day of a rental period. For example, assume that Susan has a monthly tenancy. It is August 15, and Susan has decided that she wants to move out. She must give at least 60 days' notice, which takes her to October 14. However, the termination date must be the last day of the month, so the earliest termination date that she can specify in her notice is October 31. A special rule allows a tenant to give less than 60 days' notice when the termination date is the last day of February or March. If a tenant is moving at the end of February or March, he or she may give notice by January 1 or February 1, respectively.

For a fixed-term tenancy, notice must be given at least 60 days before the termination date, and the termination date must be the last day of the fixed term. If Susan has a fixed-term tenancy ending August 31, she must give notice no later than July 2. Even if she were to give notice well before July 2—for example, on March 1—the earliest termination date will still be August 31, the last day of her fixed-term tenancy.

If a tenant moves out without giving proper notice, the tenancy is deemed to end either on the date the landlord rents the unit to a new tenant or on the earliest date that the tenant can terminate the tenancy pursuant to the Act, whichever is earlier, and the tenant is required to pay the rent owing up to this date.

There are also provisions in the Act giving tenants the right to terminate a tenancy early when a landlord breaches one of his or her obligations under the Act. If, for example, a landlord harasses a tenant, fails to maintain the rental property, alters the locking system, enters a tenant's unit illegally, withholds vital services, or interferes with a tenant's reasonable enjoyment of the rental property, the LTB can make an order terminating the tenancy, if the LTB is satisfied that termination is a reasonable remedy in the circumstances.

### Termination by the Landlord

The landlord can terminate a tenancy only for the grounds or reasons specified in the Act. Some of the reasons deal specifically with the conduct or behaviour of tenants or their guests (referred to as **fault grounds** or **termination for cause**), while other reasons do not (referred to as **no-fault grounds**).

The Act provides very specific procedural rules for each of the grounds for termination, including

**fault grounds**
grounds for termination based on the conduct or behaviour of the tenant or a guest of the tenant

**termination for cause**
termination by the landlord on fault grounds

**no-fault grounds**
grounds for termination unrelated to the conduct or behaviour of the tenant or a guest of the tenant

- the form, content, and timing of the notice of termination that must be given to the tenant;
- the earliest possible termination date that the landlord can specify on the notice of termination;
- what, if anything, a tenant can do to remedy the situation and void the notice of termination; and
- what the landlord can do if the tenant does not remedy the situation or does not move out on the termination date specified in the notice.

It is important to read these provisions very carefully. Although the process is quite similar for most grounds, the timing of the notice and the earliest possible termination date can be very different depending on the type of tenancy and the grounds for termination. For most fault grounds, the landlord can terminate the tenancy before the end of a rental period or term. For most no-fault grounds, the landlord must wait until the end of a rental period or term.

One of the most common grounds for early termination by a landlord is non-payment of rent or **arrears of rent**. Section 59 of the *Residential Tenancies Act* provides that a tenant is considered to be in arrears of rent on the day following the day on which rent is due and payable.

**arrears of rent**
unpaid rent that is owed to a landlord

Assume that Tina Tenant has a monthly tenancy, and her rent is due on the 1st of each month. It is August 10, and Tina has not paid August's rent. Her landlord, who wants to commence proceedings to terminate her tenancy as early as possible, must take the following steps:

1. The landlord must serve Tina with the proper notice of termination. For this ground, the required form is Form N4, Notice to End Your Tenancy for Non-Payment of Rent. This form is available on the LTB website. The termination date specified in the notice cannot be earlier than the 14th day after the notice is served on the tenant. If the landlord serves Tina on August 10, the earliest date that can be inserted in the notice of termination is August 24.

   This ground allows the tenant an opportunity to remedy the situation and void the notice of termination by paying the arrears of rent within 14 days after the notice is served. The landlord's notice must specify what the tenant must do, and by what date, in order to avoid termination of tenancy. Accordingly, if Tina pays all the rent owing any time before August 24, the notice will be void.

2. If Tina does not pay the rent owing by August 24, and does not move out by this date, the landlord must then commence an application before the LTB. The landlord will typically seek an order terminating the tenancy and evicting the tenant, and requiring the payment of the arrears of rent.

   The earliest date that the landlord can commence the application is the day after the termination date specified in the notice, or August 25. In other words, the landlord must wait for the remedy period to expire.

   The latest date that an application can be commenced is provided for in section 69 of the Act. For all grounds except non-payment of rent, an application may not be made more than 30 days after the termination date specified in the notice. For non-payment of rent, there is no limitation period as long as the rent remains unpaid.

The Act also provides for early termination by the landlord for the following additional "fault" grounds:

- the tenant or a guest has committed an illegal act in the rental unit or the residential complex;
- the tenant or a guest has wilfully or negligently caused damage to the rental unit or residential complex;
- the conduct of the tenant or a guest interferes with the reasonable enjoyment of the residential complex by the landlord or another tenant;

- an act or omission of the tenant or a guest seriously impairs the safety of any person; or
- there are too many persons residing in the tenant's unit.

Note that having an animal in the rental unit is not, by itself, a ground for early termination, even if the tenancy agreement contains a no-pet clause. A tenant can be evicted only if the pet has caused damage to the rental premises or disturbs the landlord or other tenants.

The Act also provides grounds for termination by the landlord at the end of a period or term. These are mostly no-fault grounds and include the following:

- the landlord personally requires possession of the rental unit (for himself or herself, for a member of his or her immediate family, or for the family's caregiver);
- a buyer of the rental unit personally requires possession of the rental unit (for himself or herself, for a member of his or her immediate family, or for the family's caregiver);
- the landlord requires possession to demolish, convert, or renovate the residential complex;
- the residential complex is being converted to a condominium; or
- the tenant has persistently failed to pay rent on time.

Whenever a landlord is seeking to terminate a tenancy early, the following questions should be considered:

- What is the ground or reason for wanting to terminate the tenancy early?
- Does the *Residential Tenancies Act* permit termination for this ground or reason?
- What section or sections of the Act deal with this ground?
- What is the earliest termination date possible?
- Is there a remedy period available to the tenant?
- What is the earliest date that the landlord can commence an application to the LTB in the event that the tenant does not move out voluntarily?

You will need to determine the answers to these questions for each ground or reason, and in each case you will probably have to look at two or three sections of the Act.

## Proceedings at the Landlord and Tenant Board

Once an application has been commenced, many procedural rules must be followed in order to obtain a hearing before an adjudicator. A landlord should be familiar with the Act, with the LTB's rules of practice, and with its interpretation guidelines. This information is available on the LTB's website.

# Implications of Buying a Residential Complex

As with other real property, the onus is on the buyer to ensure that good title is acquired on closing. In that respect, the purchase of a residential rental complex is no different from the purchase of any other property. However, the buyer of real property that has a rental component must address additional concerns.

## Vacant Possession

The buyer of a residential rental complex may or may not intend to reside there. A rental property is an income-producing asset and is often purchased solely for business or investment purposes. If the buyer intends to reside in the building after closing and the seller has agreed to provide vacant possession of a rental unit, the seller has two options if the desired unit is occupied by a tenant:

1. Try to convince the tenant to enter into an agreement with the seller (as landlord) to terminate the tenancy early.
2. Serve a notice of termination on the tenant (on behalf of the buyer) pursuant to section 49 of the Act.

For the first option, the agreement should specify a termination date well in advance of closing, so that the landlord (the seller) will have time to obtain an LTB order terminating the tenancy if the tenant does not move out as agreed.

The second option is available only if

- the residential complex does not contain more than three units;
- there is a signed agreement of purchase and sale;
- the buyer needs vacant possession personally or for a family member (or for the family's caregiver) as defined in the Act; and
- the termination date is at least 60 days after notice is given and is at the end of a period or term of the tenancy.

Once a notice is served, the landlord (the seller) can immediately commence an application to terminate the tenancy and evict the tenant. In other words, the landlord does not have to wait and see whether the tenant moves out in accordance with the notice given. If the tenant refuses to move out, the matter will proceed to a hearing. The LTB requires a declaration that the buyer does, in fact, require the unit for personal use. If the landlord is successful in the hearing, the order evicting the tenant will take effect 10 days later and can then be enforced by the sheriff's office.

This entire process may take several months. The lawyer must carefully explain the procedures and timing involved to a prospective buyer who intends to reside in the property.

## Assuming Existing Tenancies

If the buyer does not intend to reside in the rental property, the only concern will be stepping into the shoes of the seller (landlord) and assuming all existing tenancies. The buyer will want an assignment of all tenancies together with a direction to tenants instructing them to make future rent cheques payable to the new owner. Finally, an estoppel certificate or statutory declaration is required to confirm the terms and conditions of all existing tenancy agreements.

In addition, adjustments must be made for the current rent, the last month's rent deposits, and interest on those deposits. These amounts will be allocated between the seller and the buyer up to the date of closing. Adjustments are discussed in detail in Chapter 21, Document Preparation. The buyer and seller must also negotiate how they will deal with any arrears of rent outstanding on the date of closing.

The buyer will also want to confirm that the rental income declared by the seller is legal and will continue. For example, if rents include the use of a swimming pool and the pool has closed, rents could decrease. The buyer must also inquire whether there will be a reduction in realty taxes. If so, tenants may seek a reduction in rent, thereby decreasing the expected cash flow to the buyer.

Finally, the buyer should determine whether any applications relating to the residential complex are pending before the LTB.

## KEY TERMS

## REFERENCES

*Residential Tenancies Act, 2006*, SO 2006, c 17.

## REVIEW QUESTIONS

1. Jose is a tenant with a fixed-term tenancy. Does he have to move out when his fixed term expires?

2. How is a residential tenancy created?

3. How much rent can a landlord charge?

4. Can a landlord require a tenant to pay a deposit?

5. Nazrana has a monthly tenancy. Her landlord, Carlos, wants to serve her with a notice of termination for non-payment of rent on the 5th day of this month. What is the earliest date that Carlos can insert in the notice of termination he serves on Nazrana?

6. Loretta is a landlord who needs to enter her tenant's rental unit to carry out a repair. Does she have to give the tenant notice?

7. Can a tenant sublet or assign the tenancy?

8. Phillipe is a tenant with a fixed-term tenancy that expires at the end of June. He wants to move out of the rental unit. What must Phillipe do in order to terminate his tenancy by notice?

9. Sylvester recently purchased a home that is occupied by a tenant. What are the options available to Sylvester if he wishes to reside in the building after closing?

10. What issues need to be addressed if the buyer of a residential rental complex wishes to assume any existing tenancies?

# Environmental Issues

13

## LEARNING OUTCOMES

After reading this chapter, you will understand:

- The types of environmental issues that might arise in a real estate transaction

- Who is responsible for repairing environmental damage

- When a buyer may have a valid claim against a seller of a contaminated property

- What steps a buyer should take to protect against buying a contaminated property

- The application of the term *"caveat emptor"* to environmental issues

## Introduction

Any piece of land may have suffered environmental damage as a result of the conduct of previous or neighbouring owners. For example, an industry located on the property may have used toxic chemicals, or an owner of a neighbouring property may have released toxins into the environment. There may be environmental concerns with residential property as well—for example, as a result of a leak from an old fuel oil tank, or of asbestos in pipe or wall insulation. Properties that were previously rural may have been contaminated by animal waste or chemical fertilizers and pesticides.

Environmental damage is often hard to detect through a standard inspection of a property, and most home inspection contracts have a disclaimer regarding environmental hazards. As a result, it is important to consider how a buyer of land may seek protection against unknowingly assuming the liability for an environmentally contaminated piece of land.

## Overview of Environmental Law

Environmental matters in Ontario are primarily governed by the *Environmental Protection Act*, a statute administered by the Ministry of the Environment and Climate Change. The statute generally prevents any person from discharging any contaminant into the **natural environment**—that is, the air, water, or land.

**natural environment**
air, land, and water, or any combination or part thereof

In an effort to prevent or control the discharge of contaminants, the ministry is authorized under the Act to issue the following orders, as required:

- *stop orders*—to stop the source of contamination if danger is imminent;
- *control orders*—to control discharges that exist but do not pose any immediate danger;
- *preventive orders*—to prevent anticipated contamination; and
- *cleanup orders*—to clean up contamination that has actually occurred.

Under the Act, the owner of contaminated property is responsible for the cleanup and repair of environmental damage regardless of who caused the contamination.

## Implications for Buyers

A buyer who does not investigate the environmental condition of property being purchased may later discover that the property is contaminated. The buyer may then be responsible for all costs associated with the cleanup and repair of the environmental damage. If the government is forced to step in and clean up the property, a lien can be registered against the property.

The Act does not require sellers of real property to disclose that the property has been contaminated. As a result, the buyer may have no claim against the seller unless

- the seller represented that the property was *not* contaminated; or
- the seller knew about the contamination and the buyer did not know about it and could not have known about it. (This would constitute a **latent defect**.)

A prudent buyer should consider the environmental condition of the property in question before signing the agreement of purchase and sale. If there is any question about the condition of the property, the buyer should include an **environmental audit clause**, which provides the right to obtain an environmental audit or soil test of the property. (It should be noted that environmental audits cost several thousand dollars, and are done only if an environmental problem is suspected.)

If the audit discloses the existence of contamination on the property, the environmental audit clause should give the buyer the right to either terminate the transaction or insist that the seller clean up the contamination. The buyer could also negotiate to include clauses representing and warranting that the property is not contaminated, and agreeing to indemnify the buyer in the event of contamination. The buyer should be wary if the seller is seeking to sell the property "as is, where is." Without investigating the environmental condition of such a property, the buyer not only may acquire contaminated property, but may have no recourse against the seller for costs associated with cleanup and remediation.

The more difficult situation occurs where neither the seller nor the buyer is aware of the existence of contamination and the agreement of purchase and sale is silent on the issue. This is especially of concern if the property is at risk of environmental contamination, as when the property has a buried oil tank or is situated near a chemical plant or gas station.

Unfortunately for the buyer, the general principle of *caveat emptor* ("let the buyer beware") governs purchases of real property. The onus is clearly on the buyer to arrange an environmental inspection of the property. If there is an environmental concern because of the nature and/or location of the property, the buyer should

- review any existing environmental audits of the property;
- determine whether any notices or orders have been issued with respect to the property; and
- conduct a **phase I environmental assessment** of the property to determine whether contamination is likely and, if contamination is deemed likely, conduct a **phase II environmental assessment**, which includes soil and groundwater analysis.

If serious contamination is discovered, further site assessment and site remediation are required pursuant to the provisions of the *Environmental Protection Act*.

**latent defect**
defect of which the seller of a property was aware but which the buyer did not know about and could not have discovered upon reasonable inspection of the property

**environmental audit clause**
clause in the agreement of purchase and sale that provides the buyer with the right to obtain an environmental audit or soil test of the property, and that, if the audit discloses the existence of contamination on the property, gives the buyer the right to either terminate the transaction or insist that the seller clean up the contamination

*caveat emptor*
Latin term meaning "let the buyer beware"

**phase I environmental assessment**
assessment of property conducted to determine the likelihood that one or more contaminants have affected all or part of the property

**phase II environmental assessment**
assessment of property conducted to determine the location and concentration of contaminants on the property; follows completion of a phase I environmental assessment

## KEY TERMS

*caveat emptor,* 167

environmental audit clause, 167

latent defect, 167

natural environment, 166

phase I environmental assessment, 167

phase II environmental assessment, 167

## REFERENCES

*Environmental Protection Act,* RSO 1990, c E.19.

## REVIEW QUESTIONS

1. What does the *Environmental Protection Act* govern?

2. What is the risk to a buyer who does not confirm the environmental condition of the property?

3. Will the buyer of contaminated property have any claim against the seller?

4. What should a prudent buyer do in order to avoid unexpected environmental problems?

# Title Searching

# 14

## LEARNING OUTCOMES

After reading this chapter, you will understand:

- Title searching concepts and terminology
- How searches under the Registry and Land Titles systems differ
- How a title searcher conducts a Registry search
- How to search title to a property in the Land Titles system
- How to conduct an online title search
- The relevance of an execution search
- What other searches must be conducted in a purchase transaction

# Introduction

It is necessary to **search the title** to a particular piece of land to find out who owns the property and whether that person's ownership interest is subject to any other claims or encumbrances. Searching title involves checking the entries in the **abstract**, **abstract book**, or parcel register for a particular piece of land and then examining the listed documents.

Titles are most often searched in the context of a real estate transaction. When a person agrees to buy real estate, an agreement of purchase and sale is signed. The agreement states what the buyer is agreeing to buy—for example, a single-family dwelling located at 123 Elm Street in Oshawa. The agreement will also set out the size of the lot and describe specific encumbrances to which the title will be subject at the closing date (the date on which the buyer pays the seller and the seller actually transfers title to the buyer).

It is the role of the buyer's lawyer to ensure that the buyer receives the title that was promised. If the buyer is financing the purchase by way of a mortgage, the lawyer may be representing the mortgagee as well and ensuring that the mortgagee's interests are protected. In both cases, the lawyer does this by searching the title to the property, first to confirm that the seller, in fact, owns the property and then to find out what encumbrances are outstanding. If the title search discloses any encumbrances that are not listed in the agreement of purchase and sale, the buyer's lawyer will ask the seller's lawyer to remove those encumbrances before the closing.

When the deal closes, the buyer's lawyer either provides an opinion to the buyer about the state of the title and certifies that the title is free and clear of any encumbrances other than the ones agreed to in the agreement of purchase and sale or, if there is title insurance, states that title is protected by the title insurance policy and provides particulars of the policy. The title search provides the basis upon which the lawyer determines the state of title and provides this opinion or statement.

# Who Conducts the Title Search?

Land registry records are public, and anyone can gain access to them. However, most title searches are conducted by law firms acting for buyers and/or mortgagees in connection with real estate transactions. Lawyers (or their law clerks) usually conduct Land Titles system searches and hire a freelance conveyancer (or "title searcher") to conduct Registry system searches. While it is permissible for a law clerk or title searcher to search a title, the title search must be prepared for and under the supervision of a lawyer. Only a lawyer can give an opinion about title to a client. It is the lawyer's responsibility to carefully review the results of the title search so that he or she can properly certify title to the client.

# When a Title Search Is Conducted

The agreement of purchase and sale will provide the buyer with a specific amount of time in which to search title and submit any requisitions (objections to title) to the seller. If the agreement does not specify a date, the *Vendors and Purchasers Act* provides that the buyer has 30 days after the agreement is signed in which to complete the search and submit requisitions.

## Where a Title Search Is Conducted

As noted above, you, as a law clerk, will probably not be asked to conduct a title search if the property is registered in the Registry system. Instead, the title search will be carried out by a freelance title searcher. The title searcher will search the title to the property at the land registry office (LRO) for the geographic area in which the property is situated. He or she will access the abstracts online using the Teraview software and will also use the abstract books for registrations prior to the date that the property was automated.

The municipal address of the property determines the region or county and, therefore, which LRO the title searcher must go to in order to search title. For example, the city of Richmond Hill is located in York Region. If the title searcher is searching title to a property located in Richmond Hill, he or she would go to the LRO for York Region, which is located in Aurora.

You can find information about the location of registry offices and the services they provide at the following Government of Ontario website: <www.ontario.ca/home-and-community/land-registry-offices-lro>.

If the property is registered in the Land Titles system, you can conduct the title search online using the Teraview software (discussed in Chapter 7, Electronic Registration and Teraview). Because Teraview allows access to property throughout Ontario, it is not necessary to go to the LRO where the particular property is located. Instead, searches are usually done from the lawyer's office. If the lawyer does not have the Teraview software, searches can be done at any LRO.

## The Difference Between Registry System and Land Titles System Titles

As discussed in Chapter 5, Land Registration Systems, the Registry system is a notice system only. It provides notice of documents registered against title to a property; it does not guarantee the legal effectiveness of any of the documents—nor does it certify the title of the current owner. As a result, in a Registry system search, the title searcher must examine all registered documents affecting title to ensure their legal effectiveness. The Land Titles system, on the other hand, does provide a guarantee of title; title is certified. As a result, a search of title records under this system is less extensive.

## Title Searches in the Registry System

While most properties are in the Land Titles system, you may occasionally encounter a property that is registered in the Registry system, which requires a longer and more complicated search of title.

A Registry system title search involves examining the history of ownership of the property for the last 40 years prior to the date on which the real estate transaction is scheduled to close. If, for example, an agreement of purchase and sale sets a closing date of September 1, 2015, the title searcher must search title back to September 1, 1975. There are a number of steps in a Registry system search. A discussion of each of the steps follows.

## 1. Determine the Legal Description and PIN

Before the title searcher can start a search, he or she will need the property identifier number (PIN). Although the agreement of purchase and sale will not contain the PIN, it can be easily located in Teraview by searching the owner's name and/or municipal address. The title searcher may also be able to obtain the PIN from the seller's lawyer.

The title searcher also needs the legal description of the property to locate the appropriate paper abstract book for the property.

## 2. Obtain the Abstract and Abstract Book

Once the title searcher has the abstract for the property from Teraview and the abstract book showing all registrations relating to the property prior to its automation, he or she must find all registrations relating to the property over the last 40 years.

## 3. Trace Back to a Good Root of Title (Root Deed)

Section 112(1) of part III of the *Registry Act* provides that the title search period is 40 years. To establish the starting point of the search, the title searcher must count back 40 years from the closing date in the agreement of purchase and sale (known s the 40-year rule). For example, if the closing date is July 5, 2016, the starting point of the search is July 5, 1976. (In practice, most title searchers go back 40 years from the date on which they conduct the search.)

**commencement date**
starting date of the title search period

**root of title (root deed)**
first conveyance of the fee simple estate (a deed or transfer) registered after the commencement date of a title search

The title searcher must then look for the first conveyance of the fee simple estate (a deed or transfer) registered after the **commencement date**. Assume that since the commencement date in our example there have been two conveyances: the first on December 15, 1978 and the second on May 28, 2000. The deed dated 1978 is the **root of title**, or **root deed**. There is no need to search back any further.

However, if there has not been a conveyance of the fee simple estate since the commencement date (July 5, 1976), it is necessary to go back beyond 40 years and find the first conveyance of the fee simple estate registered before the commencement date. If the most recent conveyance of the fee simple estate was on March 13, 1938, this deed will be the root of title, or root deed, even though it was registered far beyond the statutory 40-year search period.

This practice has been affirmed by the Supreme Court of Canada in the case of *Fire v Longtin*. However, many real estate lawyers still prefer to start their searches with the conveyance of the fee simple estate to the person who owned the property at the commencement of the 40-year search period. Assume in our example that there is a conveyance of the fee simple estate in 1963 to Smith, and a conveyance from Smith to Tran in 1988. Smith is the person who owned the property at the commencement of the 40-year period. Some lawyers would start the search with the 1963 deed to Smith and check every document registered from then on. Based on the Supreme Court of Canada decision, however, the 1988 deed to Tran will be the root of title, and any other instruments registered on title between 1963 and July 5, 1976, such as mortgages or other liens, can be ignored (since they are outside the title search period of 40 years).

If the property being searched is a whole lot on a concession or on a plan of subdivision, then all of the documents recorded in the abstract book on the pages for that lot will be relevant to the search. However, if the property is a part of a lot on a concession or on a plan of subdivision, some of the documents recorded in the abstract book on the pages for that lot may relate to the other part or parts of the lot. As a result, the title searcher should check the description column of the abstract book to determine which entries apply to the part of the lot being searched.

## 4.   Abstract the Instruments

**Abstracting** involves examining and summarizing into **search notes** the contents of all the registered documents that affect title. The purpose of search notes is to provide the lawyer reviewing the notes with enough information to determine the state of the title to the property and any encumbrances that may be registered on title. Keep in mind that, in the Registry system, the land registrar does not guarantee the accuracy of information recorded in the abstract. Therefore, the lawyer reviewing the title search must ensure that all registered documents are legally effective.

The lawyer must be satisfied that

- the conveyance is in the proper form;
- the land is properly described;
- there is no gap in the chain of title (discussed below);
- the document was properly executed and, when required, witnessed; and
- any affidavits and other statutory requirements that affect the validity of the document have been completed.

The title searcher prepares search notes by using a separate sheet of paper for each document registered during the title search period that affects the subject land. Starting with the root deed, the title searcher copies the information from the abstract for each instrument, exactly as it appears in the abstract, often using pre-printed sheets that already contain columns similar to those in the abstract book.

(This information will later be compared with the information contained in the actual document.)

**abstracting**
process of examining and summarizing into search notes the contents of all registered documents that affect title

**search notes**
summary of the contents of all registered documents affecting title; reveals the state of the title including any encumbrances

## 5.   Obtain a Copy of All Abstracted Instruments

The title searcher then obtains a copy of every registered document that has been abstracted.

## 6. Review Each Instrument

The title searcher compares all the information copied from the abstract with the information contained in the actual document by checking the dates, names, consideration, and legal description of the property. If there are any differences, they are identified by drawing a line through any information that needs correcting and then making the correction in a different colour ink. This way, the lawyer reviewing the search knows that the information in the abstract book was incorrect. For instruments other than deeds, such as mortgages, claims for liens, and deposits, the title searcher provides a brief summary of the contents of the instrument.

Next, the title searcher must check each instrument to see if the document contains all the necessary information to make it legally effective. The search notes must be detailed enough for the lawyer reviewing them to ensure that each instrument complies with all the legal requirements in place at the time that the instrument was registered. If a document does not comply with the legal requirements, this may constitute a title defect that needs to be corrected before the transaction closes. Title search paper contains a number of abbreviations representing the legal requirements for registered documents that have been in effect over the time covered by most searches today. As the title searcher notes that a particular item appears in a document, he or she checks the appropriate box.

A sample of a Registry search can be found in the Appendix to this chapter.

## 7. Obtain the Whiteprint for the Property

**whiteprint**
copy of the plan of survey of a plan of subdivision that shows the dimensions of individual building lots

The title searcher should obtain a whiteprint of the property. A **whiteprint** is a copy of a plan of survey of the plan of subdivision on which the property is situated. It is helpful to look at the plan or obtain a whiteprint because it

- enables the title searcher to see the location of the property, as well as its relationship to adjoining and other properties;
- contains measurements of the lots on the plan, which can be used to confirm the size of the lot being purchased;
- confirms the relationship to any previous plans of subdivision at the same location; and
- reveals the location of the property in relation to main roadways or intersections and confirms that the property has access to a public road.

Figure 14.1 is an example of a whiteprint of a plan of subdivision.

If the legal description refers to a reference plan, the title searcher should also get a copy of the reference plan.

## 8. Search Adjoining Land (Planning Act Search)

**adjoining land**
property that shares a common boundary with the property being searched

The title searcher must complete a *Planning Act* search if searching title to property that is not a whole lot on a plan of subdivision. A *Planning Act* search involves a review of the history of ownership of **adjoining land**. He or she must check to see

**Figure 14.1 Whiteprint of Plan 1209, Township of Whitford**

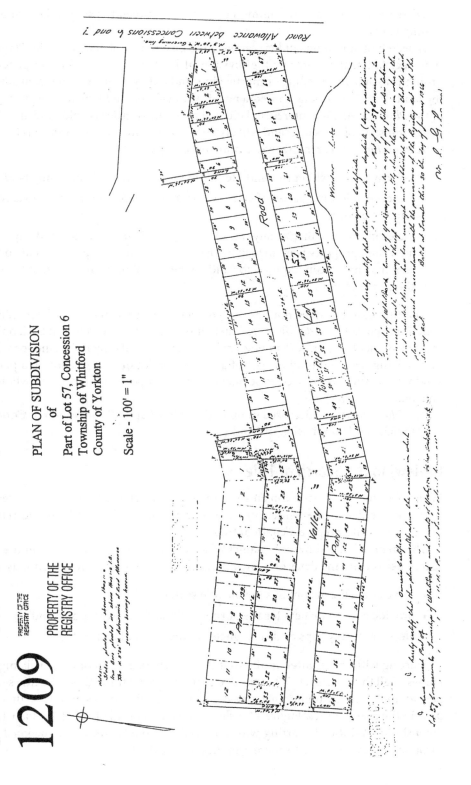

whether there was ever any common ownership between the subject land and adjoining lands.

A search of adjoining land is completed to ensure compliance with the *Planning Act*—legislation that controls the division of land in Ontario. The Act generally prohibits people from selling or mortgaging land if they retain an interest in adjoining land. There are serious consequences if a transfer of land violates the provisions of the *Planning Act*. No interest in land will pass (the transfer is void) and all subsequent transfers of the same land will also not convey any interest in the land.

A *Planning Act* search involves a number of steps:

- Looking at the whiteprint and identifying and marking all adjoining land.
- For each adjoining parcel of land, checking the deeds and transfers to ascertain the owners.
- Determining whether, at any time, the property being searched and any adjoining property were owned by the same person. If so, government consent may have been required to validate the sale of only one parcel of land by the owner of both.

The title searcher does not have to go back 40 years if there is a later transfer containing completed *Planning Act* statements; it is necessary to search back only to the date of that transfer. A *Planning Act* search is required only if the land for which title is being searched is all or part of a concession lot or part of a lot on a plan of subdivision. There is no need to search adjoining property if the land is a whole lot on a plan of subdivision.

The *Planning Act* is discussed in more detail in Chapter 9, Government Controls over the Use and Subdivision of Land.

## Reviewing the Search of Title

When the title searcher completes the search, he or she will give you the search notes and copies of the whiteprint and reference plan, if any. When you receive these, you should prepare a **chain of title**.

**chain of title**
list of all owners within the search period

The chain of title shows the names of all the registered owners during the title search period and the dates on which they acquired ownership. Its function is to

- serve as a table of contents for the title search;
- provide a list of owners for the purpose of searching executions; and
- alert you to any gaps or discrepancies in the chain of ownership.

**grantee**
person who receives title to real property

Starting with the **grantee** in the root deed, prepare a chain of title by listing the names of all the grantees in all of the deeds and transfers throughout the title search period up to and including the current owner. Copy the names exactly as they appear in the search notes. Figure 14.2 shows the chain of title for Lot 11, Plan 1209, Township of Whitford, starting with the deed to Douglas May (the diagonal line through Duncan McTavish's name signifies that he died).

**Figure 14.2    Chain of Title for Lot 11, Plan 1209, Township of Whitford**

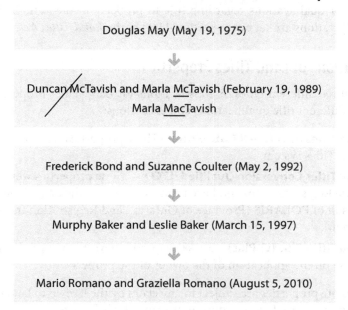

Starting with the first deed in the chain of title, make sure the grantee in one deed was the **grantor** in the next. If there are any gaps or differences, there should be an explanation in the search notes. If you look at the search notes in the Appendix, you'll see that instrument number 91764 is a deed to Duncan McTavish and Marla McTavish. However, the next deed (instrument number 153117) is just from Marla MacTavish and her name is spelled differently. The search notes explain these differences. There is a deposit of a death certificate for Duncan McTavish (instrument number 148902), which explains why he is not shown as a transferor in instrument number 153117. There is also a statutory declaration by Marla MacTavish (instrument number 170003), stating that she is one and the same person as Marla McTavish, thus explaining the different spelling of her name in instrument numbers 91764 and 153117.

**grantor**
person who transfers title to real property

## Title Searches in the Land Titles System

If the property is registered in the Land Titles system, the title search process is far simpler than it is for property registered in the Registry system. Under the Land Titles system, the state of title is guaranteed, and there is therefore no need to conduct a 40-year search. For example, if the parcel register reveals Demetre Papadepoulos as the owner, then it is guaranteed that he is the legal owner and has good title to the property, subject to any encumbrances that are noted in the register. In Land Titles, the parcel register shows only the current owner and any outstanding encumbrances. Any other entries that no longer affect title are ruled off.

In theory, you need only check the register for the parcel in question, and the register alone tells who the registered owner is and what encumbrances are outstanding. However, as stated in Chapter 5, Land Registration Systems, there are some exceptions or qualifications regarding title to property in the Land Titles system. These qualifications are set out in section 44(1) of the *Land Titles Act*.

## Classifications of Land Titles Properties

There are three different types or classifications for Land Titles properties, each of which has different title qualifications and exceptions:

**Land Titles Absolute (LT Absolute)**
properties originally in the Land Titles system; corporate existence and *Planning Act* compliance are not guaranteed

**Land Titles Conversion Qualified (LTCQ)**
properties originally in the Registry system and converted to the Land Titles system as a result of POLARIS; *Planning Act* compliance and corporate existence are guaranteed for the period prior to the date of conversion; properties remain subject to any pre-existing mature claims for adverse possession, prescription, or misdescription

**Land Titles Plus (LT Plus)**
properties upgraded from LTCQ with the additional guarantee against any mature claims for adverse possession

1. **Land Titles Absolute (LT Absolute)**—These properties were originally in the Land Titles system.

2. **Land Titles Conversion Qualified (LTCQ)**—These properties were originally in the Registry system and have been converted to the Land Titles system as a result of POLARIS (Province of Ontario Land Registration Information System).

3. **Land Titles Plus (LT Plus)**—These properties have been upgraded from LTCQ on the application of the owner of the property.

LT Absolute properties are subject to any claim by the Crown to land owned by a corporation that ceased to exist during its ownership of the land. In addition, *Planning Act* compliance is not guaranteed.

LTCQ properties guarantee *Planning Act* compliance and corporate existence but only up to the date the title was converted to LTCQ. You must still check for *Planning Act* compliance and corporate existence after the conversion date (which will be indicated on the parcel register). You must also check LTCQ properties for any pre-existing claims for adverse possession, prescription, or misdescription because these claims are not eliminated in the conversion process. As discussed in Chapter 3, Estates and Interests in Land, generally, it is not possible to acquire possessory title to land that is registered in the Land Titles system.

LT Plus properties have all the guarantees of LTCQ properties and also guarantee against any mature claims for adverse possession.

If the property is in Land Titles (either LT Absolute, LTCQ, or LT Plus), you can conduct the search from your office using the Teraview software.

## Title Searching Using Teraview

The steps for searching title using Teraview are listed below.

1. Obtain a copy of the parcel register (parcel registers are discussed in Chapter 5).

   Teraview is a pay-per-use system, and there is a cost associated with retrieving a parcel register, so it is important to make sure you have found the correct property before requesting a copy of the parcel register.

   You can obtain a copy of the parcel register using any of the following:

   • the property's unique property identifier number;

   • the municipal address;

- the owner's name; or
- the instrument number of a document registered on the title.

It is best to use the property identifier number (PIN). Every property has a unique PIN, so using the PIN guarantees that you are searching the correct property. It can be difficult to find a property in Teraview using the address. Searching by name may also be difficult, especially if the owner's name is a common one or the owner owns multiple properties.

Once you have found the correct property, retrieve the parcel register for that property by selecting "Parcel Register" at the bottom of the page, as shown in Figure 14.3.

### Figure 14.3 Retrieving the Parcel Register

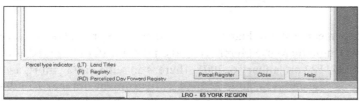

2. Obtain the whiteprint of the plan of subdivision or a copy of any other plan that affects the land.

Whiteprints are discussed above in connection with searches in the Registry system. In order to get a plan of subdivision, select "Property" and "Search by Subdivision," as shown in Figure 14.4.

### Figure 14.4 Obtaining the Whiteprint

3. Obtain a copy of the relevant instruments.

Obtain a copy of the transfer to the current owner and a copy of any other registered interests that remain outstanding. To do so, enter the instrument number in the "Instrument Reg No" field and select "Request," as shown in Figure 14.5.

### Figure 14.5 Obtaining a Copy of the Relevant Instruments

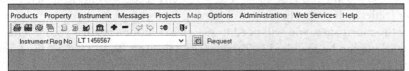

4. Review other instruments shown on the abstract.

   Make sure that the search reflects what the agreement of purchase and sale says. For example, make sure that the owners' names on title are exactly the same as the sellers' names in the agreement of purchase and sale. And if the agreement says that there is a mortgage being assumed, make sure that that mortgage is actually registered on title. Note any other outstanding mortgages or encumbrances.

5. Conduct a *Planning Act* search of adjoining property (if applicable).

   A *Planning Act* search is necessary if the land is not a whole lot on a plan of subdivision. The steps you take are the same as those set out in step 8 of the Registry search.

### Example

The sample parcel register in Figure 14.6 shows that the present owners are Francois Mercier and Huguette Marie Mercier, based on the transfer registered as instrument number LT1371122 on January 6, 2001. There is an outstanding mortgage in favour of ABC Bank, registered on June 3, 2014 as instrument number LT1394678. You should obtain copies of these two documents. You will not have to do a *Planning Act* search because the property is a whole lot on registered plan of subdivision.

## Other Searches

Whether your property is in the Registry system or the Land Titles system, there are a number of other searches that may be required.

## 1.  Execution Search (Writs of Execution)

An execution is a claim against a person resulting from a court judgment that is then registered against that person's name with the sheriff of the judicial district in which the debtor owns real property. Executions create a lien against any lands already owned by the person named in the execution at the time of filing and any lands that the person acquires after the date of filing.

As a result, for Registry properties, you must make sure that there were no executions outstanding against any owner within the 40-year search period during the time that person was the owner of the land. Make a list of all owners in the chain of title and the dates during which they were owners. You can electronically submit the names and dates to the appropriate sheriff's office for searching. Note that if title insurance is being obtained, it may not be necessary to search all names in the chain of title (see Chapter 17, Title Insurance).

For properties in Land Titles, you need to search executions only against the current owners (sellers). If your clients are obtaining a mortgage, and you are also representing the mortgagee, you will need to search executions against your clients too.

Executions can be searched in Teraview by selecting "Products" on the top toolbar, and then "Writsearch." Once on the Writsearch screen, the user selects "Writs"

## Figure 14.6   Parcel Register

**Ontario ServiceOntario**

PARCEL REGISTER (ABBREVIATED) FOR PROPERTY IDENTIFIER

PAGE 1 OF 3
PREPARED FOR JMolf001
ON 2015/06/16 AT 10:18:28

LAND
REGISTRY
OFFICE #65

12345-6789

* CERTIFIED IN ACCORDANCE WITH THE LAND TITLES ACT * SUBJECT TO RESERVATIONS IN CROWN GRANT *

PROPERTY DESCRIPTION:   PCL 170-1, SEC 65M1234; LT 170, PL 65M1234
TOWN OF NEWMARKET

PROPERTY REMARKS:

ESTATE/QUALIFIER:           RECENTLY:                        PIN CREATION DATE:
FEE SIMPLE                  FIRST CONVERSION FROM BOOK       1996/12/16
ABSOLUTE

OWNERS' NAMES                        CAPACITY    SHARE
MERCIER, FRANCOIS                    JTEN
MERCIER, HUGUETTE MARIE              JTEN

| REG. NUM. | DATE | INSTRUMENT TYPE | AMOUNT | PARTIES FROM | PARTIES TO | CERT/CHKD |
|-----------|------|-----------------|--------|--------------|------------|-----------|
| | | | | **EFFECTIVE 2000/07/29 THE NOTATION OF THE "BLOCK IMPLEMENTATION DATE" OF 1996/12/16 ON THIS PIN** | | |
| | | | | **WAS REPLACED WITH THE "PIN CREATION DATE" OF 1996/12/16** | | |
| | | | | ** PRINTOUT INCLUDES ALL DOCUMENT TYPES AND DELETED INSTRUMENTS SINCE: 1996/12/13 ** | | |
| VA41945 | 1959/05/22 | BYLAW | | | | C |
| | | *REMARKS: LN0314J, LB237508 AFFECTS ALL/PART VARIOUS LANDS (ADDED 98/01/26 BY B.WILLSON, ADLR) BY-LAW 2298* | | | | |
| LT315678 | 1986/08/21 | NOTICE AGREEMENT | | | | C |
| | | *REMARKS: (ALL/PART VARIOUS LANDS ADDED 99/01/08 AT 11:26 BY H. MOTTRAM, ADLR)* | | | | |
| LT364316 | 1987/03/10 | APL (GENERAL) | | | | C |
| | | *REMARKS: SECTION 49(5) OF THE PLANNING ACT DOES NOT APPLY* | | | | |
| 65R10429 | 1987/04/13 | PLAN REFERENCE | | | THE CORPORATION OF THE TOWN OF NEWMARKET | C |
| LT1371122 | 2001/01/06 | TRANSFER | | | MERCIER, FRANCOIS | |
| | | | | | MERCIER, HUGUETTE MARIE | |
| LT1394678 | 2014/06/03 | CHARGE | $94,000 | | ABC BANK | |

NOTE: ADJOINING PROPERTIES SHOULD BE INVESTIGATED TO ASCERTAIN DESCRIPTIVE INCONSISTENCIES, IF ANY, WITH DESCRIPTION REPRESENTED FOR THIS PROPERTY.
NOTE: ENSURE THAT YOUR PRINTOUT STATES THE TOTAL NUMBER OF PAGES AND THAT YOU HAVE PICKED THEM ALL UP.

and then "Search by Name," as shown in Figure 14.7. The user is then prompted to select a docket so that the costs associated with the writ search will go into the proper docket summary.

**Figure 14.7   Writs of Execution Name Search**

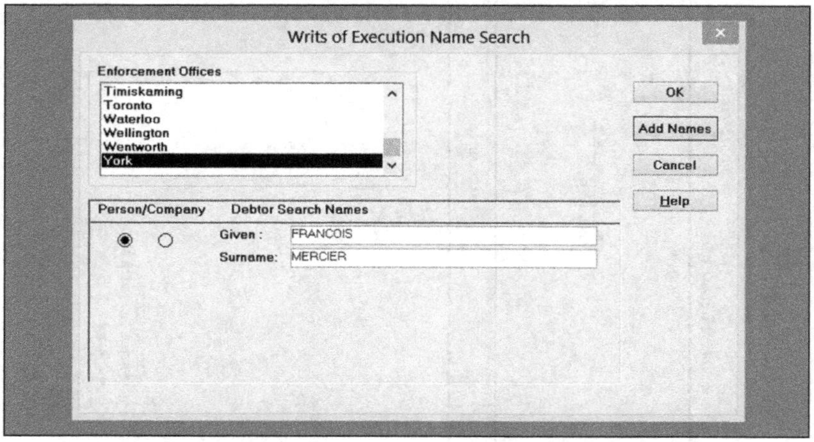

See Chapter 8, Liens Against Land, for a more complete discussion of writs of execution.

## 2. Corporate Search

If the property is in the Registry system, and there are any corporate owners on title during the 40-year search period, you must check to ensure that the corporation did not dissolve at any time during the time it owned the land. The *Business Corporations Act* provides that title to property owned by a dissolved corporation escheats to or vests in the Crown.

If your property is in the Land Titles system, a corporate search is necessary only if the present owner (the seller) is a corporation.

If, however, title insurance is being obtained (discussed in Chapter 17), corporate searches will likely not be required.

## 3. Subsearch

**subsearch**

brief examination of title records, undertaken on closing, that covers the period from the date of the title search up to the date of closing, to make sure that nothing has been registered on title since the title search was done

A **subsearch** is a brief examination of title records to update an earlier search of title. It is often performed just before registration of a transfer or mortgage to ensure that no new instruments that may affect title have been registered since the date the title search was completed. It is also performed if you are representing clients who are refinancing their property by way of a new mortgage, and you represented the clients when they purchased the property. Depending on how much time has lapsed, you may not have to do a complete search, but rather only a subsearch to make sure nothing has been registered since your previous search or subsearch.

If the property is in the Land Titles system, you need to look only at the parcel register. If the property is in the Registry system, you must check the abstract.

In both systems, on the day of closing, you must also check executions again, against the seller, and against the buyer/mortgagor if there is a mortgage being registered. Title insurance companies don't require a new execution certificate as long as the original execution search was done within a short time frame (usually seven days). Therefore, if title insurance is being obtained, executions against the buyer/mortgagor may not be required again on closing.

## KEY TERMS

abstract, 170

abstract book, 170

abstracting, 173

adjoining land, 174

chain of title, 176

commencement date, 172

grantee, 176

grantor, 177

Land Titles Absolute (LT Absolute), 178

Land Titles Conversion Qualified (LTCQ), 178

Land Titles Plus (LT Plus), 178

root of title (root deed), 172

search notes, 173

search the title, 170

subsearch, 182

whiteprint, 174

## REFERENCES

*Business Corporations Act*, RSO 1990, c B.16.

*Fire v Longtin*, [1995] 4 SCR 3, (1995), 128 DLR (4th) 767.

*Land Titles Act*, RSO 1990, c L.5.

*Planning Act*, RSO 1990, c P.13.

*Registry Act*, RSO 1990, c R.20.

*Vendors and Purchasers Act*, RSO 1990, c V.2.

## REVIEW QUESTIONS

1. Why is it necessary to search the title to property?

2. Who conducts a title search?

3. When is a title search conducted?

4. Where is a title search conducted?

5. What is the major difference between a Registry system search and a Land Titles system search?

6. What are the three different types or classifications of Land Titles properties, and what are the title qualifications and exceptions for each?

7. What are the steps in a search under the Land Titles system?

**Appendix    Registry Search Notes**

Title Search: Lot 11, Plan 1209, Township of Whitford

Present Owners: Mario Romano and Graziella Romano, as joint tenants

Outstanding Mortgages:    #635121 Bank of Montreal $320,000.00

#726341 XYZ Mortgage Ltd $15,000.00

Easements: None

Subdivision Agreement: #77286

PIN: 98765-4321 (R)

Executions: Not searched

Whiteprint of Plan 1209 enclosed.

Date of Search: March 27, 2015, by Sally Searcher

**Appendix** Continued

LOT 11 PLAN 1209 MUNICIPALITY Twp. of Whitford Page 1 of 10

| Inst. No. | Inst. Type | Inst. Date | Reg. Date | Seller/Chargor | Buyer/Chargee | Desc. |
|---|---|---|---|---|---|---|
| 77286 | Notice of Agreement | Jan. 8/74 | Jan. 15/74 | Stavros Subdivisions Ltd. | The Corporation of the Twp. of Whitfold | All + other |

○ SFCA

○ DEA/EAA
○ SFMA

○ GRANT
     FEE SIMPLE
     JT
     TEN IN COMMON
     TO USES
     AND APPOINT

○ HAB (as JT)

○ UC (4) (1))

○ REL

○ B OF DOWER (78/3/31)

○ SP CONSENT & REL

○ S & SW

○ CORP SEAL

○ ONT SUC DUTY (70/1/10-79/4/10)

   A OF MM (54/4/30)
   ONT. CO. (65/6/23)
   OTHER (82/5/15)

○ LTT AFF (21/6/1)

○ AFF OF SUB. WIT.

○ PLANNING ACT CONSENT (67/6/1)

○ AFF RE: PLAN. ACT

○ STATE RE: PLAN. ACT 1 2 3

○ AFF OF AGE (57/4/3)

○ STATE RE: AGE (85/4/1)

○ AFF OF MAR. ST. (39/6/25-78/3/31)

○ AFF OF SP. ST. (78/3/31)

○ STATE RE: SP. ST. (85/4/1)
     SP/NOT A SP/SP OF EA OTH
     NOT A MAT HOME
     REL PER SEP AGMT

○ TRANSFEREE(S) BIRTH DATE(S):

   1 _____
   2 _____

○ AFF OF PARTNER PROP 1 2 3

○ DOCUMENT GENERAL/SCHEDULE

**Lawyer for 1st party:**

**Lawyer for 2nd party:**

NOTES: Subdivision Agreement – deals mainly with roads, hydro + parkland.

**Appendix　Continued**

LOT 11　PLAN 1209　　MUNICIPALITY Twp. of Whitford Page 2 of 10

| Inst. No. | Inst. Type | Inst. Date | Reg. Date | Seller/Chargor | Buyer/Chargee | Desc. |
|---|---|---|---|---|---|---|
| 79621 | Deed | May 16/75 | May 19/75 | Stavros Subdivisions Ltd. | MAY, Douglas | All lot 11. |

✓ SFCA

○ DEA/EAA
○ SFMA

✓ GRANT
   FEE SIMPLE
   JT
   TEN IN COMMON
   TO USES
   AND APPOINT

✓ HAB (to FF)

✓ UC (4) (1))

○ REL

○ B OF DOWER (78/3/31)

○ SP CONSENT & REL

○ S & SW

✓ CORP SEAL of SSL

○ ONT SUC DUTY (70/1/10–79/4/10)

○ A OF MM (54/4/30)
   ONT. CO. (65/6/23)
   OTHER (82/6/15)

✓ LTT AFF (21/6/1)

○ AFF OF SUB. WIT.

○ PLANNING ACT CONSENT (67/6/1)

○ AFF RE: PLAN. ACT

○ STATE RE: PLAN. ACT 1 2 3

○ AFF OF AGE (57/4/3)

○ STATE RE: AGE (85/4/1)

○ AFF OF MAR. ST. (39/6/25–78/3/31)

○ AFF OF SP. ST. (78/3/31)

○ STATE RE: SP. ST. (85/4/1)
   SP/NOT A SP/SP OF EA OTH
   NOT A MAT HOME
   REL PER SEP AGMT

○ TRANSFEREE(S) BIRTH DATE(S):
   1. _____
   2. _____

○ AFF OF PARTNER PROP 1 2 3

○ DOCUMENT GENERAL/SCHEDULE

Lawyer for 1st party: Harvey Whalen
   123 Bay St.
   Toronto.

Lawyer for 2nd party: Smith + Jones
   202 Main St.
   Whitford

NOTES:

**Appendix    Continued**

LOT 11    PLAN 1209    MUNICIPALITY Twp. of Whitford Page 3 of 10

| Inst. No. | Inst. Type | Inst. Date | Reg. Date | Seller/Chargor | Buyer/Chargee | Desc. |
|---|---|---|---|---|---|---|
| 91674 | Deed | Feb.17/89 | Feb.19/89 | MAY, Douglas | McTAVISH, Duncan  McTAVISH, Marla  (j.t.) | All lot 11 |

- ○ SFCA
- ○ DEA/EAA
- ○ SFMA
- ○ GRANT
  - ○ FEE SIMPLE
  - ○ JT
  - ○ TEN IN COMMON
  - ○ TO USES
  - ○ AND APPOINT
- ○ HAB (as JT)
- ○ UC (4) (11)
- ○ REL
- ○ B OF DOWER (78/3/31)
- ○ SP CONSENT & REL

- ○ S & SW
- ○ CORP SEAL
- ○ ONT SUC DUTY (70/1/10–79/4/10)
- ○ A OF MM (54/4/30)
- ○ ONT. CO. (65/6/23)
- ○ OTHER (82/8/15)
- ○ LTT AFF (21/6/1)
- ○ AFF OF SUB. WIT.
- ○ PLANNING ACT CONSENT (67/6/1)
- ○ AFF RE: PLAN ACT
- ✓ STATE RE: PLAN. ACT (1 2 3)

- ○ AFF OF AGE (57/4/3)
- ✓ STATE RE: AGE (85/4/1)
- ○ AFF OF MAR. ST. (39/6/25–78/3/31)
- ○ AFF OF SP. ST. (78/3/31)
- ✓ STATE RE: SP. ST. (85/4/1)
  - SP/NOT A SP/SP OF EA OTH
  - NOT A MAT HOME
  - REL PER SEP AGMT
- ✓ TRANSFEREE(S) BIRTH DATE(S):
  - 1. Dec 1/48    2. Jan.18/55
- ○ AFF OF PARTNER PROP 1 2 3
- ○ DOCUMENT GENERAL/SCHEDULE

**Lawyer for 1st party:** Smith + Jones  202 Main St.  Whitford

**Lawyer for 2nd party:** Frank Milhouse  25 Wilson St.  Bakersville.

**NOTES:**

**Appendix Continued**

LOT 11  PLAN 1209   MUNICIPALITY Twp of Whitford Page 4 of 10

| Inst. No. | Inst. Type | Inst. Date | Reg. Date | Seller/Chargor | Buyer/Chargee | Desc. |
|-----------|-----------|-----------|-----------|----------------|---------------|-------|
| 148902 | Deposit | | Feb. 11/92 | Death Certificate of Duncan McTavish | | All lot 11 |

○ SFCA

○ DEA/EAA
○ SFMA

○ GRANT
  ○ FEE SIMPLE
  ○ JT
  ○ TEN IN COMMON
  ○ TO USES
  ○ AND APPOINT

○ HAB (as JT)

○ UC (4) (1)

○ REL

○ B OF DOWER (78/3/31)

○ SP CONSENT & REL

○ S & SW

○ CORP SEAL

○ ONT SUC DUTY (70/1/10-79/4/10)

○ A OF MM (54/4/30)
  ONT. CO. (65/6/23)
  OTHER (82/6/15)

○ LTT AFF (21/6/1)

○ AFF OF SUB. WIT.

○ PLANNING ACT CONSENT (67/6/1)

○ AFF RE: PLAN. ACT

○ STATE RE: PLAN. ACT 1 2 3

○ AFF OF AGE (57/4/3)

○ STATE RE: AGE (65/4/1)

○ AFF OF MAR. ST. (39/6/23-78/3/31)

○ AFF OF SP. ST. (78/3/31)

○ STATE RE: SP. ST. (85/4/1)
  ○ SP/NOT A SP/SP OF EA OTH
  ○ NOT A MAT HOME
  ○ REL PER SEP AGMT

○ TRANSFEREE(S) BIRTH DATE(S):

  1._____ 2._____

○ AFF OF PARTNER PROP 1 2 3

✓ DOCUMENT GENERAL/SCHEDULE

Lawyer for 1st party: Frank Milhouse
25 Wilson St.
Bakersville.

Lawyer for 2nd party:

NOTES: Died Nov. 22/91

**Appendix   Continued**

LOT 11   PLAN 1209      MUNICIPALITY Twp. of Whitfield   Page 5 of 10

| Inst. No. | Inst. Type | Inst. Date | Reg. Date | Seller/Chargor | Buyer/Chargee | Desc. |
|---|---|---|---|---|---|---|
| 153117 | Deed | Apr. 29/92 | May 2/92 | M<sup>ac</sup>TAVISH, Marla | BOND, Frederick COULTER, Suzanne | All lot 11 |

○  SFCA

○  DEA/EAA
○  SFMA

○  GRANT
   ○  FEE SIMPLE
   ○  JT
   ○  TEN IN COMMON
        TO USES
        AND APPOINT

○  HAB (as JT)

○  UC (4) (1)

○  REL

○  B OF DOWER (78/3/31)

○  SP CONSENT & REL

○  S & SW

○  CORP SEAL

○  ONT SUC DUTY (70/1/10-79/4/10)

○  A OF MM (54/4/30)
   ONT. CO. (65/6/23)
   OTHER (82/6/15)

○  LTT AFF (21/6/1)

○  AFF OF SUB. WIT.

○  PLANNING ACT CONSENT (67/6/1)

○  AFF RE. PLAN ACT

✓  STATE RE: PLAN. ACT ( 1 2 ③ )

○  AFF OF AGE (57/4/3)

✓  STATE RE: AGE (85/4/1)

○  AFF OF MAR. ST. (39/6/25-78/3/31)

○  AFF OF SP. ST. (78/3/31)

✓  STATE RE: SP. ST. (85/4/1)
   ☐  SP/NOT A SP/SP OF EA OTH
   ☐  NOT A MAT HOME
   ☐  REL PER SEP AGMT

✓  TRANSFEREE(S) BIRTH DATE(S):
   1. Mar. 20/60  2. May 29/63

○  AFF OF PARTNER PROP 1 2 3

○  DOCUMENT GENERAL/SCHEDULE

**Lawyer for 1<sup>st</sup> party:** Frank Milhouse
                                      25 Wilson St.
                                      Bakersville

**Lawyer for 2<sup>nd</sup> party:** Farb + Farb
                                      62 Drake Ave.
                                      Whitford

NOTES: Surname is M<sup>ac</sup>Tavish — took title as M<sup>c</sup>Tavish

O.K. — see Inst. No. 170003

**Appendix   Continued**

LOT 11   PLAN 1209   MUNICIPALITY Twp. of Whitford   Page 6 of 10

| Inst. No. | Inst. Type | Inst. Date | Reg. Date | Seller/Chargor | Buyer/Chargee | Desc. |
|---|---|---|---|---|---|---|
| 170003 | Deposit | Mar.1/97 | Mar.15/97 | Statutory Declaration by Marla McTavish | | |

- SFCA
- DEA/EAA
- SFMA
- GRANT
  - FEE SIMPLE
  - JT
  - TEN IN COMMON
  - TO USES
  - AND APPOINT
- HAB (as JT)
- UC (4) (1))
- REL
- B OF DOWER (78/3/31)
- SP CONSENT & REL

- S & SW
- CORP SEAL
- ONT SUC DUTY (70/1/10-79/4/10)
- A OF MM (54/4/30)
- ONT. CO. (65/6/23)
- OTHER (82/6/15)
- LTT AFF (21/6/1)
- AFF OF SUB. WIT.
- PLANNING ACT CONSENT (67/6/1)
- AFF RE: PLAN. ACT
- STATE RE: PLAN. ACT 1 2 3

- AFF OF AGE (57/4/3)
- STATE RE: AGE (85/4/1)
- AFF OF MAR. ST. (39/6/25-78/3/31)
- AFF OF SP. ST.(78/3/31)
- STATE RE: SP. ST. (85/4/1)
  - SP/NOT A SP/SP OF EA OTH
  - NOT A MAT HOME
  - REL PER SEP AGMT
- TRANSFEREE(S) BIRTH DATE(S):
  1 _____  2 _____
- AFF OF PARTNER PROP 1 2 3
- DOCUMENT GENERAL/SCHEDULE

**Lawyer for 1st party:** Frank Milhouse 25 Wilson St. Bakersville.

**Lawyer for 2nd party:**

NOTES: One + same person as Marla MacTavish in Inst. No 153117 and Marla McTavish in Inst. No. 91764

**Appendix Continued**

LOT 11 PLAN 1209 MUNICIPALITY Twp. of Whitford Page 7 of 10

| Inst. No. | Inst. Type | Inst. Date | Reg. Date | Seller/Chargor | Buyer/Chargee | Desc. |
|---|---|---|---|---|---|---|
| 170004 | Deed | Mar.12/97 | Mar.15/97 | BOND, Frederick COULTER, Suzanne | BAKER, Murphy BAKER, Leslie (j.t.) | All lot 11 |

- ○ SFCA
- ○ DEA/EAA
  ○ SFMA
- ○ GRANT
  - FEE SIMPLE
  - JT
  - TEN IN COMMON
  - TO USES
  - AND APPOINT
- ○ HAB (as JT)
- ○ UC (4) (1)
- ○ REL
- ○ B OF DOWER (78/3/31)
- ○ SP CONSENT & REL

- ○ S & SW
- ○ CORP SEAL
- ○ ONT SUC DUTY (70/1/10-79/4/10)
- ○ A OF MM (54/4/30)
  ONT. CO. (65/6/23)
  OTHER (82/6/15)
- ○ LTT AFF (21/8/1)
- ○ AFF OF SUB. WIT.
- ○ PLANNING ACT CONSENT (67/6/1)
- ○ AFF RE: PLAN. ACT
- ✓ STATE RE: PLAN. ACT (1 2 3)

- ○ AFF OF AGE (57/1/3)
- ✓ STATE RE: AGE (85/4/1)
- ○ AFF OF MAR. ST. (39/6/25-78/3/31)
- ○ AFF OF SP. ST. (78/3/31)
- ✓ STATE RE: SP. ST. (85/4/1)
  - SP/NOT A SP/SP OF EA OTH
  - NOT A MAT HOME
  - REL PER SEP AGMT
- ✓ TRANSFEREE(S) BIRTH DATE(S): 1. June 4/62 2. Apr.28/63
- ○ AFF OF PARTNER PROP 1 2 3
- ○ DOCUMENT GENERAL/SCHEDULE

**Lawyer for 1st party:** Farb & Farb 62 Drake Ave Whitford

**Lawyer for 2nd party:** Smith, Jones + Avery 202 Main St. Whitford

NOTES:

**Appendix   Continued**

LOT 11   PLAN 1209   MUNICIPALITY Twp. of Whitford Page 8 of 10

| Inst. No. | Inst. Type | Inst. Date | Reg. Date | Seller/Chargor | Buyer/Chargee | Desc. |
|-----------|-----------|-----------|-----------|----------------|---------------|-------|
| 635120 | Deed | Aug.2/10 | Aug.5/10 | BAKER, Murphy BAKER, Leslie | ROMANO, Mario ROMANO, Graziella (J.T.) | All lot 11 |

○ SFCA

○ ○ DEA/EAA
○ SFMA

○ GRANT
  " FEE SIMPLE
  " JT
  " TEN IN COMMON
  " TO USES
  " AND APPOINT

○ HAB (as JT)

○ UC (4) (1)

○ REL

○ B OF DOWER (78/3/31)

○ SP CONSENT & REL

○ S & SW

○ CORP SEAL

○ ONT SUC DUTY (70/1/10–79/4/10)

○ A OF MM (54/4/30)
  ONT. CO. (656/23)
  OTHER (82/6/15)

○ LTT AFF (21/6/1)

○ AFF OF SUB. WIT.

○ PLANNING ACT CONSENT (67/6/1)

○ AFF RE: PLAN. ACT

✓ STATE RE: PLAN ACT (1) 2 3

○ AFF OF AGE (57/4/3)

✓ STATE RE: AGE (85/4/1)

○ AFF OF MAR. ST. (39/6/25–78/3/31)

○ AFF OF SP. ST. (78/3/31)

✓ STATE RE: SP. ST. (85/4/1)
  SP/NOT A SP/SP OF EA OTH
  " NOT A MAT HOME
  " REL PER SEP AGMT

✓ TRANSFEREE(S) BIRTH DATE(S):
  1. July 26/78  2. Mar. 14/80

○ AFF OF PARTNER PROP 1 2 3

○ DOCUMENT GENERAL/SCHEDULE

**Lawyer for 1st party:** Smith, Jones + Avery
202 Main St.
Whitford

**Lawyer for 2nd party:** Francesca Martino
59 Park Rd.
Whitford

**NOTES:**

**Appendix Continued**

LOT 11 PLAN 1209 MUNICIPALITY Twp of Whitford Page 9 of 10

| Inst. No. | Inst. Type | Inst. Date | Reg. Date | Seller/Chargor | Buyer/Chargee | Desc. |
|-----------|-----------|-----------|-----------|----------------|---------------|-------|
| 635121 | Mortg. | Aug.2/10 | Aug.5/10 | ROMANO, Mario ROMANO, Graziella (j.t.) | BANK OF MONTREAL | All lot 11 |

O/S

- ○ SFCA
- ○ ○ DEA/EAA
- ○ ○ SFMA
- ○ GRANT
  - ○ FEE SIMPLE
  - ○ JT
  - ○ TEN IN COMMON
  - ○ TO USES
  - ○ AND APPOINT
- ○ HAB (as JT)
- ○ UC (4) (1))
- ○ REL
- ○ B OF DOWER (78/3/31)
- ○ SP CONSENT & REL

- ○ S & SW
- ○ CORP SEAL
- ○ ONT SUC DUTY (70/1/10-79/4/10)
- ○ A OF MM (54/4/30)
  - ONT. CO. (65/6/23)
  - OTHER (82/6/15)
- ○ LTT AFF (21/6/1)
- ○ AFF OF SUB. WIT.
- ○ PLANNING ACT CONSENT (67/6/1)
- ○ AFF RE: PLAN. ACT
- ○ STATE RE: PLAN. ACT 1 2 3

- ○ AFF OF AGE (57/4/3)
- ✓ STATE RE: AGE (85/4/1)
- ○ AFF OF MAR. ST. (39/6/25-78/3/31)
- ○ AFF OF SP. ST.(78/3/31)
- ✓ STATE RE: SP. ST. (85/4/1)
  - SP/NOT A SP/SP OF EA OTH
  - NOT A MAT HOME
  - REL PER SEP AGMT
- ○ TRANSFEREE(S) BIRTH DATE(S):
  - 1._____  2._____
- ○ AFF OF PARTNER PROP 1 2 3
- ○ DOCUMENT GENERAL/SCHEDULE

**Lawyer for 1st party:** Francesca Martino
59 Park Rd.
Whitford

**Lawyer for 2nd party:**

NOTES: $320,000 @ 4.5% due Aug.5, 2015
Payable 1st monthly $2,020.00

**Appendix   Concluded**

LOT 11   PLAN 1209   MUNICIPALITY Twp. of Whitford Page 10 of 10

| Inst. No. | Inst. Type | Inst. Date | Reg. Date | Seller/Chargor | Buyer/Chargee | Desc. |
|---|---|---|---|---|---|---|
| 726341 | Mort. | Mar.21/13 | Mar.23/13 | ROMANO, Mario ROMANO, Graziella (j.t.) | XYZ Mortgage Ltd. | All lot 11. |

○ SFCA

○○ DEA/EAA
   SFMA

○ GRANT
   × FEE SIMPLE
   × JT
   × TEN IN COMMON
   × TO USES
   × AND APPOINT

✓ HAB (as JT)

○ UC (4) (1))

○ REL

○ B OF DOWER (78/3/31)

○ SP CONSENT & REL

○ S & SW

○ CORP SEAL

○ ONT SUC DUTY (70/1/10-79/4/10)

○ A OF MM (54/4/30)
   ONT. CO. (65/6/23)
   OTHER (82/6/15)

✓ LTT AFF (21/6/11)

○ AFF OF SUB. WIT.

✓ PLANNING ACT CONSENT (67/6/11)

○ AFF RE: PLAN ACT

○ STATE RE: PLAN ACT 1 2 3

✓ AFF OF AGE (57/4/3)

✓ STATE RE: AGE (85/4/1)

○ AFF OF MAR. ST. (39/6/25-78/3/31)

○ AFF OF SP. ST. (78/3/31)

✓ STATE RE: SP. ST. (85/4/1)
   ✗ SP/NOT A SP/SP OF EA OTH
   ✗ NOT A MAT HOME
   ✗ REL PER SEP AGMT

○ TRANSFEREE(S) BIRTH DATE(S):
   1. _____
   2. _____

○ AFF OF PARTNER PROP 1 2 3

○ DOCUMENT GENERAL/SCHEDULE

O/S

**Lawyer for 1st party:** Francesca Martino
59 Park Rd.
Whitford

**Lawyer for 2nd party:**

**NOTES:** $15,000 @ 9% due Mar.23, 2016
Payable 1st monthly $189.00

# PART III

# The Standard Residential Real Estate Transaction

# Opening and Organizing a Real Estate File

# 15

## LEARNING OUTCOMES

After reading this chapter, you will understand:

- How to open a file

- How to create a docket in Teraview

- The importance of diarizing dates

- How to organize a file

- The purpose of a checklist

# Introduction

When opening a real estate file, you should focus on organizing the file and recording deadlines. The general principles and concerns discussed in this chapter apply in all law firms, although the specific procedures will vary from office to office.

# File Opening

open a file

start a file

Whenever a lawyer or law firm is retained to act on a matter, a file is **opened**, or started. A single client may retain a law firm to act on several different matters. There should be a separate file opened for each matter. As a law clerk, you will probably open the file.

There are a number of steps involved in opening a file. At the end, there will be a physical file in existence for keeping the relevant documents and correspondence relating to the matter. The existence of the file will be noted in various law firm records.

You must assign a name to the file. Although the procedure will vary from office to office, usually the name of the file is made up of the client's name—family name first—with a "Re:" line stating the matter to which the file relates. For example, if Harold Smith is buying a property at 123 Elm Street, Toronto, his file might be named: Smith, Harold, Re: Purchase of 123 Elm Street, Toronto.

You must make a record of the file in the law firm's general index of files. This may be accomplished manually or by computer. Usually a number is assigned to the file as well. Each lawyer or law firm has a system for assigning file numbers. Make sure there is a record of the file in the law firm's accounting system so that fees, disbursements, and moneys received with respect to the file will be accounted for.

Use a file folder to hold the documents and correspondence relating to the matter. Some law firms use specially designed real estate file folders that have checklists printed on them. Other firms use different coloured file folders for different types of files. Place a label on the folder setting out the file name and number. Note the names, addresses, and telephone numbers of the client, the other lawyer, and other relevant parties on the file folder where the information will be easy to find. Some firms have labels or other printed forms they use for recording this information.

# Creating a Docket in Teraview

As stated in Chapter 7, most law firms have the Teraview software, required to use the electronic registration system. In order to use Teraview for the transaction you must create a docket.

A docket is created by choosing "Administration" and then "Create Docket" from the top toolbar. The user then assigns an "ID" and a "Name" to the new docket, usually the law firm's internal file number for that transaction file and the client's name. For example, assume that our law firm is acting for Henry Albert Grant and Wilma Heather Grant, who are buying a property from Francois Mercier and Huguette Marie Mercier, and the law firm's internal file number is 15-3355. The ID would be

15-3355 and the name would be "GRANT," or "GRANT PURCHASE FROM MER-CIER" (or "GRANT P/F MERCIER" for short). See Figure 15.1.

**Figure 15.1    New Docket**

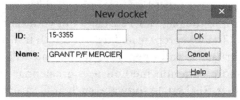

All documents associated with the client's file (such as a transfer and a charge) are located in the docket. The docket also lists all disbursements incurred on the file, including the government's fees for registering documents and obtaining execution certificates, and Teraview's fees for electronic title searching. You can find the disbursements by checking "Docket Summary" (found in the "Administration" tab). See Figure 15.2.

**Figure 15.2    Docket Summary**

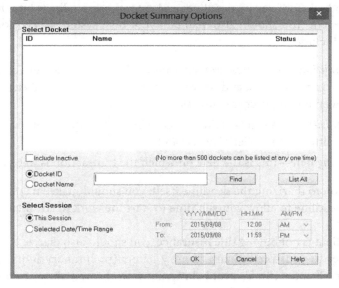

The docket summary is a very useful tool when it comes time to bill the client, and it ensures that all Teraview disbursements are captured and billed. The docket summary is discussed in greater detail in Chapter 7.

# Diarizing

In every real estate file, there will be a number of deadlines that you must not miss, including the requisition date and the closing date. These dates must be diarized. **Diarizing** is a way of reminding you and the lawyer of the dates by which work must

**diarize**
record on a calendar the dates by which work must be completed

be completed. Diarizing is done well before the deadline, so that when the date in question approaches, you can ensure that the work will be performed by that date.

There are various methods of diarizing. The simplest method uses a standard desk or pocket diary. Let's say that you are reviewing a file on January 2 and note that an important document must be prepared and delivered by February 1. You will, on January 2, turn to the page for February 1 in your diary and make an entry on that page, such as "To Do—prepare and deliver Smith transfer." When you arrive at your office on February 1 and open your diary, you will be reminded of that deadline. Another, more common method uses a calendar program installed on your personal computer. Real estate software, such as Conveyancer, also provides a calendar reminder system. When the program is opened, a calendar will appear highlighting upcoming relevant dates.

Whatever diarizing method you use, the method will work only for those dates and tasks you enter into the diarizing system. Give top priority to determining the relevant deadlines in any file and to entering those dates into the system. Failure to meet requisite deadlines may result in professional negligence claims being made against the law firm, and failure to diarize the relevant dates may result in a denial of coverage under the law firm's errors and omissions insurance policy.

Accordingly, as soon as you open the file, you should review the agreement of purchase and sale for relevant deadlines and enter those deadlines into the law firm's diarizing system. You should also maintain your own system as a backup. Dates to be diarized include

- *any condition dates*—these are dates until which the agreement of purchase and sale is conditional, and by which steps may have to be taken to firm up the agreement of purchase and sale;
- *the requisition date*—this is the date by which any requisitions on title must be submitted to the seller's lawyer; and
- *the closing date*—this is the date on which the transaction is to be completed.

In addition to diarizing the deadline itself, you should make an entry some time before the deadline to allow yourself time to start the work in advance of the actual deadline.

If your client is not buying title insurance, you should also diarize a date to check on responses to your preliminary inquiry letters (preliminary inquiry letters are discussed in Chapter 18). To avoid cluttering your diary, make one entry for all of the letters relating to a file. Let's say that on January 2 you write to the tax office, the building department, the gas company, the water department, and hydro. You can reasonably expect responses within three weeks. You should make an entry in your diarizing system for January 23, such as "Smith file—awaiting letter responses." When you check your diary on January 23, you will be reminded that you should have received responses to your letters. You will then check the Smith file and call or write to the offices that have not responded to your letters.

*Do not forget to check your diary daily.*

# File Organization

There are many different kinds of documents in a real estate file. There are letters to and from your law firm (correspondence), title searches, and various other documents. You should organize the file in such a way that the different types of documents are kept separately and can be easily identified and located.

Keep correspondence separately, either clipped together or in a separate subfile. Unless the instructing lawyer specifically requires otherwise, file both incoming and outgoing correspondence together in reverse-chronological order—that is, the oldest correspondence is at the bottom and the newest is at the top. Make a copy of every letter that is sent by the law firm, and place the copies in the file together with the original response letters.

Make notes of any telephone or other conversations, and keep these notes in the file. Some lawyers maintain a separate subfile for notes; others file notes in reverse-chronological order along with the correspondence.

Set up and label separate subfiles to hold

- all title and other search documents;
- closing documentation; and
- any mortgage documentation.

Finally, insert the agreement of purchase and sale in the file in an easily accessible location. Many lawyers attach the agreement to the inside back cover of the file folder.

# Checklists

Use a checklist in every real estate file. This is a list of the various things that must be prepared, requested, or received in a real estate file and serves as a quick way of ascertaining what is outstanding on the file at any given time. Whenever you perform a task or receive a document, make a notation on the checklist. When you want to confirm whether a document has been received, you simply look at the checklist—you will not have to search through the entire file.

If there is no checklist on the file folder itself, you should use the one in general use in the law firm, or prepare one and attach it to the inside front cover of the file. There are a lot of documents and steps to keep track of in a real estate transaction. If you do not use a checklist, you may neglect something until it is too late. Figure 15.3 is an example of a checklist for use in a purchase transaction.

### Figure 15.3   Purchase Checklist

❑ Letter to client & checklist:  Fee $ _____   Fee mrtg. $ _____   LTT _____

❑ Letter to seller's lawyer

❑ Order search from _____   Date ordered: _____

❑ Receive & review search

    ❑ Executions         OK _____   Declaration? _____

    ❑ Acknowledgment & direction for registration of transfer/deed — OR — LTT affidavit

❑ Letters to bldg./planning dept re: work orders, zoning, occupancy permits, set-backs, dev/subd. agt/heritage (if not ttl ins.)

❑ Receive & review complete (if e-reg) draft transfer

❑ Order tax certificate — ask re: local improvements, weed removal, drainage act, etc.

    ❑ Survey: Send to client              ❑ Check for encroachments, access, etc.

❑ Requisition letter                  Req. date: _____

    ❑ Title direction

    ❑ Undertaking/warranty/bill of sale: insert extra warranties as in offer

    ❑ Statutory declaration: refer to restrictions and/or compliance with agreements registered on title, etc.

❑ LSUC form of e-reg agreement: sign & send to seller's lawyer

❑ Title insurance acknowledgment: add in reference to title matters, e.g., easements, noise controls, restrictive covenants, etc.

❑ Review statement of adjustments: check accuracy of figures

    ❑ REALTY TAXES:  get copy of current tax bill — check if installments paid

❑ If property less than 2 years old, get holdback for supplemental tax assessment

❑ Utilities:  Water arrears o/s _____   Hydro arrears (if not privatized) o/s _____

    ❑ Estimated account prepared & sent         Funds reqd. $ _____

    ❑ Discharge statement              ❑ Redirection re: funds

    ❑ Undertaking to discharge signed by lawyer

❑ Closing letter to lawyer enclosing $ and documents  ❑  KEYS: to be held or delivered

❑ Closing memo to agent       ❑  LTT & reg'n transferred to spec. trust acct or sent to agent

❑ Tax department advised of change of ownership

❑ Complete & send title insurance

MORTGAGE                          Mortgagee _____

❑ Request agent to prepare mortgage

❑ Acknowledgment & direction for registration of mortgage

❑ Interim report to mortgage & request for funds _____
NET ADVANCE $ _____

❑ Acknowledgment standard charge terms [attach copy of SCT]

❑ Acknowledgment I act for all parties

❑ Insurance binder: check names, address, amount, mortgagee's name & address & if full insurable value

❑ Direction to pay funds (if required)

❑ Declaration (if required) re: principal residence, no secondary financing

❑ ID: get photocopy

❑ PAC form & VOID cheque (if required)

❑ Final report & cover letter

    ❑ Report to client & statement of account

UNDERTAKINGS completed [list on file cover]

❑ Discharge of 1st mortgage _____

❑ Proof of payment of _____

## KEY TERMS

diarize, 201
open a file, 200

## REVIEW QUESTIONS

1.  What are the steps involved in opening a file?

2.  How do you create a docket in Teraview?

3.  What is the purpose of diarizing?

4.  List and describe three dates to be diarized on the opening of a real estate purchase file.

5.  Briefly describe how a real estate file should be organized.

6.  What is the purpose of a checklist, and how is it used?

# Reviewing the Agreement of Purchase and Sale

# 16

## LEARNING OUTCOMES

After reading this chapter, you will understand:

- The importance of the preprinted clauses contained in an agreement of purchase and sale

- The types of additional clauses that may be inserted in an agreement of purchase and sale

- The significance of the various dates in an agreement of purchase and sale

- How to review an agreement of purchase and sale

- Special terms that can be added as part of a schedule to an agreement of purchase and sale

# Introduction

The agreement of purchase and sale is the document on which the entire real estate transaction is based. This chapter reviews the agreement of purchase and sale from your perspective as a law clerk who has received a fully executed agreement. It contains a clause-by-clause examination of the standard form of agreement and sale, and discusses particular items of importance, together with the steps you should take as you go through the agreement.

Most resale property transactions in Ontario are prepared on the Ontario Real Estate Association (OREA) form of agreement of purchase and sale. A copy of this form is reproduced as Figure 16.1 at the end of the chapter. (A different version of the form, used for condominium resale transactions, is reproduced as Figure 26.1.) Once you become familiar with the standard form of agreement and sale, you will review each executed agreement only for changes to the printed form and for terms set out in the schedules attached to the agreement.

# The Parties

**seller**
vendor of the property

The parties to the agreement of purchase and sale are the **seller** and the **buyer**. Some lawyers still refer to the seller as the vendor and the buyer as the purchaser. However, since the OREA form refers to buyer and seller, we use those terms in this text.

**buyer**
purchaser of the property

Different steps are required depending on which party your firm represents.

## The Seller

When you receive the completed search of title for review, you should make sure that the person named as the seller in the agreement of purchase and sale is, in fact, the registered owner of the property.

If the seller is not the registered owner, there could be complications in the transaction. For example, if the person named as the seller in the agreement of purchase and sale is a different person from the registered owner shown in the search of title, you must get a transfer on closing from the registered owner (rather than the seller) to the buyer. This situation might arise in the case of a new subdivision, where the land is still registered in the name of the developer rather than the builder, or in the case of a **flip**, where the property is purchased by a party and resold before the closing of the original purchase. New home purchases are discussed in more detail in Chapter 25.

**flip**
resale of property before the closing of the original purchase

If the seller is a corporation, you must check its corporate status. Also, you will require supporting corporate documentation on or before closing to ensure that the corporation has the proper authority to sell the property and that an authorized person has signed the agreement.

If the seller is a partnership, you must find out the names of all partners because if the sale is outside the normal course of business, all partners must sign the transfer.

If the seller is an estate, there are very particular conveyancing requirements to be met.

## The Buyer

Note the way the buyer is named in the agreement of purchase and sale. If the buyer wishes to take title in any other way, you must give the seller's lawyer a direction to that effect before the seller will give you a transfer made out in that way. For example, a direction will be necessary if only the wife signed the agreement but wishes to take title with her husband as joint tenants. If your law firm is acting for the buyer, you will have to prepare the direction. If your law firm is acting for the seller, you will have to make sure that you get a direction from the buyer on closing.

# Description of the Property

Usually the property description line of the agreement of purchase and sale contains a municipal address, followed by the dimensions of the lot and a brief description.

For search of title and registration purposes, it is easiest to start with the PIN (property identifier number). This can be obtained through Teraview.

If the property is subject to any easements (for example, a mutual driveway or an easement for repair and access), overhanging eaves, or other encroachments, they should be set out in the agreement. If any easements are specified, the buyer must accept title subject to them. If none are specified here, the buyer is not required to accept title subject to any easement subsequently disclosed on a search of title (other than minor easements for utilities and sewers). If an easement that is not mentioned in the agreement turns up on the title search, the lawyer will have to contact the client to determine whether title will be accepted subject to the easement. If the easement in question is minor, the client will often choose to close the transaction, but instructions from the client must be obtained.

If the property is part of a lot, compare the lot size as set out in the agreement of purchase and sale with the description in the last transfer of land to the property. If the property is a whole lot, compare it to the dimensions shown on the whiteprint of the plan of subdivision. Also, compare the lot size as set out in the agreement with the size of the lot as set out on any plan of survey.

With respect to plans of survey, the standard form agreement of purchase and sale requires an existing survey to be provided only if it is in the seller's possession. As soon as you receive the agreement, if there is no plan of survey attached to it, you should contact the seller's solicitor to request a copy of any survey. If the client is purchasing title insurance, an up-to-date survey is not essential, and it will not be a problem if the seller does not have a survey or does have a survey but it is not up to date. If the client is not purchasing title insurance, the lawyer and the client should discuss getting a new survey.

If the survey, the deed, or the whiteprint discloses any variation in size that is significantly different from that set out in the agreement of purchase and sale, you must immediately point this out so that the lawyer handling the file can contact the client for instructions.

# Purchase Price

The amount of money shown in this part of the agreement of purchase and sale is not the amount that will actually have to be paid by the buyer on closing. The final amount is calculated in the statement of adjustments (discussed in Chapter 21), but the purchase price is the starting point for that calculation. Mortgages assumed are deducted from the purchase price, as is any deposit paid. Other items are adjusted as well. It is the adjusted amount that the buyer must actually pay on closing.

The purchase price set out in the agreement is the amount on which land transfer tax is calculated.

# Deposit

The deposit may be paid by the buyer on presentation of the offer or upon acceptance of the offer. It is generally paid to the seller's real estate broker (the listing broker) to be held in trust pending completion of the agreement. It is then applied to the broker's commission on the transaction following closing.

Some agreements contain an added term that requires interest to be paid on the deposit. The usual provision requires the seller's broker to place the deposit into an interest-bearing account with interest being paid or credited to the buyer on or after closing. If there is such a provision in the agreement, make a note to ensure that the buyer receives the interest on or after closing.

This paragraph ends with a statement that the buyer agrees to pay the balance of the purchase price as set out in Schedule A, which is attached to the agreement. Schedule A usually contains a clause providing that the buyer will pay the balance, subject to adjustments, on completion, by bank draft, certified cheque, or wire transfer using the **Large Value Transfer System**, an electronic wire payment system, available in Canada, which allows for the transfer of large sums between participating financial institutions.

**Large Value Transfer System**
electronic wire payment system which allows for the transfer of large sums between financial institutions

# Special Terms

Following the above provision, there is a line indicating which schedule or schedules are attached. In the schedules, "customized" terms may be inserted into the agreement. Examples of such terms include:

- *Mortgages to be assumed.* Particulars of the mortgage will be set out. When you get the search of title, check to make sure that it shows a mortgage that complies with those particulars. All other mortgages must be discharged on or before closing.

- *Conditions.* The agreement of purchase and sale may be conditional until a specified date on the happening of various events such as financing, inspections, or municipal approval. Any condition date should be diarized because, depending on the condition, some action may have to be taken. If the agreement is conditional, the client will not wish to incur the expense of a title search until the agreement becomes binding.

- *Rights of inspection.*  Some agreements provide the buyer with the right to inspect the condition of the property or obtain measurements on one or more occasions before closing.
- *Survey.*  The seller may have agreed to provide an up-to-date survey.
- *Tenancies.*  If the buyer is assuming any tenancies, the details will be provided here, and you will require supporting documentation on closing.
- *Warranties.*  If the seller is making a specific warranty, such as one concerning the state of a well or septic system on a rural property, it should be set out here. Similarly, there may be warranties regarding the working order of any chattels and fixtures.

# Standard Terms

## Irrevocability (Paragraph 1)

This paragraph sets out the length of time the offer is open for acceptance by the offeree. Once the offer is accepted, this paragraph has no relevance.

## Completion Date (Paragraph 2)

The completion date is the day fixed for closing. You should make sure that the date is not a Saturday, Sunday, or statutory holiday. If it is, you must make arrangements with the other side to change the closing date. Any change to the closing date must be *confirmed in writing*.

Diarize the closing date. It is also a good idea to diarize a date approximately one week in advance of closing as a reminder to have the file ready for that date.

This paragraph states that the agreement is to be completed by no later than 6 p.m. and also states that, unless the agreement provides otherwise, **vacant possession** of the property is to be given to the buyer on closing. Vacant possession will not be provided if the property is a rental property and the premises are tenant-occupied. In this case, you will have to prepare additional documents to deal with the tenancies on closing.

**vacant possession**
free or empty of all
people and chattels

## Notices (Paragraph 3)

This paragraph deals with delivery of any notices under the agreement. The seller appoints the listing brokerage as agent for the purpose of giving and receiving notices. The buyer appoints the buyer's brokerage if the buyer has entered into a representation agreement with a brokerage. If both the buyer and seller are represented by the same brokerage, the brokerage will not be appointed as agent for the purpose of giving and receiving notices. Also, notice is deemed to be properly given, and the signatures considered original, if it is delivered to the address for service that the parties provide in the Acknowledgement section of the agreement or if it is transmitted electronically to the fax number or email address provided by the parties.

## Chattels Included (Paragraph 4)

**chattels**
movable possessions not attached to the real property

If **chattels** (movable possessions such as appliances and draperies) are included in the purchase price, they will be specified in this paragraph. Where chattels are listed, the buyer will have to allocate a value to them for the purpose of **land transfer tax** and **harmonized sales tax** calculations. The seller agrees that there will be no liens or encumbrances on any of the fixtures or listed chattels, unless specifically stated in the agreement.

**land transfer tax**
provincial (and possibly municipal) tax on the purchase of land

## Fixtures Excluded (Paragraph 5)

**harmonized sales tax (HST)**
blended federal and provincial sales tax

**Fixtures**, such as broadloom and interior doors, are automatically included in the sale of a house. However, sometimes a seller will want the right to take certain fixtures out of the house (for example, a dining room chandelier). In order for the seller to do so, those fixtures must be listed in this paragraph.

**fixtures**
immovable possessions attached to the real property, or chattels that have become attached or affixed to the real property

## Rental Items (Paragraph 6)

In order to avoid any confusion, equipment that is rented (for example, a hot water heater), and therefore not included in the purchase, is set out in this paragraph.

## HST (Paragraph 7)

This paragraph states whether harmonized sales tax (HST) is included in the purchase price or to be paid in addition to the purchase price. If the transaction is not subject to HST, the seller agrees to certify that fact.

## Title Search (Paragraph 8)

**title requisition**
request made to the seller to clear up a problem found during the search of title

This paragraph sets out the date by which the buyer (through his or her lawyer) must complete the title search and submit any **title requisitions** to the seller (through his or her lawyer). Requisitions are requests to clear up problems found with the title during the title search. This deadline is called the **requisition date**, and most title requisitions must be received by the seller by that date. If a requisition is received by the seller on or before the requisition date and the seller cannot properly answer it, the buyer may be able to negotiate a reduction in the purchase price or back out of the contract. If a requisition is received by the seller after the requisition date, the buyer may not have the right to insist on its satisfaction or resolution before closing.

**requisition date**
deadline by which the buyer must submit any title requisitions to the seller

There are different types of title requisitions. Some may be submitted until closing, while others must be submitted by the requisition date. Requisitions relating to matters of contract, matters of conveyance, and matters going to the root of title may be submitted until closing. Requisitions on matters of title not going to the root of title must be submitted by the requisition date. The distinctions between the various types of requisitions are far from clear. The most prudent course is therefore to have all of your title requisitions delivered by the requisition date. For a further discussion of title requisitions, see Chapter 19, Requisitions: An Overview, and Chapter 20, The Requisition Letter.

The buyer is given a longer period of time to submit requisitions with respect to work orders, zoning, and the insurability of the principal building. This is because there is usually a long wait to receive an answer to zoning and work order inquiries from municipal building departments. The agreement also gives the seller's consent to the release of this information. However, if the buyer is purchasing title insurance, no inquiries will be made to municipal building departments, and the extended date is irrelevant.

When you receive the agreement of purchase and sale, check the requisition date. If it is too soon after a condition date, the lawyer for the buyer may wish to have the requisition date extended to have more time to complete the search of title. Any extension of the requisition date must be agreed to by the seller and *confirmed in writing*.

Diarize the requisition date. Also make a diary entry for approximately one week before to ensure that the requisitions will be ready on time. Requisitions must be *received* by the seller on or before the requisition date, so it is not a good idea to mail the requisition letter. It is common practice to transmit the requisition letter electronically or to have it delivered by courier. If the requisition date is a weekend or holiday, the requisitions must be in the hands of the seller's lawyer *before* that date. The time period is not extended to the next business day.

## Future Use (Paragraph 9)

The previous paragraph also contains a promise that the current use of the property may be lawfully continued. This paragraph makes it clear that there is no promise that any other intended use of the property is lawful, unless the agreement specifically states that it is. If the buyer wishes to purchase the property only if it can be put to a specific use, the agreement should be stated to be conditional on that use being lawful.

## Title (Paragraph 10)

In this paragraph, the seller agrees that title is free from all encumbrances, registered restrictions, charges, and liens except:

- *As specified in the agreement of purchase and sale.* This exception would include such things as mortgages to be assumed, easements, encroachments, and so on that are specifically dealt with elsewhere in the agreement.

- *Registered restrictions that run with the land provided that such are complied with.* If any registered restrictions (also called restrictive covenants) are found during the search of title, the buyer cannot insist that they be removed from title, *provided that they have been complied with*. Accordingly, if the search discloses such restrictions, you will have to requisition proof that the restrictions have been complied with. Usually this proof takes the form of a statutory declaration or undertaking.

- *Any registered municipal agreements and registered agreements with publicly regulated utilities, provided that such have been complied with or security has been posted to ensure compliance and completion, as evidenced by a letter from the relevant municipality or regulated utility.* This exception refers to subdivision agreements. The buyer cannot insist that any of these agreements be discharged, but can only require proof of compliance or posting of security.

- *Minor easements for the supply of domestic utility or telephone services to the property or adjacent properties.* The buyer cannot object to the existence of easements that include telephone and electrical lines and sewers servicing the property and adjoining properties. This exception covers minor easements only—not hydro towers or trunk sewer lines.

- *Any easements for drainage, storm, or sanitary sewers, public utility lines, telephone lines, cable television lines, or other services that do not materially affect the present use of the property.* This exception prevents the buyer from demanding the removal of any easement for the provision of services that does not have a major impact on the present use of the property.

The paragraph goes on to describe what happens if the buyer raises an objection to the title that the seller cannot or will not correct. If the buyer makes a valid objection to the title within the requisition period that the seller cannot or will not remove, and the buyer will not waive, the agreement ends. The buyer is entitled to receive the return of the deposit but no **damages** (compensation) in addition.

**damages**
financial compensation for losses arising out of a breach of contract

The paragraph concludes by stating the effect of failing to submit a title requisition on time: unless the defect is a matter going to the root of title, the buyer is deemed to have accepted title subject to the defect. In other words, the buyer must accept title subject to any defects (other than matters going to the root of title) that were not objected to in time.

## Closing Arrangements (Paragraph 11)

This paragraph describes how the closing of the transaction will take place if it is to be done electronically. With electronic registration, the actual exchange of documents, keys, and money does not take place at the same time as the registration of the transfer. The parties agree that their lawyers will enter into a document registration agreement (DRA), or will agree to be bound by a DRA, in a form recommended by the Law Society of Upper Canada. This agreement sets out the terms of the closing.

If closing is not to be done electronically, it will take place at the appropriate land registry office.

## Documents and Discharge (Paragraph 12)

This paragraph provides that the seller is not required to produce any title documents, including a survey, unless they are within the seller's possession or control. Any survey in the seller's possession must be delivered, if requested by the buyer, as soon as possible and before the requisition date.

**institutional lender**
lender other than an individual, including a bank, trust company, credit union, or insurance company

This paragraph also deals with mortgages that are supposed to be discharged on closing. If the mortgagee is an **institutional lender** (a chartered bank, trust company, credit union, or insurance company), the buyer cannot insist that a discharge of the mortgage be registered on or before closing. If the discharge is not available in time for closing, the buyer agrees to accept the seller's solicitor's ***personal* undertaking** (discussed in Chapter 22) to obtain a discharge out of the closing funds and register the discharge within a reasonable time after closing, provided that the seller also gives the buyer

- a mortgage statement prepared by the mortgagee setting out the amount that is required to pay off the mortgage and get the discharge; and
- a direction to pay out of the closing funds the required amount directly to the mortgagee if the lawyers are not using a real-time electronic funds transfer system.

This provision is necessary because in most cases the seller will not be able to obtain a discharge of mortgage from an institutional lender in time for the closing. An institutional lender will not usually prepare a discharge of mortgage until it has actually received the discharge funds. Without this provision in the agreement of purchase and sale, the buyer does not have to accept an undertaking from the seller to discharge the mortgage, and the seller would have to have a discharge of mortgage available on closing.

If a seller is seeking to rely on the provisions of this paragraph, the seller's lawyer must, on closing, give the buyer's lawyer a direction with regard to funds, a mortgage statement, and a solicitor's personal undertaking.

This provision applies only to institutional mortgages. It does not apply to a mortgage with a private lender. Accordingly, if there is a private mortgage on title that is not being assumed by the buyer, the seller must have a discharge of that mortgage available on closing. This can put the seller in a very difficult position because the seller must discharge the mortgage in order to complete the sale but needs the money from the sale to discharge the mortgage. If your law firm is acting for a seller, and you find that there is a private mortgage on title that is not being assumed by the buyer, you will have to take special steps to make sure that the seller is in a position to provide proper title on closing.

In an electronic closing, the seller's lawyer contacts the lawyer for the private mortgagee to obtain a discharge statement. The seller's lawyer then gives a direction to the buyer's lawyer to pay directly to the mortgagee, out of the closing funds, the required amount. The lawyer for the private mortgagee will have his or her client sign an acknowledgment and direction for the discharge and agree to the registration of the discharge once the lawyer for the seller confirms that he or she has the closing proceeds in his or her possession, with the mortgage amount payable to the private lender. This confirmation is usually done by faxing to the lawyer for the private lender a copy of the certified cheque payable to the private lender. The lawyer for the seller will also give his or her personal undertaking to forward the money to the mortgagee's lawyer immediately following the closing.

In the paper system, the lawyer for the private lender will either arrange to meet the lawyers for the buyer and the seller at the land registry office, or give the discharge to the seller's lawyer to be held **in escrow** pending receipt of the discharge funds from the closing proceeds.

**personal undertaking**
a written promise given by a lawyer that is binding on the lawyer personally

**in escrow**
holding of funds or documents by a third party to be released only on certain specified conditions

There will be some mortgagees, however, who will refuse to prepare a discharge until they actually have the discharge funds. In such a case, if the seller wishes to be in a position to close the transaction, he or she will have to borrow the funds required to discharge the mortgage and repay the loan out of the proceeds of sale.

## Inspection (Paragraph 13)

In the first part of this paragraph, the buyer acknowledges having had the opportunity to inspect the property before submitting the offer, and that acceptance by the seller constitutes a binding agreement of purchase and sale. The buyer may believe that he or she was misled and may allege non-disclosure or misrepresentation, but the success of such an allegation will depend on the extent to which the buyer relied on the non-disclosure or misrepresentation. Where the matter could have been easily discovered on an inspection, this clause serves as evidence that the buyer, in fact, had the chance to inspect the property. This clause is also relied upon by the seller in a situation where the property is smaller than stated in the agreement, but the lot is fully fenced and the boundaries are apparent on examination of the property.

In the latter part of this paragraph, the buyer acknowledges having had the opportunity to include a requirement for a building inspector to examine the property, and acknowledges having waived that right (unless there is an added clause in a schedule allowing for an inspection).

## Insurance (Paragraph 14)

This paragraph states that the buildings remain at the risk of the seller until closing. This means that any loss prior to the closing date would be the seller's, not the buyer's. It is up to the seller to maintain any insurance on the property. If the buildings are substantially damaged before closing, the seller holds any insurance proceeds in trust for the buyer. The buyer has a choice: to terminate the agreement and receive a refund of the deposit, or to take the insurance proceeds and close the transaction.

This paragraph also states that the seller's insurance will not be transferred to the buyer on closing. It is up to the buyer to obtain a new insurance policy. If the buyer is assuming a mortgage or if the seller is taking back a mortgage, the buyer must give the seller proof that there is enough insurance to cover the mortgage. If the buyer is arranging a new mortgage, the buyer must give the mortgagee proof that there is enough insurance to cover the new mortgage. Even if there is no mortgage, the buyer's lawyer should always advise the buyer to arrange insurance on the premises to take effect as of the closing date. Send a letter to the buyer confirming this advice.

## Planning Act (Paragraph 15)

This paragraph provides that the agreement creates an interest in the property only if the *Planning Act* is complied with. The agreement is void if there was a contravention of the *Planning Act*. The seller also agrees to proceed diligently and pay any expenses involved in obtaining any necessary *Planning Act* consent by the closing date.

## Document Preparation (Paragraph 16)

The seller is responsible for the preparation of the transfer, with the exception of the land transfer tax affidavit, which must be prepared in registerable form at the buyer's expense. The buyer is responsible for the preparation of any mortgage back to the seller. If the buyer requests it, the seller must complete the *Planning Act* statements contained in the transfer.

## Residency (Paragraph 17)

When non-residents of Canada sell real property, the government requires them to make immediate arrangements to pay any **capital gains tax** as a result of the sale. If the seller does not pay any capital gains tax owing, the buyer will be liable for it. The buyer will have no tax liability if

**capital gains tax**
federal tax levied on the profit realized when capital property, other than a principal residence, is sold

- the seller is, in the language of the *Income Tax Act*, not a "non-resident" of Canada; or
- the seller is a non-resident but either owes no tax or has made satisfactory arrangements to pay any tax owing.

A buyer will therefore want either proof that the seller is not a non-resident of Canada or a certificate from the government stating that the non-resident seller either owes no tax or has made satisfactory arrangements for payment.

This paragraph protects the buyer by allowing the buyer a credit against the purchase price in the amount that must be paid to the Canada Revenue Agency to satisfy the non-resident seller's tax liability. In other words, the buyer may hold back sufficient funds on closing to cover the tax liability (up to 25 percent of the purchase price). The buyer will not claim this credit if the seller provides the buyer with the government certificate or provides a declaration that the seller is not a non-resident of Canada as of the date of closing.

## Adjustments (Paragraph 18)

When completing the statement of adjustments, the expenses listed in this paragraph are to be apportioned between the seller and the buyer to the date of closing. The buyer assumes responsibility as of the date of closing. Accordingly, if the closing is on the 265th day of the year, the seller's share is for 264 days and the buyer's share is for the balance of the year.

## Property Assessment (Paragraph 19)

The province of Ontario uses "current value" assessment to determine the value of a property for municipal property tax purposes. These assessment values are provided by the Municipal Property Assessment Corporation (MPAC), of which every municipality is a member.

This paragraph states that both the buyer and seller know that the property value may be reassessed, and that property taxes may change. No claims may be made against the parties, brokers, or salespeople for any such changes. The only allowable claims are for property taxes that accrued before closing.

## Time Limits (Paragraph 20)

This paragraph states that time is in all respects of the essence of the agreement. Time can be extended or abridged by agreement in writing signed by the seller and the buyer or their respective solicitors.

If a contract does not contain this kind of provision, time is not of the essence. This means that performance of the contract is not required to take place on the date specified in the agreement, but may take place any time before the contract is terminated by the other party.

With this provision, any missed deadlines are non-negotiable unless they have been waived in writing. For example, if the requisition date is missed, nothing can be done. If the closing date is missed, the deal is at an end, and the defaulting party will be liable for that result.

As a result of this provision, if the closing date, requisition date, or any other date is changed, you must confirm the change in writing. The confirming letter should always state that time is to continue to be of the essence.

## Tender (Paragraph 21)

**tender**
presentation of executed copies of all closing documents or funds to the other party in a real estate transaction

Either party may **tender** (present) money or documents to the other party, or to his or her lawyer, on the closing date. Money may be tendered by bank draft, by certified cheque, or by wire transfer using the Large Value Transfer System.

**specific performance**
court order requiring a transaction to be completed; a type of remedy for breach of contract

What is the significance of tender? If one party tries to back out of the deal, the other party may want to continue to rely on the agreement of purchase and sale, and sue for **specific performance** (a court order that the transaction be completed). To be successful in such an action, the plaintiff must prove that he or she was ready, willing, and able to complete his or her part of the bargain—in other words, ready to close on the closing date. The best evidence of this is the tender of executed copies of all necessary closing documents or funds to the other party.

## Family Law Act (Paragraph 22)

**spousal consent**
consent of the spouse of the owner on title to the transfer or mortgage of a matrimonial home, required under the *Family Law Act*

By the terms of this paragraph, the seller warrants that no **spousal consent** under the *Family Law Act* is required to complete the transaction. The seller's spouse is usually required to consent to the sale of a matrimonial home, even if the seller is the sole registered owner. Unless the spouse has signed the agreement of purchase and sale, he or she cannot be forced to consent to the ultimate transfer of title. Without the required consent, the transfer may be set aside. If spousal consent is necessary but a spouse has not signed the agreement and refuses to consent to the transfer, the buyer's only recourse is to sue the seller for breach of warranty.

Before the enactment of the *Land Registration Reform Act*, deeds and transfers contained an affidavit of age and spousal status indicating whether spousal consent was required to complete the transfer. Now there is simply an unsworn statement in the transfer. Some law firms require supporting **statutory declarations** from the seller.

## UFFI (Paragraph 23)

**UFFI** is the abbreviation for urea formaldehyde foam insulation. A number of homes were insulated with UFFI in the 1970s. It was later discovered that UFFI caused health problems, and homes that were insulated with UFFI suffered a loss in resale value.

In this paragraph, the seller warrants that, during the time the seller has owned the property, the seller has not caused the property to be insulated with UFFI, and that, to the best of the seller's knowledge, no building on the property has ever been insulated with UFFI. This warranty is stated to survive and not merge (end) on closing. Accordingly, the buyer will require the seller to deliver a warranty to this effect on closing.

## Legal, Accounting, and Environmental Advice (Paragraph 24)

The parties agree that they cannot rely on information provided by the brokerage as legal, tax, or environmental advice.

## Consumer Reports (Paragraph 25)

This paragraph warns the buyer that the seller may obtain a consumer credit report on the buyer. The seller may wish to do this if there will be a vendor-take-back mortgage from the buyer.

## Agreement in Writing (Paragraph 26)

This paragraph states that there is no other agreement except as set out in the agreement of purchase and sale and that there are no collateral warranties or representations. It also states that, where there is a conflict between the printed form and any clauses inserted in the agreement, including those in schedules, the inserted clauses govern.

This paragraph also explains that "buyer" and "seller" mean purchaser and vendor, respectively.

## Time and Date (Paragraph 27)

This paragraph states that any reference to time and date in the agreement means the time zone and date where the property is located.

## Successors and Assigns (Paragraph 28)

This paragraph states that the agreement is binding on the parties' heirs, executors, successors, and assigns. For example, if the buyer died prior to closing, the estate trustee would be bound to close the transaction, regardless of the heirs' wishes.

# Signatures of the Parties

The buyer signs the form as offeror. The seller signs the form to signify acceptance of the offer, subject to any sign-backs.

By signing the agreement, the seller is also instructing the lawyer to pay to the listing broker the unpaid balance of the real estate commission out of the proceeds of sale. Keep this responsibility in mind when your law firm is acting for the seller.

# Spousal Consent

Below the signatures of the parties, there is a place for the seller's spouse to sign the agreement. By signing, the spouse consents to the transaction pursuant to the *Family Law Act* and agrees to sign any other necessary documents.

# Information on Brokerage(s)

This section applies in transactions where there are two real estate agents or brokerages involved and confirms which one is representing each party. Usually the seller will list the property for sale with one brokerage (the listing brokerage) and the buyer will shop for a house with a different brokerage (the cooperating/buyer's brokerage). The parties deal with individual agents working for that brokerage. In most cases, the listing brokerage represents the interests of the seller, and the cooperating/buyer's brokerage represents the interests of the buyer. Sometimes both brokerages act for the seller or one brokerage acts for both seller and buyer, and these representations must be clearly outlined.

Make a note of the identity of the individual real estate agent who listed the property. The agent can be helpful in a number of situations:

- If there were several sign-backs, you may find it difficult to read the agreement, but the agent can provide assistance.
- If the agreement is conditional, the agent will provide any amending agreements waiving the condition.
- If the agreement provides for the right to inspect the property, you will make arrangements for the inspection through the agent.
- If the deal becomes jeopardized in any way, the real estate agent (whose commission is then jeopardized as well) may be able to assist in negotiating a resolution.

# Acknowledgement

Both parties sign here to acknowledge receipt of a signed agreement and identify the names and addresses of the law firms that will be representing them.

## KEY TERMS

buyer, 208

capital gains tax, 217

chattels, 212

damages, 214

fixtures, 212

flip, 208

harmonized sales tax (HST), 212

in escrow, 215

institutional lender, 214

land transfer tax, 212

Large Value Transfer System, 210

personal undertaking, 215

requisition date, 212

seller, 208

specific performance, 218

spousal consent, 218

statutory declaration, 219

tender, 218

title requisition, 212

UFFI, 219

vacant possession, 211

## REFERENCES

*Family Law Act*, RSO 1990, c F.3.

*Income Tax Act*, RSC 1985, c 1 (5th Supp), as amended.

*Land Registration Reform Act*, RSO 1990, c L.4.

*Planning Act*, RSO 1990, c P.13.

## REVIEW QUESTIONS

1. What must you do if the person named as the seller in the agreement of purchase and sale is a different person from the registered owner shown in the search of title?

2. What must you do if the seller is a corporation?

3. What must you do if the seller is a partnership?

4. What must you do if the buyer wishes to take title differently than the way he or she is named in the agreement of purchase and sale?

5. What should be done if the title search reveals an easement that is not mentioned in the agreement of purchase and sale?

6. What should you do if the agreement of purchase and sale states that interest is to be paid on the deposit?

7. What should you do if the agreement of purchase and sale is conditional until a specified date?

8. What steps may be necessary if chattels are included in the agreement of purchase and sale?

9. What steps must you take with respect to the completion date?

10. What is the requisition date, and why is it important?

11. What does the standard agreement of purchase and sale provide with respect to mortgages that are supposed to be discharged on closing? Why is this provision necessary?

12. When preparing the statement of adjustments, who is responsible for the various expenses on the date of closing?

13. What is a tender, and what is its significance?

14. Why does the agreement of purchase and sale contain a seller's warranty with respect to spousal consent under the *Family Law Act*?

15. What is UFFI? What does the agreement of purchase and sale say about it, and why?

16. Why is it a good idea to make a note of the individual agent who listed the property?

**Figure 16.1 Ontario Real Estate Association (OREA) Agreement of Purchase and Sale**

**OREA** Ontario Real Estate Association

## Agreement of Purchase and Sale

**Form 100** for use in the Province of Ontario

This Agreement of Purchase and Sale dated this .9th.......... day of ..October.......... 20.15....

**BUYER,** Henry Albert Grant and Wilma Heather Grant......., agrees to purchase from
(Full legal names of all Buyers)

**SELLER,** Francois Mercier and Huguette Marie Mercier......., the following
(Full legal names of all Sellers)

**REAL PROPERTY:**

Address .166 Valley Road...............

fronting on the .west.......... side of .Valley Road..........

in the .Town.......... Newmarket, Regional Municipality of York..........

and having a frontage of .50 feet.......... more or less by a depth of .100 feet.......... more or less

and legally described as .Lot 170, Plan 65M-1234, Town of Newmarket, Regional Municipality of York..........

..........
(Legal description of land including easements not described elsewhere) (the "property").

**PURCHASE PRICE:** Dollars (CDN$) .580,000.00..........

.Five Hundred Eighty Thousand.......... Dollars

**DEPOSIT:** Buyer submits .Upon Acceptance..........
(Herewith/Upon Acceptance/as otherwise described in this Agreement)

.Thirty Thousand.......... Dollars (CDN$) .30,000.00..........

by negotiable cheque payable to .Home Life Winners Ltd.......... "Deposit Holder"
to be held in trust pending completion or other termination of this Agreement and to be credited toward the Purchase Price on completion.
For the purposes of this Agreement, "Upon Acceptance" shall mean that the Buyer is required to deliver the deposit to the
Deposit Holder within 24 hours of the acceptance of this Agreement. The parties to this Agreement hereby acknowledge that,
unless otherwise provided for in this Agreement, the Deposit Holder shall place the deposit in trust in the Deposit Holder's
non-interest bearing Real Estate Trust Account and no interest shall be earned, received or paid on the deposit.

**Buyer agrees to pay the balance as more particularly set out in Schedule A attached.**

**SCHEDULE(S) A**.......... **attached hereto form(s) part of this Agreement.**

1. **IRREVOCABILITY:** This offer shall be irrevocable by .Buyer.......... until .8:00.......... p.m. on
(Seller/Buyer)
the .10th.......... day of .October.......... 20.15......, after which time, if not accepted, this
offer shall be null and void and the deposit shall be returned to the Buyer in full without interest.

2. **COMPLETION DATE:** This Agreement shall be completed by no later than 6:00 p.m. on the .15th.......... day
of .December.........., 20 .15...... Upon completion, vacant possession of the property shall be given to the
Buyer unless otherwise provided for in this Agreement.

**INITIALS OF BUYER(S):** ( HG/WG )     **INITIALS OF SELLER(S):** ( FM/HM )

**Form 100** Revised 2015 **Page 1 of 6**
WEBForms® Jun/2015

## Figure 16.1 Continued

3. **NOTICES:** The Seller hereby appoints the Listing Brokerage as agent for the Seller for the purpose of giving and receiving notices pursuant to this Agreement. Where a Brokerage (Buyer's Brokerage) has entered into a representation agreement with the Buyer, the Buyer hereby appoints the Buyer's Brokerage as agent for the purpose of giving and receiving notices pursuant to this Agreement. **Where a Brokerage represents both the Seller and the Buyer (multiple representation), the Brokerage shall not be appointed or authorized to be agent for either the Buyer or the Seller for the purpose of giving and receiving notices.** Any notice relating hereto or provided for herein shall be in writing. In addition to any provision contained herein and in any Schedule hereto, this offer, any counter-offer, notice of acceptance thereof or any notice to be given or received pursuant to this Agreement or any Schedule hereto (any of them, "Document") shall be deemed given and received when delivered personally or hand delivered to the Address for Service provided in the Acknowledgement below, or where a facsimile number or email address is provided herein, when transmitted electronically to that facsimile number or email address, respectively, in which case, the signature(s) of the party (parties) shall be deemed to be original.

FAX No.: 416-555-6923
(For delivery of Documents to Seller)

FAX No.: 416-555-8721
(For delivery of Documents to Buyer)

Email Address: francois@mercier.ca
(For delivery of Documents to Seller)

Email Address: henry@grant.ca
(For delivery of Documents to Buyer)

4. **CHATTELS INCLUDED:**

   stainless steel Kenmore stove
   stainless steel Kenmore refrigerator

   Unless otherwise stated in this Agreement or any Schedule hereto, Seller agrees to convey all fixtures and chattels included in the Purchase Price free from all liens, encumbrances or claims affecting the said fixtures and chattels.

5. **FIXTURES EXCLUDED:**

   dining room chandelier

6. **RENTAL ITEMS (Including Lease, Lease to Own):** The following equipment is rented and **not** included in the Purchase Price. The Buyer agrees to assume the rental contract(s), if assumable:

   hot water tank

   The Buyer agrees to co-operate and execute such documentation as may be required to facilitate such assumption.

7. **HST:** If the sale of the property (Real Property as described above) is subject to Harmonized Sales Tax (HST), then such

   tax shall be ................................................................ the Purchase Price. If the sale of the property is not subject to HST,
   (included in/in addition to)
   Seller agrees to certify on or before closing, that the sale of the property is not subject to HST.
   Any HST on chattels, if applicable, is not included in the Purchase Price.

**INITIALS OF BUYER(S):**  HG/WG   **INITIALS OF SELLER(S):**  FM/HM

## Figure 16.1    Continued

8. **TITLE SEARCH:** Buyer shall be allowed until 6:00 p.m. on the 20th............................ day of November......................., 20.15..., (Requisition Date) to examine the title to the property at Buyer's own expense and until the earlier of: (i) thirty days from the later of the Requisition Date or the date on which the conditions in this Agreement are fulfilled or otherwise waived or; (ii) five days prior to completion, to satisfy Buyer that there are no outstanding work orders or deficiency notices

   affecting the property, and that its present use( single family residential............................................................................ ) may be lawfully continued and that the principal building may be insured against risk of fire. Seller hereby consents to the municipality or other governmental agencies releasing to Buyer details of all outstanding work orders and deficiency notices affecting the property, and Seller agrees to execute and deliver such further authorizations in this regard as Buyer may reasonably require.

9. **FUTURE USE:** Seller and Buyer agree that there is no representation or warranty of any kind that the future intended use of the property by Buyer is or will be lawful except as may be specifically provided for in this Agreement.

10. **TITLE:** Provided that the title to the property is good and free from all registered restrictions, charges, liens, and encumbrances except as otherwise specifically provided in this Agreement and save and except for (a) any registered restrictions or covenants that run with the land providing that such are complied with; (b) any registered municipal agreements and registered agreements with publicly regulated utilities providing such have been complied with, or security has been posted to ensure compliance and completion, as evidenced by a letter from the relevant municipality or regulated utility; (c) any minor easements for the supply of domestic utility or telephone services to the property or adjacent properties; and (d) any easements for drainage, storm or sanitary sewers, public utility lines, telephone lines, cable television lines or other services which do not materially affect the use of the property. If within the specified times referred to in paragraph 8 any valid objection to title or to any outstanding work order or deficiency notice, or to the fact the said present use may not lawfully be continued, or that the principal building may not be insured against risk of fire is made in writing to Seller and which Seller is unable or unwilling to remove, remedy or satisfy or obtain insurance save and except against risk of fire (Title Insurance) in favour of the Buyer and any mortgagee, (with all related costs at the expense of the Seller), and which Buyer will not waive, this Agreement notwithstanding any intermediate acts or negotiations in respect of such objections, shall be at an end and all monies paid shall be returned without interest or deduction and Seller, Listing Brokerage and Co-operating Brokerage shall not be liable for any costs or damages. Save as to any valid objection so made by such day and except for any objection going to the root of the title, Buyer shall be conclusively deemed to have accepted Seller's title to the property.

11. **CLOSING ARRANGEMENTS:** Where each of the Seller and Buyer retain a lawyer to complete the Agreement of Purchase and Sale of the property, and where the transaction will be completed by electronic registration pursuant to Part III of the Land Registration Reform Act, R.S.O. 1990, Chapter L4 and the Electronic Registration Act, S.O. 1991, Chapter 44, and any amendments thereto, the Seller and Buyer acknowledge and agree that the exchange of closing funds, non-registrable documents and other items (the "Requisite Deliveries") and the release thereof to the Seller and Buyer will (a) not occur at the same time as the registration of the transfer/deed (and any other documents intended to be registered in connection with the completion of this transaction) and (b) be subject to conditions whereby the lawyer(s) receiving any of the Requisite Deliveries will be required to hold same in trust and not release same except in accordance with the terms of a document registration agreement between the said lawyers. The Seller and Buyer irrevocably instruct the said lawyers to be bound by the document registration agreement which is recommended from time to time by the Law Society of Upper Canada. Unless otherwise agreed to by the lawyers, such exchange of the Requisite Deliveries will occur in the applicable Land Titles Office or such other location agreeable to both lawyers.

12. **DOCUMENTS AND DISCHARGE:** Buyer shall not call for the production of any title deed, abstract, survey or other evidence of title to the property except such as are in the possession or control of Seller. If requested by Buyer, Seller will deliver any sketch or survey of the property within Seller's control to Buyer as soon as possible and prior to the Requisition Date. If a discharge of any Charge/Mortgage held by a corporation incorporated pursuant to the Trust And Loan Companies Act (Canada), Chartered Bank, Trust Company, Credit Union, Caisse Populaire or Insurance Company and which is not to be assumed by Buyer on completion, is not available in registrable form on completion, Buyer agrees to accept Seller's lawyer's personal undertaking to obtain, out of the closing funds, a discharge in registrable form and to register same, or cause same to be registered, on title within a reasonable period of time after completion, provided that on or before completion Seller shall provide to Buyer a mortgage statement prepared by the mortgagee setting out the balance required to obtain the discharge, and, where a real-time electronic cleared funds transfer system is not being used, a direction executed by Seller directing payment to the mortgagee of the amount required to obtain the discharge out of the balance due on completion.

13. **INSPECTION:** Buyer acknowledges having had the opportunity to inspect the property and understands that upon acceptance of this offer there shall be a binding agreement of purchase and sale between Buyer and Seller. **The Buyer acknowledges having the opportunity to include a requirement for a property inspection report in this Agreement and agrees that except as may be specifically provided for in this Agreement, the Buyer will not be obtaining a property inspection or property inspection report regarding the property.**

**INITIALS OF BUYER(S):** ( HG/WG )          **INITIALS OF SELLER(S):** ( FM/HM )

## Figure 16.1   Continued

14. **INSURANCE:** All buildings on the property and all other things being purchased shall be and remain until completion at the risk of Seller. Pending completion, Seller shall hold all insurance policies, if any, and the proceeds thereof in trust for the parties as their interests may appear and in the event of substantial damage, Buyer may either terminate this Agreement and have all monies paid returned without interest or deduction or else take the proceeds of any insurance and complete the purchase. No insurance shall be transferred on completion. If Seller is taking back a Charge/Mortgage, or Buyer is assuming a Charge/Mortgage, Buyer shall supply Seller with reasonable evidence of adequate insurance to protect Seller's or other mortgagee's interest on completion.

15. **PLANNING ACT:** This Agreement shall be effective to create an interest in the property only if Seller complies with the subdivision control provisions of the Planning Act by completion and Seller covenants to proceed diligently at Seller's expense to obtain any necessary consent by completion.

16. **DOCUMENT PREPARATION:** The Transfer/Deed shall, save for the Land Transfer Tax Affidavit, be prepared in registrable form at the expense of Seller, and any Charge/Mortgage to be given back by the Buyer to Seller at the expense of the Buyer. If requested by Buyer, Seller covenants that the Transfer/Deed to be delivered on completion shall contain the statements contemplated by Section 50(22) of the Planning Act, R.S.O.1990.

17. **RESIDENCY:** (a) Subject to (b) below, the Seller represents and warrants that the Seller is not and on completion will not be a non-resident under the non-residency provisions of the Income Tax Act which representation and warranty shall survive and not merge upon the completion of this transaction and the Seller shall deliver to the Buyer a statutory declaration that Seller is not then a non-resident of Canada;
(b) provided that if the Seller is a non-resident under the non-residency provisions of the Income Tax Act, the Buyer shall be credited towards the Purchase Price with the amount, if any, necessary for Buyer to pay to the Minister of National Revenue to satisfy Buyer's liability in respect of tax payable by Seller under the non-residency provisions of the Income Tax Act by reason of this sale. Buyer shall not claim such credit if Seller delivers on completion the prescribed certificate.

18. **ADJUSTMENTS:** Any rents, mortgage interest, realty taxes including local improvement rates and unmetered public or private utility charges and unmetered cost of fuel, as applicable, shall be apportioned and allowed to the day of completion, the day of completion itself to be apportioned to Buyer.

19. **PROPERTY ASSESSMENT:** The Buyer and Seller hereby acknowledge that the Province of Ontario has implemented current value assessment and properties may be re-assessed on an annual basis. The Buyer and Seller agree that no claim will be made against the Buyer or Seller, or any Brokerage, Broker or Salesperson, for any changes in property tax as a result of a re-assessment of the property, save and except any property taxes that accrued prior to the completion of this transaction.

20. **TIME LIMITS:** Time shall in all respects be of the essence hereof provided that the time for doing or completing of any matter provided for herein may be extended or abridged by an agreement in writing signed by Seller and Buyer or by their respective lawyers who may be specifically authorized in that regard.

21. **TENDER:** Any tender of documents or money hereunder may be made upon Seller or Buyer or their respective lawyers on the day set for completion. Money shall be tendered with funds drawn on a lawyer's trust account in the form of a bank draft, certified cheque or wire transfer using the Large Value Transfer System.

22. **FAMILY LAW ACT:** Seller warrants that spousal consent is not necessary to this transaction under the provisions of the Family Law Act, R.S.O.1990 unless Seller's spouse has executed the consent hereinafter provided.

23. **UFFI:** Seller represents and warrants to Buyer that during the time Seller has owned the property, Seller has not caused any building on the property to be insulated with insulation containing ureaformaldehyde, and that to the best of Seller's knowledge no building on the property contains or has ever contained insulation that contains ureaformaldehyde. This warranty shall survive and not merge on the completion of this transaction, and if the building is part of a multiple unit building, this warranty shall only apply to that part of the building which is the subject of this transaction.

24. **LEGAL, ACCOUNTING AND ENVIRONMENTAL ADVICE**: The parties acknowledge that any information provided by the brokerage is not legal, tax or environmental advice.

25. **CONSUMER REPORTS: The Buyer is hereby notified that a consumer report containing credit and/or personal information may be referred to in connection with this transaction.**

26. **AGREEMENT IN WRITING:** If there is conflict or discrepancy between any provision added to this Agreement (including any Schedule attached hereto) and any provision in the standard pre-set portion hereof, the added provision shall supersede the standard pre-set provision to the extent of such conflict or discrepancy. This Agreement including any Schedule attached hereto, shall constitute the entire Agreement between Buyer and Seller. There is no representation, warranty, collateral agreement or condition, which affects this Agreement other than as expressed herein. For the purposes of this Agreement, Seller means vendor and Buyer means purchaser. This Agreement shall be read with all changes of gender or number required by the context.

27. **TIME AND DATE:** Any reference to a time and date in this Agreement shall mean the time and date where the property is located.

**INITIALS OF BUYER(S):** ( HG/WG )     **INITIALS OF SELLER(S):** ( FM/HM )

**Form 100**   Revised 2015   **Page 4 of 6**

WEBForms® Jun/2015

## Figure 16.1 Continued

28. **SUCCESSORS AND ASSIGNS:** The heirs, executors, administrators, successors and assigns of the undersigned are bound by the terms herein.

| SIGNED, SEALED AND DELIVERED in the presence of: | IN WITNESS whereof I have hereunto set my hand and seal: | |
|---|---|---|
| *R. Basak* (Witness) | *H.A. Grant* (Buyer) | ● DATE Oct. 8, 2015 (Seal) |
| *R. Basak* (Witness) | *W.H. Grant* (Buyer) | ● DATE Oct. 8, 2015 (Seal) |

I, the Undersigned Seller, agree to the above offer. I hereby irrevocably instruct my lawyer to pay directly to the brokerage(s) with whom I have agreed to pay commission, the unpaid balance of the commission together with applicable Harmonized Sales Tax (and any other taxes as may hereafter be applicable), from the proceeds of the sale prior to any payment to the undersigned on completion, as advised by the brokerage(s) to my lawyer.

| SIGNED, SEALED AND DELIVERED in the presence of: | IN WITNESS whereof I have hereunto set my hand and seal: | |
|---|---|---|
| *L Saliba* (Witness) | *F. Mercer* (Seller) | ● DATE Oct. 9, 2015 (Seal) |
| *L Saliba* (Witness) | *Mercer* (Seller) | ● DATE Oct. 9, 2015 (Seal) |

**SPOUSAL CONSENT:** The Undersigned Spouse of the Seller hereby consents to the disposition evidenced herein pursuant to the provisions of the Family Law Act, R.S.O.1990, and hereby agrees with the Buyer that he/she will execute all necessary or incidental documents to give full force and effect to the sale evidenced herein.

| (Witness) | (Spouse) | ● DATE (Seal) |
|---|---|---|

**CONFIRMATION OF ACCEPTANCE:** Notwithstanding anything contained herein to the contrary, I confirm this Agreement with all changes both typed and written was finally accepted by all parties at 4:15 p.m. this 9th day of October , 20 15 . *H.A. Grant*
(Signature of Seller or Buyer)

### INFORMATION ON BROKERAGE(S)

| Listing Brokerage Home Life Winners Ltd. | Tel.No. 416-555-6922 |
|---|---|
| Morley Farquarson (Salesperson / Broker Name) | |
| Co-op/Buyer Brokerage Century 21 Sales 'R Us Ltd. | Tel.No. 416-555-8720 |
| Sandy MacPherson (Salesperson / Broker Name) | |

### ACKNOWLEDGEMENT

| I acknowledge receipt of my signed copy of this accepted Agreement of Purchase and Sale and I authorize the Brokerage to forward a copy to my lawyer. | I acknowledge receipt of my signed copy of this accepted Agreement of Purchase and Sale and I authorize the Brokerage to forward a copy to my lawyer. |
|---|---|
| *F. Mercer* (Seller) DATE Oct. 9/15 | *H.A. Grant* (Buyer) DATE Oct. 9/15 |
| *Mercer* (Seller) DATE Oct. 9/15 | *W.H. Grant* (Buyer) DATE Oct. 9/15 |
| Address for Service 166 Valley Road Newmarket, Ont. Tel.No. 905-555-3051 | Address for Service 621 Augustus Street Seneca, Ont. K1K 0T4 Tel.No. 555-555-7511 |
| Seller's Lawyer Brooks & Dunn Address 16 Any Street, Newmarket, Ont. | Buyer's Lawyer Kurtz, Emmans, Blatt & Wolf Address 321 Any Street, Seneca, Ontario K1K 6L2 |
| Email fbrooks@brooksdunn.ca | Email jwolf@kebw.ca |
| 905-555-6789 Tel.No. 905-555-6790 FAX No. | 416-555-3872 Tel.No. 416-555-3873 FAX No. |

**FOR OFFICE USE ONLY**      **COMMISSION TRUST AGREEMENT**

To: Co-operating Brokerage shown on the foregoing Agreement of Purchase and Sale:
In consideration for the Co-operating Brokerage procuring the foregoing Agreement of Purchase and Sale, I hereby declare that all moneys received or receivable by me in connection with the Transaction as contemplated in the MLS® Rules and Regulations of my Real Estate Board shall be receivable and held in trust. This agreement shall constitute a Commission Trust Agreement as defined in the MLS® Rules and shall be subject to and governed by the MLS® Rules pertaining to Commission Trust.

DATED as of the date and time of the acceptance of the foregoing Agreement of Purchase and Sale.

| (Authorized to bind the Listing Brokerage) | Acknowledged by: *A. Macpherson* (Authorized to bind the Co-operating Brokerage) |
|---|---|

**Form 100**   Revised 2015   **Page 5 of 6**

WEB*Forms*® Jun/2015

## Figure 16.1   Concluded

### Schedule A
**Agreement of Purchase and Sale**

**Form 100** for use in the Province of Ontario

This Schedule is attached to and forms part of the Agreement of Purchase and Sale between:

**BUYER,** Henry Albert Grant and Wilma Heather Grant ...................................................................................., and

**SELLER,** Francois Mercier and Huguette Marie Mercier ...................................................................................

for the purchase and sale of .166 Valley Road ...................................................................................

Newmarket, Regional Municipality of York . dated the .9th ........................... day of .October ........................., 20.15..... .

Buyer agrees to pay the balance as follows:

The Buyer agrees to pay the balance of the purchase price, subject to adjustments, by bank draft, certified cheque, or wire transfer using the Large Value Transfer System.

This offer is conditional upon the inspection of the subject property by a home inspector at the Buyer's expense, and the obtaining of a report satisfactory to the Buyer at the Buyer's sole and absolute discretion. Unless the Buyer gives notice in writing delivered to the Seller not later than 8:00 p.m. on October 16, 2015 that this condition is fulfilled, this offer shall be null and void, and the deposit returned to the Buyer in full without deduction. The Seller agrees to cooperate in providing access to the property for the purpose of this inspection. This condition is included for the benefit of the Buyer and may be waived at the Buyer's sole option by notice in writing to the Seller within the time period stated herein.

This form must be initialed by all parties to the Agreement of Purchase and Sale.

**INITIALS OF BUYER(S):** ( HG/WG )      **INITIALS OF SELLER(S):** ( FM/HM )

**Form 100**   Revised 2015   **Page 6 of 6**

WEB*Forms*® Jun/2015

# Title Insurance

# 17

## LEARNING OUTCOMES

After reading this chapter, you will understand:

- The difference between a lawyer's title opinion and title insurance

- Why title insurance is important

- What title insurance covers and what is exempt

- A lawyer's duty regarding title insurance advice to a client

- The implications of title insurance on buying property

# Introduction

Buyers of real property want to be sure that they are getting good title to the property. At one time, a buyer's only option was to rely on the legal opinion of the lawyer handling the purchase transaction certifying that the buyer was getting good and marketable title to the property. Now, buyers can choose how to protect their interests: they can either (1) rely on the lawyer's **title opinion** (also called certification of title), or (2) take out a title insurance policy.

When title insurance was first offered, it appealed particularly to buyers who did not have an up-to-date survey of their property. The insurance companies insured against any problems that an up-to-date survey might have revealed, and the title insurance premium was considerably cheaper than the cost of a new survey. In recent years, title insurance has become an increasingly popular option for buyers and for the lawyers representing them.

**title opinion**
lawyer's statement as to whether or not the buyer has good title to the property

# Certification of Title Versus Title Insurance

If a buyer chooses to rely on the lawyer's title opinion, it is the lawyer's responsibility to perform all the necessary searches, make all the required inquiries, and take all the appropriate steps to ensure that the buyer receives good and marketable title to the property. If it turns out later that there is a problem with the title, the buyer contacts the lawyer to correct it. If the lawyer is not able to correct the problem, the buyer can sue the lawyer for negligence, and the lawyer may make a claim under the law firm's mandatory errors and omissions insurance. The buyer will have to prove that the lawyer acted negligently to be able to receive compensation for the loss. If the lawyer acted reasonably or had no way of discovering the problem—for example, in the case of fraud—then there may not be a valid cause of action, in which case the buyer will not be compensated. In addition, a buyer cannot make a claim against the lawyer for a problem that arises after the purchase transaction is completed, such as a transfer, lien, or charge fraudulently registered once the buyer is the owner.

If the buyer chooses to take out a title insurance policy, the policy protects the buyer against most title problems whether they arise before or after the purchase transaction is completed. If a problem arises with title, the buyer (or the buyer's lawyer) contacts the insurance company to correct it. There is no need to sue the lawyer and establish negligence on the lawyer's part. The buyer need only prove that a problem exists that is covered by the policy purchased, and the buyer is then covered for damages or the cost of clearing title.

Under the Law Society of Upper Canada's *Rules of Professional Conduct*, lawyers are obligated to advise their buyer-clients of the choices available for assuring title. The provisions of the rules are discussed more fully under the heading "The Role of the Lawyer When Title Insurance Is Purchased," below.

# What Is Title Insurance?

Title insurance is insurance that shares many of the features of home insurance or car insurance. With home insurance or car insurance, you pay a premium to protect you in the event that you suffer loss or damage to your home or your car. With title insurance, you pay a premium to protect you against loss or damage suffered as a result of problems with title to your property.

All other insurers—life, home, automobile—assess the degree of risk involved in a particular insurance policy before issuing the policy. Title insurers are no different. Before agreeing to provide coverage for a particular title, they assess the degree of risk with respect to the specific property to decide on which risks they are willing to assume and the premium they will charge to do so. A title insurer reviews the state of the title to the property before issuing a policy just as a home insurer might physically inspect the property. A title insurer may exclude certain risks that it is not prepared to cover, just as a home insurer might exclude coverage against the risk of flood to a house located on a flood plain. However, the premium for title insurance is paid only once, with no annual renewals, unlike other types of insurance in which insurance premiums are paid on a schedule, usually annually. A title insurance policy is usually obtained at the time the property is purchased, and/or when a mortgage is being registered, but it may also be purchased by existing homeowners who did not obtain title insurance when the home was purchased. Title insurance must be ordered by a lawyer, on behalf of the homeowner or mortgagee.

# Whom Does Title Insurance Protect and for How Long?

Title insurance policies can be issued in favour of both buyers of real property and lenders of money secured by real property. In fact, some lenders require that title insurance be taken out as a condition of granting a loan.

A policy issued in favour of a buyer, called an owner's policy, remains in effect as long as the insured has title to the property. Some policies also continue to protect those who have received title because of the owner's death or as a result of a transfer to them by way of gift or for nominal consideration—for example, a spouse or child of the owner.

A lender's policy covers the principal amount of the mortgage and may be required only for the duration of the loan—in other words, for the time that the mortgage remains on title. The lender is covered in the event that it acquires the property as a result of default, by realizing on the security, and suffers loss with respect to a risk covered under the policy.

# What Types of Losses Are Covered Under a Title Insurance Policy?

Each title insurance policy lists the risks or losses that the policy will cover and those that it will not cover (exclusions). Generally, the owner of a title insurance policy is insured against title problems that were in existence at the time the policy was purchased, both "on title" and "off title." "On-title" matters are those that are reflected in the registered title to the property and include

- conflicting ownership interests in the property;
- any charge, lien, or encumbrance on or other defect in the title;
- unmarketability of title; and
- lack of a right of access to and from the property, if title to the insured property turns out to be different from that shown in the policy for whatever reason, including past fraud or forgery.

"Off-title" matters are those that are not reflected in the registered title to the property and include

- work orders;
- zoning issues;
- defects that would have been revealed by an up-to-date survey, including encroachments; and
- realty tax arrears.

Title insurance policies may also offer protection for defects that arise after the policy is purchased, including fraud, encroachments, and certain construction liens (if they arose before closing but are registered after closing).

Most policies include "gap coverage." This protects the insured from title problems that may arise as a result of a failure to register documents on the closing date for reasons such as traffic problems that delay couriers or power outages. For example, if a transaction is scheduled to close on a Friday and Teraview cannot be accessed because of a power outage, the buyer can still move in and the two lawyers will undertake to complete the registration on Monday. If a title problem arises between the Friday and the Monday, the buyer and the mortgagee will be protected with gap coverage.

Standard exclusions from coverage include

- problems that the purchaser agreed to accept (in the agreement of purchase and sale);
- certain government rights in the land;
- certain expropriations;
- environmental and conservation authority issues; and
- native land issues.

# How Much Does Title Insurance Cost?

The cost of title insurance is determined by the purchase price of the property. The one-time premium is approximately $325 to $375 for a resale home costing less than $500,000. The premium goes up by approximately $1 for each $1,000 in price over $500,000. If the buyer is arranging a mortgage, the lender will be covered as well for an additional premium of approximately $50. If title insurance is being purchased for a lender only, such as on a refinance, the premium is much less than for a purchase.

In addition to the cost of the policy, the buyer will also have to pay the lawyer's legal fees and disbursements for the searches and inquiries required by the title insurance company.

Depending on the searches required by the insurance company before issuing the policy, the overall cost of the insurance premium plus lawyer's fees and disbursements may be less than the legal fees and disbursements involved in obtaining a lawyer's opinion on title. (For a more complete discussion, see "The Role of the Lawyer When Title Insurance Is Purchased," below.)

# Title Insurance Companies and Their Policies

There are a number of insurance companies offering title insurance in Ontario—several private title insurance companies and TitlePLUS, which is administered by the Lawyers' Professional Indemnity Company (LawPRO). The main private title insurers in Ontario are First Canadian Title, Stewart Title, and Chicago Title.

There is no standard policy currently in use in Ontario, but there are similarities among all the policies in use. The body of the policy outlines what is included in the policy coverage. The policy will contain a number of schedules. Usually, the first schedule, Schedule A, describes the property covered and the amount of insurance. It also provides the name of the insured (either the owner or the lender, depending on the type of policy), a description of the estate or interest in land covered under the policy (usually fee simple if it's an owner's policy), and the name of the title holder of the fee simple estate or other interest in land. The second schedule, Schedule B, usually lists exceptions—both standard, preprinted exceptions and property-specific exceptions to the policy. The preprinted policy form may also contain exclusions from coverage. Any risk that is excluded from coverage by either the standard exclusions in the preprinted policy or the exceptions in Schedule B will not be covered by the insurance policy.

# The Role of the Lawyer When Title Insurance Is Purchased

A lawyer must still be involved in a real estate purchase transaction involving title insurance. In fact, only a lawyer can arrange title insurance on behalf of a buyer, and only after getting written instructions from the client to obtain title insurance on the client's behalf. Figure 17.1 is a direction to the lawyer to obtain title insurance.

The lawyer will carry out most of the same steps involved in a purchase without title insurance. He or she will

- open and organize a file;
- review the agreement of purchase and sale;
- advise the client on how to take title to the property;
- prepare or review all the necessary documents;
- prepare for the closing, including the execution of documents by the client;
- close the transaction and register the documents;
- notify utilities and government offices of the change in ownership; and
- provide the client with a **reporting letter**.

When the client chooses to purchase a title insurance policy, the lawyer applies for it on the buyer's behalf. The lawyer must still search title to the property because the insurance company will require a title opinion from the lawyer before issuing a policy. However, the lawyer may not have to conduct as thorough a title search as would be required if he or she were certifying title to the buyer. Also, all insurers are willing to waive certain off-title searches and inquiries that would otherwise be required.

All title insurers in Ontario waive the following searches or inquiries:

- execution searches against prior owners;
- corporate status certificates for prior owners;
- proof of subdivision agreement compliance; and
- an up-to-date survey of the property.

Depending on which insurer provides the policy, some or all of the following searches or inquiries will also be waived:

- hydro, water, and gas certificates;
- tax certificates;
- evidence of building and zoning compliance;
- unregistered hydro easement inquiries;
- conservation authority clearance; and
- proof of restrictive covenant status.

By waiving these searches, the insurer is agreeing to accept the risk of or "insure over" these potential problems. If the lawyer discovers a title defect in the course of the searches required by the insurer, the lawyer can ask the insurer to insure over the known defect or problem in whole or in part for the buyer and/or the lender. This will ensure that the problem does not become an exception to the coverage provided under the policy.

The choice of insurer may affect the way in which various steps in the application process are completed. Some conveyancing software—for example, Conveyancer—

**Figure 17.1   Direction to Lawyer to Obtain Title Insurance**

## ACKNOWLEDGMENT AND DIRECTION FROM PURCHASER

**TO:**   Kurtz, Emmans, Blatt & Wolf
Barristers & Solicitors

**RE:**   GRANT purchase from MERCIER
166 Valley Road, Newmarket

This will confirm that you, as my lawyer, have reviewed and explained to me the various options available to protect my ownership interests arising from the purchase of the above property, and that, in particular, you have explained the advantages and disadvantages of protecting my interests through the purchase of title insurance as compared to a lawyer's opinion on title.

I hereby instruct you to proceed by way of the purchase of title insurance from _____ Title Insurance Company.

**DATED** at _____ of _____ , this _____ day of _____ , 2015.

_____

HENRY ALBERT GRANT

_____

WILMA HEATHER GRANT

provides access to certain insurers, allowing the lawyer to complete the policy. If a lawyer prefers to use TitlePLUS, he or she must complete a questionnaire and submit it to the insurer. The insurer will then issue a policy.

The lawyer also has an important role to play in advising the client with respect to the insurance policy itself. For example, the lawyer may advise the client about which insurer to choose, and the premium to be paid. The lawyer may also review the initial report from the insurer to determine what coverage is excluded from the policy and to make sure that the client is properly named in the policy as the insured, the property is properly described in the policy, and there are no title problems that should be resolved instead of being insured over. When the final policy is issued, the lawyer may review it to ensure that it complies with the commitment.

The role of the lawyer with respect to title insurance in real estate conveyancing is dealt with in the *Rules of Professional Conduct*. Rules 3.2-9.4 to 3.2-9.7 state:

> 3.2-9.4  A lawyer shall assess all reasonable options to assure title when advising a client about a real estate conveyance and shall advise the client that title insurance is not mandatory and is not the only option available to protect the client's interests in a real estate transaction.
>
> **Commentary**
> A lawyer should advise the client of the options available to protect the client's interests and minimize the client's risks in a real estate transaction. The lawyer should be cognizant of when title insurance may be an appropriate option. Although title insurance is intended to protect the client against title risks, it is not a substitute for a lawyer's services in a real estate transaction.
>
> The lawyer should be knowledgeable about title insurance and discuss with the client the advantages, conditions, and limitations of the various options and coverages generally available to the client through title insurance. Before recommending a specific title insurance product, the lawyer should be knowledgeable about the product and take such training as may be necessary in order to acquire the knowledge.
>
> 3.2-9.5  A lawyer shall not receive any compensation, whether directly or indirectly, from a title insurer, agent or intermediary for recommending a specific title insurance product to their client.
>
> 3.2-9.6  A lawyer shall disclose to the client that no commission or fee is being furnished by any insurer, agent, or intermediary to the lawyer with respect to any title insurance coverage.
>
> **Commentary**
> The fiduciary relationship between lawyer and client requires full disclosure in all financial dealings between them and prohibits the acceptance of any hidden fees by the lawyer, including the lawyer's law firm, any employee or associate of the firm, or any related entity.
>
> 3.2-9.7  If discussing TitlePLUS insurance with the client, a lawyer shall fully disclose the relationship between the legal profession, the Society, and the Lawyers' Professional Indemnity Company (LawPRO).

Under rule 6.1-6.1 of the *Rules of Professional Conduct*, these matters must be dealt with by the lawyer, and cannot be delegated to a law clerk. According to the rule, a lawyer may not permit a non-lawyer to

- provide advice to a client with respect to any insurance, including title insurance, without supervision;
- present insurance options or information regarding premiums to a client without supervision;
- recommend one insurance product over another without supervision; or
- give legal opinions regarding the insurance coverage obtained.

# Fraud and Title Insurance

In recent years there has been a dramatic increase in real estate title fraud in Ontario. The following examples illustrate ways in which title fraud can be perpetrated:

1. A fraud artist obtains title to a property by registering a fraudulent transfer or deed of land transferring title to himself or herself. The fraudster then arranges a mortgage on the property with a bank and registers the mortgage against title. The fraudster makes no mortgage payments. The owner first becomes aware of the scheme when the bank serves a notice of sale as a result of the default.

2. A married woman arranges a mortgage on property owned by her and her husband, without notice to the husband. She has an accomplice pose as her husband when the mortgage documents are signed, and then receives the proceeds from the mortgage. Her husband does not find out about the mortgage until they are going through a divorce, and the property is sold.

3. A lawyer breaches his undertaking to use proceeds from closing to pay off and discharge an outstanding mortgage. The lawyer instead disappears with the money, and title to the property remains subject to the prior mortgage.

In cases similar to these, innocent homeowners have either lost their homes or been left with properties subject to hefty mortgages.

When title insurance was first introduced, it was the only way an innocent homeowner could protect against title fraud. Without title insurance, if a homeowner lost his or her home to a fraudster, the only recourse was to apply to the Land Titles Assurance Fund. It was a time-consuming, and often costly, procedure that only provided the homeowner with money to compensate for the lost property; it did not restore title to the homeowner.

After much media coverage on the subject of title fraud, the Ontario government enacted Bill 152, the *Ministry of Government Services Consumer Protection and Service Modernization Act, 2006*, which amended the *Land Registration Reform Act* and the *Land Titles Act*.

Sections 155 and 156 of the *Land Titles Act* now read:

> **Fraudulent dispositions**
>
> 155. Subject to this Act, a fraudulent instrument that, if unregistered, would be fraudulent and void is, despite registration, fraudulent and void in like manner.
>
> **Offences**
>
> 156(1)  A person is guilty of an offence if the person fraudulently procures or attempts to fraudulently procure a fraudulent entry on the register, an erasure or deletion from the register or an alteration of the register.

**Penalty**

(2) A person who is convicted of an offence under this section is liable to,

(a) a fine of not more than $50,000 or imprisonment for a term of not more than two years less a day, or both, if the person is an individual; and

(b) a fine of not more than $250,000, if the person is a corporation.

Ownership of property can no longer be lost as a result of a falsified mortgage, fraudulent sale, or a counterfeit power of attorney. There is a streamlined and expedited Land Titles Assurance Fund process for victims of fraud. For most cases of fraud, title will be returned to the owner who was on title immediately before the fraud and a decision on compensation will be made within 90 days. In addition, an individual who is convicted is subject to a fine of up to $50,000 and/or imprisonment of up to two years, and a corporation is subject to a fine of up to $250,000.

Shortly after passage of this legislation, the Court of Appeal confirmed, in the case of *Lawrence v Maple Trust Company*, that a mortgage that had been obtained on the basis of a fraudulent transfer of title was not valid.

Even though the law now states that a fraudulent document will not defeat the rights of the true owner, it has become more and more common for buyers to obtain title insurance when purchasing property because it is much simpler to make a claim than to litigate. As mentioned above, some lenders actually insist on title insurance. If the lender insists on title insurance and the same lawyer is acting for both the buyer and the lender, the buyer will be required to obtain title insurance. Furthermore, although the legislation protects current homeowners from any subsequent title fraud against their property, it does not do the same for buyers. A lawyer acting for a buyer of land in the Land Titles system can no longer rely on the title index as an accurate reflection of the state of the title. There may have been a fraudulent transaction in the past that is not evident on the title index. When the fraud is discovered, title will be restored to the owner who was registered immediately before the fraud. Thus, lawyers will be unable to certify title to their clients and will have to rely on title insurance policies to insure against the possibility of a prior undiscovered fraud.

## KEY TERMS

reporting letter, 234

title opinion, 230

## REFERENCES

Bill 152, *Ministry of Government Services Consumer Protection and Service Modernization Act, 2006*, SO 2006, c 34.

*Land Registration Reform Act*, RSO 1990, c L.4.

*Land Titles Act*, RSO 1990, c L.5.

Law Society of Upper Canada, *Rules of Professional Conduct* (Toronto: LSUC, 2000), online: <http://www.lsuc.on.ca/WorkArea/DownloadAsset.aspx?id=2147486159>.

*Lawrence v Maple Trust Company*, 2007 ONCA 74.

## REVIEW QUESTIONS

1. How is the buyer protected against potential title problems in a transaction where title insurance is not purchased?

2. How is the buyer protected against potential title problems in a transaction where title insurance has been purchased?

3. How does title insurance affect the work that has to be done on a file?

4. How frequently does a person have to pay a premium for title insurance?

5. How long does a title insurance policy stay in effect in the case of an owner's policy?

6. What types of losses are covered under a title insurance policy?

7. Under the *Rules of Professional Conduct*, can a lawyer receive a fee from a title insurance company for using its policy?

8. How does title insurance protect against fraudulent transactions?

9. Under what circumstances might a lawyer not be able to rely on a Land Titles title index as an accurate reflection of the state of the title?

# Preliminary Matters

# 18

## LEARNING OUTCOMES

After reading this chapter, you will understand:

- What information you must get from your client before you can prepare the documents required for a real estate purchase

- The preliminary letters you may write to or for your client

- The relevance of title insurance when drafting letters

- What searches and inquiries may be necessary if there is no title insurance

- Specialized inquiries that may be required in a transaction

# Introduction

Once you have opened the file, reviewed the agreement of purchase and sale, and diarized the relevant dates, you must perform a number of tasks designed to obtain the information you need before the transaction can close. The specific tasks involved will depend on whether the client decides to purchase title insurance. The lawyer handling the file must advise the client of the options available, and the client must decide early on which to choose. Some of the preliminary inquiry letters discussed in this chapter will not be necessary if the client purchases title insurance, but each file must be dealt with individually by checking the title insurance policy. Any letters in this chapter may be signed by a law clerk or a lawyer.

# Preliminary Letter to the Buyer

You may send a preliminary letter or email to or telephone the buyer confirming that your firm is representing him or her in the purchase of the property, advising the buyer of various aspects of the transaction, and requesting whatever information you need. Questions may include the following:

- If there are two buyers, do they want to take title as joint tenants or as tenants in common?
- Are the names shown on the agreement of purchase and sale the buyer's full given names?
- What is the buyer's birthdate?
- Is the buyer financing the purchase by way of a mortgage? If so, who is the mortgagee, and what are the terms of the mortgage?

You must get answers to these questions before you can proceed with any document preparation. Figure 18.1, at the end of the chapter, is an example of a preliminary letter to the buyer.

# Title Insurance

You must determine whether or not title insurance is being obtained for the buyer and lender, if applicable, before ordering a search of title or sending any further letters. Although a title search is always required whether or not there is title insurance, both the extent of the title search and the need for off-title searches will depend on whether and what kind of title insurance is being obtained.

# Search of Title

The next matter that you must deal with is the title search. Start by using the property identifier number (PIN) to find out whether the property is registered in the Registry or Land Titles system. If the property is registered in the Registry system, a full 40-year search will be required, and you will likely have to make arrangements to have the title searched by an experienced title searcher. If the property is in Land Titles, you can do the search from your office using the Teraview software. See Chapter 14, Title Searching, for a more complete discussion.

If you are not doing the title search yourself, you must give instructions to the title searcher. You can do this orally or in writing. If you give the title searcher oral instructions, make a note in the file setting out the name of the title searcher, the date you made the request for the title search, and any instructions you provided.

You must give the title searcher sufficient information on which to act, including

- the date by which you require the search;
- the requisition date;
- a description of the land—if possible, the lot and plan or concession number; if not, the municipal address and the land registry office in which the land is registered;
- the dimensions of the property;
- the names of the current registered owners;
- the kind of search you require—if the land is registered in the Registry system, you should request a full 40-year search, unless your law firm has previously certified title to the property, in which case, you should request a search only from the date that your law firm previously certified title;
- whether abutting lands should be searched for *Planning Act* compliance—this will be necessary if the land in question is part of a lot;
- what instruments, if any, should be copied; and
- which names should be searched for executions—in a 40-year search, you will have to search against all owners in the chain of title; if a mortgage is being taken back by the seller, you will have to search against the buyer as well (your law firm may choose to search executions through Teraview).

Regarding this last point, note that if title insurance is being obtained, executions against all the owners in a 40-year search will not be required. Also, be sure to advise the title searcher accordingly so that money is not spent needlessly.

Figure 18.2 is an example of a title search request.

## Independent Conveyancer for Closing

If the property is in the Registry system, someone will have to attend at the land registry office for the closing. If your law firm uses independent conveyancers, you should book one to ensure that the conveyancer will be available on the date of closing.

## Electronic Closing

Usually you will be dealing with Land Titles properties, and there will be no attendance at the land registry office on closing. Instead, the lawyers will either sign a document registration agreement (DRA) or agree to be bound by the terms of the

DRA, which sets out their respective obligations on closing. See Figure 7.5 in Chapter 7 for an example of a DRA.

## Preliminary Letter to the Seller's Solicitor

Find out the name of the seller's solicitor by checking the Acknowledgement section of the agreement of purchase and sale, or by telephoning the real estate agent. It is customary to write to, email, or telephone the seller's solicitor to confirm that your firm is acting for the buyer and to request a survey and a statement of adjustments, and to advise how the client is taking title. The law firm acting for the seller will often send a similar preliminary letter or email to your law firm to confirm that it is acting for the seller. Figure 18.3 is an example of a preliminary letter to the seller's solicitor.

## Hydro, Gas, and Metered Water Accounts

Some lawyers will write to the utility companies servicing the property to arrange for a final meter reading the day before closing and to advise the utility companies of the impending change of name on the account. Other lawyers will advise their clients to make those arrangements. See Figures 18.4, 18.5, and 18.6 for examples of letters to the water department, hydro company, and gas company requesting meter readings.

Some utility companies now require that lawyers complete forms online, rather than sending in actual letters.

## Municipal Tax Certificate

If your client is not obtaining title insurance, you must obtain a tax certificate from the municipality in which the property is located to confirm the current amount of the realty taxes and whether there are any arrears, because tax arrears constitute a lien on the land. Although title insurance covers tax arrears, even with title insurance some lawyers prefer to obtain a tax certificate to avoid the possibility of having to make a claim on title insurance, since the information is so easily attainable. You may also use this information to review the statement of adjustments when you receive it from the seller's solicitor. Figure 18.7 is an example of a letter requesting a municipal tax certificate.

## Searches That May Be Necessary if There Is No Title Insurance

The remaining letters and searches will usually be required only if title insurance is not being obtained. Sometimes, however, one or more of these letters and searches may be required even if title insurance is being obtained. Since title insurance typically insures only against problems of which the buyer and his or her lawyer are unaware, if the lawyer knows of or suspects a problem, the lawyer may need to do a search or send a letter to determine the extent of the problem in order to advise the client and get instructions on how to proceed. For example, if there is a known encroachment, the title insurance company will not insure the buyer for that problem. In that case, the lawyer may do a search to determine the extent of the encroachment in order to advise the client and get instructions.

## Personal Property Security Act (PPSA) Search

If chattels of significant value are included in the agreement of purchase and sale, you may wish to conduct a PPSA search against the seller to make sure that the chattels are free of encumbrances.

## Water Department, Sewers, and Drains

If you haven't already requested this information when requesting a final meter reading, you may write to the water department of the municipality in which the property is located to find out the status of the water account. You need this information because water account arrears can be added to the tax account and then become a lien against the land. You also need this information to check the statement of adjustments if the water account is billed on a flat-rate basis.

You also want to find out

1. whether the property is serviced by water and storm and sanitary sewers, and, if so, whether the sewer and water connections are completed and fully paid for; and
2. whether there are any easements or rights of way for drains, sewers, and water pipes.

The first item is particularly important for new houses, although there are older houses as well, even within urban areas, that are not connected to the municipal sewers. If there are any easements, the buyer's lawyer will have to determine whether they fall within the scope of the utility easements provided for in the agreement of purchase and sale.

Figure 18.8 is an example of a letter to the water department.

## Building Department

You may also write a letter to the building department of the municipality in which the property is located to find out

1. whether the size of the building and its location on the lot comply with applicable zoning bylaws;
2. what the permitted use of the property is; and
3. whether or not there are any outstanding work orders against the property.

You will have to provide a copy of an up-to-date survey of the property to get the first item of information. If a building has been constructed contrary to the relevant zoning bylaws, a demolition order could conceivably be issued against the building. If the intended use of the property is contrary to the relevant zoning bylaws, the municipality may be able to get a court order to prohibit the intended use. Finally, if there are outstanding work orders against the property, the new owner will be required to make the mandated repairs to the property at the new owner's expense.

Depending on the municipality, you will receive different types of answers to this letter. Many municipalities decline to provide an opinion as to compliance with the relevant bylaws. Instead, they simply give the number of the relevant bylaw and leave it to the buyer's lawyer to review it and decide whether the property complies. If you receive that kind of letter, you must get a copy of the relevant bylaw and give it to the lawyer handling the file.

Very often a building was erected or a property was used in a particular way before the passage of the current bylaw. Zoning bylaws are rarely retroactive, and the existing size and location of the buildings and use of the property may be allowed to continue as a legal non-conforming use. To qualify as such, the use of the property or the size and location of the buildings, as the case may be,

- must not have changed since the bylaw was enacted; and
- must have complied with the bylaw in effect when the building was constructed or the use started.

Few, if any, municipalities will provide an opinion that the property qualifies as a legal non-conforming use. The law firm acting for the buyer will be required to provide it. In order to give that opinion, you will have to

- find out the date of the enactment of the existing bylaw;
- find out the date of the construction of the building or commencement of its present use, as the case may be;
- obtain a copy of the bylaw in effect at the time the construction or use, as the case may be, started; and
- obtain evidence that the construction or use, as the case may be, has not changed since the bylaw came into effect.

In order to obtain the last item, you may have to requisition a statutory declaration from the seller. In addition, you can check the municipal building department files to find out whether any building permits have been issued for the property.

Figure 18.9 is an example of a letter to the building department.

## Unregistered Hydro Easements

Under the Ontario *Electricity Act, 1998*, hydro easements may be created that are not registered on title. These easements occur most often in rural or cottage areas, but it is possible for one to exist on an urban property that has not been subdivided. To find out whether there are any unregistered hydro easements affecting the property, write to Hydro One at the appropriate regional office or inquire online at <https://www.services.hydroone.com/lvr>.

Figure 18.10 is an example of a letter to Hydro One.

# Specialized Inquiries

In some transactions, additional inquiries may be required, depending on the nature of the property.

## Septic Tanks

If the property is not connected to the municipal sewer system, you must write to the health department of the relevant municipality to ensure that the septic tank has been approved by the department. Figure 18.11 is an example of a letter to the health department.

## Ontario Heritage Act

If a property has been "designated" under the *Ontario Heritage Act*, the owner's right to make alterations or improvements to the property is limited. Clearly, the application of this Act is not a concern in most transactions. However, if there is any doubt, write an inquiry letter to the clerk of the relevant municipality.

## Conservation Authority

If a property is designated as being within a fill line or flood plain, no building on the property or change in the grading pattern of the property is permitted without a permit from the appropriate conservation authority. Again, this designation is not a concern in all transactions. If there is any question, write to the local conservation authority to determine whether the property has been specially designated. This may well be of concern even if the property is located within an urban area. If the property is near a ravine, contains a stream, or is in a low-lying area, it may be a designated property.

## New Homes

If the property includes a newly constructed home, it is important to make sure that the builder is enrolled with the Tarion Warranty Corporation, which administers the *Ontario New Home Warranties Plan Act*. This inquiry can be made online at <http://www.tarion.com/_layouts/buildersearch/builder_search.aspx>. The procedures involved in the purchase of a new home are discussed in Chapter 25.

## Other Specialized Inquiries

Depending on the nature of the transaction, you may need to make additional inquiries to

- the Ministry of the Environment about a pollutant;
- the Ministry of Transportation about limitations on construction if the property is within 800 metres of a Queen's highway;

- the fire marshal's office about work orders; and
- the health department about work orders.

# Addresses and Fees

Before you can write any of the letters described in this chapter, you must find out the address of the appropriate department or company, and confirm the fee (if any) charged for the information provided. There are a number of ways to obtain this information:

- Your law firm may maintain a master file containing this information.
- Your law firm may have a solicitor's desk book that you can check.
- You can telephone the relevant municipality.
- You can find the information online.

If a fee is payable, remember to enclose a cheque with your letter.

# REFERENCES

*Electricity Act, 1998*, SO 1998, c 15, Schedule A.

*Ontario Heritage Act*, RSO 1990, c O.18.

*Ontario New Home Warranties Plan Act*, RSO 1990, c O.31.

*Personal Property Security Act*, RSO 1990, c P.10, as amended.

*Planning Act*, RSO 1990, c P.13.

# REVIEW QUESTIONS

1. Why would you send a preliminary letter to the client?

2. What information should you give to a title searcher?

3. What is a PPSA search, and when do you need one?

4. Why would you write a preliminary letter to the seller's solicitor?

5. Why would you obtain a municipal tax certificate?

6. Sandine is buying a house and your law firm is acting. He has instructed the firm to order title insurance on his behalf. Would you have to write to the utility companies and, if so, for what purpose?

**Figure 18.1    Preliminary Letter to the Buyer**

*Date*

Mr. Henry Grant and Ms. Wilma Grant
621 Augustus Street
Seneca, Ontario
K1K 0T4

Dear Mr. and Ms. Grant:

Re:    Grant purchase from Mercier
        166 Valley Road, Newmarket

We acknowledge receipt of a copy of your agreement of purchase and sale for the above property, which is closing on December 15, 2015, and wish to thank you for requesting us to act on your behalf.

If you are financing the purchase by means of a mortgage, please let us know, and advise the lending institution ("lender") that we are acting for you. You should know that if we do the mortgage work for you, we will also be representing the lender's interests, and any information we receive about the transaction from either party cannot be kept confidential from the other party. If a conflict of interest should occur between you and the lender, we may be obliged to stop acting for both of you. Such a conflict is very rare.

If there is a mortgage, you will need to insure the property for at least the amount of the mortgage. We will need from your insurance agent a binder letter, indicating the name of the insuring company, the effective date, the expiry date, the amount of coverage, and the names of the mortgagees, with a certified copy of the policy to follow.

If you have an up-to-date plan of survey of the property, please forward it to us.

Before the closing date, you will need to attend at our offices to sign documents, and to provide a certified cheque to cover a) the amount to be paid to the seller; b) land transfer tax and registration costs; c) the cost of title insurance, if applicable; and d) our account. We will advise you several days before the closing date what the exact amount of the certified cheque should be, and will arrange for an appointment with us.

We will contact you shortly to obtain the full name and birthdate of each person who will be shown as an owner on the deed, and to discuss the purchase of title insurance. In the interim, if you have any questions, please feel free to contact us.

Yours very truly,

Kurtz, Emmans, Blatt & Wolf
Per:

**Figure 18.2   Title Search Request**

| | |
|---|---|
| FILE NAME | FILE NO. |
| REQUESTED BY | |
| DATE OF REQUEST | DATE REQUIRED |
| DATE OF CLOSING | REQUISITION DATE |
| DESCRIPTION OF LAND | MUNICIPALITY |
| MUNICIPAL ADDRESS | |
| DIMENSIONS OF PROPERTY | |
| REGISTERED OWNERS | |
| PIN | |

**Instructions**
( )   Full 40-year search (Registry)
     Attached:   ( )   Agreement of purchase and sale
                ( )   Survey
( )   Full search (Land Titles)
( )   Search abutting lands
( )   Subsearch only
     From date
     From instrument no.
     Purpose of subsearch
( )   Attached previous search

Obtain copies of the following instruments:
( )   Registered agreements
( )   Outstanding mortgages
     ( )
     ( )
     ( )
     ( )
( )   Register the following documents:

**Special Instructions**

## Figure 18.3 Preliminary Letter to the Seller's Solicitor

*Date*

Brooks & Dunn
Barristers and Solicitors
16 Any Street
Newmarket, Ontario
L0L 1T1

Dear Sir or Madam:

Re:    Grant purchase from Mercier
        166 Valley Road, Newmarket
        Closing Date: December 15, 2015
        Our File No.: 15-1925

Please be advised that I act for the buyers in the above transaction and I understand that you represent the sellers.

My clients will take title to the property as follows:

| Full Name | Birthdate |
|---|---|
| GRANT, Henry Albert | March 27, 1952 |
| GRANT, Wilma Heather | March 18, 1955 |
| As joint tenants | |

Kindly provide the following at your earliest convenience:

Draft Deed
Statement of Adjustments
Plan of Survey

I trust the foregoing to be satisfactory.

Yours very truly,

Kurtz, Emmans, Blatt & Wolf
Per:

**Figure 18.4   Letter to the Water Department**

*Date*

Water Department
Town of Newmarket
*Address*

Dear Sir or Madam:

Re:   Grant purchase from Mercier
       166 Valley Road, Newmarket
       Closing Date: December 15, 2015
       Our File No.: 15-1925

I am the solicitor for Henry Albert Grant and Wilma Heather Grant, the buyers in the above transaction, which is scheduled to be completed on December 15, 2015.

Kindly arrange for the water meter to be read on the said closing date.

For your reference, the solicitor for the seller is:

Brooks & Dunn
Barristers and Solicitors
16 Any Street
Newmarket, Ontario
L0L 1T1

Thank you for your cooperation.

Yours very truly,

Kurtz, Emmans, Blatt & Wolf
Per:

**Figure 18.5    Letter to the Local Hydro Company**

*Date*

Newmarket Hydro
*Address*

Dear Sir or Madam:

Re:    Grant purchase from Mercier
        166 Valley Road, Newmarket
        Closing Date: December 15, 2015
        Our File No.: 15-1925

I am the solicitor for Henry Albert Grant and Wilma Heather Grant, the buyers in the above transaction, which is scheduled to be completed on December 15, 2015.

Kindly arrange for the hydro meter to be read on the said closing date.

For your reference, the solicitor for the seller is:

Brooks & Dunn
Barristers and Solicitors
16 Any Street
Newmarket, Ontario
L0L 1T1

Thank you for your cooperation.

Yours very truly,

Kurtz, Emmans, Blatt & Wolf
Per:

**Figure 18.6    Letter to the Local Gas Company**

*Date*

Enbridge Inc.
Billing Clerical Department
*Address*

Dear Sir or Madam:

Re:    Grant purchase from Mercier
       166 Valley Road, Newmarket
       Closing Date: December 15, 2015
       Our File No.: 15-1925

I am the solicitor for Henry Albert Grant and Wilma Heather Grant, the buyers in the above transaction, which is scheduled to be completed on December 15, 2015.

Kindly arrange for the gas meter to be read on the said closing date.

For your reference, the solicitor for the seller is:

Brooks & Dunn
Barristers and Solicitors
16 Any Street
Newmarket, Ontario
L0L 1T1

Thank you for your cooperation.

Yours very truly,

Kurtz, Emmans, Blatt & Wolf
Per:

**Figure 18.7 Letter Requesting a Municipal Tax Certificate**

*Date*

Tax Department
Town of Newmarket
*Address*

Dear Sir or Madam:

Re:   Grant purchase from Mercier
        166 Valley Road, Newmarket

We are the solicitors for Henry Albert Grant and Wilma Heather Grant, the buyers in the above transaction, which is scheduled to close on December 15, 2015.

Would you please provide us with a tax certificate showing:

- the arrears of taxes, if any;
- a statement showing current taxes;
- any charges for work orders, snow shovelling, demolition, water, or other public utilities;
- any other statutory charges, liens, or levies including local improvement rates that may be collectable by you.

Enclosed is our cheque in the amount of $ _____ , in payment of your fee, together with a stamped self-addressed envelope.

Thank you for your attention to this matter.

Yours very truly,

Kurtz, Emmans, Blatt & Wolf
Per:

**Figure 18.8   Letter to the Water Department**

*Date*

Water Department
Town of Newmarket
*Address*

Dear Sir or Madam:

Re:   Grant purchase from Mercier
       166 Valley Road, Newmarket

We are the solicitors for Henry Albert Grant and Wilma Heather Grant, the buyers in the above transaction, which is scheduled to close on December 15, 2015.

Would you please advise us whether or not there are any arrears of water payments owing with respect to the subject property?

Would you also please advise us whether or not this property is serviced by water and storm and sanitary sewers, and, if so, whether or not all drains, sewers, and water connections servicing this property are completed and paid for in full?

We would also like to know whether or not you have any claim for easements or rights of way for drains, sewers, and water pipes that would affect this property.

Enclosed is our cheque in the amount of $ _____ , in payment of your fee, together with a stamped self-addressed envelope.

Thank you for your attention to this matter.

Yours very truly,



Kurtz, Emmans, Blatt & Wolf
Per:

**Figure 18.9 Letter to the Building Department**

*Date*

Building Department
Town of Newmarket
*Address*

Dear Sir or Madam:

Re: Grant purchase from Mercier
166 Valley Road, Newmarket

We are the solicitors for Henry Albert Grant and Wilma Heather Grant, the buyers in the above transaction, which is scheduled to close on December 15, 2015.

Would you please provide us with the following information with respect to the subject property:

- zoning, zoning bylaw number, and date of the zoning bylaw;
- the number and date of any part lot control bylaw with respect to the property;
- whether the land complies with the lot area, lot frontage, and lot depth requirements;
- whether the building complies with the height, floor area density, and set-back requirements;
- whether there are any prohibitions or limitations with respect to the use of the land and building;
- whether all other relevant bylaws and ordinances have been complied with; and
- whether there are any outstanding work orders or stop-work orders or notices of violation with respect to the property? Would you please advise us of the amount of money advanced, if any, and the unpaid amount outstanding for development charges in respect of any past work orders or notices of violation?

Enclosed is our cheque in the amount of $ _____ , in payment of your fee, together with a copy of the survey with respect to the property and a stamped self-addressed envelope.

Thank you for your assistance in this matter.

Yours very truly,


Kurtz, Emmans, Blatt & Wolf
Per:

**Figure 18.10   Letter to Hydro One**

---

*Date*

Hydro One
*Address*

Dear Sir or Madam:

Re:   Grant purchase from Mercier
       166 Valley Road, Newmarket

---

We are the solicitors for Henry Albert Grant and Wilma Heather Grant, the buyers in the above transaction, which is scheduled to close on December 15, 2015.

Would you please advise us whether or not Hydro One claims any easements under the *Electricity Act, 1998* with respect to the subject property?

Enclosed is our cheque in the amount of $ _____ , in payment of your fee, together with a copy of the survey with respect to the property and a stamped self-addressed envelope.

Thank you for your assistance in this matter.

Yours very truly,


Kurtz, Emmans, Blatt & Wolf
Per:

**Figure 18.11    Letter to the Health Department**

*Date*

Health Department
Regional Municipality of York
*Address*

Dear Sir or Madam:

Re:    Grant purchase from Mercier
       166 Valley Road, Newmarket

We are the solicitors for Henry Albert Grant and Wilma Heather Grant, the buyers in the above transaction, which is scheduled to close on December 15, 2015.

Would you please advise us whether or not the septic tank located on the property has been approved by the local health unit? In order to facilitate future servicing, would you also please provide us with a copy of the diagram showing the location of the septic tank and tile bed?

If jurisdiction over the property lies with the Ministry of the Environment, please advise us by telephone.

Enclosed is our cheque in the amount of $ _____ , in payment of your fee, together with a stamped self-addressed envelope.

Thank you for your assistance in this matter.

Yours very truly,



Kurtz, Emmans, Blatt & Wolf
Per:

# Requisitions: An Overview

# 19

## LEARNING OUTCOMES

After reading this chapter, you will understand:

- The importance of requisitions in a real estate transaction

- The different categories of requisitions

- The procedure for requisitions

- What the sources of requisitions are

- The importance of a title search as a source of requisitions

- How to review a search of title to determine what requisitions to make

# Introduction

This chapter deals with the steps you must take arising from the matters discussed in Chapter 18, Preliminary Matters—the search of title and the responses to your inquiry letters.

You and the lawyer handling the file must decide whether the searches and answers to your inquiry letters disclose a satisfactory state of affairs. If not, you must take steps to resolve the disclosed problems by way of a request made to the seller to do so. These requests are known as **requisitions**.

This chapter deals with requisitions in general and reviews those matters that give rise to requisitions. The drafting of requisitions will be dealt with in Chapter 20, The Requisition Letter.

The word "requisition," in its widest sense, means anything the buyer formally requires of the seller in a real estate transaction—the correction of a title defect, the production of a document, or any other thing to which the buyer is entitled. The purpose of making a requisition may be simply to remind the other party of a contractual obligation, or it may be to preserve the buyer's rights under the contract with respect to an alleged title defect. All requisitions are based on the provisions in the agreement of purchase and sale. It is therefore always essential to read the agreement of purchase and sale before preparing requisitions.

The making of a requisition may give rise to the buyer's right to terminate the agreement of purchase and sale under paragraph 10 of the agreement. For this to occur, the requisition must deal with one of the matters referred to in paragraph 10; the seller (acting in good faith) must be unwilling or unable to remove, remedy, satisfy, or obtain insurance in favour of the buyer against the defect; and the buyer must be unwilling to waive the requisition. The buyer cannot rely on a title defect to terminate the agreement of purchase and sale unless the buyer makes a requisition with respect to that defect.

**requisition**
request made to the seller to clear up problems revealed by the title search and other inquiries

# Categories of Requisitions

There are different categories of requisitions. The distinction between these categories is important primarily for determining whether or not the time limit in paragraph 8 of the agreement of purchase and sale set for the making of requisitions (the requisition date) applies to a particular requisition. As noted in Chapter 16, some requisitions may be submitted until closing, while others must be submitted by the requisition date. Requisitions relating to matters of contract, matters of conveyance, and matters going to the root of title may be submitted until closing. Requisitions on matters of title not going to the root of title must be submitted by the requisition date. The distinctions between the various types of requisitions are far from clear. The most prudent course is therefore to have all of your title requisitions delivered by the requisition date.

**requisition going to the root of title**
requisition based on a defect that calls into question the legal enforceability/validity of the title

## Requisitions on Title

**requisition on title**
query of directives made by the buyer that asks the seller to remedy problems with title

Requisitions on title raise objections to the title, based on the title search, and set out specific corrective actions that the buyer requires. Requisitions on title are either **requisitions going to the root of title** or other **requisitions on title**.

Requisitions going to the root of title are those that call into question the validity of the seller's title to the property, or that raise very serious defects in the seller's title— so serious that, if required to accept title, the buyer would not be receiving title at all or would be receiving something substantially different from what he or she contracted for. As stated above, requisitions going to the root of title may be submitted up until the closing date.

Other requisitions on title include all requisitions flowing from the search of title that are not requisitions going to the root of title, and that do not fall under the category of requisitions on conveyance or requisitions on contract. As stated above, these requisitions must be made by the requisition date.

## Requisitions on Conveyance

**Requisitions on conveyance** deal with matters related to the documentation that the seller is required to deliver on closing. They require the seller to produce an effective conveyance of the property, assuming that the seller has the ability to do so. If the seller is unable to do so, the requisition is not one on conveyance but a requisition on title.

requisition on
conveyance
requisition that requires
the seller to produce an
effective conveyance,
assuming that the seller
has the ability to do so

## Requisitions on Matters of Contract

**Requisitions on matters of contract** are for specific things that the buyer is entitled to receive under the contract and are determined by the provisions in the agreement of purchase and sale. For example, if the contract states that the seller agrees to obtain a consent from the committee of adjustment for a minor variance, the buyer will request that the seller produce this document. Strictly speaking, it is not necessary to requisition those matters because the obligation already exists under the contract. However, it is good practice to remind the seller's lawyer of the specific things that the buyer expects under the terms of the agreement of purchase and sale. As stated above, requisitions on matters of contract may be made up until the closing date.

requisition on matters of
contract
requisition for specific
things that the buyer
is entitled to receive
under the contract

## Requisitions on Matters of Zoning and Building Bylaws

These matters have been held to be matters of land use and not matters of title. However, the wording of the particular agreement of purchase and sale may also cause some of these matters to be matters of contract.

# Procedure for Requisitions

To be valid, a requisition must set out a specific objection to or problem with the particular title and must then require a specific solution (or propose one or more alternative solutions).

Before you can determine what requisitions to make, you must, *under the supervision of the lawyer handling the file*, read the agreement of purchase and sale, obtain and review a proper search of title, send out and receive responses to any preliminary letters, and review an up-to-date survey of the property, if available. Only then can you determine what, if any, problems exist and what requisitions should be made. In general, both parties to a real estate transaction want the deal to close, so there will usually be a great deal of cooperation between the parties. There is therefore no need to be adversarial when drafting the requisitions. However, the requisitions must be sufficiently particular for the buyer's lawyer to be able to rely on them if problems arise.

# Results of Preliminary Letters as a Source of Requisitions

In Chapter 18 we discussed the various preliminary letters that may be required in a real estate purchase. As we noted, usually many of those letters will be required only if title insurance is not being obtained. However, if preliminary inquiry letters are sent, be sure to read the responses to the letters to see if they disclose any matters that might give rise to a requisition.

## Municipal Tax Certificate

If the municipal tax certificate discloses that taxes have been paid up to or beyond the closing date, no requisition will be necessary, and the taxes will simply be adjusted on the statement of adjustments.

   If the tax certificate discloses arrears of taxes—and particularly if the arrears are substantial—the matter should be dealt with in the requisition letter. The requisition will set out the particulars of the state of the tax account and require proof on closing of payment of the taxes. Taxes will be adjusted in the statement of adjustments on the basis that they have been paid up until closing (because, as of closing, they will have been). Often payment of the tax arrears will be made out of the closing funds. In such a case, the seller will provide a direction to the buyer that the appropriate portion of the closing funds be made payable to the municipality and delivered to the seller's solicitor. The seller's solicitor will then provide a personal undertaking to the buyer to deliver the cheque to the municipality and to bear any responsibility for further penalties.

## Water Department, Sewers, and Drains

If water charges are calculated on a flat-rate basis, they may be dealt with in the same way as municipal realty taxes. If the water charges are metered, however, the final balance will not be ascertainable until after closing. However, you should make sure that all bills delivered before closing have been paid. Request that evidence of that payment be provided on closing. If necessary, arrangements can be made for payment of any outstanding bills out of the closing proceeds, following the procedure applicable to tax certificates above.

   The final bill will be delivered to the seller after closing. To ensure that the seller will pay the final water bill, you must require delivery of an undertaking signed by the seller to that effect. However, if the bills have historically been large, you can call the water department to get an estimate of the final bill and request that the seller's lawyer provide an undertaking to hold back sufficient money from the closing proceeds to pay it.

If the letter from the water department discloses the existence of an easement more significant than that required to be assumed by the terms of the agreement of purchase and sale, you must ask the seller to obtain a release of the easement from the municipality. There is virtually no possibility that the seller will be able to obtain such a release, but by making the requisition, the buyer's rights under the agreement of purchase and sale are preserved.

If a significant easement is disclosed by the response from the water department, it will be necessary to obtain the buyer's written instructions on how to proceed. Even though the buyer is not required to accept title subject to this easement, the buyer may choose to close regardless.

## Building Department

As discussed in Chapter 18, Preliminary Matters, the first step following receipt of the letter from the building department is to fill in the details necessary to analyze the response.

You must review the cited zoning bylaws to determine the existing permitted use. If it is not as specified in the agreement of purchase and sale, you must requisition an amendment to the bylaw, a variance to allow the use, or satisfactory evidence that the use constitutes a legal non-conforming use. Advise the client of the potential problem.

If the location of the building does not comply with existing zoning provisions, again, you must requisition an amendment to the bylaw, a variance to allow the use, or satisfactory evidence that the use constitutes a legal non-conforming use. Again, you must advise the client.

If it appears that the location of the building or use of the premises may constitute a legal non-conforming use, you cannot simply rely on the seller to provide the necessary evidence. You must also try to collect evidence that may resolve the question. For example, there may be declarations of possession registered on title that establish a continuous use or that the physical state of the buildings has not changed since before the date the current bylaw was enacted.

A survey pre-dating the bylaw can help to establish a legal non-conforming use as to building location if the buyer can confirm that there have been no changes to the structure since the date of the survey. If there have been changes made to the structure, ask the municipality whether building permits were issued and, if so, whether they seem to cover the work done. If building permits were issued, it is possible that there will not be a problem with zoning. Ordinarily, a building permit is issued only if the work complies with the existing zoning requirements or if a variance has been obtained.

In addition to getting independent evidence, you should require the seller to provide as much evidence as possible—in particular, a declaration of possession that addresses the issue of use or location of the structures. Even if the seller's ownership does not extend back beyond the passage of the current bylaw, the seller may possess statutory declarations from previous owners that can, when added together, establish continuity of use or the physical state of the buildings.

If there are outstanding work orders, you must requisition their rectification and removal. If the seller is unwilling to do this, you should obtain written instructions from the client about whether to accept title subject to the outstanding work orders. Occasionally, a buyer will agree to assume responsibility for the work orders in return for a reduction in the purchase price in an amount equal to the amount required for the repairs. In such a case, the client should be advised that the work may well end up costing more than estimated.

### Unregistered Hydro Easements

If the response from Hydro One states that there is an unregistered easement, you must decide whether it is one that falls within the category of easements that the buyer is required to accept. If it does not, you must request that the seller obtain a discharge of the easement from Hydro One. It is most unlikely that such a discharge can be obtained, but by making the requisition, you protect the buyer's rights under the agreement of purchase and sale. You must also get the client's written instructions.

On a practical note, do not notify the client as each problem arises. Rather, it is a good practice to review the state of the title with the client once the search, the survey, and the replies to the preliminary letters have been reviewed.

## The Survey as a Source of Requisitions

As stated in Chapter 17, Title Insurance, title insurance insures against any problems that an up-to-date survey might have revealed, and it is therefore very common today to complete a transaction without a survey. If a survey is obtained, an up-to-date plan of survey of the property can disclose one or more of the following problems:

- the property being purchased is the wrong property—not the property the buyer had in mind;
- the property being purchased is the wrong size;
- buildings on the property being purchased encroach on someone else's property;
- buildings on someone else's property encroach on the property being purchased; or
- there is a right of way over the property being purchased that is not in accordance with the agreement of purchase and sale.

### The Wrong Property

This is a concern that almost never arises in urban transactions. In the unlikely event that such a problem does arise, you must get the client's written instructions as soon as possible.

### The Wrong Size

If the property shown on the survey is smaller than described in the legal description, or smaller than the size indicated by the dimensions in the agreement of purchase and sale, the buyer's rights will depend on a number of circumstances, including the extent of the discrepancy and whether the size of the property was apparent on examination of the property. If the extent of the discrepancy is large enough, the buyer may either seek an abatement (reduction) in the purchase price or terminate the transaction. The client must give specific, written instructions.

If you discover a discrepancy in size, in order to preserve the buyer's rights under the agreement of purchase and sale, you must requisition resolution of the matter. The requisition should point out the deficiency, referring to the survey (and the most recent transfer if it discloses the problem as well), and should require a correcting transfer. Note that the words "more or less" in the agreement will forgive minor discrepancies in the legal description.

## Encroachments on Other Property

The survey may show that buildings or structures encroach on adjoining property. For example, the fence may be located partly on the neighbouring property, the eaves of the house may hang over the neighbouring property, or the front steps may be located on municipal property.

An encroachment by a building or structure on adjoining property is not a problem if the owner of the other property consents or if the encroachment has existed long enough to establish possessory title. If the survey discloses an encroachment, you must submit a requisition on the matter. The requisition should set out the particulars of the encroachment and seek proof of consent of the other owner or satisfactory evidence of possessory title.

## Encroachments on Property Being Purchased

If the survey discloses that adjoining buildings or structures are encroaching on the property being purchased, the buyer's rights will depend on the nature and extent of the encroachment. If the encroachment is minor, the buyer may be obliged to accept title notwithstanding the encroachment. If the encroachment is major, however, the buyer may be entitled to terminate the transaction or seek an abatement in the purchase price. You must get the client's written instructions.

If you find this kind of encroachment, you must submit a requisition on the matter. The requisition should set out the particulars of the encroachment and require its removal. Although the seller will generally not be able to have the encroachment removed (there may, in fact, be possessory title), the requisition is made to protect the buyer's rights under the agreement of purchase and sale.

## Rights of Way

If the survey discloses the existence of a right of way over the property that has not been provided for in the agreement of purchase and sale, you must submit a requisition on the matter. The requisition should set out the particulars of the right of way and require its removal. Although the seller may not be in a position to have the right of way removed, you must make the requisition to protect the buyer's rights under the agreement of purchase and sale. The client may be entitled to seek an abatement or to terminate the transaction. You will need specific written instructions from the client.

# The Title Search as a Source of Requisitions

When the search notes are received from the title searcher, you must review them to determine the answers to a number of questions:

- Is the parcel the size expected?
- Does the search start with a good root of title?
- Is the chain of title connected?
- Have all mortgages been discharged?
- Are there any other outstanding matters?
- Are there any mortgages to be assumed?
- Are there any outstanding executions?
- Are there any other possible concerns?
- Do the instruments conform with all formal requirements?
- Are there any inconsistencies in affidavits?
- Have adjoining properties been searched?

We discuss the title search review process generally under this heading. In the Appendix to this chapter you will find a detailed review of two title searches—a Registry system search and a Land Titles system search. In Chapter 20, the review of the title search will be used to draft a requisition letter.

## Size of the Parcel

Compare the measurements shown on the whiteprint of the plan of subdivision (or the metes and bounds description in the most recent transfer/deed) with the dimensions stated in the agreement of purchase and sale. They should be the same.

## Good Root of Title

If the property is in the Registry system, there must be a good root of title.

A good root of title (or root deed) will be the first conveyance after the commencement date of the search (40 years before the date of closing), or a certificate of title, or a Crown patent.

## Chain of Title

Starting with the earliest grant in the chain of title, all grants to date should be listed. In any conveyance, the grantor should be the same person as the grantee in the previous conveyance. The last person in the chain should be the same person as the seller.

## Discharge of Mortgages

All mortgages, other than mortgages to be assumed by the buyer, should have been discharged. Review the search to make sure that all these mortgages have been discharged. Make a list of all mortgages that are still outstanding, and requisition a discharge of each.

The search should contain sufficient particulars of any outstanding mortgage (including the date and time of registration, the registration number, and the parties) to enable the person closing the deal to be sure that the discharge produced on or before closing or promised by a personal undertaking is proper. The search should also contain sufficient information (the mortgage terms, the name and address of the mortgagee, and the mortgage number) to allow the buyer's law firm to follow up on the discharge and ensure that one will be available.

## Other Outstanding Matters

Review the search of title again for any other liens, charges, agreements such as sub-division agreements, restrictive covenants, bylaws, or other matters that have not been adequately dealt with. Make a note of any outstanding items, and determine what, if any, action is required—for example, a discharge, evidence of compliance, etc. Requisition the required action, and then take any necessary follow-up steps with third parties. The search should contain sufficient particulars to allow you to do this.

### Subdivision Agreements

The search of title may disclose an outstanding subdivision agreement. Paragraph 10 of the agreement of purchase and sale requires the buyer to accept title subject to such agreements, provided that they have been complied with. You must requisition proof of compliance or posting of security to secure compliance. If title insurance is not being obtained, it is not enough to rely on the seller to look after this matter. In addition, you should write a letter to the relevant municipality to ascertain whether a discharge is available and, if not, whether the agreement has been complied with or adequate security posted. Figure 19.1, at the end of this chapter, is an example of this kind of letter. If title insurance is being obtained, it will insure against any such problems, and the follow-up letter is not necessary.

### Restrictive Covenants

The search of title may disclose outstanding restrictive covenants (registered restrictions running with the land). Under the agreement of purchase and sale, the buyer must accept title subject to these restrictions, provided that they have been complied with. Accordingly, you must requisition evidence that the restrictions have been complied with. Again, in addition to making the requisition, you should contact any third party involved to try to obtain evidence of compliance.

## Mortgages to Be Assumed

If the agreement of purchase and sale states that the buyer is to assume an existing mortgage, make sure that you instruct the title searcher to obtain a photocopy of the mortgage for review. When you review the search, look at the mortgage to confirm that the terms of the mortgage registered on title comply with the terms of the mortgage as described in the agreement of purchase and sale.

If the mortgage on title matches the description of the mortgage to be assumed in the agreement of purchase and sale, you must requisition confirmation that the mortgage on title is the mortgage to be assumed. You will also requisition the production of a mortgage statement on closing that confirms the balance outstanding on the mortgage and states that the mortgage is in good standing. You should also write to the mortgagee, asking for a mortgage statement. Figure 19.2 is an example of this letter.

If the mortgage on title differs from the description of the mortgage to be assumed in the agreement of purchase and sale, you must requisition either production and registration of an amending agreement that amends the mortgage to conform with the terms of the agreement, or a discharge of the existing mortgage and replacement with a mortgage containing the appropriate terms. Rather than an amending agreement or a new mortgage, the seller may provide a mortgage statement, signed by the mortgagee, confirming that the terms of the mortgage, in fact, comply with the terms in the agreement. In most circumstances, production of this kind of a mortgage statement will be satisfactory.

You must also review any mortgage to be assumed to make sure that there are no restrictions on assumability. If the mortgage is not assumable by a buyer, it will be necessary to requisition an amendment to the mortgage or a discharge of the existing mortgage and replacement with a mortgage that complies with the agreement. If the mortgage requires the approval by the mortgagee of any subsequent buyer, it is necessary to requisition the approval. Review the agreement of purchase and sale to determine who is responsible for obtaining this approval. In any event, ask the mortgagee what steps must be taken by the buyer to be approved, and advise the buyer accordingly.

## Executions

If the client has chosen not to obtain title insurance and the property is registered in the Registry system, it is standard procedure to search executions against all owners during the 40-year search period. The search notes should therefore include a sheriff's certificate containing a list of names and indicating whether there are any executions against the persons named.

If there are outstanding executions against any person in the chain of title during their period of ownership, you must requisition removal of the execution. If the execution disclosed on the certificate is, in fact, outstanding against the seller or a prior owner, the seller will be required to have the execution removed before closing, usually by paying the amount of the judgment.

Often, however, the execution disclosed on the certificate turns out to be not against the seller or a prior owner, but rather against someone with a similar name. In that case, you will requisition production of sufficient evidence to ensure that the person named in the execution is not the same person as the person in the chain of title. In the Land Titles system, if the amount of the execution is $50,000 or more, you will need a letter from the execution creditor or from the execution creditor's lawyer that the owner or former owner of the property is not the same person as the execution debtor. If the amount is less than $50,000, an affidavit from the owner is sufficient.

## Other Possible Concerns

The search of title may disclose matters that require additional attention.

### Deeds Under Power of Sale

If the search of title discloses a deed under power of sale, you must review the mortgage to get particulars of the power of sale, including the default period and notice period. If there is no power of sale contained in the mortgage, part II of the *Mortgages Act* governs the notice and default periods.

Check that there is a declaration deposited on title stating that the required default has taken place (default for the period in the mortgage or the Act) and that service of the notice has been effected on the required parties (see part III of the *Mortgages Act* regarding parties). There must be a statement by the mortgagee or by the lawyer representing the mortgagee that the sale complies with part III (and, where there is no power of sale in the mortgage, with part II) of the *Mortgages Act*.

Section 35 of the *Mortgages Act* provides that a statutory declaration is conclusive evidence of compliance with the power of sale provisions and is sufficient to give good title. However, the statutory declaration must make sense on the surface. In other words, if it is clear that there was no proper default, notice period, or service on all parties, the buyer cannot rely on the statutory declaration.

### Final Orders of Foreclosure

Where the search reveals a final order of foreclosure, check the order to make sure that it contains the proper legal description and that all persons with an interest on title subsequent to the mortgage, as well as the spouse of the mortgagor, are identified as being foreclosed.

### Construction Liens and Certificates of Action

Where the search of title discloses a construction lien on title, review the search to ensure that the lien has been properly discharged. The lien itself may be discharged by either registration of a discharge of lien or a court order. If a certificate of action has been registered as well, a court order is required for it to be properly vacated or removed. The court order must state that the certificate of action is vacated and, where applicable, the lien is discharged.

If either the lien or the certificate of action is outstanding, you must requisition that the lien be discharged or the certificate of action be vacated.

### Corporations

In reviewing the search of title, make a note of all corporate owners on title and the dates during which they owned the property. If title insurance is not being obtained, you must arrange for a corporate search of each corporation to confirm that it was in existence during the time the property was owned. If the corporate existence lapsed at any time during its ownership of the property, the land escheats, or reverts to the Crown.

Although there is software that enables online corporate searches, most residential real estate law firms get their corporate searches done by a service provider—for example, Dye & Durham or OnCorp.

If title insurance is being obtained, it will likely insure against any such problems, in which case a corporate search is not necessary.

### Transfers by an Estate

recital
statement that sets
out facts on which a
document is based

If the search is in the Registry system, and it discloses a transfer by an estate or if the seller is an estate, a special form of transfer containing a number of specific **recitals** will be required. A notarial copy of the certificate of appointment of estate trustee, with or without a will, must also be registered on title. In addition, if the deceased died between 1970 and 1979, an Ontario succession duty release must be registered on title.

If the property is in Land Titles, and the seller is an estate, the estate trustee must first register a transmission application, registering the estate trustee as the owner of the deceased's property. The application must contain a compliance with law statement by the lawyer for the estate, stating that debts have been paid in full, and setting out the particulars of the appointment of the estate trustee, which must still be in full force and effect.

### Rights of Way

If the agreement of purchase and sale states that the property includes a right of way over another property, it is necessary to search the title to the servient tenement to ensure that the right of way is registered against that property.

## Formal Requirements

Many statutes affecting the registration requirements of various instruments have come into and gone out of effect during the period of time covered by a 40-year Registry system search. Accordingly, the formalities required of each instrument will differ for different dates in the search period.

You can find lists of these different requirements and their relevant dates in various title-searching manuals. These lists set out, for example, the effective dates for certain affidavits, as well as other technical requirements in force from time to time. A list of dates that were important for searches in the Registry system is reproduced in Figure 19.3.

For each instrument abstracted, the title searcher should have checked off boxes to indicate various items that appear in the instruments. When reviewing the search notes, you must check the notes for each instrument and compare them with the various items on one of the lists to ensure that the instrument complies with the technical requirements in effect at the relevant time.

## Inconsistencies in Affidavits

Review the contents of affidavits of marital status and spousal status to make sure there is no inconsistency from one transaction to the next. If a deed contains a statement or affidavit that the property is not a matrimonial home, but there is a previous affidavit on title with respect to the same parties that contradicts it, you cannot rely on the latter statement or affidavit. You will have to requisition evidence that explains the contradiction.

## Adjoining Property

If the property being purchased is part of a lot, it may be necessary to search adjoining properties to ensure compliance with the *Planning Act*. This is not required if a part lot exemption bylaw is registered on title, if a consent to the severance has been registered in the past, or if a transfer containing the completed *Planning Act* statements has been registered on title. It is not necessary to search adjoining properties if the property being purchased is a whole lot, unless there is registered on title a bylaw that states that the plan of subdivision is no longer deemed to be a registered plan of subdivision for the purposes of section 50(3) of the *Planning Act*.

If any contravention of the *Planning Act* is disclosed, you must requisition the obtaining and registration of a consent to the severance.

# Follow Up on All Requisitions

If problems are disclosed when reviewing the title search, survey, and responses to preliminary letters, it is not sufficient to simply requisition a correction of the matter—you cannot rely on the seller to rectify matters. Depending on whether or not title insurance is being obtained, you may have to take other steps as well. For example, you may have to

- contact municipalities for occupancy permits, releases, or confirmation of compliance with subdivision agreements;
- contact third-party lawyers with regard to executions, affidavits, or technical deficiencies; and
- contact mortgagees for statements or discharges.

If title insurance is being obtained, contact the insurer to make sure that it will insure over the problem that has been discovered.

## KEY TERMS

recital, 272

requisition, 262

requisition going to the root of title, 262

requisition on conveyance, 263

requisition on matters of contract, 263

requisition on title, 262

## REFERENCES

*Fire v Longtin*, [1995] 4 SCR 3, 128 DLR (4th) 767.

*Mortgages Act*, RSO 1990, c M.40.

*Planning Act*, RSO 1990, c P.13.

*Registry Act*, RSO 1990, c R.20.

*Vendors and Purchasers Act*, RSO 1990, c V.2.

## REVIEW QUESTIONS

1. What is the purpose of making a requisition?

2. What are the implications of making a requisition?

3. The seller's lawyer receives a requisition setting out a general problem with the state of title without requesting any solution. Is this a valid requisition?

4. The buyer's lawyer has just obtained the tax certificate and it discloses arrears of taxes. What should the lawyer do?

5. Georgette is buying a home from Svitlana and the final water bill will be delivered to Svitlana after the closing takes place. Water charges on the property are metered and Georgette is concerned about what will happen if Svitlana does not pay the final bill. What should Georgette's lawyer do?

6. You work for a lawyer who is representing a buyer in a real estate transaction. The letter you received from the building department states that there are outstanding work orders against the property. In addition, it appears that the location of the building on the property does not comply with existing zoning provisions. What should the lawyer do?

7. What should you do if the response from Hydro One states that there is an unregistered easement?

8. Your firm represents the buyer in a real estate transaction. An up-to-date plan of survey discloses that the property is smaller than the description in the agreement of purchase and sale and that there are buildings that encroach on the adjoining property. The survey also discloses the existence of a right of way over the property that is not provided for in the agreement of purchase and sale. What should the lawyer in your firm requisition from the seller?

9. What requisition should be made if there are mortgages on title other than any mortgages to be assumed?

10. What requisition is made if the search of title discloses an outstanding subdivision agreement?

11. Your firm represents the buyer in a real estate transaction. The search of title discloses an outstanding restrictive covenant that prohibits the owner from installing a satellite dish on the property. The buyer wants to know if he is bound by this restriction. Advise him.

12. What requisition is made if there is a mortgage to be assumed? What are the three possible requisitions to make if the buyer is assuming a mortgage?

13. What requisition is made if there are outstanding executions against any person in the chain of title?

# APPENDIX
# Reviewing the Search of Title: Two Examples

Whether the property is in the Land Titles system or the Registry system, you must review the title search to determine what requisitions are necessary. As you will see, the process is much simpler if the property is in the Land Titles system. In this Appendix, we review two title searches, first a Registry system search and then a Land Titles system search.

## Reviewing a Registry System Search

We start with a review of the search notes for the 40-year Registry system search of Lot 11, Plan 1209, Township of Whitford, found in the Appendix at the end of Chapter 14. In the next chapter, these search notes will serve as the basis for the drafting of requisitions on title.

### Is the Parcel the Right Size?

This property is a whole lot, so you must review the whiteprint of the plan of subdivision to make sure that the dimensions of the lot are the same as the dimensions specified in the agreement of purchase and sale. A copy of the whiteprint can be found in Chapter 14 as Figure 14.1. Assume that the dimensions shown on the whiteprint are satisfactory.

### Does the Search Start with a Good Root of Title?

Assuming that the search was conducted in March 2015, our root of title is the deed to Douglas May registered on May 19, 1975 as instrument number 79621. This is the oldest deed that is within the 40-year search period.

### Is the Chain of Title Connected?

The chain of title as disclosed in the search notes can be found in Chapter 14 as Figure 14.2. The diagonal line through Duncan McTavish's name signifies that he died, leaving Marla McTavish as the surviving joint tenant. There appears to be no break in the chain of title.

### Have All Mortgages Been Discharged?

The cover page of the search notes discloses two outstanding mortgages: instrument number 635121 from Romano and Romano to Bank of Montreal, and instrument number 726341 from Romano and Romano to XYZ Mortgage Ltd. You must review the agreement of purchase and sale to determine whether these mortgages are to be discharged or assumed.

### Are There Any Other Outstanding Matters?

The search discloses a number of matters that must be examined.

#### INSTRUMENT NUMBER 77286

Instrument number 77286 is a notice of agreement relating to a subdivision agreement between Stavros Subdivisions Ltd. and the Corporation of the Township of Whitford. Paragraph 10 of the agreement of purchase and sale requires the buyer to accept title subject to any municipal agreements, as long as they have been complied with. You should requisition proof of compliance with this agreement in the form of a letter from the township. If no title insurance is being obtained, you should also write to the Township of Whitford yourself, to make sure that the terms of the subdivision agreement have been complied with.

#### INSTRUMENT NUMBER 153117

Instrument number 153117 is a deed from Marla MacTavish alone. There is also a death certificate for Duncan McTavish (deposited as instrument number 148902), which provides proof of his death. Thus, there is sufficient evidence that Marla MacTavish had the right to convey the property on her own as the surviving joint tenant.

Another concern with this document is a spelling discrepancy between Marla *Mc*Tavish in instrument number 91764 and Marla *Mac*Tavish in instrument number 153117. This, however, is explained in deposit number 170003, which is a statutory declaration by Marla McTavish, explaining that she is one and the same person as Marla MacTavish in instrument number 153117 and Marla McTavish in instrument number 91764. Therefore, no requisitions are necessary with respect to these documents.

### Have All Formal Requirements Been Met?

The lawyer must check each instrument against the important dates listed in Figure 19.3 to ensure that it complies with the various registration requirements in effect at the relevant time.

### Are There Outstanding Executions?

The search notes provided by the title searcher may not include a sheriff's certificate, if your law firm can search executions through Teraview, as discussed in Chapter 7. Let's assume that executions are searched against all names disclosed in the chain of title, and they are clear.

### Potential Solutions to Problems

When reviewing a search of title, keep in mind the following basic principles because they may provide an answer to potential title problems.

The first possible solution is "the 40-year rule." The combined effect of the various sections of part III of the *Registry Act* is that title is not affected by any question more than 40 years old if there have been conveyances during that 40-year search period. If there have been no conveyances during that period, you must search back to the last recorded conveyance.

In fact, *Fire v Longtin* confirmed the 40-year rule. In other words, it is not necessary to look for a root deed outside the 40-year period, provided that there is a conveyance some time within the 40-year period. Notwithstanding this decision, some lawyers prefer to look for the conveyance to the person who owned the property at the commencement of the 40-year search period, while relying on the 40-year rule to answer any questions with regard to intervening registrations between the root deed and the closing date of the current transaction.

Another potential solution is addressed by the *Vendors and Purchasers Act* provision with respect to recitals as discussed above, regarding instrument number 153117.

## Reviewing a Land Titles System Search

Next we review a Land Titles system search by examining the parcel register for Lot 170, Plan 65M-1234, Town of Newmarket, found in Chapter 14 as Figure 14.6.

As discussed in Chapter 5, under the Land Titles system, the government guarantees the accuracy of title to land and the parcel register always reflects the current state of title. As a result, many of the questions we have to ask in reviewing a Registry system search do not apply to a Land Titles system search, as illustrated by a review of those questions with respect to this Land Titles property:

1. *Is the parcel the right size?* This question must be answered for a Land Titles property. You should obtain a whiteprint of the plan of subdivision and review it.

2. *Does the search start with a good root of title?* This is not a concern for an Land Titles property.

3. *Is the chain of title connected?* This is not a concern for a Land Titles property.

4. *Have all mortgages been discharged?* This question must be answered for a Land Titles property. In this case, the parcel register shows one outstanding mortgage. You must review the agreement of purchase and sale to determine whether or not this mortgage is to be discharged.

5. *Are there any other outstanding matters?* This question must be answered for a Land Titles property. However, there will be far fewer outstanding instruments than in a Registry system search. In this case, instrument LT315678, the notice of agreement with the Corporation of the Town of Newmarket, is the only outstanding instrument of any concern. Paragraph 10 of the agreement of purchase and sale requires the buyer to accept title subject to any municipal agreements, as long as they have been complied with. You should requisition proof of compliance with this agreement in the form of a letter from the town. If no title insurance is being obtained, you should also write

to the Town of Newmarket yourself, to make sure that the terms of the subdivision agreement have been complied with.

6. *Have the formal requirements of outstanding documents been met?* This is not a concern for a Land Titles property because all Land Titles documents are reviewed before they are accepted for registration.

7. *Are there executions outstanding?* It is necessary to search executions against the current owners only.

**Figure 19.1   Subdivision Agreement Letter**

*Date*

Building Department
*Name of municipality*
*Address*

Dear Sir or Madam:

Re:   *Name of transaction*
       *Address of property*

We are the solicitors for _____ , the purchaser(s) in the above transaction, which is scheduled to close on (*date*).

Our search of title has disclosed the following agreements registered on title:

- Instrument number _____ , dated (*date*) and registered on (*date*) between (*subdivider*) and (*municipality*)
- Instrument number _____ , dated (*date*) and registered on (*date*) between (*subdivider*) and (*municipality*)

With respect to each of the above agreements, please advise us

- whether all the terms and provisions of the agreement have been complied with, or whether there are any outstanding items still to be completed;
- if the agreement has been complied with, whether a release is available;
- if there are still outstanding items, whether you hold adequate security to guarantee completion of all outstanding matters;
- whether there are any outstanding levies or other charges; and
- whether any occupancy provisions of the agreement have been complied with.

We enclose a stamped, self-addressed envelope for your convenience, together with our cheque payable to _____ in the amount of $_____, in payment of your fee.

Thank you for your assistance in this matter.

Yours very truly,

**Figure 19.2 Letter Requesting Mortgage Statement for Assumption Purposes**

*Date*

*Mortgagee's name*
*Mortgagee's address*

Dear Sir or Madam:

Re: Your mortgage with (*vendor's name*)
     *Address of property*
     *Mortgage number*

We act for _____ , the purchaser(s) in the above transaction, which is scheduled to close on (*date*). Pursuant to the agreement of purchase and sale, our clients are assuming the mortgage that you hold.

Please forward a mortgage statement to us setting out the amount of principal and interest outstanding as of the closing date and the terms of the said mortgage including the interest rate, the payment date and period, the balance due date, and the amount and frequency of each payment.

As well, please confirm that the said mortgage may be assumed by our clients, and that it is in good standing.

Thank you for your assistance in this matter.

Yours very truly,

## Figure 19.3    Important Dates Affecting Registration Requirements

| Date | | Requirement |
| --- | --- | --- |
| June 1 | 1921 | Land transfer tax affidavit |
| June 1 | 1929 | Affidavit of celibacy |
| January 1 | 1937 | All documents perforated with the word "registered" |
| June 25 | 1939 | Affidavit of age and marital status required by men in deed or mortgage where wife has joined to bar her dower |
| April 30 | 1954 | Affidavit of mortmain for corporations (revoked June 23, 1965) |
| April 1 | 1957 | Affidavit of age required by men and women<br><br>Affidavit of marital status by men in deed or mortgage if no one joins in as wife |
| January 1 | 1959 | Dominion estate tax consents required (revoked January 1, 1972) |
| May 8 | 1964 | Retail sales tax clearance (repealed April 1, 1976) |
| July 1 | 1964 | Affidavit of age required in power of attorney, lease, assignment of lease and mortgage<br><br>Affidavit of marital status may be sworn by either spouse<br><br>Instruments must contain the surname and at least one given name of grantee other than a corporation |
| June 23 | 1965 | No affidavit of mortmain required for Ontario companies |
| January 1 | 1967 | Affidavit of age required on discharge of mortgage |
| May 3 | 1967 | Power of consent under *Planning Act* transferred from Planning Board to committees of adjustment or Ministry of Municipal Affairs |
| June 15 | 1967 | Prior violations of subdivision and part lot control requirements of *Planning Act* are forgiven |
| May 3 | 1968 | *Planning Act* 10-acre consent rule cancelled |
| May 13 | 1969 | Affidavit of marital status required any time wife joins in a document |
| June 27 | 1969 | Conveyance of land as gift made subject to subdivision and part lot control under *Planning Act* |
| January 1 | 1970 | Succession duty consent required (repealed April 10, 1979) |
| June 27 | 1970 | *Planning Act* subdivision and part lot control applies throughout Ontario |

**Figure 19.3 Continued**

| Date | | Requirement |
|---|---|---|
| April 28 | 1971 | Simultaneous conveyances prohibited under *Planning Act* |
| September 1 | 1971 | Age of majority changed to 18 years from 21 years |
| January 1 | 1972 | Dominion estate tax consent requirement cancelled<br>Affidavit of residence—section 116 of the *Income Tax Act* |
| January 1 | 1973 | All new subdivisions must be registered in Land Titles system |
| April 1 | 1973 | Retail sales tax on chattels paid at registry office |
| July 1 | 1973 | All tax sales registered before July 1, 1973 pursuant to *Municipal Affairs Act* and *Assessment Act* confirmed under *Tax Sales Confirmation Act* |
| August 1 | 1973 | Registration of notice of agreement of purchase and sale, option to purchase or assignment good for one year under *Registry Act* |
| December 17 | 1973 | Partial discharge of mortgage subject to subdivision and part lot control under *Planning Act* |
| April 10 | 1974 | Affidavit of residency by purchaser to be included in deed, *Land Speculation Tax Act* affidavit or lien clearance to be inserted in deed (repealed October 24, 1978) |
| April 1 | 1976 | Retail sales tax clearance cancelled |
| March 31 | 1978 | *Family Law Reform Act* abolishes dower unless previously vested; creates statutory right of possession by spouse to matrimonial home; affidavits required |
| October 24 | 1978 | *Land Speculation Tax Act* repealed |
| December 15 | 1978 | *Planning Act* contravention of consent requirements forgiven except where judgment or court order provides otherwise |
| March 31 | 1979 | Once *Planning Act* consent is given to convey a parcel, further consent not required for subsequent sale |
| April 10 | 1979 | Succession duty consent cancelled |
| November 30 | 1979 | Corporation tax lien must be registered against property to be effective |
| July 1 | 1980 | Requirement to register estate tax consent cancelled |
| June 26 | 1981 | *Planning Act* consent required for partition orders |

**Figure 19.3    Concluded**

| Date | | Requirement |
|---|---|---|
| June 15 | 1982 | *Mortmain and Charitable Uses Act* repealed |
| April 2 | 1983 | *Construction Lien Act* in force |
| August 1 | 1983 | *Planning Act, 1983* in force |
| November 1 | 1984 | *Land Registration Reform Act* in force in County of Oxford, *Planning Act* statements available; *Planning Act* affidavits not required |
| January 1 | 1985 | *Municipal Tax Sales Act* in force |
| April 1 | 1985 | *Land Registration Reform Act* in force in all of Ontario |
| March 1 | 1986 | *Family Law Act* in force; new statements regarding matrimonial home |
| March 31 | 1988 | Vested dower rights extinguished unless notice of claim registered |

# The Requisition Letter

# 20

## LEARNING OUTCOMES

After reading this chapter, you will understand:

- How to compose a requisition letter

- The standard requisitions that apply to almost every purchase transaction

- How to draft specific requisitions arising from a title search

- How to draft specific requisitions arising from responses to inquiry letters

- The questions you must ask yourself when you make a requisition

# Introduction

This chapter examines the standard form of requisition letter and provides examples of specific requisitions based on the search notes for the Registry system search of Lot 11, Plan 1209, Township of Whitford (found in the Appendix to Chapter 14 and reviewed in the Appendix to Chapter 19) and the Land Titles system search for Lot 170, Plan 65M-1234, Town of Newmarket taken from the parcel register, found as Figure 14.6 in Chapter 14 and reviewed in the Appendix to Chapter 19.

To be valid, a title requisition must identify a specific objection to a particular title, a specific solution, and possibly one or more alternative solutions. Thus, the letter should not contain generalized, unnecessary requisitions. However, in order to protect the client's rights, you should requisition what the buyer is entitled to on closing according to the terms of the agreement of purchase and sale.

# Review of the Standard Requisition Letter

Figure 20.1, at the end of the chapter, is a sample requisition letter containing the requisitions that would arise in the purchase of Lot 170, Plan 65M-1234, Town of Newmarket. Note that the letter must be signed by a lawyer.

## Preamble

Note that the first sentence of the opening paragraph states that the requisitions are made without prejudice. The wording in the paragraph parallels some of the wording of paragraph 10 of the agreement of purchase and sale, which gives the buyer the right to negotiate or waive requisitions once made. If the buyer raises an objection to the title that the seller is unable or unwilling to remove, remedy, or satisfy, the buyer may waive the requisition so that the seller cannot use this failure as a reason for terminating the deal. However, if the buyer chooses not to waive it, the buyer then has the right to refuse to close the deal.

## Standard Requisitions

There are a number of requisitions that will be made in almost every transaction. They cover standard conveyancing requirements (for example, declarations of possession) and basic contract rights (for example, keys and vacant possession on closing). Samples of these requisitions are found in paragraphs 1 through 13 of Figure 20.1.

## Documents to Be Executed

In most transactions, the buyer will require the delivery of certain documents on closing in addition to the transfer. It is the usual practice for the buyer's lawyer to prepare documents such as declarations of possession, general undertakings, and warranties, to ensure that they are in a form satisfactory to the buyer. Sometimes, however, the seller's lawyer will still prepare his or her own documents for the seller to sign.

When documents are prepared by the buyer's lawyer for execution by the seller, it is usual to enclose the documents in the requisition letter, as indicated in paragraph 14, so that they may be executed by the seller and delivered on closing.

## Specific Requisitions on Title

The next portion of the requisition letter, starting at paragraph 15, sets out the specific requisitions relating to particular issues of title. As discussed in Chapter 19, Requisitions: An Overview, the sources of these requisitions will be

- the preliminary letters;
- the title search; and
- the plan of survey.

## Signature

The requisition letter must be prepared for signature by the lawyer handling the file and must be signed by the lawyer. Law clerks cannot sign the requisition letter.

# Drafting Specific Requisitions Arising from the Search of Title

This section examines examples of specific requisitions that might arise from a review of the search of title. The purpose of this review is twofold: (1) to provide a sense of the difference between a good and a bad requisition, and (2) to provide examples of how to draft a requisition. First we review a Registry system search and then we review a Land Titles system search.

## Registry System Search

The requisitions below are drafted in March 2015, and are based on the search notes for Lot 11, Plan 1209, Township of Whitford, found in the Appendix to Chapter 14 and reviewed in the Appendix to Chapter 19.

### Instrument Number 77286

This instrument is a notice of agreement that contains a subdivision agreement with the Township of Whitford. Because paragraph 10 of the agreement of purchase and sale states that the buyer must accept title subject to any registered agreements with municipalities as long as they have been complied with, the buyer cannot demand its removal. However, you must requisition proof from the municipality that the subdivision agreement has been complied with. If title insurance is not being obtained, you must also write to the Township of Whitford for evidence of compliance. If title insurance is being obtained, it will insure against any such problems, and the follow-up letter is not necessary. (See page 1 of the search notes, Appendix, Chapter 14.)

The requisition would read as follows:

> Instrument number 77286 is a notice of agreement containing a subdivision agreement between Stavros Subdivisions Ltd. and the Corporation of the Township of Whitford registered January 15, 1974.
>
> REQUIRED:   On or before closing, satisfactory evidence from the Township of Whitford that the terms of the said agreement have been complied with or that adequate security has been posted.

Whenever you make a requisition, you must ask yourself the following questions:

1. What is the likely answer to this requisition?
2. What answer would I like to receive?
3. What can I do to answer the requisition?
4. What will I do if the requisition cannot be answered to my satisfaction?

With respect to this requisition, those questions would be answered as follows:

1. The likely answer will be "Please satisfy yourself." As mentioned earlier, you should write to the Township of Whitford yourself, to make sure there has been compliance with the subdivision agreement. You may ask why you need to make a requisition if you know that the answer will be "Please satisfy yourself." You must do so to protect the rights of the buyer under the agreement of purchase and sale, if title insurance is not being obtained, in case the evidence obtained shows non-compliance with the subdivision agreement.
2. You would like to receive proof of compliance by way of letter from the municipality. Because you can obtain the letter yourself, without assistance from the seller, "Please satisfy yourself" is an acceptable answer.
3. Write to the municipality directly for an answer.
4. If the answer from the municipality discloses non-compliance with the subdivision agreement, and the buyer is not obtaining title insurance, the buyer will have to decide whether to complete the transaction.

### Instrument Number 635121

This instrument is a mortgage in favour of the Bank of Montreal. Let's assume that this mortgage is not one that the buyer has agreed to assume. Since the mortgagee is a chartered bank, according to the terms of the agreement of purchase and sale, if a discharge is not available on closing (as is most likely the case), the buyer is obliged to accept the seller's lawyer's personal undertaking to obtain and register a discharge of the mortgage. The seller's lawyer will also have to provide a mortgage statement from the bank and a direction regarding funds from the seller, directing that the amount required to discharge the mortgage be paid directly to the bank out of the closing funds.

The requisition would read as follows:

> Instrument number 635121 is a mortgage from Mario Romano and Graziella Romano in favour of the Bank of Montreal, registered August 5, 2010, securing the principal sum of $320,000.00. Pursuant to the terms of the agreement of purchase and sale, this mortgage is to be discharged.

> REQUIRED:   On or before closing, registration of a good and valid discharge of the said mortgage or, in the alternative, on or before closing, production of the seller's lawyer's personal undertaking to obtain, out of the closing funds, a discharge in registerable form and to register same on title within a reasonable time after completion, and production of a mortgage statement prepared by the mortgagee setting out the balance required to obtain the discharge, together with a direction executed by the seller directing payment to the mortgagee of the amount required to obtain the discharge out of the balance due on completion.

The only acceptable answer to this requisition is an agreement by the seller's lawyer to register a discharge, either on closing (unlikely) or within a reasonable time after closing, provided all the above requirements are met.

### Instrument Number 726341

This instrument is a mortgage in favour of XYZ Mortgage Ltd. If this is a mortgage that the buyer has not agreed to assume, it will give rise to a requisition to discharge the mortgage.

Because it is not an "institutional" mortgage as defined in paragraph 12 of the agreement of purchase and sale, you must requisition that a discharge be registered on or before closing. You will not accept an undertaking to obtain and register a discharge. This requisition should read as follows:

> Instrument number 726341 is a mortgage registered on March 23, 2013 from Mario Romano and Graziella Romano in favour of XYZ Mortgage Ltd., securing the principal sum of $15,000.00. By the terms of the agreement of purchase and sale, the said mortgage is to be discharged.

> REQUIRED:   On or before closing, registration of a good and valid discharge of the said mortgage. Please note that we will not accept an undertaking in this regard.

## Land Titles System Search

The following requisitions are based on the parcel register for Lot 170, Plan 65M-1234, Town of Newmarket, found in Figure 14.6 in Chapter 14 and reviewed in the Appendix to Chapter 19.

### Instrument Number LT1394678

Instrument number LT1394678 is a charge in favour of ABC Bank (which is a chartered bank). Let's assume that this charge is not one that the buyer has agreed to assume. Since the chargee is a chartered bank, the charge is treated the same way as instrument number 635121 in the Registry system search. According to the terms of the agreement of purchase and sale, if a discharge is not available on closing (as is most likely the case), the buyer is obliged to accept the seller's lawyer's personal undertaking to obtain and register a discharge of the charge. The seller's lawyer will also have to provide a mortgage statement from the bank and a direction regarding funds from the seller, directing that the amount required to discharge the charge be paid directly to the bank out of closing funds.

The requisition should read as follows:

> Instrument number LT1394678 is a charge registered June 3, 2014 from Francois Mercier and Huguette Mercier in favour of ABC Bank securing the principal sum of $94,000.00.
>
> REQUIRED:    On or before closing, production and registration of a good and valid discharge of this mortgage. In the alternative, on or before closing, production of the seller's lawyer's personal undertaking to obtain, out of the closing funds, a discharge in registerable form and to register same on title within a reasonable time after completion, and production of a mortgage statement prepared by the mortgagee setting out the balance required to obtain the discharge, together with a direction executed by the seller directing payment to the mortgagee of the amount required to obtain the discharge out of the balance due on completion.

The only acceptable answer to this requisition is an agreement by the seller's lawyer to register a discharge, either on closing (unlikely) or within a reasonable time after closing, provided all the above requirements are met.

### Instrument Number LT315678

Instrument number LT315678 is a notice of agreement with the Corporation of the Town of Newmarket dated August 21, 1986. It is treated the same way as instrument number 77286 in the Registry system search. You should requisition proof of compliance with this agreement in the form of a letter from the town. If no title insurance is being obtained, you should also write to the Town of Newmarket yourself, to make sure that the terms of the agreement have been complied with.

The requisition would read as follows:

> Instrument number LT315678 is a notice of agreement with the Corporation of the Town of Newmarket dated August 21, 1986.
>
> REQUIRED:    On or before closing, satisfactory evidence from the Town of Newmarket that the terms of the said agreement have been complied with or that adequate security has been posted.

## Drafting Specific Requisitions Arising from Responses to Preliminary Letters

This section examines examples of specific requisitions that might arise from responses to the preliminary inquiry letters dealt with in Chapter 18, Preliminary Matters, most often sent out only if the client is *not* buying title insurance. The letters address issues such as municipal taxes, utilities, and building department concerns. If title insurance is being obtained, these letters are generally not sent out, and so no specific requisitions will arise. However, these issues are still addressed in the requisition letter in the standard requisitions discussed above.

## Municipal Tax Certificate

Suppose the municipal tax certificate discloses arrears of 2014 taxes (prior year's taxes) in the amount of $1,850.00 plus penalties of $90.00 and arrears of current taxes in the amount of $1,200.00 plus penalties of $30.00. The requisition would read as follows:

> Township of Whitford tax certificate dated March 9, 2015 discloses arrears of 2014 taxes in the amount of $1,850.00 plus penalties of $90.00 and arrears of 2015 taxes in the amount of $1,200.00 plus penalties of $30.00.
>
> REQUIRED:   On or before closing, satisfactory evidence that the said arrears and penalties have been paid in full.

## Water Accounts

Suppose the response from the water department discloses arrears of $300.00. The requisition would read as follows:

> By letter from the Township of Whitford Water Department, dated March 9, 2015, we were advised that the water account on the subject property is in arrears in the amount of $300.00.
>
> REQUIRED:   On or before closing, satisfactory evidence that the said arrears together with any penalties for late payment have been paid in full.

## Sewers and Drains

Suppose the response from the water department discloses the existence of a storm sewer easement. Paragraph 10 of the agreement of purchase and sale requires the buyer to accept title subject to easements for storm sewers, provided they do not materially affect the present use of the property. You would have to discuss this easement with the buyer. If he or she confirms that it does not materially affect the present use of the property, you will not make a requisition.

## Unregistered Hydro Easements

If the response from Hydro One discloses an unregistered hydro easement that materially affects the present use of the property (and is therefore not an easement that the buyer is required to accept, according to paragraph 10 of the agreement), the requisition would read as follows:

> By letter from Hydro One dated March 10, 2015, a copy of which is attached, we were advised that the property is subject to an unregistered easement pursuant to the *Electricity Act, 1998*. The said easement materially affects the present use of the property.
>
> REQUIRED:   On or before closing, production of a release of the said easement.

## Building Department

Suppose that the response from the building department discloses a contravention of the bylaw governing side yard set-backs and the existence of two outstanding work orders. The requisition would read as follows:

> By letter dated March 10, 2015, we were advised by the building department of the Township of Whitford that the location of the buildings on the property contravenes the provisions of bylaw number _____ in that the side yard set-backs of the buildings are insufficient.
>
> REQUIRED:  On or before closing, amendment of the said bylaw, specifically exempting the subject property from the application of the said bylaw in this regard; or, in the alternative, a minor variance to the bylaw, approved by the committee of adjustments, permitting the said side yard set-backs; or, in the further alternative, satisfactory evidence that the existing side yard set-backs qualify as a legal non-conforming use if, in fact, they do.

> By letter dated March 10, 2015, a copy of which is attached, we were advised by the building department of the Township of Whitford that there are outstanding work orders against the subject property.
>
> REQUIRED:  On or before closing, satisfactory evidence that all work required pursuant to the said work orders has been completed to the satisfaction of the building department and that the said work orders have been released.

## Effect of Title Insurance

If the buyer in this transaction is purchasing title insurance, you may not have sent many of the preliminary inquiry letters, and there would therefore be no corresponding requisitions.

# Following Up on Requisitions

As previously discussed in Chapter 19, Requisitions: An Overview, if there is a title problem, it is not sufficient to simply submit a requisition. If the buyer wants to close the transaction, you must take all reasonable steps to solve the problem by contacting the lawyers who prepared earlier documents and anyone else who may have the information that you need.

The requisition letter can be thought of as a checklist of everything that is required from the seller in order to close the transaction. And there is no harm in requisitioning something that may not be necessary. It is much better to requisition something and receive "Please satisfy yourself" as a response than to omit a potential issue.

# Requisitions from the Seller's Perspective

It is the seller's lawyer's responsibility to answer all valid requisitions. If the law firm acted for the seller in the purchase of the property, valid requisitions should have been submitted at that time, and the answers will likely be in the firm's purchase file for the property. If the firm acted in the purchase and failed to submit a valid requisition at that time, the firm may find itself subject to a claim for professional negligence arising out of its work on the purchase transaction.

If the seller's law firm did not act for the seller in the original purchase of the property, the law firm that did act should be contacted with respect to any requisitions that the seller's lawyer cannot answer. The previous lawyer may have an answer in the original file. If not, that lawyer may be sued for professional negligence by the seller if the problem existed at the time of the seller's purchase. The seller's lawyer may also have to contact a third party (or that party's lawyer) who can provide a solution to the problem.

## REFERENCES

*Construction Lien Act*, RSO 1990, c C.30.

*Electricity Act, 1998*, SO 1998, c 15, Schedule A.

*Family Law Act*, RSO 1990, c F.3.

*Income Tax Act*, RSC 1985, c 1 (5th Supp), as amended.

*Planning Act*, RSO 1990, c P.13.

## REVIEW QUESTIONS

1. What four questions must you ask yourself when making a requisition?

2. What must the seller's lawyer do when requisitions are received from the buyer's lawyer?

3. The search of title discloses a charge registered on October 15, 2015 as instrument number 12345 from Jennifer Annistone to Bradley Pitts in the principal amount of $100,000.00. According to the agreement of purchase and sale, this mortgage is to be discharged. Draft the appropriate requisition.

4. The search of title reveals a subdivision agreement registered on title. When the buyer's lawyer requisitioned proof that the agreement has been complied with, the seller's lawyer responded "Please satisfy yourself." Is that an acceptable response? Explain.

**Figure 20.1   Requisition Letter**

*Date*

Brooks & Dunn
Barristers and Solicitors
16 Any Street
Newmarket, Ontario
L0L 1T1

Attention: Fred Brooks

Dear Sir:

Re:   Grant purchase from Mercier
        166 Valley Road, Newmarket
        Closing Date: December 15, 2015
        Our File No.: 15-1925

Without prejudice to the rights of my client under the agreement of purchase and sale, and reserving the right to submit such further and other requisitions as may be deemed necessary from time to time as well as the right to waive any or all of them, I wish to raise the following requisitions:

1.   REQUIRED:   Draft transfer/deed of land, engrossed as follows:

| **Full Name** | **Birthdate** |
| --- | --- |
| GRANT, Henry Albert | March 27, 1952 |
| GRANT, Wilma Heather | March 18, 1955 |
| As joint tenants | |

2.   REQUIRED:   An up-to-date survey of the subject lands. Please advise immediately if one is not available.

3.   REQUIRED:   Statement of adjustments, in duplicate.

4.   REQUIRED:   On or before closing, satisfactory evidence of compliance with the following legislation:

   a)   the *Family Law Act*, Ontario;

   b)   section 116 of the *Income Tax Act*, Canada;

   c)   the *Planning Act*, Ontario, including completion of the *Planning Act* statements in the transfer/deed of land;

   d)   the *Construction Lien Act*, Ontario.

## Figure 20.1 Continued

5. REQUIRED: On or before closing, satisfactory evidence that there are no executions affecting title to the subject property.

6. REQUIRED: On or before closing, production and delivery of evidence that all buildings situate on the lands herein are located entirely within the limits thereof, that possession has been consistent with registered title to the property, and that there are no encumbrances, liens, rights of way, easements, encroachments, restrictions, or agreements of any kind affecting the property which are not disclosed by the registered title.

7. REQUIRED: On or before closing, evidence that there are no work orders outstanding and that the lands and premises and all structures erected thereon comply with all bylaws, standards, and regulations enacted or passed by the Town of Newmarket and any other governmental body or department having jurisdiction thereover.

8. REQUIRED: On or before closing, evidence that:

   a) there are no arrears of municipal taxes or other municipal charges or assessments, including penalties, and that taxes have been paid in accordance with the statement of adjustments; and

   b) payment of water, hydro, and gas are not in arrears and that each shall be paid to the date of closing.

9. REQUIRED: On or before closing, satisfactory evidence that the property has not been insulated with urea formaldehyde foam insulation.

10. REQUIRED: On or before closing, satisfactory evidence that the fixtures affixed to the lands and buildings, and the chattel property included in the purchase price, are the property of the sellers and are not subject to any conditional sales contract, chattel mortgage, or lien note and that the sellers are the absolute owners of all such fixtures and chattels, free of any encumbrances.

11. REQUIRED: An opportunity for my client to perform a final inspection of the premises.

12. REQUIRED: On closing, keys and vacant possession, subject to any tenancy which the buyer has expressly agreed to assume pursuant to the agreement of purchase and sale.

13. REQUIRED: On or before closing, evidence that this transaction is not subject to harmonized sales tax.

**Figure 20.1   Concluded**

14.   REQUIRED:   That the following documents, which are enclosed herewith, be executed by the sellers and returned to my office, in duplicate, on or before closing:

a)   seller's undertakings;

b)   warranties/bill of sale;

c)   declaration of possession;

d)   statutory declaration re HST.

15.   Instrument number LT1394678 is a charge registered June 3, 2014 from Francois Mercier and Huguette Marie Mercier in favour of ABC Bank securing the principal sum of $94,000.00.

REQUIRED:   On or before closing, production and registration of a good and valid discharge of this mortgage. In the alternative, on or before closing, production of the seller's lawyer's personal undertaking to obtain, out of the closing funds, a discharge in registerable form and to register same on title within a reasonable time after completion, and production of a mortgage statement prepared by the mortgagee setting out the balance required to obtain the discharge, together with a direction executed by the seller directing payment to the mortgagee of the amount required to obtain the discharge out of the balance due on completion.

16.   Instrument number LT315678 is a notice of agreement with the Corporation of the Town of Newmarket dated August 21, 1986.

REQUIRED:   On or before closing, satisfactory evidence from the Town of Newmarket that the terms of the said agreement have been complied with or that adequate security has been posted.

Yours very truly,


Kurtz, Emmans, Blatt & Wolf
Per:

# Document Preparation 21

## LEARNING OUTCOMES

After reading this chapter, you will understand:

- Which documents must be prepared for the closing of a residential real estate transaction

- Which law firm usually prepares which documents

- The reasons why each document is necessary

- How to prepare the documents

- The differences between Land Titles (electronic) documents and Registry (paper) documents

- How to calculate the entries in a statement of adjustments

# Introduction

Once all of your requisitions have been satisfactorily answered, you must begin to think about the closing of the transaction and the documents that will be required for the closing. Some of the documents are prepared by the buyer's lawyer and others are prepared by the seller's lawyer. Often one party's lawyer prepares documents that must be signed by the other party. However, that party's lawyer may choose to prepare his or her own version of the documents instead.

Note that although we have been referring to the "buyer" and "seller," some of the documents still refer to "purchaser" and "vendor."

The buyer's lawyer usually prepares

- a direction regarding title;
- a purchaser's undertaking to readjust;
- the land transfer tax affidavit;
- the land transfer tax statement (if the property is in the Land Titles system);
- any mortgage documents;
- undertakings regarding the discharge of mortgages;
- a bill of sale;
- warranties with respect to chattels (may be combined with the bill of sale);
- a statutory declaration regarding writs of execution;
- a statutory declaration of possession;
- an *Income Tax Act* declaration;
- a realty tax declaration;
- a vendor's general undertaking; and
- a statutory declaration regarding harmonized sales tax (HST).

The seller's lawyer usually prepares

- a statement of adjustments;
- a direction regarding funds; and
- the transfer.

Both lawyers prepare an acknowledgment and direction for their respective clients.

# Buyer's Documents

There are very few documents that the buyer must execute. The buyer's primary obligation on closing is to give money to the seller. All title obligations are those of the seller.

## Direction Regarding Title

The direction regarding title is a document given to the seller by the party who signed the agreement of purchase and sale as buyer. It authorizes the seller to deliver a transfer of land naming someone else as the transferee. This direction is technically necessary only if title is being taken in a name different from that of the buyer in the agreement of purchase and sale. For example, a direction is required if the buyer named in the agreement is John Smith and John Smith wants the transfer to be in favour of any of the following: John James Smith, John Smith and Jane Smith as joint tenants, or Fred Jones. If John Smith wants the transfer/deed to simply name John Smith as transferee, no direction is necessary.

Although a direction regarding title is not necessary if the name of the transferee is exactly the same as the name of the buyer in the agreement of purchase and sale, it is usual to give a direction regarding title anyway to confirm the birthdate(s) to be inserted in the transfer, and to state how the transferees are taking title (for example, as joint tenants or as tenants in common). For example, if John Smith and Mary Smith signed the agreement of purchase and sale, and both John Smith and Mary Smith are going on title, the direction will disclose their dates of birth and whether they are taking title as joint tenants or tenants in common.

From the perspective of the seller, remember that, in the absence of a direction signed by the buyer named in the agreement of purchase and sale, the seller must deliver a transfer to that buyer as named in the agreement and to no one else.

Figure 21.1, at the end of the chapter, is an example of a direction regarding title.

## Purchaser's Undertaking to Readjust

When calculating the balance due on closing, various costs and expenses are allocated between the seller and the buyer to the time of closing. This allocation is calculated in the statement of adjustments (discussed later in this chapter). The buyer gives an undertaking to readjust in case it turns out that any items on the statement of adjustments were incorrectly adjusted in the buyer's favour. To readjust means to pay back any amount improperly or incorrectly credited to the buyer. (The seller also undertakes to readjust in the vendor's general undertaking, discussed later in this chapter.)

Figure 21.2 is a sample purchaser's undertaking to readjust.

## Land Transfer Tax Affidavit (Registry Properties)

If the property is still in the Registry system, a paper land transfer tax affidavit (previously called an affidavit of residence and of value of the consideration) must be sworn by the buyer and inserted in the transfer of land before registration. It provides the government with the information necessary to calculate the land transfer tax payable by the buyer as a result of the transfer. The standard form of agreement of purchase and sale provides that the affidavit is to be prepared by the buyer. This approach is consistent with the form of the affidavit itself, which may be completed only by the transferee or his or her agent.

The following discussion deals with the completion of the affidavit, a copy of which is reproduced as Figure 21.3. The actual calculation of the taxes is dealt with in Chapter 22, Closing the Transaction.

### The Preamble

Complete the preamble by inserting the PIN (property identifier number), lot and plan number, city and municipality, transferor(s), and transferee(s).

### Paragraph 1

Check the box that appropriately describes the deponent. The transferee usually swears the affidavit, and therefore box (a) and box (d) (if the transferees are spouses of one another) are most commonly checked. The affidavit is rarely sworn by the solicitor for the transferee.

### Paragraph 2

This paragraph sets out the allocation of the total consideration and is the most complicated paragraph to complete. The calculation of land transfer tax and HST will be based on these figures.

Land transfer tax is essentially a provincial sales tax payable on the sale of land, just as HST is a sales tax payable on the sale of goods. In most real estate transactions, some chattels (movable items) are included in the purchase price. Accordingly, part of the purchase price is allocated to the chattels and part to the land. HST should be paid on the value of the chattels and land transfer tax on the value of the land. The affidavit requires this allocation of the purchase price between land and chattels.

When you complete this paragraph, you should fill in line (i), Total Consideration, first. The amount to be inserted is the purchase price found at the top of the agreement of purchase and sale and *not* the adjusted amount found in the statement of adjustments.

Next, complete line (g) by inserting the value of all chattels. When completing this line, remember that the HST rate is significantly higher than the land transfer tax rate. Accordingly, most buyers wish to allocate little, if any, value to the chattels. Get the client's instructions on the allocation. When doing this, review with the client the chattels included in the purchase price and advise the client that generally there must be some value placed on the chattels. The chattels included in the purchase price are listed in paragraph 4 of the agreement of purchase and sale. Keep in mind that real estate agents often insert items that are really fixtures (immovable items), such as broadloom, storm windows, and screens. When reviewing this paragraph with the client, you must determine which of the listed items are, in fact, chattels. Insert the value that the client allocates to the chattels in line (g). Keep notes of your discussions with the client. If you have any concern about this valuation issue, ask the lawyer handling the file to deal with it.

Next, deduct the amount of the value of the chattels from the total consideration. Insert the result in line (f), which is stated to be the value of the land, building, fixtures, and goodwill subject to land transfer tax.

Next, complete line (b), Mortgages. Only two types of mortgages are relevant to this line: (i) mortgages being assumed (mortgages already registered on title and being credited against the purchase price) and (ii) mortgages being taken back by the seller. Do not include any new mortgages being arranged by the buyer with a third party.

With respect to mortgages being assumed, insert the amount shown on the statement of adjustments (if you have received one) as the principal and interest outstanding as of the closing date. If the seller has not yet given you a statement of adjustments, you can get this information from a mortgage statement for assumption purposes obtained from the mortgagee.

For mortgages being taken back by the seller, insert the principal amount of the mortgage.

Paragraphs (c), (d), and (e) deal with other types of consideration that are rarely encountered in residential real estate transactions. Complete them only if they apply to the transaction.

Once these paragraphs have been completed, total the amounts from line (b) to (e). (It's best to do this calculation on a separate sheet of paper.) Take your calculated total and deduct it from the amount set out in line (f). The resulting amount is the total of the moneys to be paid in cash. Insert this amount in line (a). Because adjustments are not dealt with in this affidavit, the amount inserted in line (a) is rarely the same as the balance due on closing.

## Paragraph 3

Complete this paragraph only if the consideration exceeds $400,000 and state whether the property is a single-family residence. This statement is required because the rate of tax changes in cases where the consideration exceeds $400,000 if the property is a single-family residence.

When completing this paragraph, you must review with the client the definition of "single family residence" in section 1(1) of the *Land Transfer Tax Act* because the affidavit states that the client has reviewed the definition. You should get a copy of the statute and allow the client to read the appropriate section. If the client has any question on the meaning of the section (certainly if the question is one you can't answer with total confidence), you must refer the client to the lawyer handling the file.

## Paragraph 4

Where the consideration is nominal, you must complete this paragraph to state whether the property is subject to any encumbrances. This information is necessary because, where a transfer is made for "natural love and affection," land transfer tax is still payable on the amount of any assumed encumbrances except when the transfer is between spouses.

## Paragraph 5

If the consideration is nominal, you must describe the relationship between the transferor and the transferee, and state the purpose of the conveyance. This paragraph is not usually completed when fair market value is paid for the property. It is required in the case of transfers for "natural love and affection" or where former spouses convey property in divorce or *Family Law Act* settlements.

If you have to complete this paragraph, contact the land transfer tax office to find out the specific wording you should use in the particular situation.

### Attestation

Complete the attestation to set out the date and place the affidavit is sworn.

### Property Information Record

At the bottom of the affidavit is a property information record that is self-explanatory.

### School Tax Support

Completion of this section is voluntary and, if the client wishes, may be completed by the client at the time of execution.

## Land Transfer Tax Statements (Land Titles Properties)

If the property is in the Land Titles system, the buyer's lawyer prepares an electronic land transfer tax statement for inclusion in the transfer that has been messaged through Teraview from the seller's lawyer. It contains similar information to that in the affidavit. Figure 21.4 is an example of the land transfer tax statement.

## Mortgage Documents

If the buyer is financing the transaction by way of a mortgage from a third-party mortgagee (such as a financial institution or a relative) or a vendor-take-back mortgage, the buyer's lawyer usually prepares the mortgage documents. A detailed discussion of these documents is found in Chapter 29, Acting for the Mortgagee.

## Undertakings Regarding the Discharge of Mortgages

If there is a mortgage registered on title that the buyer has not agreed to assume under the terms of the agreement of purchase and sale, the mortgage must ordinarily be discharged on closing. However, if the mortgage is from an institutional lender, the buyer is required to accept the personal undertaking of the seller's lawyer to obtain the discharge and register it at a later date.

If the buyer has agreed to accept an undertaking to discharge a mortgage, you must make sure that the form of undertaking given is satisfactory. It is essential that the undertaking be the personal undertaking of the seller's lawyer and not an undertaking given by the lawyer on behalf of the seller only. The undertaking must bind the seller's lawyer and not merely the seller. The undertaking to obtain and register a discharge of the mortgage must be stated unconditionally. It is not enough for the undertaking to require the lawyer to use his or her best efforts. To comply with the requirements of the agreement of purchase and sale, there should be a statement that the discharge will be obtained and registered within a reasonable period of time.

When an undertaking is being accepted on the closing of the transaction, you will also have to get the appropriate mortgage statement and direction regarding payment of the funds.

Most banks will prepare *and* register discharges, and then advise the seller's lawyer of the registration particulars. The seller's lawyer will, in turn, advise the buyer's lawyer. Notwithstanding this possibility, the wording of the undertaking should obligate the seller's lawyer to register the discharge.

Figure 21.5 is an example of an acceptable form of undertaking.

## Statutory Declaration Regarding Writs of Execution

If there are executions against a name similar to that of the seller, a statutory declaration will be required to clarify that the executions are not in fact against the seller. Figure 21.6 is an example of the declaration. If the amount of the execution exceeds $50,000, this declaration will have to be executed by the lawyer for the seller.

## Statutory Declaration of Possession

This document is a declaration sworn by the seller setting out certain facts concerning the seller's possession of the land. A declaration of possession can clear up title defects, such as adverse possession, if the land is registered in the Registry system. Possessory interests do not usually exist in the Land Titles system, and so this declaration is not ordinarily required if the property is in the Land Titles system. However, the declaration is often expanded to include sworn statements to support the statement as to age and spousal status contained in the transfer, other recitals in the transfer, or matters such as the residency of the seller. As a result, some lawyers request one as a matter of course, because of the other matters dealt with in the declaration.

There are many variations of the standard form of declaration of possession. Some buyers' lawyers are content to have the seller's lawyer prepare the declaration of possession. Others may want to prepare the declaration themselves and forward it to the seller's lawyer for signing to make sure that it addresses the matters necessary to clear up any title questions. When you prepare a declaration of possession, you must customize the standard form to coincide with the facts of the particular title and transaction.

In addition to requiring the seller to execute the declaration of possession prepared, the buyer's lawyer will ask the seller's lawyer to deliver any declarations of possession from previous owners that may be in the seller's possession. A series of declarations of possession may establish continuity of possession over a period of 10 or 20 years sufficient to defeat a claim made against the title.

Figure 21.7 is an example of a statutory declaration of possession. The various paragraphs deal with the following matters:

- Paragraphs 1 through 4 establish continuity of possession and could address possible adverse possession claims that might be advanced against the property.

- Paragraph 5 deals with compliance with the *Planning Act*.
- Paragraph 6 is a statement as to residency within the meaning of the *Income Tax Act*.
- Paragraph 7 could help to establish that an old survey is still up to date and may be relied upon.

As stated above, sometimes the lawyer will add in a sworn statement to support the statements as to age and spousal status contained in the transfer.

## Income Tax Act Declaration

The buyer's lawyer must obtain a sworn declaration as to the seller's residency within the meaning of section 116 of the *Income Tax Act*. If the seller is a non-resident, additional income tax may be payable on the sale, and if it is not paid by the seller, the buyer may be responsible. If the declaration discloses that the seller is a non-resident, the buyer will require evidence that the tax has been paid or that satisfactory arrangements for payment have been made with the government.

A separate declaration is not required if appropriate wording is included in the statutory declaration of possession. The appropriate wording states that the seller is, or is not, a non-resident. This language parallels the language used in the *Income Tax Act*. See paragraph 6 of Figure 21.7 for an example of appropriate wording in a statutory declaration of possession. If there is no declaration of possession, a separate declaration will be required. See Figure 21.8.

## Realty Tax Declaration

If your client is purchasing title insurance and you did not write a letter to the tax department to obtain a tax certificate, you may require proof from the seller that the realty taxes are not in arrears. This can be done by way of a statutory declaration by the seller, together with a receipted tax bill. Figure 21.9 is an example of a realty tax declaration. It should be noted that, even if this declaration is not obtained from the seller, title insurance will pay outstanding taxes as long as the seller signs an undertaking to pay outstanding taxes (usually contained in the vendor's general undertaking discussed below).

## Warranties and Bill of Sale

It is customary for the seller to execute a document containing a number of warranties that will survive the closing of the transaction. Figure 21.10 is an example of such a document.

The standard form of agreement of purchase and sale contains a warranty that the seller has not insulated the property with UFFI (urea formaldehyde foam insulation) and that, to the best of the seller's knowledge, the property has never been insulated with UFFI. Paragraph 1 of Figure 21.10 is an example of a UFFI warranty. The document also contains warranties that no damage has occurred to the property since it was inspected by the buyer, and that there are no construction liens or work orders.

When chattels are included in the agreement of purchase and sale, the buyer's lawyer may require the delivery of a bill of sale that covers all the chattels. The bill of sale is often combined with the warranties.

## Vendor's General Undertaking

The buyer's lawyer usually requires the seller to execute a general undertaking designed to protect and extend beyond closing a number of the buyer's rights under the contract.

Figure 21.11 is an example of a vendor's general undertaking. In it, the seller undertakes:

- To deliver vacant possession on closing (assuming that is a term of the agreement of purchase and sale), and to provide all keys.

- To pay all utility charges to closing. These charges are generally metered, so a final bill cannot be prepared until after the final reading, which takes place on the day before closing. This undertaking covers payment of that final bill. Although arrears no longer form a lien against the property, the buyer may prefer to know that the charges have been paid.

- To pay all arrears of taxes and to readjust the taxes if necessary. If there are arrears of realty taxes disclosed in the tax certificate, this undertaking is not adequate to protect the buyer. Instead, the seller's lawyer should be required to hold back a sufficient portion of the closing funds and to personally undertake to pay the arrears out of those funds. The undertaking to readjust covers the situation where the taxes have not been assessed and are estimated on the statement of adjustments or where there is an error in the adjustment on the statement of adjustments, as a result of either incorrect information provided by the municipality or a miscalculation. If there is an error, the seller agrees to pay to the buyer any amount incorrectly credited to the seller.

- To leave on the premises any chattels and fixtures specified in the agreement, free of encumbrances.

- To readjust any items on the statement of adjustments as necessary.

- To supply fuel oil in accordance with the statement of adjustments (where applicable). If the house is heated by oil, the seller fills up the fuel tank on the day before closing and, on the statement of adjustments, charges the buyer for a full tank of oil at the current cost per litre multiplied by the number of litres in the tank. If the seller does not leave a full tank of oil on the premises, the buyer may sue on this undertaking.

- To make all payments on any mortgage being assumed by the buyer that fall due on or before closing and to readjust if necessary. The buyer should not rely on this undertaking with respect to the payment of the mortgage. At the time of closing, the seller should provide evidence that all payments have, in fact, been made. If any mortgage payment has not been made, a sufficient portion of the funds should be paid to the seller's lawyer and the buyer should obtain the lawyer's personal undertaking to pay any outstanding amount.

## HST Declaration

HST is not generally payable on the resale of a residential property. If HST is payable on a transaction, it is the obligation of the seller to collect the tax and remit it to the government. However, if HST is payable on the transaction and the seller fails to obtain it from the buyer and submit it, the government has the power to assess the tax against either the seller or the buyer. The buyer should be protected against this risk by obtaining a statutory declaration regarding HST from the seller. Paragraph 7 of the agreement of purchase and sale requires the seller to certify that the agreement is not subject to HST if such is the case.

Most law firms acting for the buyer will require the seller to swear a statutory declaration with regard to HST. Figure 21.12 is an example of this declaration.

# Seller's Documents

## The Statement of Adjustments

The statement of adjustments is the document that identifies the exact amount the buyer has to pay on closing. The document is prepared by the seller's lawyer and shows the calculations to determine the balance due on closing. A law clerk doing real estate work must know how to do this calculation—to be able to prepare a statement of adjustments if you are working for the seller's lawyer and to be able to review a statement of adjustments if you are working for the buyer's lawyer.

The terms "Purchaser" and "Vendor" are still used in the statement of adjustments itself even though the parties are referred to as "Buyer" and "Seller" in the agreement of purchase and sale. As a result, in the discussion that follows we use the terms "Purchaser" and "Vendor" in our examples, and the terms "Buyer" and "Seller" in our comments and explanations.

### Items to Be Adjusted

You calculate the balance due on closing by starting with the purchase price in the agreement of purchase and sale and then apportioning various prepaid expenses between the seller and the buyer to the date of closing. Items to be adjusted include such expenses as mortgages being assumed, fuel costs, unmetered utilities, realty taxes, and rents.

### Format of the Statement of Adjustments

The document is titled "Statement of Adjustments" and identifies the transaction, including the name of the buyer, the name of the seller, and the address of the property. It also states the date as of which adjustments are made. This date will usually be the day of closing.

The statement of adjustments is divided into three columns. The first column contains a description of the item being adjusted and may include some calculations. The second column is headed "Credit Purchaser" and the third column is headed "Credit Vendor."

Figure 21.13 is the statement of adjustments for our transaction.

## *Adjustment for the Day of Closing*

The standard form of agreement of purchase and sale states that the day of closing is to be apportioned to the buyer. This means that the buyer assumes responsibility for the particular expense—and starts paying it—as of the day of closing.

## *Calculations and Credits*

Before you can apportion the various items between the seller and the buyer, you must determine what number day of the year the closing is taking place—is it the 5th day (January 5), the 25th day (January 25), or the 325th day (November 21)? In our transaction, the closing date is December 15, which is day number 349. You can find this information in many desk diaries, which show the place of each date in the numerical sequence for the year and also, on any particular day, how many days are left in the year, or you can Google this information.

Once you know the day of the year, convert the relevant expense to a **per diem** (daily) amount and then allocate it between the parties. For an expense paid on a yearly basis, the per diem amount is obtained by dividing the amount of the yearly payment by 365. For an expense paid on a monthly basis, the per diem amount is obtained by dividing the amount of the monthly payment by 30 or 31. Once you know the per diem amount, you must multiply that amount by the correct number of days to take you to the day of closing. Remember that the seller is responsible for expenses up to and including the day *before* closing. Any amount that the seller is entitled to receive is added to the purchase price and is considered a credit to the seller. Any amount that the buyer is entitled to receive is deducted from the purchase price and is considered a credit to the buyer.

**per diem**
per day; for each day; daily

## *An Example*

The following is a step-by-step explanation of the various items in a statement of adjustments based on the example in Figure 21.13.

### SALE PRICE

The sale price is always the first item in the statement of adjustments. Use the total sale price found in the agreement of purchase and sale. The amount is placed in the "Credit Vendor" column because it is an amount the seller is entitled to receive.

> SALE PRICE                              580,000.00

### DEPOSIT

This item is always next and is also found in the agreement of purchase and sale. Since this amount has already been paid by the buyer, it is deducted from the sale price and credited to the buyer.

> DEPOSIT
> Paid to broker                         30,000.00

### REALTY TAXES

An adjustment is usually made for realty taxes because the seller will rarely have paid the exact amount of tax owing to the date of closing. If the seller has paid more than that amount, the seller is entitled to a credit for the overpayment. If the seller has paid less than that amount, the buyer is entitled to a credit in the amount of the seller's underpayment.

To adjust for realty taxes, you must first find out the total amount of tax payable for the year and how much of the tax the seller has actually paid. You obtain this information from the seller's tax bills, or by writing to the tax department of the municipality.

If the closing date is very early in the year, the municipality may not yet have set its taxes. In that case, the adjustment is made on the basis of the previous year's taxes. Since the current year's taxes will almost certainly be higher, the past year's taxes are increased by a stated percentage for the purposes of the adjustment.

> REALTY TAXES
>
> (*Current year*) taxes estimated at $5,100.00
>    (based on (*previous year*) taxes of $5,000.00 plus 2 percent)

This is the kind of situation where undertakings to readjust are necessary because the adjustment is based on an estimate.

If your request for tax information is made a little later in the year, you may find that the municipality has set interim taxes for the first six months of the year, but not the final taxes for the whole year. In that case, the adjustment is made on the basis of the interim levy on the assumption that the final taxes will be twice the interim levy. The example below assumes an interim levy of $2,600.00.

> REALTY TAXES
>
> (*Current year*) taxes estimated at $5,200.00

If you are able to obtain the final tax amount for the year, the adjustment will reflect that.

> REALTY TAXES
>
> (*Current year*) taxes of $5,200.00

Once you find out the total amount of the taxes, you must calculate how much of those taxes should have been paid by the seller. First, you must calculate the per diem amount of taxes. Divide the amount of the taxes (actual or estimated) by 365. Then multiply the per diem amount by the number of days from the beginning of the year until the day before the closing date. (Remember that taxes for the closing date are the buyer's responsibility.) This amount is the seller's share and is set out in the statement of adjustments. Assuming we have a final tax levy of $5,200.00, and a closing date of December 15, the information would appear as follows:

> REALTY TAXES
>
> 2015 taxes of $5,200.00
> Vendor's share: 348 days = $4,957.81

Next, you must set out the amount that the seller has actually paid. If the seller has paid less than the seller's share of the taxes, the buyer should be credited with the difference. If the seller has paid more than the seller's share of the taxes, the seller is credited with the overpayment. The following is an example of an adjustment for an underpayment:

> REALTY TAXES
>
> 2015 taxes of $5,200.00
> Vendor's share: 348 days = $4,957.81
> Vendor has paid: $3,610.14
> Difference: $1,347.67
> Credit purchaser                               1,347.67

The following is an example of an adjustment for an overpayment (as in our example in Figure 21.13):

> REALTY TAXES
>
> 2015 taxes of $5,200.00
> Vendor's share: 348 days = $4,957.81
> Vendor has paid: $5,200.00
> Difference: $242.19
> Credit vendor                               242.19

## UTILITIES

Gas, electricity, and water are usually metered. In that case, no adjustment is necessary, and the statement of adjustments would contain the following entry:

> HYDRO, GAS, WATER
> Metered, no adjustment

Sometimes water charges will not be metered but will be billed on a flat-rate basis. In that case, there must be an adjustment for the water charges. There are three steps involved in the calculation:

1. Find out the amount payable for the current billing period. Get this information from the municipal water department.
2. Find out how much the seller has paid. Again, this information comes from the water department.
3. Calculate how much should have been paid by the seller. Take the billed amount and divide it by the number of days *in the billing period* to get a per diem amount. For example, a quarterly bill for the second quarter (April, May, June) would be divided by 91 days. Multiply the per diem amount by the number of days that have elapsed since the *start of the billing period* (this will not necessarily be the beginning of the year).

For example, assume that the closing date is May 15, water is billed quarterly at the rate of $100.00 per quarter, and the first and second quarters' bills have been paid.

For the purposes of the statement of adjustments, the first quarter is not relevant. Divide the second quarter bill of $100.00 by the number of days in the quarter (91). This gives you a per diem amount of $1.0989. Multiply this amount by 44, which is the number of days from the start of the second quarter (April 1) until the day of closing. This gives you a total of $48.35, which is the seller's share. Since the seller has paid $100.00, the seller is entitled to a credit of $51.65.

### INSURANCE

Under the standard form of agreement of purchase and sale, insurance policies are not assumed by the buyer and there will be no adjustment for insurance.

### BALANCE DUE ON CLOSING

Once all of the adjustments have been calculated, you must calculate the balance due on closing. First, total the "Credit Vendor" column. From that total deduct all of the items in the "Credit Purchaser" column. The difference is the balance due on closing. Insert this amount on the line above the total of the "Credit Purchaser" column. To double-check your calculations, add up the figures in the "Credit Purchaser" column—the total should be the same as the total for the "Credit Vendor" column. For example:

| | | |
|---|---|---|
| BALANCE DUE ON CLOSING | 550,242.19 | |
| | 580,242.19 | 580,242.19 |

## *Other Possible Adjustments*

There may be adjustments for rent, common expenses, mortgages that the buyer is assuming, mortgages back to the seller, fuel oil, and, on newly constructed homes, various inspection and installation fees. Approach the calculations for these adjustments in the same way you would those discussed above. Below are examples of adjustments for an assumed mortgage, for a mortgage back to the seller, and for fuel oil.

### MORTGAGE ASSUMED

Assumed mortgages are rarely seen during times of low interest rates and low inflation. However, if a buyer agrees to assume an existing mortgage, the buyer is agreeing to take over the seller's debt on closing. This assumed debt is part of the purchase price and is deducted from the amount the buyer has to pay on closing. Accordingly, the outstanding principal amount of the mortgage after the date of the last mortgage payment constitutes a credit to the buyer.

> FIRST MORTGAGE ASSUMED
> Principal outstanding as of
> December 1, 2015                            42,563.00

In addition to crediting the buyer with the amount of the outstanding principal of the mortgage, there will almost always be a credit in favour of the buyer for interest payable on the mortgage. This credit is given because, some time after closing, the buyer will have to make a mortgage payment, and that payment will include principal and interest. Because mortgage interest is payable "not in advance," the mortgage payment will include interest for the period of time since the last payment. For example, if mortgage payments are due on the 1st of each month, the payment made on January 1 will include interest for the period December 1-31. If the closing date is December 15, the buyer should not have to pay the interest for the period before the closing, which is the seller's responsibility. Because the January 1 payment that the buyer will make will include interest for all of December, the buyer is entitled to a credit for 14 days' worth of interest paid on the seller's behalf.

To calculate the interest, you must calculate the per diem amount of interest on the principal amount of the mortgage. For example, if the interest rate is 4 percent per annum on the principal amount shown above, the per diem amount is calculated as follows:

$$\frac{\$42{,}563.00 \times 0.04}{365} = \$4.664$$

Then multiply the per diem amount of interest by the number of days to be credited to the buyer. In this case, it would be 14 days:

$$\$4.664 \times 14 = \$65.30$$

The full entry for the assumed mortgage would therefore look like this:

FIRST MORTGAGE ASSUMED

| | |
|---|---|
| Principal outstanding as of December 1, 2015 | 42,563.00 |
| Interest at 4% for 14 days | 65.30 |

The seller's lawyer gets this mortgage information by asking the mortgagee for a mortgage statement for assumption purposes. You should get a copy of the mortgage statement from the seller on closing to verify the figures in the statement of adjustments. Some buyers' lawyers will not wait until closing to get a copy of the mortgage statement from the seller's lawyer but will contact the mortgagee directly for a mortgage statement. That way the lawyer can verify the adjustments before the closing or prepare the statement of adjustments if the buyer's lawyer doesn't.

The example above shows the principal balance and then a separate calculation of the interest to the date of closing. Many mortgage statements provide a combined amount of principal and interest to a date specified in the mortgage statement (usually the closing date, as requested by the seller). If the mortgage statement shows a combined amount, place that figure in the statement of adjustments. It is not necessary to break the figure down into principal and interest. Instead, the statement of adjustments would simply state:

| | |
|---|---|
| Principal and interest outstanding as of December 15, 2015 | 42,628.30 |

### SECOND MORTGAGE BACK

If the seller agrees to take a mortgage back from the buyer, the buyer is given a credit for the principal amount of that mortgage. The credit is given because the buyer does not have to pay that portion of the closing price in cash. The seller is accepting the mortgage instead of cash. Since the statement of adjustments calculates the amount payable on closing, this amount is deducted from the purchase price and is therefore credited to the buyer.

> SECOND MORTGAGE
> Back to seller                                     25,000.00

No adjustment is necessary for interest, because interest starts to accrue only as of the date of closing.

### FUEL OIL

As noted above, if the house being purchased is heated by oil, the seller is required to fill the oil tank on the day before closing (the seller's lawyer should remind the seller to do so), and the buyer must pay the seller for the full tank of oil. This charge is shown as a credit to the seller on the statement of adjustments. The seller's lawyer will find out from the seller the capacity of the oil tank in litres (the standard tank holds 900 litres). Then you must find out the current cost per litre of home fuel oil. You can obtain this information by calling any supplier of home fuel oil. The adjustment will set out the capacity of the tank and the price of the oil. For example:

> FUEL OIL
> 900 litres @ $1.02/litre (including HST)
> Credit vendor                                     918.00

## *The Statement of Adjustments from the Buyer's Perspective*

As previously stated, the statement of adjustments is a document that is supposed to be prepared by the seller's law firm. When you work for the buyer's law firm, you must know how to check the calculations in the statement of adjustments and how to verify the information on which the calculations are based. Sometimes, however, the buyer's law firm receives adjustments over the telephone at the last minute, or not at all. The buyer's lawyer will then have to calculate the adjustments.

When you receive the statement of adjustments, first confirm the accuracy of the amounts used in the calculations by checking them against the information you obtained from your own sources.

- Look at the agreement of purchase and sale to confirm the purchase price, the deposit, and the principal amount of any mortgage back to the seller.
- Write to the appropriate municipal offices to confirm the realty tax and utilities figures. If title insurance is purchased, this will not be necessary.
- Write to the mortgagee for a mortgage statement to confirm the principal of and interest on any mortgages the buyer is assuming.

After you have verified the figures, check the seller's calculations to make sure they are correct.

If any mortgages are being assumed, you must also check that the principal outstanding is close to the principal amount that was set out in the agreement of purchase and sale. It is possible that the seller forgot about payments made on the mortgage. In that case, the principal balance will be lower than expected, and so the credit to the buyer will also be lower. The buyer will then require more funds than expected to close. If there is a major difference, the buyer may not be able to come up with enough funds to close and may choose to end the transaction. Even if the buyer chooses to proceed with the transaction, the buyer will need enough time to arrange for the additional funds required to close. Therefore, advise the buyer of any difference as soon as possible.

## Direction Regarding Funds

The buyer's lawyer (on behalf of the buyer) must make the balance due on closing payable to the person named as the seller in the agreement of purchase and sale unless the seller gives the buyer a written direction to make the balance payable to someone else. The seller will usually want at least some of the closing balance to be payable elsewhere. If there is a mortgage to be discharged on closing, the seller will direct that an amount equal to the outstanding balance of the mortgage be made payable directly to the mortgagee. If there are water or tax arrears, the seller may direct that an amount equal to the arrears be made payable to the municipality. Finally, the seller's lawyer will usually insist that the balance of closing funds be made payable to the law firm to make sure that the law firm will have enough money to fulfill any undertakings it has given and to deduct its own legal fees.

The seller's lawyer will usually have the seller sign a direction stating that the closing funds are to be payable to the law firm or "as they may in writing direct." The seller's lawyer will usually not know the exact amounts that will have to be paid to third parties until just before closing. This kind of direction allows the law firm the flexibility to redirect the closing funds as required once the lawyer has the final information on amounts owing, such as mortgages to be discharged and tax arrears. The seller will not have to come in again to sign another direction.

Figure 21.14 is an example of a direction regarding funds signed by the seller.

Figure 21.15 is an example of a redirection regarding funds signed by the seller's lawyer.

# A Word About Undertakings

Undertakings may be given and signed by a client or the client's lawyer. If the undertaking is given and signed by the client, it is binding on the client only, and the lawyer has no responsibility to ensure that it is fulfilled. Depending on the way it is worded, if the undertaking is given and signed by the lawyer, it may bind only the client or it may bind the lawyer.

## Undertakings on Behalf of the Client

Undertakings on behalf of the client, although executed by the lawyer, bind only the client. These undertakings are rare and are usually given at the last minute, when the lawyer cannot arrange for the client to give one. The lawyer gets verbal approval from the client, and signs on behalf of the client. For the lawyer to escape personal liability, the undertaking must clearly state, "I/We hereby undertake on behalf of the seller/buyer, and without personal liability, as follows: ..." For example, if a seller improperly removed a fixture, the lawyer could undertake on behalf of the client to return it.

## Personal Undertakings

These are undertakings that are binding on the lawyer. An undertaking signed by a lawyer will bind the lawyer unless it is clearly stated to be without personal liability.

Lawyers give this kind of undertaking only if it is absolutely necessary and only with respect to items totally within the lawyer's control—for example, an undertaking to discharge an institutional mortgage where the lawyer has received a mortgage statement from the mortgagee and is receiving funds sufficient to discharge the mortgage.

Most undertakings are anticipated and are therefore prepared before closing. However, sometimes unforeseen matters arise. On the day of closing, you may be requested to give or accept additional undertakings. You should never give or accept an undertaking without first obtaining instructions from the lawyer handling the file.

# Transfer of Title

A document that actually transfers title from the seller to the buyer is required in every real estate transaction. If the property is in the Land Titles system, the documents will be electronic and completed in Teraview. If the property is in the Registry system, a paper form of transfer will be used. A paper transfer is shown as Figure 21.16 and the electronic form of transfer is shown as Figure 21.17.

The buyer's lawyer will ask for a draft of the transfer (whether it is paper or electronic) to review before the closing. When you receive it, you must review it to make sure that it has been properly completed. When reviewing the transfer, be sure to check the following:

- All transferors should be named as they were in the transfer by which they took title. The names should be set out with the family name first (in upper-case letters) followed by the first given name in full, followed by any other given names in full. Initials are not permitted. If the transfer is created in Teraview, the names will be accurate because they are pre-populated into the document based on the information on the title.

- All transferees should be named in accordance with the instructions of the buyer's lawyer to the seller's lawyer. Make sure that the correct birthdates are set out.

- The legal description should agree with the legal description in the last instrument registered on title. If you are using Teraview, this information will be correct because it is pre-populated based on the information on the title.

- Transferors must certify that they are at least 18 years old and include one of the following statements to indicate compliance with the provisions of the *Family Law Act*:

  - I am not a spouse.

  - We are spouses of one another. (This statement is used in cases where both spouses are registered owners and are therefore both parties to the transfer as transferors.)

  - I am a spouse.

  In the first case, because there is no spouse with an interest under the *Family Law Act*, no further statement is required. In the second case, both spouses are parties to the conveyance and therefore explicitly consent to the conveyance, and, again, no further statement is required. In the third case, however, where the statement indicates the existence of a spouse who is not a party to the conveyance as an owner, the transfer must also contain one of the following statements to demonstrate compliance with the provisions of the *Family Law Act*:

  - The person consenting below is my spouse. (In this case, the non-titled spouse must complete the spousal consent.)

  - The property transferred is not ordinarily occupied by me and my spouse, who is not separated from me, as our family residence.

  - I am separated from my spouse and the property transferred was not ordinarily occupied by us at the time of our separation as our family residence.

  - The property is not designated under section 20 of the *Family Law Act* as a matrimonial home by me and my spouse, but there is such a designation of another property as our matrimonial home, which has been registered and which has not been cancelled.

  - My spouse has released all rights under part II of the *Family Law Act* by a separation agreement.

  - The transaction is authorized by court order under section 23 of the *Family Law Act*, registered as instrument number _____, which has not been stayed.

  - The property transferred is released from the application of part II of the *Family Law Act* by court order registered as instrument number _____, which has not been stayed.

  The consent of the non-titled spouse is required only in the first case.

- In addition to indicating compliance with the *Family Law Act*, the statement must disclose facts that are consistent with the knowledge of the buyer's lawyer. Do not accept a statement setting out facts that are inconsistent with other evidence on the title—for example, a statement that the transferor is not a spouse when a previous mortgage indicates that there is a spouse.

- Make sure that the *Planning Act* statements have been completed if the buyer's lawyer has asked the seller to complete them. These statements confirm compliance with the provisions of the *Planning Act*. Completion of these statements is not required for the purpose of registration. However, the standard form of agreement of purchase and sale states that these statements must be completed by the seller if required by the buyer.

## Document Prepared by Both Lawyers

**acknowledgment and direction**
document signed by a party to a real estate transaction authorizing his or her lawyer to sign and release a document electronically on his or her behalf

Both lawyers must also prepare an **acknowledgment and direction** for their clients to sign with respect to each document that the lawyers will be registering on title. For a seller, this is usually the transfer; for the buyer, this is usually the transfer and the charge. This acknowledges the client's understanding of the electronic documents and authorizes the buyer's lawyer to complete the transaction on behalf of the client by way of electronic registration. It also directs the lawyer to enter into any necessary escrow closing agreement with the other lawyer. Furthermore, it provides a warranty as to the client's identity. This document is essential when using the e-reg system because the documents submitted for registration are not physically signed by the client. Figure 21.18 is an example of an acknowledgment and direction.

Both lawyers must also sign, or confirm in writing that they agree to be bound by, the document registration agreement, discussed in Chapter 7.

# KEY TERMS

acknowledgment and direction, 318

per diem, 309

# REFERENCES

*Family Law Act*, RSO 1990, c F.3.

*Income Tax Act*, RSC 1985, c 1 (5th Supp), as amended.

*Land Transfer Tax Act*, RSO 1990, c L.6.

*Planning Act*, RSO 1990, c P.13.

# REVIEW QUESTIONS

1. Which documents does the buyer's lawyer usually prepare?

2. Which documents does the seller's lawyer usually prepare?

3. What is a direction regarding title, and why is one necessary?

4. What is an undertaking to readjust, and why is one necessary?

5. Why is the land transfer tax statement or affidavit necessary?

6. When is the buyer required to accept an undertaking to discharge a mortgage? What should such an undertaking state?

7. What is a statutory declaration regarding writs of execution, and when is one necessary?

8. What is a statutory declaration of possession, and why is one necessary?

9. What is the *Income Tax Act* declaration, and why is one necessary?

10. What is a vendor's general undertaking, and why is one necessary?

11. What is the statement of adjustments, and why is one necessary?

12. Is an adjustment made for insurance in the statement of adjustments?

13. After all the adjustments are made, how is the balance due on closing calculated in the statement of adjustments?

14. What is the direction regarding funds, and why is one necessary?

15. What is an HST declaration, and when is one necessary?

16. What is an undertaking on behalf of a client?

17. What is a personal undertaking?

18. What type of document is required to transfer title of a Registry property, and who prepares it?

19. What is the acknowledgment and direction in an e-reg transaction, and why is one necessary?

20. The current annual property taxes for the property being purchased are $3,650, of which the seller has paid $1,000. The transaction is scheduled to close on March 31. Calculate the adjustment.

**Figure 21.1   Direction Regarding Title**

### DIRECTION RE TITLE

**TO:**          Francois Mercier and Huguette Marie Mercier

**AND TO:**    Brooks & Dunn
                Barristers and Solicitors

**RE:**          Grant purchase from Mercier
                166 Valley Road, Newmarket

---

WE HEREBY AUTHORIZE AND DIRECT you to engross the deed or transfer with respect to the above transaction as follows:

| Full Name | Birthdate |
|---|---|
| GRANT, Henry Albert | March 27, 1952 |
| GRANT, Wilma Heather | March 18, 1955 |
| As joint tenants | |

AND FOR SO DOING this shall be your good, sufficient, and irrevocable authority.

DATED at _____ , this _____ day of December, 2015.


_____
Henry Albert Grant


_____
Wilma Heather Grant

**Figure 21.2   Purchaser's Undertaking to Readjust**

**UNDERTAKING TO READJUST**

**TO:**       Francois Mercier and Huguette Marie Mercier

**AND TO:**   Brooks & Dunn
            Barristers and Solicitors

**RE:**       Grant purchase from Mercier
            166 Valley Road, Newmarket

---

IN CONSIDERATION of and notwithstanding the closing of the above transaction, we hereby undertake to readjust the statement of adjustments after closing should the same be found to contain any errors or omissions, forthwith upon written demand.

**DATED** at _____ , this _____ day of December, 2015.


                                    _____
                                    Henry Albert Grant


                                    _____
                                    Wilma Heather Grant

## Figure 21.3 Land Transfer Tax Affidavit

**Ontario**

Ministry of Finance
Audit Branch
Land Taxes
33 King Street West
PO Box 625
Oshawa ON L1H 8H9

Property Identifier(s) No.

**Land Transfer Tax Affidavit**
*Land Transfer Tax Act*

*Ce formulaire est disponible en français*
**Refer to Instructions on reverse side.**

**In the Matter of the Conveyance of** *(insert brief description of land)* _____

_____

**BY** *(print names of all transferors in full)* _____

**TO** *(print names of all transferees in full)* _____

*I* _____

*have personal knowledge of the facts herein deposed to and Make Oath and Say that:*

1. I am *(place a clear mark within the square opposite the following paragraph(s) that describe(s) the capacity of the deponents):*

   ☐ (a) the transferee named in the above-described conveyance;

   ☐ (b) the authorized agent or solicitor acting in this transaction for the transferee(s);

   ☐ (c) the President, Vice-President, Secretary, Treasurer, Director or Manager authorized to act for _____
   (the transferee(s));

   ☐ (d) a transferee and am making this affidavit on my own behalf and on behalf of *(insert name of spouse)* _____
   who is my spouse.

   ☐ (e) the transferor or an officer authorized to act on behalf of the transferor company and ☐ I am tendering this document for registration and
   ☐ no tax is payable on registration of this document.

2. *The total consideration for this transaction is allocated as follows:*

   (a) Monies paid or to be paid in cash ............................................ $ _____

   (b) Mortgages  (i) Assumed *(principal and interest)* ......................... $ _____

   (ii) Given back to vendor ............................................ $ _____

   (c) Property transferred in exchange *(detail below in para. 5)* .................. $ _____

   (d) Other consideration subject to tax *(detail below)* ......................... $ _____

   (e) Fair market value of the lands *(see Instruction 2(c))* ...................... $ _____

   (f) Value of land, building, fixtures and goodwill subject to
   Land Transfer Tax *(Total of (a) to (e))* ................................... $ _____  $ _____

   (g) Value of all chattels - items of tangible personal property ................ $ _____

   (h) Other consideration for transaction not included in (f) or (g) above ......... $ _____

   (i) Total Consideration ................................................ $ _____

   *All blanks must be filled in. Insert Nil where applicable.*

3. To be completed where the value of the consideration for the conveyance exceeds $400,000.00.
   I have read and considered the definition of "single family residence" set out in subsection 1(1) of the Act. The land conveyed in the above-described conveyance:

   ☐ does not contain a single family residence or contains more than two single family residences;

   ☐ contains at least one and not more than two single family residences; or

   ☐ contains at least one and not more than two single family residences and the lands are used for other than just residential purposes. The transferee has
   accordingly apportioned the value of consideration on the basis that the consideration for the single family residence is $ _____ and the
   remainder of the lands are used for _____ purposes.

   **Note:** Subsection 2(1)(b) imposes an additional tax at the rate of one-half of one per cent upon the value of the consideration in excess of $400,000.00 where
   the conveyance contains at least one and not more than two single family residences and 2(2) allows an apportionment of the consideration where the
   lands are used for other than just residential purposes.

4. If consideration is nominal, is the land subject to any encumbrance? ☐ Yes ☐ No

5. Other remarks and explanations, if necessary. _____

_____

Sworn/affirmed before me in the _____

_____

this _____ day of _____ , 20 _____

_____
Signature(s)

A Commissioner for taking Affidavits, etc.

**Property Information Record**

A. Describe nature of instrument: _____

B. (i) Address of property being conveyed *(if available)* _____

(ii) Assessment Roll No. *(if available)* _____

C. Mailing address(es) for future Notices of Assessment under the *Assessment Act* for property being conveyed
_____

**For Land Registry Office Use Only**

Registration No.

Registration Date *(Year/Month/Day)*

Land Registry Office No.

D. (i) Registration number for last conveyance of property being conveyed *(if available)* _____

(ii) Legal description of property conveyed: Same as in D (i) above. ☐ Yes ☐ No ☐ Not Known

E. Name(s) and address(es) of each transferee's solicitor: _____

**School Support (Voluntary Election)** *(See reverse for explanation)*

|  | Yes | No |
|---|---|---|
| (a) Are all individual transferees Roman Catholic? | ☐ | ☐ |
| (b) If Yes, do all individual transferees wish to be Roman Catholic Separate School Supporters? | ☐ | ☐ |
| (c) Do all individual transferees have French Language Education Rights? | ☐ | ☐ |
| (d) If Yes, do all individual transferees wish to support the French Language School Board (where established)? | ☐ | ☐ |

**Note: As to (c) and (d) the land being transferred will receive French Public School Board Election unless otherwise directed in (a) and (b).**

0449E (2013/01)  © Queen's Printer for Ontario, 2013  Disponible en français  Page 1 of 2

## Figure 21.4   Electronic Land Transfer Tax Statement

---

### LAND TRANSFER TAX STATEMENTS

In the matter of the conveyance of:        Parcel 170-1, Section 65M-1234

---

BY:     MERCIER, FRANCOIS
        MERCIER, HUGUETTE MARIE

TO:     GRANT, HENRY ALBERT                                              %(all PINs)
        GRANT, WILMA HEATHER                                            %(all PINs)

---

1.  GRANT, HENRY ALBERT AND GRANT, WILMA HEATHER

    I am

    ☐ (a) A person in trust for whom the land conveyed in the above-described conveyance is being conveyed;

    ☐ (b) A trustee named in the above-described conveyance to whom the land is being conveyed;

    ☑ (c) A transferee named in the above-described conveyance;

    ☐ (d) The authorized agent or solicitor acting in this transaction for _____ described in paragraph(s) (_) above.

    ☐ (e) The President, Vice-President, Manager, Secretary, Director, or Treasurer authorized to act for _____ described in paragraph(s) (_) above.

    ☐ (f) A transferee described in paragraph ( ) and am making these statements on my own behalf and on behalf of _____ who is my spouse described in paragraph (_) and as such, I have personal knowledge of the facts herein deposed to.

---

2.  I have read and considered the definition of "single family residence" set out in subsection 1(1) of the Act. The land being conveyed herein:

    contains at least one and not more than two single family residences.

---

3.  **The total consideration for this transaction is allocated as follows:**

    | | |
    |---|---:|
    | (a) Monies paid or to be paid in cash | 580,000.00 |
    | (b) Mortgages   (i) assumed (show principal and interest to be credited against purchase price) | 0.00 |
    |   (ii) Given Back to Vendor | 0.00 |
    | (c) Property transferred in exchange (detail below) | 0.00 |
    | (d) Fair market value of the land(s) | 0.00 |
    | (e) Liens, legacies, annuities and maintenance charges to which transfer is subject | 0.00 |
    | (f) Other valuable consideration subject to land transfer tax (detail below) | 0.00 |
    | (g) Value of land, building, fixtures and goodwill subject to land transfer tax (total of (a) to (f)) | 580,000.00 |
    | (h) VALUE OF ALL CHATTELS - items of tangible personal property | 0.00 |
    | (i) Other considerations for transaction not included in (g) or (h) above | 0.00 |
    | (j) Total consideration | 580,000.00 |

---

**PROPERTY Information Record**

A. Nature of Instrument:     Transfer

                            LRO  65     Registration No.                 Date:

B. Property(s):             PIN  12345-6789     Address           Assessment
                                                                  Roll No

C. Address for Service:     166 Valley Road
                            Newmarket, Ontario
                            L3H 3B3

D. (i) Last Conveyance(s):  PIN  12345-6789     Registration No.

   (ii) Legal Description for Property Conveyed : Same as in last conveyance?  Yes ☑  No ☐  Not known ☐

**Figure 21.5 Undertaking to Discharge Mortgage**

---

<u>**UNDERTAKING**</u>

**TO:**      Henry Albert Grant and Wilma Heather Grant

**AND TO:**      Kurtz, Emmans, Blatt & Wolf
Barristers and Solicitors

**RE:**      Mercier sale to Grant
166 Valley Road, Newmarket

---

IN CONSIDERATION of and notwithstanding the closing of the above-noted transaction, we hereby personally undertake to obtain and register a good and valid cessation of the charge registered as instrument number LT1394678 in favour of ABC Bank.

Without limiting the generality of the foregoing, with respect to each mortgage or charge referred to above, we personally undertake as follows:

a)      to forthwith pay to the mortgagee or person lawfully entitled thereto all moneys required to fully pay out and discharge such mortgage;

b)      to obtain and register a proper form of discharge as soon as possible after closing and to forthwith thereafter provide you with registration particulars thereof.

**DATED** at _____ , this _____ day of December, 2015.


Brooks & Dunn

Per: _____

**Figure 21.6   Statutory Declaration Regarding Executions**

<u>STATUTORY DECLARATION RE EXECUTIONS</u>

LAND TITLES ACT

IN THE MATTER OF Parcel 170-1 in the Register for Section 65M-1234

AND IN THE MATTER OF certain writs of execution in the hands of the Sheriff of York Region, copies of which have been filed in the Land Registry Office for the Land Titles Division of York Region as numbers _____.

WE, Francois Mercier and Huguette Marie Mercier, of the Town of Newmarket, in the Regional Municipality of York,

DO SOLEMNLY DECLARE that:

1.   We are the registered owners of the land entered as Parcel 170-1, Section 65M-1234.

2.   We are not the same persons as _____, the judgment debtors named in writ of execution number _____, wherein _____ _____, as plaintiff, was awarded $_____ plus $_____ costs.

SEVERALLY DECLARED BEFORE ME at the          )
_____          )
                                                                          )
in the Province of Ontario                                    )
                                                                          )   _____
this _____ day of December, 2015              )   Francois Mercier
                                                                          )
_____          )   _____
A Commissioner, etc.                                        )   Huguette Marie Mercier

**Figure 21.7  Statutory Declaration of Possession**

**IN THE MATTER OF** title to:
Lot 170, Plan 65M-1234
166 Valley Road, Newmarket

**AND IN THE MATTER OF** the sale thereof from
Francois Mercier and Huguette Marie Mercier to
Henry Albert Grant and Wilma Heather Grant

We, Francois Mercier and Huguette Marie Mercier, SOLEMNLY DECLARE that:

1. We are the absolute owners of the above-mentioned lands and either personally or by our tenants have been in actual, peaceable, continuous, exclusive, open, undisturbed, and undisputed possession and occupation thereof, and of the houses and other buildings used in connection therewith throughout our period of ownership of the property.

2. We are not aware of any person or corporation having any claim or interest in the said lands or any part thereof adverse to or inconsistent with registered title and are positive that none exists.

3. Possession and occupation of the above lands by the vendors have been undisturbed throughout by any action, suit, or other proceedings or adverse possession or otherwise on the part of any person whomsoever and during such possession and occupation, no payment has ever been made or acknowledgment of title given by the undersigned, or, so far as we know, by anyone else, to any person in respect of any right, title, interest, or claim upon the said lands.

4. To the best of our knowledge and belief, the buildings used in connection with the premises are situate wholly within the limits of the lands above described, and there is no dispute as to the boundaries of the said lands. Except as may be registered on title, we have never heard of any claim of easement affecting the lands, either for light, drainage, or right of way or otherwise.

5. We do not retain the fee or the equity of redemption in, or a power or right to grant, assign, or exercise a power of appointment with respect to any land abutting the lands being conveyed in the subject transaction.

6. We are not non-residents of Canada within the meaning of section 116 of the *Income Tax Act* (Canada) nor will we be non-residents of Canada at the time of closing.

7. We have carefully examined the survey prepared by _____ and dated _____, a copy of which is attached hereto, and have compared our knowledge of the buildings situate on the subject property with those shown on the said survey. The survey accurately describes the property and buildings on the subject property as they exist today and there are no other buildings, additions, decks, swimming pools, outbuildings, or any other structures not shown on such survey.

**Figure 21.7    Concluded**

AND WE make this solemn declaration conscientiously believing it to be true, and knowing that it is of the same force and effect as if made under oath.

SEVERALLY DECLARED BEFORE ME at the          )
_____          )
                                                                )
in the Province of Ontario                                )
                                                                )    _____
this _____ day of December, 2015          )    Francois Mercier
                                                                )
_____          )    _____
A Commissioner, etc.                                    )    Huguette Marie Mercier

**Figure 21.8 Income Tax Act Declaration**

---

<u>**STATUTORY DECLARATION RE SECTION 116 OF THE INCOME TAX ACT**</u>

CANADA        ) IN THE MATTER OF 166 Valley Road,
             ) Newmarket
PROVINCE OF ONTARIO  )
             )
             ) AND IN THE MATTER OF the sale thereof
             ) from Francois Mercier and Huguette Marie
             ) Mercier to Henry Albert Grant and Wilma
             ) Heather Grant

WE, Francois Mercier and Huguette Marie Mercier, of the Town of Newmarket,

  DO SOLEMNLY DECLARE, that

1. We are not and will not be at the time of closing the above-noted transaction a non-resident of Canada within the meaning of section 116 of the *Income Tax Act* of Canada.

AND WE make this solemn declaration conscientiously believing it to be true, and knowing that it is of the same force and effect as if made under oath.

SEVERALLY DECLARED BEFORE ME at the )
_____ )
             )
in the Province of Ontario      )
             ) _____
this _____ day of December, 2015 ) Francois Mercier
             )
_____ ) _____
A Commissioner, etc.       ) Huguette Marie Mercier

**Figure 21.9  Realty Tax Declaration**

**STATUTORY DECLARATION RE REALTY TAXES**

| | | |
|---|---|---|
| CANADA | ) | IN THE MATTER OF 166 Valley Road, |
| | ) | Newmarket |
| PROVINCE OF ONTARIO | ) | |
| | ) | |
| | ) | AND IN THE MATTER OF the sale thereof |
| | ) | from Francois Mercier and Huguette Marie |
| | ) | Mercier to Henry Albert Grant and Wilma |
| | ) | Heather Grant |

WE, Francois Mercier and Huguette Marie Mercier, of the Town of Newmarket,

DO SOLEMNLY DECLARE, that

1.   We are the registered owners of the above-mentioned property and as such have knowledge of the matters herein deposed to.

2.   The 2015 realty taxes are in the amount of $5,200.00.

3.   All 2015 realty tax installments have been paid in accordance with the statement of adjustments. There are no arrears of realty taxes in connection with the property.

4.   There are no outstanding hydro, water, and gas accounts, and all utility accounts will be paid up to the date of closing.

AND WE make this solemn declaration conscientiously believing it to be true, and knowing that it is of the same force and effect as if made under oath.

| | | |
|---|---|---|
| SEVERALLY DECLARED BEFORE ME at the | ) | |
| _____ | ) | |
| | ) | |
| in the Province of Ontario | ) | |
| | ) | _____ |
| this _____ day of December, 2015 | ) | Francois Mercier |
| | ) | |
| _____ | ) | _____ |
| A Commissioner, etc. | ) | Huguette Marie Mercier |

## Figure 21.10 Warranties and Bill of Sale

### WARRANTIES AND BILL OF SALE

**TO:**      Henry Albert Grant and Wilma Heather Grant

**AND TO:**      Kurtz, Emmans, Blatt & Wolf
Barristers and Solicitors

**RE:**      Grant purchase from Mercier
166 Valley Road, Newmarket

### WARRANTIES

We, Francois Mercier and Huguette Marie Mercier, being the vendors in the above transaction, hereby warrant as follows:

1. THAT during the time we have owned the property, we have not caused any building on the property to be insulated with insulation containing urea formaldehyde, and that to the best of our knowledge, no building on the property contains or has ever contained insulation that contains urea formaldehyde. If the building is part of a multiple unit building, this warranty shall only apply to that part of the building which is the subject of this transaction.

2. THAT no damage has occurred to the property, including the buildings situate on the subject property as well as the chattels and fixtures included in the purchase price, since the same were inspected by the purchaser.

3. THAT no work, construction, or alterations have been done on the premises, or material supplied thereto, which could result in a lien being registered under the *Construction Lien Act*.

4. THAT, as at the date of closing of this transaction, there are no work orders or deficiency notices outstanding and affecting the subject property and, if any should exist, they shall be rectified at our expense forthwith upon demand.

5. THAT the warranties contained in the agreement of purchase and sale, as well as those contained herein, shall survive closing.

6. THAT any work to be done to the subject property by the vendors as stipulated in the agreement of purchase and sale shall be completed prior to closing in a good and workmanlike manner.

7. THAT the chattels and fixtures included in the agreement will be in good working order on completion. This warranty shall survive and not merge on completion of this transaction.

### BILL OF SALE

**Figure 21.10   Concluded**

IN CONSIDERATION of the closing of the within transaction, the undersigned, being the vendors of the subject property, do hereby sell, transfer, and convey to the purchaser the chattels and fixtures included in the purchase price as specified in the agreement of purchase and sale; and we covenant that we are the lawful owners thereof and that we have the right to transfer and convey the same and that such chattels and fixtures are free of all encumbrances, liens, and claims of any kind whatsoever.

**DATED** at _____ , this _____ day of December, 2015.


_____
Francois Mercier


_____
Huguette Marie Mercier

**Figure 21.11    Vendor's General Undertaking**

**UNDERTAKING**

**TO:**        Henry Albert Grant and Wilma Heather Grant

**AND TO:**   Kurtz, Emmans, Blatt & Wolf
             Barristers and Solicitors

**RE:**        Grant purchase from Mercier
             166 Valley Road, Newmarket

In consideration of and notwithstanding the closing of the above-noted transaction, we hereby undertake as follows:

1.   To deliver up vacant possession of the premises on closing and all keys to the premises.

2.   To pay all hydroelectric, water, and gas charges, if any, to the date of closing.

3.   To pay all arrears of taxes and penalties, including local improvement rates, and to readjust realty taxes and local improvement rates for the current year, if necessary.

4.   To leave on the premises the chattels and fixtures specified in the agreement of purchase and sale herein, free of encumbrances, liens, charges, or claims of any kind whatsoever.

5.   To readjust any of the items shown on the statement of adjustments, if necessary.

6.   To have the oil tank filled in accordance with the statement of adjustments at our expense on the day before closing.

7.   To make all payments under the existing mortgage(s) being assumed by the purchasers that fall due on or before the closing date, and to readjust the amounts credited to the purchasers with respect to the principal balance and interest owing and tax account status of the existing mortgage(s) being assumed by the purchasers, if necessary.

**DATED** at _____ , this _____ day of December, 2015.


_____
Francois Mercier


_____
Huguette Marie Mercier

**Figure 21.12  Statutory Declaration Regarding HST**

**IN THE MATTER OF** Harmonized Sales Tax ("HST") provisions of the *Excise Tax Act* (Canada), as amended (the "Act")

**AND IN THE MATTER OF** the sale of:
Lot 170, Plan 65M-1234
166 Valley Road, Newmarket, from Francois Mercier and Huguette Marie Mercier to Henry Albert Grant and Wilma Heather Grant

We, Francois Mercier and Huguette Marie Mercier, SOLEMNLY DECLARE that:

1.   The above property is occupied as a residential unit, and all parts of the property are reasonably necessary for the use and enjoyment of the property as a place of residence for individuals.

2.   We did not acquire the property or carry on any construction or renovation of the property in the course of business or adventure or concern in the nature of trade.

3.   We have not claimed an input tax credit under the Act in respect of the acquisition of the property or an improvement to it.

4.   No part of the property is capital property used primarily in a business of ours.

5.   The sale is not being made in the course of a business or adventure or concern in the nature of trade of ours in respect of which we have filed an election under the Act.

6.   The property is a "used residential complex" and the sale of the property is exempt from HST under section 2 and, if applicable, section 9 of part I of schedule V of the Act, and we make this declaration to be delivered to the purchaser with intent that it be relied upon by the purchaser in claiming such exemption as a statement in writing or certificate delivered to the purchaser pursuant to section 194 of the Act.

AND WE make this solemn declaration conscientiously believing it to be true, and knowing that it is of the same force and effect as if made under oath.

SEVERALLY DECLARED BEFORE ME at the            )
_____            )
                                                                                      )
in the Province of Ontario                                          )
                                                                                      )        _____
this _____ day of December, 2015                 )        Francois Mercier
                                                                                      )
_____            )        _____
A Commissioner, etc.                                                )        Huguette Marie Mercier

**Figure 21.13 Statement of Adjustments**

---

### STATEMENT OF ADJUSTMENTS

VENDOR:      Francois Mercier and Huguette Marie Mercier
PURCHASER:  Henry Albert Grant and Wilma Heather Grant
PROPERTY:   166 Valley Road, Newmarket, Ontario

Adjusted as of December 15, 2015

|  | Credit Purchaser | Credit Vendor |
|---|---|---|
| SALE PRICE |  | 580,000.00 |
| DEPOSIT Paid to Broker | 30,000.00 |  |
| REALTY TAXES 2015 taxes of $5,200.00 Vendor's share: 348 days = $4,957.81 Vendor has paid: $5,200.00 Difference: $242.19 Credit vendor |  | 242.19 |
| HYDRO, GAS, WATER Metered, no adjustment |  |  |
| BALANCE DUE ON CLOSING | 550,242.19 |  |
|  | 580,242.19 | 580,242.19 |

**Figure 21.14    Direction Regarding Funds**

### DIRECTION REGARDING FUNDS

**TO:**   Henry Albert Grant and Wilma Heather Grant

**AND TO:**  Kurtz, Emmans, Blatt & Wolf
Barristers and Solicitors

**RE:**   Grant purchase from Mercier
166 Valley Road, Newmarket

---

You are hereby authorized and directed to make the balance due on closing payable to our solicitors Brooks & Dunn, in trust, or as they may in writing direct, and for so doing this shall be your good, sufficient, and irrevocable authority.

**DATED** at _____ , this _____ day of December, 2015.


_____
Francois Mercier


_____
Huguette Marie Mercier

**Figure 21.15    Redirection Regarding Funds**

### REDIRECTION REGARDING FUNDS

**TO:**          Henry Albert Grant and Wilma Heather Grant

**AND TO:**    Kurtz, Emmans, Blatt & Wolf
                Barristers and Solicitors

**RE:**          Grant purchase from Mercier
                166 Valley Road, Newmarket

---

You are hereby authorized and directed to make the balance due on closing payable as follows:

1.    To: ABC Bank                $93,111.23
2.    Brooks & Dunn, in trust     $457,130.96
                                   _____
                                   $550,242.19

and for so doing, this shall be your good and sufficient authority.

**DATED** at _____ , this _____ day of December, 2015.

Brooks & Dunn

Per:

## Figure 21.16    Transfer (Paper)

Province
of
Ontario

DYE & DURHAM CO. INC.—Form No. 970
Amended NOV. 1992

# Transfer/Deed of Land

Form 1 — Land Registration Reform Act

**A**

**FOR OFFICE USE ONLY**

New Property Identifiers

Additional:
See
Schedule ☐

Executions

Additional:
See
Schedule ☐

(1) **Registry** ☐    **Land Titles** ☐    (2) Page 1 of    pages

(3) **Property Identifier(s)**    Block    Property    Additional: See Schedule ☐

(4) **Consideration**    Dollars $

(5) **Description**    This is a:    Property Division ☐    Property Consolidation ☐

(6) **This Document Contains**    (a) Redescription New Easement Plan/Sketch ☐    (b) Schedule for: Description ☐    Additional Parties ☐    Other ☐    (7) **Interest/Estate Transferred** Fee Simple

(8) **Transferor(s)** The transferor hereby transfers the land to the transferee and certifies that the transferor is at least eighteen years old and that

Name(s)    Signature(s)    Date of Signature  Y  M  D

(9) **Spouse(s) of Transferor(s)** I hereby consent to this transaction
Name(s)    Signature(s)    Date of Signature  Y  M  D

(10) **Transferor(s) Address for Service**

(11) **Transferee(s)**    Date of Birth  Y  M  D

(12) **Transferee(s) Address for Service**

(13) **Transferor(s)** The transferor verifies that to the best of the transferor's knowledge and belief, this transfer does not contravene section 50 of the Planning Act.
Date of Signature  Y  M  D    Date of Signature  Y  M  D
Signature.    Signature.
**Solicitor for Transferor(s)** I have explained the effect of section 50 of the Planning Act to the transferor and I have made inquiries of the transferor to determine that this transfer does not contravene that section and based on the information supplied by the transferor, to the best of my knowledge and belief, this transfer does not contravene that section. I am an Ontario solicitor in good standing.
Name and Address of Solicitor    Date of Signature  Y  M  D
Signature.

**Planning Act — OPTIONAL**

Affix Statement by Solicitor for Transferee(s) here if necessary

(14) **Solicitor for Transferee(s)** I have investigated the title to this land and to abutting land where relevant and I am satisfied that the title records reveal no contravention as set out in subclause 50 (22) (c) (ii) of the Planning Act and that to the best of my knowledge and belief this transfer does not contravene section 50 of the Planning Act. I act independently of the solicitor for the transferor(s) and I am an Ontario solicitor in good standing.
Name and Address of Solicitor    Date of Signature  Y  M  D
Signature.

(15) **Assessment Roll Number of Property**    Cty.  Mun.  Map  Sub.  Par.

(16) **Municipal Address of Property**

(17) **Document Prepared by:**

**FOR OFFICE USE ONLY**

**Fees and Tax**

Registration Fee
Land Transfer Tax

Total

## Figure 21.17  Transfer (Electronic)

| LRO # 65  **Transfer** | | **In preparation** on 2015 07 02 | at 10:21 |
|---|---|---|---|
| *This document has not been submitted and may be incomplete.* | | yyyy mm dd | Page 1 of 2 |

### Properties

| | | | |
|---|---|---|---|
| *PIN*  12345-6789 | LT | *Interest/Estate* | Fee Simple |
| *Description*  Parcel 170-1, Section 65M-1234 | | | |

*Address*    166 Valley Road
Newmarket, Ontario

### Consideration

*Consideration*    $ 580,000.00

### Transferor(s)

The transferor(s) hereby transfers the land to the transferee(s).

| | |
|---|---|
| *Name* | MERCIER, FRANCOIS |
| | Acting as an individual |
| *Address for Service* | 97 Brook Street |
| | Newmarket, Ontario |
| | L3H 1V2 |

I am at least 18 years of age.

HUGUETTE MARIE MERCIER and I are spouses of one another and are both parties to this document

This document is not authorized  under Power of Attorney by this party.

| | |
|---|---|
| *Name* | MERCIER, HUGUETTE MARIE |
| | Acting as an individual |
| *Address for Service* | 97 Brook Street |
| | Newmarket, Ontario |
| | L3H 1V2 |

I am at least 18 years of age.

FRANCOIS MERCIER and I are spouses of one another and are both parties to this document

This document is not authorized  under Power of Attorney by this party.

### Transferee(s)

| | | Capacity | Share |
|---|---|---|---|
| *Name* | GRANT, HENRY ALBERT | Joint tenant | |
| | Acting as an individual | | |
| *Date of Birth* | 1952 03 27 | | |
| *Address for Service* | 166 Valley Road | | |
| | Newmarket, Ontario | | |
| | L3H 3B3 | | |
| *Name* | GRANT, WILMA HEATHER | Joint tenant | |
| | Acting as an individual | | |
| *Date of Birth* | 1955 03 18 | | |
| *Address for Service* | 166 Valley Road | | |
| | Newmarket, Ontario | | |
| | L3H 3B3 | | |

# Figure 21.17   Continued

LRO # 65   **Transfer**                                              **In preparation**  on  2015 07 02     at  10:21

*This document has not been submitted and may be incomplete.*                              yyyy mm dd      Page 2 of 2

| *Calculated Taxes* |
| --- |

*Provincial Land Transfer Tax*          $8,075.00

## Figure 21.17 **Concluded**

---

**LAND TRANSFER TAX STATEMENTS**

In the matter of the conveyance of:  Parcel 170-1, Section 65M-1234

---

| | | |
|---|---|---|
| BY: | MERCIER, FRANCOIS | |
| | MERCIER, HUGUETTE MARIE | |
| TO: | GRANT, HENRY ALBERT | %(all PINs) |
| | GRANT, WILMA HEATHER | %(all PINs) |

---

1. GRANT, HENRY ALBERT AND GRANT, WILMA HEATHER

    I am

    ☐ (a) A person in trust for whom the land conveyed in the above-described conveyance is being conveyed;

    ☐ (b) A trustee named in the above-described conveyance to whom the land is being conveyed;

    ☑ (c) A transferee named in the above-described conveyance;

    ☐ (d) The authorized agent or solicitor acting in this transaction for ____ described in paragraph(s) (_) above.

    ☐ (e) The President, Vice-President, Manager, Secretary, Director, or Treasurer authorized to act for ____ described in paragraph(s) (_) above.

    ☐ (f) A transferee described in paragraph ( ) and am making these statements on my own behalf and on behalf of _____ who is my spouse described in paragraph (_) and as such, I have personal knowledge of the facts herein deposed to.

---

2. I have read and considered the definition of "single family residence" set out in subsection 1(1) of the Act. The land being conveyed herein:

    contains at least one and not more than two single family residences.

---

3. **The total consideration for this transaction is allocated as follows:**

| | |
|---|---|
| (a) Monies paid or to be paid in cash | 580,000.00 |
| (b) Mortgages  (i) assumed (show principal and interest to be credited against purchase price) | 0.00 |
| (ii) Given Back to Vendor | 0.00 |
| (c) Property transferred in exchange (detail below) | 0.00 |
| (d) Fair market value of the land(s) | 0.00 |
| (e) Liens, legacies, annuities and maintenance charges to which transfer is subject | 0.00 |
| (f) Other valuable consideration subject to land transfer tax (detail below) | 0.00 |
| (g) Value of land, building, fixtures and goodwill subject to land transfer tax (total of (a) to (f)) | 580,000.00 |
| (h) VALUE OF ALL CHATTELS - items of tangible personal property | 0.00 |
| (i) Other considerations for transaction not included in (g) or (h) above | 0.00 |
| (j) Total consideration | 580,000.00 |

---

**PROPERTY Information Record**

A. Nature of Instrument:  Transfer

    LRO  65  Registration No.  Date:

B. Property(s):  PIN  Address  Assessment Roll No

C. Address for Service:  166 Valley Road
Newmarket, Ontario
L3H 3B3

D. (i) Last Conveyance(s):  PIN  12345-6789  Registration No.

(ii) Legal Description for Property Conveyed : Same as in last conveyance?  Yes ☑  No ☐  Not known ☐

## Figure 21.18   Acknowledgment and Direction

### ACKNOWLEDGEMENT AND DIRECTION

**TO:**           Judith Marlene Wolf _____
                   (Insert lawyer's name)

**AND TO:**     JUDITH M WOLF LAW OFFICE _____
                   (Insert firm name)

**RE:**           GRANT purchase from MERCIER, 166 Valley Road, Newmarket _____ ('the transaction")
                   (Insert brief description of transaction)

**This will confirm that:**

- I/We have reviewed the information set out in this Acknowledgement and Direction and in the documents described below (the "Documents"), and that this information is accurate;

- You, your agent or employee are authorized and directed to sign, deliver, and/or register electronically, on my/our behalf the Documents in the form attached.

- You are hereby authorized and directed to enter into an escrow closing arrangement substantially in the form attached hereto being a copy of the version of the Document Registration Agreement, which appears on the website of the Law Society of Upper Canada as of the date of the Agreement of Purchase and sale herein. I/We hereby acknowledge the said Agreement has been reviewed by me/us and that I/We shall be bound by its terms;

- The effect of the Documents has been fully explained to me/us, and I/we understand that I/we are parties to and bound by the terms and provisions of the Documents to the same extent as if I/we had signed them; and

- I/we are in fact the parties named in the Documents and I/we have not misrepresented our identities to you.

- I, _____, am the spouse of _____, the (Transferor/Chargor), and hereby consent to the transaction described in the Acknowledgment and Direction. I authorize you to indicate my consent on all the Documents for which it is required.

### DESCRIPTION OF ELECTRONIC DOCUMENTS

The Document(s) described in the Acknowledgement and Direction are the document(s) selected below which are attached hereto as "Document in Preparation" and are:

☐     A Transfer of the land described above.

☐     A Charge of the land described above.

☐     Other documents set out in Schedule "B" attached hereto.

Dated at    _____ , this  _____ day of  _____ , 20___ .

**WITNESS**

(As to all signatures, if required)

_____      _____
                                      HENRY ALBERT GRANT

                                      _____
                                      WILMA HEATHER GRANT

                                        _____

                                          _____

# Closing the Transaction

# 22

## LEARNING OUTCOMES

After reading this chapter, you will understand:

- How the buyer prepares to complete a real estate transaction

- How the seller prepares to complete a real estate transaction

- How to determine and calculate the taxes payable on closing by a buyer of real property

- When harmonized sales tax is payable by a buyer of real property

- How a real estate transaction is finally completed

- How a closing is completed electronically

# Introduction

After the closing documents have been prepared, you must turn your attention to preparation for the closing itself. It is at the closing that the buyer receives title to the property and the seller receives payment. The buyer's lawyer wants to make sure that there are sufficient funds on hand to close the transaction and that the buyer gets exactly what was contracted for. The seller's lawyer wants to make sure that the appropriate payment is received on behalf of the seller and that the seller can deliver title as promised.

The actual steps involved in closing the transaction will depend on whether the closing is completed electronically.

# Organization from the Buyer's Perspective

If the buyer's lawyer and law clerk have been well organized, used checklists, and diarized as they've gone along, there should be very little left to do as the closing date approaches.

## Monetary Issues

To prepare for closing, you must know how much the buyer has to pay to complete the transaction and to whom the money must be paid. You received this information from the statement of adjustments and the direction regarding funds, prepared by the seller's lawyer. (Both of these documents are discussed in Chapter 21, Document Preparation.)

You must also calculate how much the buyer will have to pay for

- provincial land transfer tax;
- municipal land transfer tax (if the property is located in the City of Toronto and it contains at least one and not more than two single-family residences);
- harmonized sales tax (HST), if any;
- registration fees;
- the title insurance premium, if any; and
- legal fees and disbursements.

### Calculating the Provincial Land Transfer Tax

Provincial land transfer tax is calculated using the information in the land transfer tax affidavit or statement (discussed in Chapter 21; see Figure 21.3). Land transfer tax is payable on the amount shown in paragraph 2, line (f), "Value of land, building, fixtures and goodwill subject to Land Transfer Tax."

The land transfer tax rates are

- ½ of 1 percent (0.005) on the first $55,000;
- 1 percent (0.01) on the amount from $55,000.01 to $250,000;

- 1½ percent (0.015) on the amount from $250,000.01 to $400,000; and
- 2 percent (0.02) on the amount over $400,000 if the property contains at least one and not more than two single-family residences. Otherwise, the rate remains at 1½ percent (0.015).

| Value of Consideration | Provincial Land Transfer Tax Rate |
|---|---|
| The first $55,000 | 0.5% (0.005) |
| On the amount from $55,000.01 to $250,000 | 1% (0.01) |
| On the amount from $250,000.01 to $400,000 | 1.5% (0.015) |
| Amount over $400,000* | 2% (0.02) |

\* If the property contains at least one and not more than two single-family residences. Otherwise, the rate remains at 1.5%.

As a shortcut, you may do the calculation based on the scale set out below:

- If the consideration is less than or equal to $55,000, simply multiply the amount of the consideration by 0.005.
- If the consideration is greater than $55,000 but is not greater than $250,000, multiply the amount of the consideration by 0.01 and then deduct $275.
- If the consideration is greater than $250,000 but is not greater than $400,000, or the consideration is greater than $400,000 but does not contain at least one and not more than two single-family residences, multiply the amount of the consideration by 0.015 and then deduct $1,525.
- If the consideration is greater than $400,000, and the property contains at least one and not more than two single-family residences, multiply the amount of the consideration by 0.02 and then deduct $3,525.

| Value of Consideration (VC) | Shortcut Formula |
|---|---|
| Less than or equal to $55,000 | VC × 0.005 |
| Between $55,000.01 and $250,000 | VC × 0.01 − $275 |
| Between $250,000.01 and $400,000 | VC × 0.015 − $1,525 |
| Greater than $400,000* | VC × 0.02 − $3,525 |

\* If the property contains at least one and not more than two single-family residences. Otherwise, use the shortcut formula in row 3.

For example, if the consideration on the sale of a single-family residence is $650,000, the calculation can be done in *either* of the following two ways:

1. For the first $55,000: $55,000 × 0.005 = $275

   For $55,000 to $250,000: $195,000 × 0.01 = $1,950

   For $250,000 to $400,000: $150,000 × 0.015 = $2,250

   For $400,000 to $650,000: $250,000 × 0.02 = $5,000

   Total provincial land transfer tax: $9,475

or

2. ($650,000 × 0.02) − $3,525 = $13,000 − $3,525 = $9,475

If the property contains three or more residential units, the rate does not increase again after $400,000.

It is important to advise first-time homebuyers that they are entitled to a rebate of up to $2,000 of the provincial land transfer tax. This rebate is available only to someone who has never owned property anywhere in the world, and not just Ontario. The rebate is $2,000 or the total amount of the land transfer tax, whichever is lower.

### Calculating the Municipal Land Transfer Tax

If the property is located in the City of Toronto and it contains at least one and not more than two single-family residences, municipal land transfer tax must also be paid. The rates are as follows:

- ½ of 1 percent (0.005) on the first $55,000;
- 1 percent (0.01) on the amount from $55,000.01 to $400,000;
- 2 percent (0.02) on the amount over $400,000.

If the property contains more than two single-family residences, the rate applied to the amount over $400,000 is 1½ percent (0.015) rather than 2 percent.

| Value of Consideration | Municipal Land Transfer Tax Rate |
| --- | --- |
| The first $55,000 | 0.5% (0.005) |
| On the amount from $55,000.01 to $400,000 | 1% (0.01) |
| Amount over $400,000* | 2% (0.02) |

\* If the property contains more than two single-family residences, the rate applied to the amount over $400,000 is 1.5%.

As a shortcut, you may do the calculation based on the scale set out below:

- If the consideration is less than or equal to $55,000, multiply the amount of the consideration by 0.005.
- If the consideration is between $55,000.01 and $400,000, multiply the amount of the consideration by 0.01, and subtract $275.

- If the consideration is greater than $400,000, multiply the amount of the consideration by 0.02 (or by 0.015 if the property contains more than two single-family residences) and subtract $4,275.

| Value of Consideration (VC) | Shortcut Formula |
|---|---|
| Less than or equal to $55,000 | VC × 0.005 |
| Between $55,000.01 and $400,000 | VC × 0.01 − $275 |
| Greater than $400,000* | VC × 0.02 − $4,275 |

  \* If the property contains more than two single-family residences, multiply the amount of the consideration by 0.015 instead of 0.02 and subtract $2,275.

For example, if the consideration on the sale of a single-family residence in the City of Toronto is $650,000, the calculation can be done in *either* of the following two ways:

1. For the first $55,000: $55,000 × 0.005 = $275

   For $55,000 to $400,000: $345,000 × 0.01 = $3,450

   For $400,000 to $650,000: $250,000 × 0.02 = $5,000

   Total municipal land transfer tax: $8,725

or

2. ($650,000 × 0.02) − $4,275 = $13,000 − $4,275 = $8,725

First-time homebuyers are exempt from municipal land transfer tax on purchase prices up to $400,000. They have to pay tax on amounts over $400,000, at the rate of 2 percent. For example, if the purchase price of the property is $350,000, no municipal land transfer tax is payable. If the purchase price of the property is $480,000, the buyer will pay 2 percent of the amount over $400,000, or 2 percent of $80,000.

## Calculating the Harmonized Sales Tax

Harmonized sales tax is payable on the value of the chattels included in the transaction. The calculation of this tax is based on the information contained in the land transfer tax affidavit. To calculate the amount of harmonized sales tax payable, multiply the amount shown in paragraph 2, line (g), "Value of all chattels," by 13 percent. For example, if the value of chattels is $2,000, the HST payable is $2,000 × 0.13 = $260.

If the home being purchased is newly built or substantially renovated, harmonized sales tax is also payable at the same rate on the value of the land, building, fixtures, and goodwill. Buyers of new or substantially renovated homes may be eligible for a refund of up to $24,000 of the provincial portion (8 percent) of this tax, but only if the buyer warrants that he or she or an immediate family member will be using the property as his or her residence. Since HST is usually included in the price for new homes, this rebate goes to the builder, not the buyer. If the property is a resale home, HST is not payable on the value of the land, building, and fixtures.

### Registration Fees Payable on Closing

The buyer pays to register the transfer and any mortgages other than a vendor-take-back mortgage. The seller pays to register any mortgage back and any discharges of mortgage or other documents required to clear the title of encumbrances. At the time of publication, the registration fee for electronic registrations was $71.30 (including a Teraview fee of $11.30) for each instrument of any kind; however, registration fees increase regularly. If the document is being registered in the paper system, there is no Teraview fee and the registration fee is $60.

### Obtaining Funds from the Client

You must obtain sufficient funds from the buyer to cover the balance due on closing, the provincial land transfer tax, the municipal land transfer tax (if any), the harmonized sales tax (if any), and the registration fees. In addition, most law firms will want the client to give the firm enough money to cover the legal fees and disbursements for the transaction.

**disbursements**
a lawyer's out-of-pocket expenses

The lawyer will set the amount to be charged for fees. You will need to calculate the total amount of **disbursements**. Disbursements are the out-of-pocket expenses that your firm has paid or will pay with respect to the transaction, such as the costs of a title search, an execution certificate, a tax certificate, registration fees, postage, and courier charges. Sometimes the title insurance premium will be included as a disbursement as well, and other times it will be calculated as a separate item.

### Mortgage Proceeds

If the client is financing part of the purchase by way of a mortgage, you will need to know exactly how much the mortgagee will be providing on the closing date. The amount may well be less than the principal amount of the mortgage. For example, if the interest adjustment date is different from the closing date, an amount for interest is deducted from the amount advanced under the mortgage. If the mortgage is a

**high ratio mortgage**
a mortgage for more than 80 percent of the value of the property

**high ratio mortgage** (a mortgage for more than 80 percent of the value of the property), an amount may be deducted for insurance. The money received from the mortgagee will be applied to the purchase price and will reduce the amount of money to be provided directly by the buyer.

## One Week Before Closing

Start your final preparation for closing *at least* one week before the closing date.

### Review the File

- Make sure that all preliminary letters, the requisition letter, and any follow-up letters sent by the law firm have been answered and that the answers are satisfactory.
- Update public utility account and tax information in the case of a long closing or if the original responses revealed arrears that the seller's solicitor indicated would be paid before closing. If title insurance is being obtained for the transaction, this step will likely not be necessary.

### Contact the Client

- You must advise the client of the amount of money to be provided.
- Set up an appointment for the client to deliver the funds and to sign all documents.
- Remind the client to arrange insurance coverage for the property as of the closing date. If the buyer is arranging new mortgage financing, the client will have to provide to the mortgagee particulars of the insurance coverage, and the lawyer will require a **binder letter** in order to confirm that the mortgagee is named on the policy.
- Check that the client has taken all steps necessary for any mortgage approvals, whether there are new mortgages or mortgages being assumed.

**binder letter**
a letter from an insurance company confirming that the property will be insured as of a specific date, and showing the amount of coverage, and the names of the mortgagees

### Prepare the Statutory Declaration Regarding Executions

If there are any executions outstanding against a name similar to that of the buyer, prepare a statutory declaration regarding executions to be sworn by the client. In the declaration, deal specifically with any executions outstanding at the time the declaration is drafted. The buyer will swear that he or she is not one and the same as the person in each execution. If the execution is over $50,000, a statutory declaration must be sworn by the buyer's lawyer that the buyer and the debtor are not the same person. The buyer's lawyer will want confirmation from the creditor before signing such a declaration.

### Confirm Arrangements for a Conveyancer

If the closing is taking place at the registry office, rather than electronically, your firm may be using an outside conveyancer to attend at the closing. In that case, re-confirm the conveyancer's availability and time preferences, and make arrangements for the pickup and delivery of the file.

### Prepare the Closing Memo or Closing Checklist

The closing memo is a document that sets out all steps to be taken, documents and other things to be exchanged on closing, and registration instructions. In the unlikely event that the closing is at the registry office, you will need to prepare a closing memo for the conveyancer or other person actually attending at the registry office. If the closing is electronic, you should prepare a closing memo for yourself in the form of a checklist.

The preparation of the closing memo or closing checklist is discussed below.

## The Day Before Closing/Morning of Closing

Make sure you know how the closing cheques are to be payable, requisition or prepare the cheques, and have them signed and certified, as necessary. If the closing is electronic, your firm may instead make an arrangement to deposit the balance due on closing directly into the trust account of the seller's lawyer.

If the closing is taking place at the registry office, arrange the specific time for the closing, and exchange the names of the persons attending for the buyer and seller.

# Buyer's Closing Memo or Closing Checklist

The contents of the closing memo or closing checklist will depend on whether the closing is taking place at the registry office or is electronic because the steps in each type of closing are different. In both cases, refer to the requisition letter. If it was drafted properly, it will list all items required on closing.

## Registry Closing

The closing memo for a registry office closing has four main parts:

1. preliminary steps to take;
2. documents and items to get;
3. documents and items to give; and
4. registration instructions.

### Preliminary Steps

These steps will be the same in every registry office closing.

#### UPDATE SEARCH OF TITLE

The closing memo should instruct the conveyancer to subsearch from the last instrument shown in the search.

If a particular instrument was to be registered prior to closing, specify it in the closing memo, with instructions to ensure that it has been registered. Examples include a discharge of mortgage, a mortgage, a mortgage amending agreement, or a release.

Attach the search of title to the closing memo so that it is available, if necessary, to cross-check a recent registration. The search notes also provide the conveyancer with the last instrument number registered in the abstract at the time of the search. This indicates to the conveyancer where to start the subsearch.

#### UPDATE EXECUTION SEARCH

Set out the details of any executions you are aware of and for which satisfactory arrangements, such as delivery of an affidavit, have been made. If an execution was to be discharged by closing, give particulars in the memo so that the conveyancer can confirm that the execution has, in fact, been discharged.

### Documents and Items to Get

Under this heading, list all documents and other items to be obtained from the seller on closing. This list will be based on the requisition letter. The memo should provide sufficient explanation and copies of draft documents to be obtained.

## TRANSFER/DEED OF LAND

The transfer provided on closing must be in the same form as the draft transfer previously submitted by the seller and approved by the buyer's lawyer. The memo should instruct the conveyancer to compare the documents, and the draft should be attached.

## MORTGAGES TO BE ASSUMED

If a mortgage is being assumed, the conveyancer must obtain

- a mortgage statement for assumption purposes showing a balance outstanding in the same amount as that shown on the statement of adjustments (which should be attached)—the memo should specify what the outstanding principal and interest should be;
- a copy of the mortgage, if not already provided by the title searcher; and
- particulars of the mortgage number and address for payment.

## MORTGAGES TO BE DISCHARGED

If a mortgage is to be discharged on or before closing, instruct the conveyancer to make certain either that the discharge has already been registered or that a discharge will be registered before registration of the transfer. The memo must provide full registration particulars of the mortgage to be discharged so that the conveyancer can check the validity of the discharge.

## UNDERTAKINGS TO DISCHARGE MORTGAGES

If, by the terms of the agreement of purchase and sale, or otherwise, the buyer has agreed to accept an undertaking to discharge a mortgage, the memo must instruct the conveyancer to obtain

- a mortgage statement for discharge purposes;
- the seller's signed direction, and a redirection that the appropriate amount of funds is to be made payable to the mortgagee; and
- the seller's lawyer's personal undertaking to discharge the mortgage under the terms set out in the agreement of purchase and sale—the memo should set out the precise wording that is acceptable.

## EXECUTED COPIES OF DOCUMENTS FORWARDED TO THE SELLER FOR SIGNATURE

The memo should advise the conveyancer to obtain executed copies of the documents previously prepared by your law firm and forwarded (usually with the requisition letter) to the seller for execution. These documents include undertakings, warranties, and declarations of possession. Copies of the draft documents should be attached so that the conveyancer can verify that the executed documents are in the proper form. These documents are discussed in detail in Chapter 21.

### DOCUMENTS REQUIRED TO ANSWER REQUISITIONS

The closing memo should specify any documents that are required to answer requisitions. These documents may be ascertained by reading the requisition letter, the answers to requisitions, and any follow-up correspondence. If, as an answer to a requisition, the seller agreed to provide something, it should be listed so that the conveyancer will obtain it from the seller on closing.

### KEYS

Unless alternative arrangements were made for the delivery of keys to the buyer, at least one key must be obtained on closing.

### DIRECTION REGARDING FUNDS

Before closing, the seller's lawyer will have advised the buyer's lawyer of the manner in which closing funds are to be paid and the closing cheques will have been prepared accordingly. The conveyancer should be told to obtain a direction regarding funds in accordance with the cheques provided.

This part of the memo should conclude by instructing the conveyancer to conduct a careful subsearch of the property and to insert the land transfer tax affidavit in the transfer (three copies should be attached).

## Documents and Items to Give

Under this heading, list all the documents and other items to be given to the seller on closing.

### MORTGAGE BACK

If this is applicable, the buyer's lawyer provides the vendor-take-back mortgage.

### CERTIFIED CHEQUES

A certified cheque or cheques made payable as instructed by the seller should be attached to the memo and particulars of the cheques provided. The conveyancer should be reminded (if instructions have not already been provided) to ensure that the appropriate direction regarding funds is provided by the seller.

### DIRECTION REGARDING TITLE

See Chapter 21, Document Preparation, for a discussion of this document.

### UNDERTAKING TO READJUST

See Chapter 21, Document Preparation, for a discussion of this document.

### ADDITIONAL ITEMS

The memo should also specify the additional items delivered with the memo, such as the file and cheques for registration, land transfer tax, and other fees.

### *Registration Instructions*

You must specify what documents the conveyancer should register and the required order of registration. If the seller is to register a discharge, it should be registered before your conveyancer registers anything. If the seller is registering a vendor-take-back mortgage, make sure it is registered in the correct sequence with your conveyancer's documents. (If it is a second mortgage, it must be registered after the first mortgage.)

## Electronic Closing Checklist

If the transaction is closing electronically, as is most likely the case, the parties do not meet at the registry office to exchange documents and funds, and register. Instead, the parties exchange the documents to be registered on title, such as transfers and charges, electronically. The closing funds and documents that are not registered on title are delivered by courier. In some cases it may be possible to wire or transfer funds between branches of financial institutions. You will then update the search and register the documents electronically. The buyer's checklist on an electronic closing reflects these steps.

### *Documents to Get*

With the exception of the transfer, you will receive most of the same documents as you would in a registry office closing. Instead of receiving them on closing, however, you will receive them by courier in advance of the closing. Your checklist should list all of the documents you will receive and will contain the same information as a registry office closing memo.

### *Documents to Give*

You will give the same documents as you would in a registry office closing. Instead of delivering them on closing, however, you will deliver them by courier in advance of the closing. Your checklist should list all of the documents you will give and will contain the same information as a registry office closing memo.

### *Subsearch/Executions*

It is necessary to conduct a subsearch before registering the transfer, to make sure that title has not changed since the title search was done, except for required registrations such as a discharge of mortgage, a mortgage, a mortgage amending agreement, or a release. If a particular instrument was to be registered, specify it in the checklist. Teraview will automatically search executions against the seller, unless the seller is an estate. If the seller is an estate, you will have to search executions against the deceased. If the buyer has arranged a mortgage and you are also acting for a mortgagee, you will have to search executions against the buyer. If title insurance is being obtained for the transaction, however, it may not be necessary to re-search executions against the buyer. That's because the title insurance policy will protect the lender against any new executions as long as the original execution search was completed within a short period of time before the closing, usually one to two weeks.

### *Day of Closing*

Courier all non-registerable documents and certified cheques to the seller's lawyer.

# Closing the Transaction

A registry office closing will almost certainly be handled by an outside conveyancer, so we discuss the procedure on an electronic closing only.

If the closing memo or closing checklist has been properly prepared, the closing should go smoothly.

In an electronic transaction both the seller's lawyer and the buyer's lawyer enter into a document registration agreement (DRA) prior to the closing date. The DRA sets out the escrow closing procedure to be followed in closing the transaction.

**off-title documents**
documents that are required for closing but are not registered on title

The seller's lawyer sends **off-title documents** (documents that are not registered) and a key by courier to the buyer's lawyer. The buyer's lawyer sends off-title documents and closing funds by courier to the seller's lawyer. The seller's lawyer checks the buyer's documents, and when satisfied that they are acceptable and that the closing proceeds have been received, he or she accesses Teraview, releases the transfer for registration, and advises the buyer's lawyer that this has been done. Then the registering party (usually the buyer's lawyer) logs onto Teraview and conducts a subsearch to verify that title to the property has not changed since the title search was done (or that any required documents have been registered). The registering party then searches executions (which will be done automatically against the seller) and registers the transfer and any other registerable documents, such as mortgages, released for registration.

When a law firm obtains the Teraview licence and user access, arrangements are made regarding payment of land transfer tax and registration fees. Usually they are debited from the firm's general account. When a document is registered electronically, the registration fees and land transfer tax, if applicable, will be debited at the end of the day.

## KEY TERMS

binder letter, 349

disbursements, 348

high ratio mortgage, 348

off-title documents, 354

## REVIEW QUESTIONS

1. Tom Cruiser is buying a single-family residence in Oakville, Ontario, for $805,000. According to the land transfer tax affidavit, the value of the land, building, fixtures, and goodwill subject to land transfer tax is $800,000 and the value of chattels included in the transaction is $5,000. Calculate the land transfer tax and the harmonized sales tax (HST) payable on the transaction.

2. Assume that Tom Cruiser (from question 1) has never owned a home before, anywhere in the world. What is the amount of the provincial land transfer tax rebate he is entitled to?

3. Saraya Jones recently purchased a home in downtown Toronto. What taxes will Saraya be required to pay on closing?

4. Guillermo recently bought a home from Sanjaya and arranged a mortgage to finance the purchase. Sanjaya agreed to discharge the mortgage currently registered on title. The closing is taking place next week. Who will pay the registration fees on closing?

5. What is the purpose of a closing memo or closing checklist for a registry office closing?

6. What searches must be updated during a registry office closing?

7. Your firm's client is the buyer in a real estate transaction and the firm's conveyancer is attending the closing. The buyer has arranged a first and second mortgage to finance the purchase. What documents must the conveyancer register, and in what order must he or she register them?

8. How are documents exchanged between the parties when the closing takes place electronically?

9. How is land transfer tax paid in an electronic closing?

# Buyer's Post-Closing Procedure

# 23

## LEARNING OUTCOMES

After reading this chapter, you will understand:

- How to deal with mortgages and other financial matters after closing

- The procedure for dealing with other outstanding matters after closing

- What a reporting letter is and why it is important in a real estate transaction

- What matters should be addressed in a reporting letter

- Who signs the reporting letter in a real estate transaction

- When a real estate file may be closed

## Introduction

Once the transaction has closed, you will need to call the buyer to let him or her know the deal has closed and to make arrangements for the buyer to pick up the key. You will then need to attend to the post-closing matters that remain outstanding.

## Mortgages and Other Financial Matters

It may be a while before you send the final reporting letter to the client, and tax installments or mortgage payments may fall due in the meantime. Therefore, immediately after the closing, you should send a letter to the buyer advising of any payments that must be made in the near future. Give the buyer enough information to make the payment, such as the mortgage number, the address of the mortgagee, and the amount of the monthly payment.

If there are any mortgages, whether newly arranged or assumed by the buyer, obtain an amortization schedule for the client. As discussed in Chapter 6, Charges/Mortgages and illustrated in Figure 6.4, an amortization schedule sets out the breakdown of each mortgage payment between principal and interest and the remaining principal balance after each payment. Most law firms have computer programs that will allow you to print an amortization schedule.

## Undertakings

If your law firm accepted any undertakings on closing, diarize each undertaking for the appropriate period of time. When the time is up, forward reminder letters until all outstanding undertakings have been fulfilled.

## Interest on Deposit

Some agreements of purchase and sale provide that the deposit be paid into an interest-bearing account, with interest to be paid to the buyer on closing. If that is the case, send a letter to the listing broker requesting a cheque payable either to the buyer directly or to your law firm. Diarize the letter for a reasonable period of time and follow up with the broker if necessary.

## Post-Closing Letters

Write a letter to the tax department, advising of the change in ownership. This is done to make sure that future notices are addressed to the buyer and not to the seller. Figure 23.1, at the end of this chapter, is an example of a letter to the tax department.

# Reporting Letter

At the end of the transaction, the buyer's law firm writes a reporting letter to the client. The reporting letter on a purchase can be quite long and complex if there is no title insurance. It summarizes the main provisions of the agreement of purchase and sale, describes the procedures on closing, and explains the items in the statement of adjustments. The letter may also contain a statement setting out the manner in which the closing funds were applied, but more often, that information will be provided in an enclosed trust ledger statement. The letter goes on to **certify title** and explains any limitations to the certification. The reporting letter concludes by listing the documents that are enclosed with the letter.

**certify title**
describe the state of the owner's title, including any limitations

If the client has purchased a title insurance policy, the reporting letter is much shorter. Certification of title is not required, and the letter will instead provide particulars about the insurance policy. In addition, it will set out the details of any mortgages arranged or assumed, and an explanation of the statement of adjustments. It may also contain a statement setting out the manner in which the closing funds were applied, but more often that information will be provided in an enclosed trust ledger statement. Again, the reporting letter concludes by listing the documents that are enclosed with the letter.

Preparation of a reporting letter when there is no title insurance can be time-consuming, and many lawyers and law clerks are slow to forward one. It is best to deal with the reporting letter as soon as possible because, subject to following up on any undertakings, the file is then completed and may be billed. Also, clients appreciate receiving the reporting letter sooner rather than later.

# Review of a Reporting Letter in a Transaction Without Title Insurance

Figure 23.2 is an example of a very comprehensive reporting letter for a purchase, typical of a letter that would be used if title insurance was not purchased. The letter also contains some clauses that may be used in a reporting letter if title insurance was purchased, and they are noted as such. The precedent includes alternative paragraphs for different situations, and is likely more comprehensive than necessary in most cases. When using the precedent, you must choose only the paragraphs appropriate to your transaction and amend them as required. Do not simply follow the precedent blindly.

The following is a discussion of the clauses contained in Figure 23.2.

## Opening Paragraph

The opening paragraph simply confirms that the transaction has been completed.

## Agreement of Purchase and Sale

This paragraph specifies the key terms of the agreement of purchase and sale, including the date of the agreement; the seller's name; the municipal address of the property; and the main financial terms of the contract, such as the purchase price, the amount of the deposit, and the amount of any mortgages to be assumed or given back to the seller.

## Closing

The first paragraph confirms the closing date. If the closing was postponed from the original closing date, the next paragraph specifies the original date and the rescheduled one.

In the unlikely event that the transaction was not completed electronically, the next two paragraphs provide particulars of the date of closing and the registration number(s) of registered documents.

If the closing was completed electronically, as is the case in the vast majority of transactions, the remaining paragraphs provide particulars of the electronic closing, including how much money was paid, exactly how the buyers took title, and full registration particulars.

## Land Transfer Tax

This paragraph sets out the amount of land transfer tax (provincial and municipal, if applicable), harmonized sales tax, and registration fees that were paid on closing.

## New First Mortgage Arranged

Use the paragraphs under this heading if a new first mortgage has been arranged. These paragraphs explain the repayment terms of the mortgage, including the principal amount, interest rate, term, and monthly payments. You should also enclose and explain the amortization schedule. Explain any prepayment privileges or other special terms, such as municipal tax payments to be included with the payments of principal and interest.

The letter then provides sufficient information to enable the buyer to make the monthly payments—the mortgage number, address of the mortgagee, and date of payments, including the date of the first payment.

Following that explanation, the letter reports the registration particulars of the mortgage and confirms enclosure of a copy of the mortgage and the standard charge terms. This group of mortgage paragraphs should conclude with confirmation of the amount of money received from the mortgagee and applied toward the balance due on closing.

Note: These paragraphs can also be used in a transaction in which title insurance was purchased.

## New Second Mortgage Arranged

If a new second mortgage has been arranged with a third party, the reporting letter should cover the same matters as for a new first mortgage.

Note: These paragraphs can also be used in a transaction in which title insurance was purchased.

## Statement of Adjustments

This paragraph refers to the statement of adjustments enclosed. The entries in the statement of adjustments are explained in the paragraphs that follow.

Note: This paragraph (and those that follow under this heading) can also be used in a transaction in which title insurance was purchased.

### Deposit

This paragraph confirms the amount of the deposit and that the buyer was given a credit in that amount in the statement of adjustments.

### First Mortgage Assumed

Use the paragraphs under this heading if the buyer has assumed an existing first mortgage. These paragraphs explain the entry in the statement of adjustments, and the provisions and payment particulars of the mortgage in the same detail as for a new mortgage.

### Second Mortgage Back to Seller

Use the paragraphs under this heading if the seller is taking back a second mortgage. In that case, the buyer will be given a credit in the statement of adjustments. The paragraphs explain this adjustment and the provisions and payment particulars of the mortgage in the same detail as for a new mortgage.

### Realty Taxes

These paragraphs explain the adjustment for realty taxes in the statement of adjustments and advise the client that the tax department has been notified of the change in ownership.

### Fuel Oil

Insert this paragraph if the house is heated by oil. It explains the adjustment for fuel oil in the statement of adjustments and reminds the buyer to check the tank to make sure that the seller fulfilled the undertaking to leave a full tank.

### Water Charges

Insert this paragraph if there was an adjustment for water charges.

### Utilities

This paragraph deals with metered utilities. The paragraph confirms that the meters were read before closing, that final bills will be sent to the seller, and that future bills will be sent to the buyer.

### Balance Due on Closing

This paragraph confirms the amount of the balance due on closing.

## Statement of Funds and Disbursements

This statement outlines the receipt and disbursements of closing funds. The statement, also called a trust statement, specifies the source of all funds paid to your firm for the transaction—usually from the buyer and one or more mortgagees. It also specifies to whom the funds were paid on and after the closing. This statement specifies

- the payees and amounts of all cheques delivered to the seller's lawyer on closing—cheques may have been payable to a mortgagee, the municipality, or a utility, as well as to the seller's law firm;
- the amount paid to the Ministry of Finance for land transfer tax, harmonized sales tax, and registration fees;
- the amount paid to your law firm for legal fees and disbursements; and
- the amount of any balance owing to the client or to your law firm.

Notice that the statement of funds and disbursements is set up in columns. The amount of all funds received is placed in the right-hand numerical column and the amount of all funds disbursed is placed in the left-hand numerical column. These two columns must balance.

It is more common to provide a separate trust ledger statement than to include a statement of funds and disbursements in the reporting letter. That approach is used in the reporting letter for our specific transaction later in this chapter.

## Insurance

In your preliminary letter to the buyers, you advised them to arrange insurance coverage for the property. Before closing, you should have obtained particulars of the insurance policy. This paragraph confirms the importance of maintaining adequate insurance coverage.

Note: This paragraph can be used in a transaction in which title insurance was purchased.

## Survey

There are several paragraphs dealing with the survey to choose from, depending on the circumstances.

The first paragraph is used when the client instructed your firm to have a new survey prepared. The second paragraph is used when the seller provided you with an existing up-to-date survey. Both of these paragraphs outline the particulars of the survey. The precedent paragraphs state that the buildings are wholly within the lot lines, with no encroachments. If that is not the case, your law firm should have advised the client before the closing, and this paragraph will confirm these earlier discussions and the instructions given by the client at that time. In addition, the title certification will be qualified to reflect this situation and the lawyer handling the file will most likely want to be involved in the drafting of this part of the reporting letter.

The third paragraph is used in the situation where the survey provided by the seller pre-dates additions or renovations to the buildings and, therefore, the survey is not helpful in determining whether the existing buildings comply with current bylaws. It will be necessary to limit the certification of the title paragraph accordingly. In this situation, the lawyer handling the file should have discussed this matter with the client before closing and should have explained the implications of closing the transaction without an up-to-date survey. The client's instructions to proceed without an up-to-date survey should have been confirmed in writing. The reporting letter should *not* be the first time the client is advised of this situation.

The fourth paragraph is used in cases where no survey was available, and the client instructed your law firm to proceed with the closing without obtaining a survey. The certification of title paragraph will have to be limited accordingly. Again, the client should have had this situation explained, with any instructions to proceed without an up-to-date survey confirmed in writing at that time. The paragraph should confirm these previous instructions.

## Municipal Bylaws

This part of the letter describes the results of the building department inquiries. There are two choices. The first paragraph is used when the building department advised your client that the municipal bylaws were complied with.

The second paragraph is used where the survey shows that the location of the buildings does *not* comply with existing bylaws, *but* the property is exempt from the application of the bylaws because the buildings were erected before the passage of the current bylaws and complied with the previous bylaws. (See Chapter 9, Government Controls over the Use and Subdivision of Land, for a discussion of the requirements for a legal non-conforming use.)

## Restrictions

This paragraph is included if there are any restrictive covenants on title. Under the terms of the standard form agreement of purchase and sale, the buyer must accept title subject to any restrictive covenants on title so long as they have been complied with. This paragraph therefore specifies the restrictions, states that the client was required to accept title subject to them, and refers to the evidence that was obtained to ensure that the restrictions have been complied with.

Note: This paragraph can be used in a transaction in which title insurance was purchased, but will not address evidence of compliance with the restrictions.

## Subdivision Agreements

This paragraph is inserted if there are any outstanding subdivision agreements on title. The standard form agreement of purchase and sale requires that the buyer accept title subject to subdivision agreements, provided that the agreements have been complied with or adequate security has been posted.

The paragraph identifies the agreements that are outstanding and states that the terms of the agreement of purchase and sale require the buyer to accept title subject to them. The paragraph then confirms that the agreements have been complied with or adequate security has been posted.

## Easements

If the title was subject to an easement, insert a paragraph setting out the details of the easement. There are two paragraphs to choose from, depending on whether the easement is one the client is required to accept under the agreement of purchase and sale, either as part of the standard terms or by a special paragraph.

If the buyer is required to accept title subject to the easement, use the first paragraph in the precedent. This paragraph sets out the details of the easement and states that the client is required to accept title subject to it under the terms of the agreement of purchase and sale. The precedent deals with the right of the builder to enter for inspection and repairs. Other common easements are utility easements and easements for access to and from adjoining properties.

On occasion, there will be an easement registered on title that the buyer decides to accept even though the terms of the agreement of purchase and sale do not require such acceptance. In that case, use the second paragraph in the precedent. That paragraph sets out the nature of the easement and confirms the client's instructions to close notwithstanding the fact that he or she is not required to do so. The reporting letter should *not* be the first time the client hears about this matter. The lawyer handling the file should have discussed this matter with the client before the closing and should have obtained instructions confirming the client's wishes in writing.

If there was an easement registered on title that was discharged before closing, there is no need to make reference to it in the reporting letter.

Note: These paragraphs can be used in a transaction in which title insurance was purchased.

## Family Law Act

You may use this standard paragraph no matter what *Family Law Act* statement was included in the transfer, provided that the *Family Law Act* was complied with. If it was not, the deal should not have closed.

## Warranties and Bill of Sale

A document containing warranties and a bill of sale should have been obtained on closing, and this paragraph should be inserted in the reporting letter.

## Title

This is the section in which your law firm gives a title opinion (certifies title) subject to any limitations referred to in the body of the letter. This section is not used if there is title insurance because the lawyer will not be giving a title opinion.

The first paragraph summarizes the key searches—title, taxes, and executions. If the tax or execution searches disclosed a problem, it should have been resolved before closing, and the standard wording with respect to executions can still be used. With respect to taxes, the paragraph should set out what the arrears were and the arrangements that were made for their payment.

The second paragraph contains the key words "we are of the opinion that *(name(s) of buyer(s)) (has/have)* a good and marketable title in fee simple to the said lands [*where applicable*—as joint tenants and not as tenants in common] and that the title was, at the date of closing, free from encumbrance, save for … ." The paragraph must list any exceptions, such as

- mortgages, whether new, assumed, or given back to the seller;
- subdivision agreements;
- restrictions;
- easements; and
- other title problems, if any exist.

Any exceptions should have been fully discussed earlier in the letter under the appropriate headings.

If the opinion is limited because there was no up-to-date survey or no survey at all, after the words "we are of the opinion that," the following words should be inserted: "subject to any discrepancy that may be shown by an up-to-date survey of the property."

## Concluding Paragraph

The concluding paragraph lists the documents enclosed, which should include

- the statement of adjustments;
- the duplicate registered transfer or a copy of the electronic transfer;
- a copy of any mortgage and standard charge terms;
- the survey;
- the title insurance policy (if applicable); and
- any other documents received on closing.

Note: This paragraph can be used in a transaction in which title insurance was purchased.

## Signature

The reporting letter must be prepared for signature by the lawyer handling the file and must be signed by the lawyer. Law clerks may not sign the reporting letter.

# Review of a Reporting Letter Generated by Conveyancer in a Transaction with Title Insurance

Title insurance is purchased in the vast majority of residential purchases. In addition, most real estate firms use computer software, such as Conveyancer, throughout the transaction, including in the preparation of the reporting letter. The software generates a reporting letter based on the information that has been entered into the file as the transaction progressed, and makes the process of completing the reporting letter simple.

Figure 23.3 is the reporting letter for our specific transaction, as created in Conveyancer. As you can see, the letter is much shorter and does not deal with many of the issues that are explained in the longer letter. In particular, many of the title issues, such as municipal bylaws and subdivision agreements, are not addressed because title insurance was obtained and there is therefore no need to conduct those searches. In addition, there is no certification of title clause, since the title is protected by the title insurance policy, which is enclosed with the letter.

## Opening Paragraph

The opening paragraph simply confirms that the transaction has been completed.

## Title

The first paragraph of this section confirms that title is protected by the title insurance policy, and states the name of the insurance company and the policy number. It confirms that the policy is attached and advises the buyer to follow the procedures set out in the policy if a claim should arise.

The following paragraphs then go on to confirm how title was taken, with complete names, dates of birth, and capacity, and confirm the registration date and number of the transfer.

## Mortgage Arranged

This section explains the terms of the new mortgage that was arranged. It sets out the interest rate, and the amount and frequency of each payment, and the first payment date. If there is more than one mortgage, either arranged or assumed, there will be a separate section for each mortgage.

## Insurance

This paragraph explains the importance of fire and liability insurance and the necessity of maintaining fire insurance for at least the value of the mortgage(s).

## Statement of Adjustments

This paragraph refers to the statement of adjustments enclosed. Sometimes the letter explains each entry on the statement of adjustments in detail, as is done in the Figure 23.2 reporting letter, and other times the letter just refers to the statement of adjustments that is enclosed.

## Enclosures

This paragraph lists all of the documents that are enclosed with the report.
   It is important to enclose the following:

1. Transfer—to show the client's ownership.
2. Statement of adjustments—to show the client the balance due on closing.
3. Mortgage(s)—to show the terms of any new mortgage. If a mortgage was assumed, information such as a copy of the original mortgage as well as an assumption statement should be enclosed.
4. Amortization schedule.
5. Title insurance policy—with all of the relevant schedules attached.
6. Statement of account—to show how much was paid to the law firm.
7. Trust ledger statement—to show a clear accounting of how all of the money was received by the firm and how it was disbursed.

## Signature

The reporting letter must be prepared for signature by the lawyer handling the file and must be signed by the lawyer. Law clerks may not sign the reporting letter.

# Statement of Account

Prepare a statement of account setting out the fees and disbursements your law firm is charging the client with respect to the purchase transaction. Follow the format used by your firm. Make sure that you retain funds for payment of the account before releasing any funds to the client. The format used for a statement of account varies from law firm to law firm. If your firm uses software, such as Conveyancer, the software creates the statement of account.

## Trust Ledger Statement

This statement contains the same information as a statement of funds and disbursements incorporated into the body of the reporting letter, as discussed earlier in this chapter. As stated, it is more common to provide a separate trust ledger statement than to include a statement of funds and disbursements in the reporting letter.

See Figure 23.4 for an example of a trust ledger statement.

## Closing the File

Do not close the file until all post-closing matters have been completed, including the fulfillment of any undertakings. At that time, follow the standard procedure of your law firm.

## KEY TERMS

certify title, 359

## REFERENCES

*Family Law Act*, RSO 1990, c F.3.

## REVIEW QUESTIONS

1. Why should you send a letter to the buyer right after closing, advising him or her of mortgage or tax payments?

2. What is an amortization schedule?

3. You work for a law firm and the firm received undertakings on closing. What steps must you take after closing?

4. In what circumstances might a real estate broker owe a buyer money following closing?

5. Why do you write to the tax department following closing?

6. What is the function of a reporting letter to the client?

7. When should you close the file?

## Figure 23.1    Letter to the Tax Department

*Date*

Tax Department
Town of Newmarket
*Address*

Dear Sir or Madam:

Re:               Grant purchase from Mercier
                  166 Valley Road, Newmarket
Closing Date:  December 15, 2015
Our File No.:  15-1925

---

Please be advised that we are the solicitors for Henry Albert Grant and Wilma Heather Grant who, effective December 15, 2015, purchased the property described above.

Kindly amend your records to show our clients:

GRANT, Henry Albert and Wilma Heather

as the new owners of the property.

We would therefore request that you forward a copy of the current tax bill and all future notices and bills to the new owner of the property at:

166 Valley Road, Newmarket, Ontario

Thank you for your cooperation in this matter.

Yours very truly,

Kurtz, Emmans, Blatt & Wolf
Per:

**Figure 23.2    Reporting Letter to the Buyer (generic)**

*Date*

*Buyer's name*
*Buyer's address*

Re:          *Name of transaction*
             *Address and municipality*

Dear (*buyer's name*):

We are pleased to confirm completion of this transaction and would like to make our report to you.

**Agreement of Purchase and Sale**

On (*date*) you entered into an agreement with (*seller's name*) for the purchase of the property municipally known as (*address of property*). The purchase price was $(*purchase price*) and a deposit of $(*deposit*) was paid at that time. [*Where applicable*—You also agreed to assume a first mortgage in the principal amount of $(*principal amount of first mortgage*)]. The balance of the purchase price, after adjustments, was to be paid by cash or certified cheque on closing.

**Closing**

This transaction closed as scheduled on (*date of closing*), and adjustments were made as of that date.

[*Use the following paragraph if the closing was postponed.*]

This transaction was originally scheduled to close on (*date*), but was postponed [*where applicable*—a number of times]. The transaction ultimately closed on (*date of closing*), and adjustments were made as of that date.

[*Use the following paragraphs if the transaction was not closed electronically.*]

At that time, we attended at the (*name and location of land registry office*) and handed over a (*series of*) cheque(s) in the amount of $(*balance due on closing*), being the balance due on closing as set out in the enclosed statement of adjustments. In return, we received a transfer of land endorsed as follows:

BUYER'S LAST NAME, *first name*                    *buyer's birthdate (yr-mo-date)*

BUYER'S LAST NAME, *first name*                    *buyer's birthdate (yr-mo-date)*

[*where applicable*—as joint tenants.]

This transfer of land was registered in (*name, location, and number of land registry office*) on (*closing date*) as instrument number (*number*).

[*Use the following paragraphs if the transaction was closed electronically.*]

**Figure 23.2 Continued**

Prior to closing, we delivered to the seller a (*series of*) cheque(*s*) in the amount of $(*balance due on closing*), being the balance due on closing as set out in the enclosed statement of adjustments. In return, the seller released the transfer for registration endorsed as follows:

BUYER'S LAST NAME, *first name*                    *buyer's birthdate (yr-mo-date)*

BUYER'S LAST NAME, *first name*                    *buyer's birthdate (yr-mo-date)*

[*where applicable*—as joint tenants.]

This transfer was registered electronically on (*closing date*) as instrument number (*number*).

**Land Transfer Tax**

Before closing, you completed (*an affidavit or a statement*) under the *Land Transfer Tax Act*. Based on that document, on closing, we paid provincial land transfer tax in the amount of $(*amount*) and harmonized sales tax in the amount of $(*amount*) to the Ministry of Finance [*where applicable*—and municipal land transfer tax in the amount of $(*amount*) to the Treasurer, City of Toronto] from the funds deposited to your credit in our trust account. We also paid registration fees of $(*amount*) from the funds deposited to your credit in our trust account.

**New First Mortgage** [*Use these paragraphs where a new first mortgage is arranged.*]

On your instructions, we prepared a first charge/mortgage in favour of (*name of mortgagee*). This charge/mortgage secures the principal sum of $(*amount*) with interest at (*rate*)% per annum and is repayable by equal monthly installments of $(*amount*) on account of principal and interest. The installments commence on the (*day*) day of (*month*), (*year*) up to and including the (*day*) day of (*month*), (*year*) when the balance, if any, of the principal sum is to be paid.

The monthly installments will be applied first to pay the interest calculated on the principal outstanding from time to time, and the balance of the monthly installments will be applied to reduce the principal.

[*Explain amortization schedule as follows:*] We are enclosing an amortization schedule for this mortgage. The schedule shows how much of each monthly payment is applied to principal and to interest and how much of the principal balance remains outstanding after each payment.

[*Where applicable, include details of any prepayment provisions. Refer to the mortgage for details.*]

[*Where applicable, include details of any tax payment provisions. Refer to the mortgage for details.*]

[*Provide mortgage payment information as follows:*] Your first monthly payment under this charge/mortgage falls due on (*date*) and, if not being taken from your account automatically, should be made payable to (*mortgagee's name*) at (*mortgagee's address*). Please note your mortgage reference number (*number*) on your payments and in any correspondence with the mortgagee.

**Figure 23.2   Continued**

[*Provide registration particulars as follows:*] This charge/mortgage was registered on title on (*date*) as instrument number (*number*). We enclose a copy of the charge/mortgage together with the standard charge terms.

[*Provide details of mortgage money received as follows:*] Before closing, we received a cheque from (*name of mortgagee*) in the amount of $(*amount*). This cheque was deposited into our trust account and applied to the balance due on closing.

**New Second Mortgage** [*Use this paragraph if a new second mortgage is arranged.*]

In accordance with the agreement of purchase and sale, we prepared a second charge/mortgage in favour of (*name of mortgagee*).

[*See New First Mortgage for other paragraphs.*]

**Statement of Adjustments**

Before closing, the seller's lawyer provided us with a statement of adjustments that identified the balance you were required to pay on closing. A copy of the statement of adjustments is enclosed, and the entries and calculations on the statement of adjustments are explained in the following paragraphs.

**Deposit**

When you signed the agreement of purchase and sale, you paid a deposit of $(*amount*). You were given a credit in that amount on the statement of adjustments.

**First Mortgage Assumed** [*Use these paragraphs where a first mortgage is assumed.*]

On closing, you assumed a charge/mortgage in favour of the (*mortgagee's name*), securing the principal sum of $(*original principal amount*). At the time of closing, the outstanding principal and interest under that mortgage totalled $(*amount*) as confirmed by the enclosed mortgage statement from the mortgagee dated (*date*). You were given a credit in this amount on the statement of adjustments.

[*Insert paragraph explaining monthly payments—see New First Mortgage.*]

[*Insert amortization schedule paragraph.*]

[*Insert prepayment privilege paragraph where applicable.*]

[*Insert tax payment paragraph where applicable.*]

[*Insert payment information paragraph.*]

We enclose a copy of the charge/mortgage together with the standard charge terms.

**Figure 23.2   Continued**

**Second Mortgage Back to Seller** [*Use these paragraphs if the seller takes back a second mortgage.*]

In accordance with the agreement of purchase and sale, you executed a second charge/mortgage in favour of the seller, securing the principal amount of $(*amount*). You were given a credit in this amount on the statement of adjustments.

[*Insert paragraph explaining monthly payments—see New First Mortgage.*]

[*Insert amortization schedule paragraph.*]

[*Insert prepayment privilege paragraph where applicable.*]

[*Insert tax payment paragraph where applicable.*]

[*Insert payment information paragraph.*]

[*Insert registration particulars paragraph.*]

**Realty Taxes** [*These paragraphs should explain the realty tax adjustment and must be drafted according to the transaction—for example, if the seller had paid taxes for the entire year:*]

The realty taxes for (*year*) in the amount of $(*total annual taxes*) have been paid in full by the seller. Because the seller's share of the realty taxes was only $(*seller's share of taxes*), the seller was allowed a credit for this item on the statement of adjustments in the amount of $(*amount*).

We have advised the tax department of your purchase of the property and have requested that all future tax bills be sent to you.

**Fuel Oil** [*Use this paragraph if the property is heated by oil.*]

The seller agreed to leave a full tank of fuel oil on closing and was given a credit for the cost of the fuel in the amount of $(*amount*) on the statement of adjustments. Please check to make sure that the fuel oil tank is, in fact, full, and advise us immediately if that is not the case.

**Water Charges** [*If there was an adjustment for water charges, use this paragraph to explain the water charge adjustment—for example, if the seller had paid more than his or her share:*]

The seller paid $(*amount*) for water charges for the period from _____ to _____. Because the seller's share of the water charges was only $(*seller's share of water charges*), the seller was allowed a credit for this item on the statement of adjustments in the amount of $(*amount*).

**Utilities**

We arranged for the utility meters to be read before closing and for final bills to be sent directly to the seller. We have also notified the utilities that you are now the owner(s) of the property and that all future utility bills are to be sent to you.

**Figure 23.2   Continued**

**Balance Due on Closing**

The balance due on closing as calculated in the statement of adjustments was $(*amount*).

**Statement of Funds and Disbursements**

The funds to complete this transaction were received and disbursed by us as follows:
[*Set out the source of all funds and how the funds were paid out. For example:*]

| | | |
|---|---|---|
| Received from (*mortgagee*) | | $150,000.00 |
| Received from (*client's name*) | | 131,000.00 |
| Paid to (*seller's mortgagee*) in accordance with seller's direction regarding funds (enclosed) re: seller's first mortgage | $177,818.75 | |
| Paid to (*seller's law firm*), in trust in accordance with seller's direction regarding funds (enclosed) | 98,390.02 | |
| Paid to the Ministry of Finance for land transfer tax, harmonized sales tax, and registration of transfer and charge | 2,830.00 | |
| Paid to (*buyer's law firm*) for fees and disbursements | 1,225.50 | |
| Balance owing to you | 735.73 | |
| | $281,000.00 | $281,000.00 |

**Insurance** [*Set out the particulars of the client's insurance coverage. For example:*]

We wish to confirm that you made arrangements for insurance with (*name of insurance company*) as policy number (*number*). This policy is for $(*amount*) and expires on (*date*). (*Name of mortgagee*) is shown as first mortgagee.

**Survey** [*Choose one of the following paragraphs.*]

[*When a new survey has been prepared:*]

In accordance with your instructions, we obtained a new survey of the property from [*name of surveyor*], Ontario Land Surveyors. The survey, dated (*date*), indicates that the buildings are located wholly within the lot lines and that there are no other buildings encroaching on or over the property.

[*When an up-to-date survey was provided by seller:*]

The seller provided us with a survey of the land and building thereon prepared by (*name of surveyor*), Ontario Land Surveyors, dated (*date*). This survey indicates that the buildings are located wholly within the lot lines and that there are no other buildings encroaching on or over the property. The seller has confirmed by way of statutory declaration that there have been no changes to land and buildings since the date of the survey.

**Figure 23.2   Continued**

[*When the survey does not show present location of buildings on the lands:*]

The seller provided us with a survey prepared by (*name of surveyor*) dated (*date*). As we previously advised you, the survey shows the dimensions of the land but does not show the present location of the buildings on the land. You instructed us to proceed with the transaction notwithstanding this fact. Our opinion on title is therefore subject to any discrepancy that may be disclosed by an up-to-date survey showing the present location of the buildings on the land. [*Under the heading "Title," below, insert the following words: "subject to any discrepancy that may be shown by an up-to-date survey of the property" after the words "Based on the above searches."*]

[*When no survey is available:*]

We advised you that there was no survey of the property, and you instructed us to proceed with the transaction notwithstanding this fact. Our opinion on title is therefore subject to any discrepancy that may be disclosed by an up-to-date survey showing the location of the buildings on the land. [*Under the heading "Title," below, insert the following words: "subject to any discrepancy that may be shown by an up-to-date survey of the property" after the words "Based on the above searches."*]

**Municipal Bylaws** [*Choose one of the following paragraphs, unless a minor variance was or is necessary.*]

[*When property complies with bylaws:*]

We were advised by the building department of (*name of municipality*) that, based on the above survey, the location of the buildings on the property complied with all municipal bylaws at the time of closing.

[*When property is a legal non-conforming use:*]

Based on the above survey, we have been advised by the building department of (*name of municipality*) that the buildings erected on the property do not comply with the zoning bylaw in effect at this time. However, because the buildings were erected before the enactment of the zoning bylaw presently in force, they are exempt from its provisions.

**Restrictions** [*Set out the particulars of any restrictive covenants—for example, if there were restrictions against altering the grading or drainage.*]

[*If no title insurance has been purchased:*]

As we discussed before closing, the property is subject to a restriction that you must comply with for a period of seven years from (*day, month, year*), against the alteration of grades, catch basins, or obstruction of drainage. By the provisions of the agreement of purchase and sale, you were required to accept title subject to restrictions, provided that they were complied with. In this regard, on closing, we obtained the statutory declaration of the seller that, to the best of the seller's knowledge, the restrictions have been complied with.

**Figure 23.2  Continued**

[*If title insurance has been purchased:*]

As we discussed before closing, the property is subject to a restriction that you must comply with for a period of seven years from (*day, month, year*), against the alteration of grades, catch basins, or obstruction of drainage.

**Subdivision Agreements** [*Set out the particulars of any subdivision agreements. For example:*]

At the time of closing, a subdivision agreement between (*name of developer*) and (*name of municipality*) was registered on title as instrument number (*number*). By the provisions of the agreement of purchase and sale, you were required to accept title subject to subdivision agreements provided they have been complied with. We were advised by (*name of municipality*) that the terms and conditions of this subdivision agreement have been complied with to date and that sufficient securities have been deposited with the municipality to ensure the completion of services and of all other obligations of the owner.

**Easements** [*If there are any easements, choose one of the following paragraphs.*]

[*If the easement is in accordance with the agreement of purchase and sale, set out the particulars—for example, if there is an easement in favour of the builder to enter for repairs:*]

By the terms of the agreement of purchase and sale, you agreed to accept the title subject to the right of the builder to enter upon the land in order to inspect the premises, to carry out the necessary repairs to the building upon the land, and to complete its obligations under the subdivision agreement, this right of re-entry to be for a period of five years from the date of closing.

[*If the easement is not provided for in the agreement of purchase and sale, set out the particulars—for example, if there is a right of way over part of the property:*]

Even though you were not required to do so under the agreement of purchase and sale, you agreed to accept title to the property subject to a right of way over a strip of land 1.23 metres wide by 16.20 metres long in favour of the owners of the property immediately to the east of your property, to provide access to maintain the building on that adjoining property and for the purpose of free and unobstructed access to the rear yard of that adjoining property. This easement is shown on the survey as part 15. In addition, you have a right in the nature of an easement over the property immediately to the west of your property for the same purposes. This easement is shown on the survey as part 14.

**Family Law Act**

The seller completed a statement pursuant to the provisions of the *Family Law Act* setting out facts that indicated that there was compliance with the Act.

**Warranties and Bill of Sale**

On closing, we obtained a warranty from the seller warranting that, during the time the seller has owned the property, the seller has not caused any building on the property to be insulated with

**Figure 23.2 Concluded**

insulation containing urea formaldehyde, and that to the best of the seller's knowledge, no building on the property contains or has ever contained insulation that contains urea formaldehyde. We also obtained warranties that no damage has occurred since your inspection, no work has been done that could result in a lien being registered, there are no work orders or deficiency orders, and the chattels and fixtures are in working order on completion. Also included in this document is a bill of sale for the chattels that were included in the agreement of purchase and sale.

**Title**
[*Use the following two paragraphs if title insurance has not been obtained.*]

We have made a full and proper search of the title to this property. We have obtained a certificate from the treasurer of (*name of municipality*) showing that there are no arrears of taxes on the above-mentioned property. We have searched in the office of (*name and location of land registry office*) and have satisfied ourselves that, at the time of closing, there were no executions outstanding affecting the title to the said lands.

Based on the above searches, we are of the opinion that (*name(s) of buyer(s)*) (*has/have*) a good and marketable title in fee simple to the said lands [*where applicable*—as joint tenants and not as tenants in common] and that the title was, at the date of closing, free from encumbrance, save for [*list any encumbrances:*]

    1.
    2.
    3.

Because this transaction is now completed, we enclose the following documents:

1. statement of adjustments;
2. duplicate transfer/deed of land number (*number*);
3. copy of charge/mortgage of land number (*number*), together with standard charge terms;
4. seller's undertaking;
5. warranties and bill of sale;
6. direction regarding funds [*where applicable*—and redirection of funds];
7. statutory declaration;
8. survey;
9. (*other*);
10. (*other*).

We also enclose our statement of account, which we trust will meet with your approval.

This completes our report to you. If you have any questions in connection with this transaction, please do not hesitate to contact us. We are pleased to have assisted you in this matter.

Yours very truly,

(*Buyer's lawyer*)

Encls.

**Figure 23.3   Reporting Letter to the Buyer (specific to our transaction)**

*Date*

Henry Albert Grant and Wilma Heather Grant
166 Valley Road
Newmarket, Ontario
L3H 3B3

Dear Mr. and Mrs. Grant:

Re:        Your purchase from Mercier
         166 Valley Road, Newmarket
         Closing Date: December 15, 2015
         Our File No.: 15-1925

We are pleased to now submit our reporting letter in relation to your purchase of the above property, which transaction was completed on December 15, 2015.

**TITLE**

In accordance with your instructions, your title to the property is protected under a title insurance policy issued by Title Insurance Company as policy number 1234567. Schedules identifying the property and the insured, and listing additional exceptions as well as affirmative assurances relating to matters not covered, excluded or excepted, are attached to the title insurance policy. Your copy of the policy, including schedules, is enclosed with this report. Should you ever be required to file a claim, it is important that you follow the procedures set out in the policy.

Title to the property was taken in the following manner:

| Full Name | Birthdate |
|---|---|
| GRANT, Henry Albert | March 27, 1952 |
| GRANT, Wilma Heather | March 18, 1955 |
| As joint tenants | |

We are enclosing herewith the duplicate registered transfer/deed, the original of which we registered on your behalf on December 15, 2015 as instrument number YR234567.

**Figure 23.3 Continued**

**FIRST MORTGAGE ARRANGED**

Mortgagee:          Data Bank of Canada

Address:           111 Richmond Street
Toronto, Ontario
M1B 1B1

Loan Number:     271925

Principal:         $280,000.00

Interest Rate:     3%

Payments:        $740.00 (monthly)

First Payment Date:  February 1, 2016

The standard charge terms filed as number 225577 are incorporated by reference into this mortgage.

**INSURANCE**

It is of the utmost importance to maintain adequate fire and liability coverage on the property and we wish to confirm that you arranged fire insurance effective from the date of closing. Although it is recommended that the amount of coverage be for replacement cost, it is necessary to maintain, at the very least, coverage in an amount not less than the aggregate secured by any mortgages on the property from time to time, and, in addition, the interests of such mortgagees must be noted on the policy.

**STATEMENT OF ADJUSTMENTS**

We are enclosing herewith a copy of the statement of adjustments, which contains details of the various adjustments to the purchase price. The statement is used so as to determine the cash balance that you were required to pay to the seller on closing. The figures on the right-hand side are credits to the seller (and, as such, are added onto the purchase price) while those on the left are credits to you.

You will see from the statement of adjustments that you were charged with the purchase price of $580,000.00 and you received credit with the deposit moneys that you had already paid. With respect to realty taxes, the statement shows the seller's proportionate share of the annual tax bill for the period from January 1, 2015 to the date of closing as well as the amount actually paid by the seller on this account. The difference between these two figures appears as an adjustment to the purchase price.

The balance due on closing was determined by adding to the sale price the credits to the seller as shown in the right-hand column of the statement of adjustments, and deducting therefrom the credits to the buyer as set out in the left-hand column.

**Figure 23.3   Concluded**

**ENCLOSURES**

We are enclosing the following documents:

> Transfer number LT234567.
> Statement of adjustments.
> Copy of first mortgage.
> Amortization schedule.
> Title insurance policy number 1234567.
> Our statement of account.
> Our trust ledger statement.

We trust that this transaction has been completed to your satisfaction and if you have any questions or comments, please do not hesitate to contact our office.

Yours very truly,


Kurtz, Emmans, Blatt & Wolf
Per:


Encls.

**Figure 23.4    Trust Ledger Statement**

Mr. Henry Albert Grant and Wilma Heather Grant

Re:                    Your purchase from Mercier
                        166 Valley Road, Newmarket
                        Our File No.: 15-1925

**TRUST LEDGER STATEMENT**

| | | |
|---|---|---|
| Received from 1st mortgagee—Data Bank of Canada | | $280,000.00 |
| Received from you | | 280,184.87 |
| Paid to vendor on closing | $550,242.19 | |
| Paid Ontario Land Transfer Tax | 8,075.00 | |
| Paid title insurance premium | 375.00 | |
| Paid legal fees and disbursements | 1,492.68 | |
| | $560,184.87 | $560,184.87 |

THIS IS OUR STATEMENT HEREIN
Kurtz, Emmans, Blatt & Wolf
Per:

E. & O. E.

# Acting for the Seller

# 24

## LEARNING OUTCOMES

After reading this chapter, you will understand:

- What information and documents a seller must provide his or her lawyer when selling property

- What a lawyer for the seller must do *before* closing

- What a lawyer for the seller must do *after* closing

- How to prepare a reporting letter to the seller, including a statement of funds and disbursements

- When a sale file can be closed

# Introduction

The previous chapters have covered the residential real estate transaction mostly from the perspective of the buyer. This chapter examines the transaction from the seller's point of view.

In a residential real estate sale, the seller's law firm will

- open and organize a file;
- review the agreement of purchase and sale;
- gather information about the property and the state of title;
- prepare the statement of adjustments;
- receive and respond to the buyer's requisition letter;
- prepare or review the necessary closing documents;
- prepare for the closing;
- ensure that the seller properly executes all documents;
- close the transaction;
- fulfill any undertakings given on closing; and
- provide the client with a reporting letter.

## Opening and Organizing the File

The first step is to open and organize a file for the sale transaction. Obtain or prepare a checklist and insert it in the file. Figure 24.1, at the end of the chapter, is an example of a sale checklist.

After reviewing the agreement of purchase and sale, diarize any outstanding condition dates, the requisition date, and the closing date. As the file progresses, diarize the dates on which you expect responses to any letters that you send out. See Chapter 15, Opening and Organizing a Real Estate File, for a discussion of this topic.

## Reviewing the Agreement of Purchase and Sale

Review the agreement of purchase and sale to determine what matters you will need to attend to and what documents you will have to prepare to close the deal. See Chapter 16, Reviewing the Agreement of Purchase and Sale, for a discussion of this topic.

## Gathering Information About the Property and the State of Title

Ask your client to provide you with the following:

- transfer;
- survey;

- reporting letter the seller received when the property was purchased;
- details of outstanding mortgages;
- any declarations of possession;
- receipted tax bills;
- information about how the property is heated;
- information about spousal status; and
- information about residency status.

# Preparing the Statement of Adjustments

See Chapter 21, Document Preparation, for a discussion of the statement of adjustments.

# Receiving and Responding to the Requisition Letter

See Chapter 19, Requisitions: An Overview, and Chapter 20, The Requisition Letter, for a discussion of requisitions.

# Preparing or Reviewing Closing Documents

See Chapter 21, Document Preparation, for a discussion of closing documents.

# Preparation for Closing

## One Week Before Closing

The following steps should be taken *at least* one week before the closing.

### Review the File

Review the file to find out what requisitions have to be answered and to confirm that the documentation necessary to do so is in the file or expected shortly.

### Check Mortgages to Be Discharged

If there are mortgages to be discharged, make sure that either you have the discharge or arrangements have been made for the mortgagee's lawyer to register a discharge on closing. (Usually, when the mortgagee sends a discharge statement, it includes a statement that the mortgagee will register the discharge upon receipt of the funds.) Check that you have received a mortgage statement for discharge purposes and that you have advised the buyer's lawyer to make the appropriate amount of funds payable to the mortgagee. Also check that you have prepared the direction regarding funds.

### Check Mortgages for Which an Undertaking to Discharge Will Be Given

If an undertaking to discharge a mortgage will be acceptable, check that you have received a mortgage statement for discharge purposes and that you have prepared a direction regarding the payment of the appropriate amount of funds to the mortgagee. Also check that you have prepared the lawyer's personal undertaking to obtain a discharge.

### Check Mortgages to Be Assumed

If the buyer is assuming a mortgage, you will have to provide a mortgage statement for assumption purposes and a copy of the mortgage. If any steps were required by the buyer in order to assume the mortgage—for example, obtaining the approval of the mortgagee or executing an assumption agreement—contact the buyer's lawyer to confirm that these steps have been taken.

### Contact the Client

Contact the client to make arrangements for attendance at your office to execute the transfer and other closing documents. Also, remind the client to cancel insurance on the premises but only *after* you have called to confirm that the deal has closed.

### Get the Keys

Unless alternative arrangements have been made for the transfer of keys to the buyer, the seller must provide at least one key for delivery on closing. The remaining keys are usually left in the house.

### Finalize How Funds Are to Be Payable

Determine how the closing funds are to be payable (for example, funds may have to be directed to discharge a mortgage or to pay tax arrears), then prepare the appropriate redirection regarding funds. Finally, tell the buyer's law firm to whom the cheques should be made payable.

### Check Non-Resident Seller Requirements

If the seller is a non-resident, you must make arrangements for payment of the capital gains and obtain the appropriate certificate.

### Prepare the Closing Memo

If the property is in the Registry system, and the closing is taking place in the registry office, prepare a closing memo that will be the mirror image of the buyer's closing memo as discussed in Chapter 22. If there are any documents to be registered, give clear instructions as to the order of registration. Make sure that a key and all relevant documents are attached.

If the closing is in the Land Titles system, prepare a checklist setting out the closing funds and all the documents you will require from the buyer before releasing the electronic transfer for registration.

## The Day Before Closing/Morning of Closing

If the closing is taking place in the registry office, arrange the specific time for closing and make sure that you give the conveyancer enough money to pay for any registrations.

If the closing is taking place electronically, courier a key and all non-registerable documents to the buyer's lawyer. This can be done on the closing date or before.

# Closing

See Chapter 22, Closing the Transaction, for a discussion of closing procedures on behalf of the seller.

If there is a private mortgage to be discharged, you must courier the discharge funds to the lawyer for the mortgagee, to be held in escrow until the transfer is registered. Upon notification of the registration of the transfer, the lawyer for the mortgagee must register a discharge.

# Seller's Post-Closing Procedure

There are a number of matters that the seller's law firm has to attend to after the closing of the transaction.

## Mortgages and Financial Undertakings

If the firm gave an undertaking to discharge any mortgages, forward the discharge funds to the mortgagee as soon as possible, preferably on the day of closing. Interest on the mortgage continues to accrue each day until the funds are actually received by the mortgagee. If the law firm delays in delivering the discharge funds to the mortgagee, your firm may have to pay the extra interest.

Retain enough money in the law firm's trust account to cover any undertakings provided on closing for payment of utility or tax arrears.

## Forward Funds to the Client

After covering the law firm's fees and disbursements, forward the balance of the closing funds to the client as soon as possible. Obtain your client's instructions—your client may want to pick up the cheque, have it delivered, or have it deposited directly into a bank account. Proceeds of sale are generally very large, and the client will not want to lose interest on the money. If you delay in forwarding the money to the client, your firm may have to pay the client for any interest lost.

## Real Estate Commission

The deposit will ordinarily have been paid to the seller's real estate broker, and, once the transaction has closed, it is used to pay the real estate commission on the transaction. If the deposit is not enough to cover the real estate commission, you will have to pay the balance of the commission from the closing proceeds. It is not usually necessary to calculate the amount of the commission because you will likely receive a letter from the broker setting out the amount owed.

If the deposit is greater than the amount of the commission on the transaction, forward a letter to the broker asking that the excess amount be sent immediately to your client. Diarize a date approximately two weeks later to call your client to determine whether the payment was received.

## Follow Up on Undertakings

Take steps to follow up on all undertakings given personally by the law firm. Diarize to ensure that a mortgagee provides or registers a discharge of mortgage, or that outstanding property taxes or utility arrears have been paid. A copy of the discharge of mortgage for our transaction is shown as Figure 24.2. Remind the client of any undertakings he or she must fulfill—for example, to pay the final water bill.

## Tax Department

Write to the municipal tax department, advising it to change its records to show the buyer as the new owner. Even though a similar letter will likely be sent by the buyer's law firm (see Figure 23.1), you want to ensure that the seller is no longer billed for taxes. Some firms send similar letters to the various utility companies, or advise their clients to make sure they have notified all utilities.

## Reporting Letter

Although a reporting letter to the seller is not as long and detailed as a reporting letter to the buyer, there is still a tendency to delay its preparation. Clients appreciate receiving one sooner rather than later.

The letter specifies key terms in the agreement of purchase and sale, summarizes the closing procedure, and explains the statement of adjustments. It concludes by explaining how funds were received and disbursed. Figure 24.3 is a sample reporting letter to the seller. It includes alternative paragraphs for use in different situations. When using the precedent, you must choose the paragraphs appropriate to the situation and amend them as required. Do not simply follow the precedent blindly.

### Preamble

The opening paragraph confirms completion of the transaction.

### Agreement of Purchase and Sale

This paragraph sets out the date of the agreement, the name of the buyer, the address of the property, the sale price, and the amount of the deposit.

### Closing

This paragraph confirms the closing of the transaction, sets out the amount of money received, and confirms that, in exchange, your firm handed over a transfer of land to the buyer. If the transaction was completed electronically, this paragraph will state that the transfer was released for registration.

## Mortgages

The reporting letter covers any mortgages assumed by the buyer and explains the adjustment in the statement of adjustments. Make sure you confirm in the letter that, although the buyers have assumed your client's mortgage, the client may be responsible for all payments under the mortgage until it is discharged, if the buyer fails to make any payments. (The client should have been advised of this obligation before closing.)

If the seller took a mortgage back, the paragraph sets out the principal amount of the mortgage and states that the buyer was credited with that amount on the statement of adjustments. Payment particulars are also set out, and an executed copy of the mortgage, the standard charge terms, and an amortization schedule are enclosed. Identify any special provisions in the mortgage, such as prepayment privileges.

## Realty Taxes

This paragraph explains the municipal realty tax adjustment on the statement of adjustments.

## Fuel Oil

This paragraph explains the fuel oil adjustment on the statement of adjustments and confirms that the seller filled the tank prior to closing.

## Water

This paragraph explains any adjustment for water on the statement of adjustments if water is not metered.

## Other Adjustments

There should be a paragraph, under the appropriate heading, explaining any other item on the statement of adjustments. For example, there may be an adjustment for rental payments if there are tenants living on the property.

## Mortgage Discharged

This paragraph describes the steps taken if the seller had an outstanding mortgage that was required by the agreement of purchase and sale to be discharged.

## Real Estate Commission

The agreement of purchase and sale directs the seller's lawyer to pay any remaining balance outstanding on the real estate commission. The deposit will already have been applied against the commission and is usually sufficient. If the deposit is insufficient, the reporting letter should set out the deficiency and state that it has been paid from the proceeds of the sale. If the deposit is greater than the amount of the commission, the reporting letter should state that you have asked the real estate broker to forward the excess amount directly to the seller.

### Statement of Funds and Disbursements

The statement covering receipt and disbursement of funds shows receipt of the balance due on closing and how those funds have been applied.

The amount of the balance due on closing appears in the right-hand numerical column and the amount of all payments your firm made from the proceeds appears in the left-hand numerical column. Payments from the proceeds might include:

- the balance of the real estate commission;
- money paid to discharge a mortgage;
- money paid on account of utility or other arrears;
- money retained in trust on account of other undertakings that has not yet been disbursed—for example, money held back on account of work orders that have to be cleared; and
- your law firm's fees and disbursements.

The sum remaining after deducting these items is the net proceeds.

### Net Proceeds

Include a paragraph stating how the net proceeds have been dealt with. Although the reporting letter may not be prepared for a while, sellers almost always want to receive the proceeds on the day of closing. Accordingly, the proceeds will likely have been paid to the seller by cheque or deposited into a bank account before the preparation of the reporting letter.

### Concluding Paragraph

The concluding paragraph lists the documents being enclosed. Generally, there are few documents following a sale. Although the seller signed a number of documents that were delivered to the buyer, in most cases there is no need to provide copies of them. Once the property has been sold, they are of little interest to the seller. Generally, the only documents enclosed are the statement of adjustments, the statement of account, and an executed copy of any mortgage given back to the seller, together with the standard charge terms.

### Signature

The reporting letter must be prepared for signature by the lawyer handling the file and must be signed by the lawyer. It may not be signed by a law clerk.

## The Reporting Letter for Our Transaction

Figure 24.4 is a reporting letter for our transaction.

### Agreement of Purchase and Sale

This section confirms completion of the transaction, and sets out the date of the agreement, the address of the property, the sale price, and the amount of the deposit.

### Statement of Adjustments

This section explains the adjustments that were made on closing, including the purchase price, the deposit, and the taxes, so that the seller can understand the balance due on closing.

### Previous First Mortgage

This section explains the money that was paid to the existing mortgagee in order to discharge the mortgage. It confirms the amount that was paid and that the lawyer will obtain a discharge of the mortgage and make sure that the discharge is registered.

### Real Estate Commission

The agreement of purchase and sale directs the seller's lawyer to pay any remaining balance outstanding on the real estate commission. In our case, the deposit was greater than the amount of the commission, so the reporting letter states that you have asked the real estate broker to forward the excess amount directly to the seller.

### Net Proceeds

This paragraph states how the net proceeds have been dealt with. In this transaction we are assuming that the proceeds were paid to the seller by cheque or deposited into a bank account before the preparation of the reporting letter.

### Statement of Funds and Disbursements

There is no statement of funds and disbursements in this letter. Instead we provide this information to the client by way of a trust ledger statement, shown as Figure 24.5.

### Concluding Paragraph

The concluding paragraph lists the documents being enclosed. Generally, the only documents enclosed are the statement of adjustments, a copy of the discharge statement, the statement of account, and the trust ledger statement.

### Signature

The reporting letter must be prepared for signature by the lawyer handling the file and must be signed by the lawyer. It may not be signed by a law clerk.

## Statement of Account

Prepare a statement of account setting out your firm's fees and disbursements on the sale transaction. The law firm will have kept sufficient funds to pay the account before releasing the closing funds to the client.

## Closing the File

Do not close the file until all post-closing matters have been completed, including performance of any undertakings. At that time, follow the standard procedure of the law firm.

# REVIEW QUESTIONS

1. What dates should you diarize if you are acting for the seller?

2. If there is a mortgage being paid off, what document do you prepare to advise the buyer's lawyer how funds are to be payable?

3. If a mortgage is being discharged, why is it important for the seller's lawyer to deliver funds to the mortgagee as soon as possible after closing?

4. The buyer's deposit is usually made payable to the real estate broker in trust. When the transaction closes, the broker can take the deposit from the trust account and apply it to the real estate commission.

    a. What if the deposit is not enough to cover the commission?

    b. George and Almaida sold their property. The deposit was $40,000 and was paid to the real estate broker. The total commission was $34,400. Will George and Almaida get the difference back, and if yes, how?

5. Why is a legal opinion not included in the seller's reporting letter?

6. What is the purpose of the seller's lawyer's reporting letter?

## Figure 24.1   Sale Checklist

SALE TRANSACTION

SELLER(S) _____     BUYER(S) _____

SPOUSE _____     BUYER'S SOLICITOR _____

ADDRESS _____     ADDRESS _____

_____     _____

PHONE   BUS _____     PHONE_____

       RES _____

NEW ADDRESS _____

_____

_____     _____

CLOSING DATE_____     REQUISITION DATE _____

RESPONSIBLE SOLICITOR_____     REQUISITIONS SUBMITTED _____

_____     REQUISITIONS ANSWERED _____

- ❑ Letter to client
- ❑ Letter to buyer's lawyer
- ❑ Receive from client: tax bill, old title documents, annual mortgage information letter, mortgage & SCT, survey, oil bill, etc.
- ❑ Receive & review requisition letter (including title direction) — amend documents enclosed
- ❑ Prepare statement of adjustments
  - ❑ check if water metered or billed semi-annually (in old city of Toronto)
  - ❑ oil heat — remind client to order last fill & confirm size of tank & current price for oil
- ❑ Reply to requisition letter
  - ❑ forward amended documents prepared by buyer's solicitor or prepare & send own form of undertaking/warranty/bill of sale & declaration
- ❑ Order mortgage statement for discharge purposes
- ❑ Receive & review discharge statement
  - ❑ check prepayment penalty & provisions in mortgage (only 3 months if mortgage over 5 years old)
  - ❑ discharge to be registered by mortgagee
  - ❑ discharge amount set out in statement $ _____
  - ❑ send to buyer's lawyer
- ❑ Send survey to buyer's lawyer
- ❑ Sign & send LSUC form of e-reg agreement to buyer's lawyer if not received
- ❑ Prepare transfer and acknowledgment & direction for registration of transfer
- ❑ Get commission statement from realtor
- ❑ Send commission statement & discharge statement to client for review
- ❑ Prepare & send estimated account
- ❑ Prepare direction re: funds and redirection re: funds
- ❑ Undertaking to discharge — to be signed by lawyer
- ❑ Arrange meeting with client to sign & review closing documents
- ❑ Get photocopy ID
- ❑ Prepare closing memo to agent
- ❑ Prepare letter to mortgagee sending money & requesting acknowledgment of receipt
- ❑ Prepare letter to realtor sending balance of commission or advising of closing & requesting balance to be sent to client

POST-CLOSING
- ❑ Undertakings complied with (list on file cover)
- ❑ Report to client & statement of account

# Figure 24.2    Register of a Discharge

LRO # 65    **Discharge Of Charge**    **In preparation** on 2015 07 08    at 09:15

*This document has not been submitted and may be incomplete.*    yyyy mm dd    Page 1 of 1

## Document to be Discharged

| Registration No. | Date | Type of Instrument |
|---|---|---|
| YR2115116 | 2015 06 23 | Charge/Mortgage |

## Discharging Party(s)

This discharge complies with the Planning Act. This discharge discharges the charge.

| | |
|---|---|
| *Name* | ABC Bank |
| | Acting as a company |
| *Address for Service* | 47 Anywhere Road |
| | Toronto, Ontario |
| | M0M 1M0 |

This document is not authorized under Power of Attorney by this party.

## Figure 24.3 Sample Reporting Letter to the Seller

*Date*

*Seller's name*
*Seller's address*

Re:                *Name of transaction*

Dear (*seller's name*):

We are pleased to confirm completion of this transaction and would like to make our report to you.

**Agreement of Purchase and Sale**

On (*date of agreement*) you accepted the offer of (*buyer's name*) to purchase (*address of property*). The agreement of purchase and sale provided for a sale price of $(*amount*). A deposit of $(*amount*) was paid, with the balance of the purchase price to be paid by certified cheque on closing, subject to adjustments.

**Closing**

[*Use this paragraph if the closing was not completed electronically.*]

On (*date of closing*), we received a (*series of*) certified cheques(s) in the amount of $(*balance due on closing*), being the balance due on closing calculated in accordance with the enclosed statement of adjustments. In exchange, we handed over a transfer endorsed in favour of the buyers.

[*Use this paragraph if the closing was completed electronically.*]

Prior to the closing, we received a (*series of*) cheque(s) in the amount of $(*balance due on closing*), being the balance due on closing calculated in accordance with the enclosed statement of adjustments. In exchange, we released the transfer for electronic registration.

**Mortgage Assumed** [*Use this paragraph if there was a mortgage assumed by the buyer.*]

On closing, the buyer assumed a first mortgage in favour of (*name of mortgagee*) on which there was the outstanding sum of $(*amount*) for principal and interest from (*date of last payment*) to (*date of closing*) in the amount of $(*amount*). The buyer was credited with both of these amounts on the statement of adjustments.

As we previously advised you, should the buyer fail to make a payment or payments, you may be responsible for the mortgage until it is discharged.

**Mortgage Taken Back** [*Use this paragraph if the seller took back a second mortgage.*]

**Figure 24.3   Continued**

In accordance with the agreement of purchase and sale, you took back a second charge/mortgage securing the principal amount of $(*amount*). The buyers were given a credit in this amount on the statement of adjustments.

The charge/mortgage was registered on title on (*date of closing*) as instrument number (*number*). We enclose an executed copy of the charge/mortgage together with the standard charge terms.

This charge/mortgage secures the principal sum of $(*amount*) with interest at (*rate*)% per annum and is repayable by equal monthly installments of $(*amount*) on account of principal and interest. The installments commence on the (*day*) day of (*month*), (*year*) up to and including the (*day*) day of (*month*), (*year*) when the balance, if any, of the principal sum is to be paid to you.

The monthly installments will be applied first to pay the interest calculated on the principal moneys from time to time outstanding, and the balance of the monthly installments will be applied in reduction of the principal.

[*Explain amortization schedule as follows:*] We are enclosing an amortization schedule for this mortgage. The schedule shows how much of each monthly payment is applied to principal and to interest and how much of the principal balance remains outstanding after each payment.

[*Where applicable, include details of any prepayment provisions. For example:*]

The buyer has the privilege, at any time when not in default under the mortgage, to prepay all or any part of the outstanding principal balance without notice or bonus.

**Realty Taxes** [*This paragraph should explain the realty tax adjustment—for example, if the seller paid the realty taxes in full:*]

The realty taxes for (*year*) in the amount of $(*total annual taxes*) were paid in full by you. Because your share of the realty taxes was only $(*seller's share of taxes*), you were allowed a credit for this item on the statement of adjustments in the amount of $(*amount*).

**Fuel Oil** [*Insert this paragraph if the property is heated by oil:*]

You left a full tank of fuel oil on the premises and were therefore allowed a credit of $(*amount*) for this item on the statement of adjustments.

**Water Charges** [*If there was an adjustment for water charges, insert a paragraph to explain this adjustment—for example, if the vendor paid more than his or her share of the water charges:*]

You paid $(*amount*) for water charges for the period from _____ to _____. Because your share of the water charges was only $(*seller's share of water charges*), you were allowed a credit for this item on the statement of adjustments in the amount of $(*amount*).

**Utilities**

**Figure 24.3 Continued**

Arrangements were made for the utility meters to be read before closing. Final bills will be forwarded to you. Please pay them promptly upon receipt.

**Mortgage Discharged** [*Use this paragraph if a mortgage was discharged on closing.*]

At the time of closing, there was an outstanding mortgage in favour of (*name of mortgagee*). By the terms of the agreement of purchase and sale, you were required to discharge this mortgage. A mortgage statement obtained from (*name of mortgagee*) showed an outstanding balance of $(*amount*) owing as of the date of closing. Accordingly, we delivered a cheque in the amount of $(*amount*) to (*name of mortgagee*) and have arranged for the mortgage to be discharged.

**Real Estate Commission**

We have paid the balance of the commission due to (*real estate broker*) in the amount of $(*amount*).

**Statement of Funds and Disbursements**

[*Set out the balance due on closing and how the funds were paid out. For example:*]

The following is the manner in which the closing funds were received and disbursed in this transaction:

| | | |
|---|---|---|
| Balance due on closing | | $271,554.60 |
| Paid (*name of mortgagee*) | $172,359.14 | |
| Paid (*name of broker*) balance of real estate commission | 2,500.00 | |
| Our fee and disbursements | 987.50 | |
| Net proceeds | 95,707.96 | |
| | $271,554.60 | $271,554.60 |

**Net Proceeds** [*Insert one of the following paragraphs.*]

[*If proceeds were picked up by client:*]

We wish to confirm that on (*date*) you came to our office and picked up our trust cheque in the amount of $(*amount of net proceeds*).

[*If proceeds were delivered to client:*]

We wish to confirm that on (*date*) we delivered to you our trust cheque in the amount of $(*amount of net proceeds*).

[*If proceeds were deposited into client's bank account:*]

**Figure 24.3    Concluded**

On your instructions, on (*date*), we deposited the sum of $(*amount of net proceeds*) to your credit into (*bank account and branch*).

As this matter is now complete, we enclose the following documents:

1. statement of adjustments;
2. our statement of account;
3. [*list any other documents enclosed*].

This completes our report to you. If you have any questions in connection with this transaction, please do not hesitate to contact us. We are pleased to have assisted you in this matter.

Yours very truly,

(*Seller's lawyer*)

Encls.

**Figure 24.4   Reporting Letter for Our Transaction**

Francois Mercier and Huguette Marie Mercier
97 Brook Street
Newmarket, Ontario
L3H 1V2


Dear Mr. and Mrs. Mercier:

Re:            Your sale to Grant
               166 Valley Road, Newmarket
               Our File No.: 15-1111

We are pleased to now submit our reporting letter in relation to your sale of the above property.


**AGREEMENT OF PURCHASE AND SALE**

This transaction was completed in accordance with the agreement of purchase and sale executed by you and the buyer. The sale price was $580,000 with $30,000 being paid as a deposit and the balance payable to you by certified cheque on closing subject to adjustments.

The transaction was completed on December 15, 2015.


**STATEMENT OF ADJUSTMENTS**

The statement of adjustments sets out closing adjustments between you and the buyer, calculated as at December 15, 2015.

The statement reflects a credit to you in the amount of $580,000, being the sale price of the property, and a credit to the buyer for the deposit moneys of $30,000.

REALTY TAXES—For the purpose of adjustments, the 2015 taxes are $5,200. Since your prorated share of the taxes for the period from January 1, 2015 to December 15, 2015 amounted to $4,957.81 whereas you had paid $5,200 on this account, you received credit in the statement of adjustments with the sum of $242.19.

BALANCE DUE ON CLOSING—After accounting for the foregoing adjustments, the buyer was required to pay the balance due on closing in the amount of $550,242.19.

For details as to the disbursement of funds received by our office, please refer to our trust ledger statement, which is enclosed.

**Figure 24.4   Concluded**

**PREVIOUS FIRST MORTGAGE**

From the funds that we received from the buyer on the closing of this transaction, we forwarded the sum of $93,111.23 so as to discharge the previous first mortgage in favour of ABC Bank.

The amount required to discharge this mortgage was determined in accordance with the mortgage statement for discharge purposes obtained by our office, and we are enclosing a copy thereof for your reference.

We will be obtaining and registering a discharge of this mortgage as soon as possible after closing.

**REAL ESTATE COMMISSION**

Insofar as the deposit moneys of $30,000 held by the real estate broker exceeded the commission payable of $26,100 plus HST, the broker was instructed to refund the difference to you, being $507, promptly after closing.

**NET PROCEEDS**

The sum of $456,237.12 was paid to you following the closing of the transaction. You will see that this amount is reflected on the enclosed trust ledger statement.

**ENCLOSURES**

We are enclosing the following documents:

> Statement of adjustments.
> Copy of first mortgage statement for discharge purposes.
> Statement of account.
> Trust ledger statement.

We trust that this transaction has been completed to your satisfaction. If you have any questions or comments, please do not hesitate to contact our office.

Yours very truly,


Brooks & Dunn
Per:

Encls.

**Figure 24.5 Trust Ledger Statement**

Mr. Francois Mercier and Ms. Huguette Marie Mercier

Re:       Your sale to Grant
             166 Valley Road, Newmarket
             Our File No. 15-1111

**TRUST LEDGER STATEMENT**

| | | |
|---|---:|---:|
| Received from buyer on closing | | $550,242.19 |
| Paid to discharge previous 1st mortgage—ABC Bank | $ 93,111.23 | |
| Paid legal fees and disbursements | 893.84 | |
| Paid to you following closing | 456,237.12 | |
| | $550,242.19 | $550,242.19 |

THIS IS OUR STATEMENT HEREIN
Brooks & Dunn
Per:

E. & O. E.

# PART IV

# Other Residential Real Estate Transactions

# Purchase of a New Home

# 25

## LEARNING OUTCOMES

After reading this chapter, you will understand:

- The mandatory requirements for an agreement of purchase and sale of a new home, by way of the addendum

- What warranties protect buyers of new homes, and for how long

- Builders' obligations if the completion of the construction of a new home is delayed

- Special concerns regarding searches in a new home purchase

- What additional adjustments may be made in the statement of adjustments for a new home purchase

# Introduction

Buying a newly built home is different from buying a resale home. While a resale home is a finished product that can be inspected prior to closing, a new home is typically purchased before construction has even begun, based on a model home or the builder's plans. For this reason, the agreement of purchase and sale will address various risks and issues associated with the construction of a new home. Because of these differences in the agreement of purchase and sale, there are additional concerns that arise for lawyers acting on such a transaction. The builder or seller and the buyer approach the issues concerning the construction and purchase of a new home from different perspectives. Generally, builders want to be protected from the uncertainties beyond their control that are inherent in the building process. Some examples of events that could delay or compromise completion of the deal as promised include bad weather, unavailability of construction materials, and labour disruptions. Builders want some flexibility with regard to completion dates and delays, and the ability to substitute construction materials if necessary.

The buyer, on the other hand, wants the home to be completed on time, to be of the quality promised, and to be free from any defects. The buyer wants some protection against unlimited delays and extensions of closing dates, and against improper substitution of construction materials. The buyer also wants some warranty against defective materials or construction that will extend beyond the closing date. This chapter examines these concerns.

# The New Home Agreement of Purchase and Sale

The agreement of purchase and sale for a new home is typically drafted by the builder and therefore tends to be one-sided in the builder's favour. There are some standard forms of agreement created by various building and construction associations for their members. In practice, however, most builders continue to use their own form of agreement of purchase and sale. Although there are some warranty protections that new home builders are legally required to provide and cannot contract out of, builders can and do draft agreements that provide them with a great deal of flexibility.

# Ontario New Home Warranties Plan Act

The *Ontario New Home Warranties Plan Act* is the governing legislation dealing with new home purchases. It outlines the extensive warranty protection provided to buyers and sets out the responsibilities of new home builders and sellers.

The Act applies to all new homes sold in Ontario and is administered by Tarion Warranty Corporation, formerly the Ontario New Home Warranty Program (ONHWP). Tarion is a private company that regulates new home builders and protects the rights of new home buyers by

- registering new home builders and sellers;
- enrolling new homes for warranty coverage;
- investigating illegal building practices;
- resolving warranty disputes between homeowners and builders; and
- educating new home buyers about their rights.

Under the Act, every builder or seller of a new home must register with Tarion. In addition, the builder or seller must enroll the new home in Tarion's warranty program before construction commences. Builders typically pass the enrollment fees on to the buyer in the agreement of purchase and sale.

Every new home agreement of purchase and sale must include an addendum prescribed by the regulations under the Act. This mandatory addendum contains important information about the new home transaction that will be of particular concern to the buyer. For example, the addendum

- clarifies the rights of the seller;
- provides Tarion's registration and enrollment details of the builder and the home;
- contains provisions dealing specifically with extensions and delays;
- advises buyers to seek legal advice before signing the agreement of purchase and sale;
- provides the builder's contact information; and
- sets out the requirements for arbitration for disputes arising from the termination of the agreement of purchase and sale.

If there is any conflict between provisions in the addendum and the agreement of purchase and sale, the provisions in the addendum will prevail.

Tarion maintains a guarantee fund that is financed entirely by registration, renewal, and enrollment fees. If a builder fails to complete the purchase agreement or breaches any statutory warranty obligations, Tarion will use this fund to pay the claims of any buyers.

Detailed information about Tarion is available at <www.tarion.com>.

## New Home Warranties

Under Tarion, every seller of a new home provides warranties for the following:

1. deposit protection;
2. defects in work and materials;
3. major structural defects;
4. substitution of materials; and
5. delays in completion.

Warranty coverage begins as soon as the buyer is in possession of the new home and remains in effect until the warranty period expires, even if the property is resold. The total maximum coverage for each home is $300,000, for homes with a possession date on or after July 1, 2006.

### Deposit Protection

The buyer's deposit on a new home is protected up to a maximum of $40,000 per home. If the sale is not completed, through no fault of the buyer, the buyer can make a deposit claim.

Any deposit moneys paid in excess of this amount are not protected. If the agreement of purchase and sale provides for a deposit greater than $40,000, the buyer should ensure that the excess amount is payable to the builder's/seller's solicitor in trust, to be released only when the transaction closes.

### Defects in Work and Materials

New home buyers have two warranty protections against defects in work and materials. The builder warrants that for the year immediately following possession, the home

- is properly constructed, in accordance with the Ontario *Building Code Act, 1992*;
- is free from unauthorized substitutions;
- is free of defects in materials; and
- is fit for habitation—in other words, is ready to live in.

The builder also warrants that for the two years immediately following possession, the home is free from

- water penetration through basement or foundation walls;
- water penetration into the building envelope that is caused by defects in materials or work such as caulking, windows, and doors;
- defects in materials or work related to the electrical, plumbing, and heating systems;
- defects in materials or work that cause exterior cladding (brickwork, or aluminum or vinyl siding) to detach, displace, or deteriorate; and
- violations of the Ontario *Building Code Act*'s health and safety provisions.

### Major Structural Defects

The builder warrants that for seven years immediately following possession, the home is free from any major structural defects. A "major structural defect" is defined in the *Administration of the Plan* regulation under the *Ontario New Home Warranties Plan Act*, in respect of a home built after June 30, 2012, as

> any defect in work or materials in respect of a building, including a crack, distortion or displacement of a structural load-bearing element of the building, if it,
>> (i)  results in failure of a structural load-bearing element of the building,

(ii) materially and adversely affects the ability of a structural load-bearing element of the building to carry, bear and resist applicable structural loads for the usual and ordinary service life of the element, or

(iii) materially and adversely affects the use of a significant portion of the building for usual and ordinary purposes of a residential dwelling and having regard to any specific use provisions set out in the purchase agreement for the home.

The Act provides some exceptions to this coverage. These include major structural defects resulting from

- flood damage;
- dampness that is not caused by the failure of a load-bearing portion of the building;
- damage to drains or sewers;
- damage to finishes;
- damage arising from acts of God, acts of the owner, acts of the owner's tenants and/or guests, or acts of war;
- malicious damage; or
- damage by insects or rodents, unless due to construction that did not meet the standards of the Ontario *Building Code Act*.

### Substitution of Materials

The agreement of purchase and sale typically provides the builder with the right to substitute materials if those originally specified are not available. While this makes practical sense from the builder's point of view, buyers need assurance that they will not end up with a significantly different home with respect to quality and appearance.

Tarion offers protection to the buyer against improper substitution of materials by the builder. Where the agreement of purchase and sale specifies that the buyer is entitled to select certain items of construction or finishing, the builder is not permitted to substitute these items without the buyer's written consent, giving the buyer an opportunity to make an alternative selection. For example, if the buyer has personally selected tiles, cabinets, bathroom fixtures, or paint colours, the buyer must consent if substitutions are to be made. The buyer must be notified in writing of the builder's inability to provide the buyer's selection. The buyer is then given seven days to make another selection, failing which the builder may substitute materials of equal or better quality.

For items that the buyer is entitled to receive under the agreement but is not entitled to choose, the builder can substitute only items of equal or better quality. For example, if the buyer is entitled to a certain model of washing machine, which is unavailable, the builder must provide a washing machine of equal or better quality.

### Delays in Completion for Agreements Signed After June 30, 2008

Agreements signed after June 30, 2008 must contain a Tarion addendum that outlines closing details, including a Statement of Critical Dates, which sets out the expected closing date and the latest possible dates allowed for extensions. The addendum also contains important information about the property being purchased, such as when construction is likely to start; whether water and sewer services are available; and whether there are any conditions precedent in the agreement, which, if not met, would result in early termination of the agreement. (Only certain early termination conditions are permitted, and most involve obtaining external approval, or the occurrence of an external event. Examples of such conditions are consent to the creation of a lot; obtaining a certificate of approval of a septic system; and completion of services such as roads, water lines, and sewer lines for the property or surrounding area.)

### FIRM CLOSING DATE

When a builder is fairly sure of completing a house by a specific date, he or she will provide a firm closing date in the Statement of Critical Dates, and an outside closing date, which is 365 days after the firm closing date, and is the latest possible closing date.

### TENTATIVE CLOSING DATES

When a builder is unsure of the exact date that the home will be completed, the builder may provide two tentative closing dates, a firm closing date, and an outside closing date in the Statement of Critical Dates. This allows the builder to extend the closing date twice, each by up to 120 days, without paying compensation. The first tentative closing date is the date by which the builder expects to complete the home. The second tentative closing date adds up to 120 days to the first tentative closing date. The firm closing date extends the second tentative closing date by up to 120 days.

If the builder has to delay beyond the first tentative closing date, the builder must give the buyer written notice of the delay at least 90 days before the first tentative closing date; otherwise, the first tentative closing date becomes the firm closing date. Similarly, if the builder has to delay beyond the second tentative closing date, the builder must give written notice of the delay at least 90 days before the second tentative closing date; otherwise, the second tentative closing date becomes the firm closing date. The outside closing date is 365 days after the earlier of the second tentative closing date and the firm closing date. For example, a builder might provide a Statement of Critical Dates as follows:

| | |
|---|---|
| First tentative closing date | November 15, 2015 |
| Second tentative closing date | March 15, 2016 |
| Firm closing date | July 13, 2016 |
| Outside closing date | March 15, 2017 |

If the closing date is going to be delayed beyond November 15, 2015, the builder must give the buyer notice of the delay no later than August 17, 2015 (90 days before November 15). If there is a further delay beyond March 15, 2016, the buyer must receive notice of the delay by December 15, 2015 (90 days before March 15).

**DELAYED CLOSING DATES**

If the home is not completed by the firm closing date, the builder must set a delayed closing date, and the buyer is entitled to "delayed closing compensation" for living expenses of $150 per day for each day of delay, until the delayed closing date or termination of the agreement, up to a maximum of $7,500. Receipts are not required. Compensation is also payable for costs incurred, such as extra moving or storage expenses, but receipts for those expenses must be provided.

Delayed closing compensation is not payable if the delay was due to any extraordinary circumstance that was not the fault of the seller. Such extraordinary circumstances would include a strike, fire, explosion, act of God, civil insurrection, act of war or terrorism, or pandemic. In these cases, the builder is obligated to advise the buyer of the delay and keep him or her informed as to its length.

If the home is not completed by the outside closing date, the buyer has 30 days from the outside closing date to terminate the agreement and is entitled to delayed closing compensation and a refund of all deposits paid, plus interest.

More information on delayed closing warranties can be found on the Tarion website at <www.tarion.com>.

## Pre-Delivery Inspection

When the home is complete, the buyer must arrange for a pre-delivery inspection (PDI) to be conducted before he or she moves in. During this inspection, the buyer should identify any unauthorized substitutions as well as any items that are damaged, missing, incomplete, or not working properly. All deficiencies are noted on a special PDI form, which provides a written record of the condition of the home as it existed before the buyer moved in.

During the PDI, the buyer will sign a certificate of completion and possession. This certificate confirms the official date of possession and activates the warranty coverage for the new home. The buyer will also confirm receipt of a homeowner information package. This package explains the rights and responsibilities of the new home buyer under the Act. It also explains the procedure to be followed by the buyer when requesting warranty service. The homeowner information package can be found on the Tarion home page at <www.tarion.com>.

# Additional Concerns and Steps

A lawyer acting for the buyer of a new home will have the same concerns, and must take the same steps, as those involved in the purchase of a resale residential property. There are some additional concerns and steps as well.

## Special Concerns Regarding Searches

There are special concerns at the search and inquiry stage of a new home purchase.

## Mortgages

The search of title may disclose a **blanket mortgage** on the entire development for millions of dollars. Usually the agreement of purchase and sale will require the buyer to accept the builder's undertaking to provide a partial discharge of the mortgage within a reasonable period of time after closing.

## Restrictions on Title

As is the case in resale agreements, the buyer of a new home must take title subject to any registered restrictions, easements, and agreements. The new home agreement will usually also require the buyer to accept future and potential easements, restrictions, and agreements entered into by the seller between the time the agreement is entered into and the closing date. It is very important for the buyer to check the "permitted encumbrances" clause in the new home agreement to determine the nature and scope of any potential title restrictions.

## Tarion Search

In addition to the usual searches and letter inquiries, a lawyer acting on the purchase of a new home must contact Tarion to ensure that the builder or seller has, in fact, registered with Tarion and that the new home has, in fact, been enrolled in the new home warranty program. The registration information is often attached to the agreement of purchase and sale.

# Adjustments on Closing

The statement of adjustments in a new home purchase will be different from that for a resale home, primarily because the agreement of purchase and sale of a new home generally allows the builder to pass a number of expenses on to the buyer.

## Enrollment Fees

The agreement of purchase and sale may provide that the cost of enrollment under Tarion will be added to the purchase price. The cost depends on the purchase price of the property.

## Utility Connections

The agreement of purchase and sale of a new home usually allows the builder to pass on to the buyer any charges paid to a utility for the connection of services or the installation of meters.

## New Housing Rebate

HST of 13 percent is payable on new homes. This amount, however, is usually included in the purchase price. If the buyer will be using the house as his or her primary place of residence, or the principal residence of an immediate family member, the buyer may be eligible for a rebate of some of the provincial part of the HST, up to $24,000. Most new home agreements of purchase and sale assume that the buyer qualifies for this rebate, and therefore the purchase price will reflect the discounted HST amount. If it turns out that the buyer does not qualify for the rebate, the purchase price will be increased by way of an adjustment in the seller's favour.

## Realty Taxes

For resale properties, the adjustment of realty taxes on closing is based on actual taxes assessed. For new homes, before construction is complete, taxes are calculated on the basis that the land is vacant; therefore, they do not provide an accurate indication of what the taxes will be once the construction has been completed and the property separately assessed. Accordingly, on closing, the taxes are adjusted as if they had been assessed on the completed property and as if the seller had paid them in full at this higher rate. By adjusting taxes in advance, the seller avoids having to go after the buyer for any additional taxes owing after closing. Once a supplementary tax bill is issued, the seller will pay the taxes and the taxes will be readjusted, if necessary, in accordance with the undertakings to readjust that are exchanged on closing. If the seller has overestimated the new taxes, the seller will refund money to the buyer. If the seller has underestimated the new taxes, the buyer will have to pay the difference.

## KEY TERMS

blanket mortgage, 412

## REFERENCES

*Administration of the Plan*, RRO 1990, Reg 892.

*Building Code Act, 1992*, SO 1992, c 23, as amended.

*Ontario New Home Warranties Plan Act*, RSO 1990, c O.31.

## REVIEW QUESTIONS

1. What is the *Ontario New Home Warranties Plan Act*?

2. How is the *Ontario New Home Warranties Plan Act* administered?

3. What must a buyer of a new home do to protect his or her statutory warranty rights?

4. What is an "addendum"?

5. What happens if a builder fails to fulfill the purchase agreement or breaches any statutory warranty obligations?

6. For what items does a seller of a new home provide warranties?

7. When does warranty coverage begin and end?

8. What can a buyer of a new home do if the builder delays completion without complying with the Act?

9. What takes place during the pre-delivery inspection?

10. How are realty taxes adjusted on the closing of a new home purchase?

## DISCUSSION QUESTIONS

1. Sally is purchasing a new home. The builder is registered with Tarion, and the home has been enrolled in the warranty program. The builder's form of agreement of purchase and sale provides for a deposit of $50,000. The agreement also provides that the builder can substitute materials if necessary.

   a. Sally is nervous about giving so much money as a deposit. What advice should Sally's lawyer give her?

   b. Sally is excited about being able to choose some of the items in her new home (lighting and plumbing fixtures, cabinets, carpets, tiles, and paint colours) but is concerned about the builder being able to make changes. She is worried that she will not like the quality or appearance of substitutions that are made by the builder. What advice should Sally's lawyer give her?

2. Ramona purchased a new home that is enrolled in the warranty program and had a firm closing date of September 30, 2015. On July 25, the builder sent Ramona a letter notifying her that the closing date was being extended to October 25 because of a shortage of bricks. Ramona is very upset about these delays and wants to know whether she is entitled to any compensation. Explain your answer.

# Purchase of a Condominium

# 26

## LEARNING OUTCOMES

After reading this chapter, you will understand:

- The steps involved when purchasing a resale condominium

- What a status certificate is and what information it provides

- How to search executions in a condominium resale

- The steps involved when purchasing a new condominium

- Why there are two stages to the closing of a new condominium purchase

- What happens during the interim occupancy period of a new condominium purchase

# Introduction

If the client is purchasing a condominium, the steps and procedures for the transaction are mostly the same as those for the purchase of a residential property owned in fee simple. This chapter discusses the main differences, which arise because of the nature of condominium ownership. As discussed in Chapter 11, Condominiums, the buyer will become the sole owner in fee simple of the condominium unit and a part owner (tenant in common with all of the other unit owners) of the common elements of the condominium corporation. The buyer will also become a member of the condominium corporation that manages and administers the condominium property.

# Purchase of a Resale Condominium

## Agreement of Purchase and Sale

The standard form of agreement of purchase and sale for a resale condominium is different from the one used in the purchase of a resale residential property owned in fee simple. Both the Ontario Real Estate Association (OREA) and the Toronto Real Estate Board (TREB) have a standard form of agreement to be used for the purchase of a resale condominium. In addition to the usual clauses in an agreement of purchase and sale, the seller agrees to give the buyer copies of the key condominium documentation, and the seller makes representations about the amount of the common expenses and the financial status of the condominium corporation. (See the discussion below under the heading "Status Certificate.")

A copy of the OREA form of agreement of purchase and sale for a condominium resale is reproduced as Figure 26.1, at the end of the chapter.

## Title Search

All condominiums are registered in the Land Titles system. There is a separate parcel register or title index for each unit in a condominium. You must examine the title index to verify the state of title to the unit being purchased.

In addition to the dwelling unit, there may be parking units and storage units. Parking and storage units are sometimes designated as exclusive-use common elements, and are sometimes separate units, depending on how the condominium was initially set up. If the parking/storage units are separately deeded, there will be a separate parcel register for each.

## Execution Search

The execution search in a condominium resale differs from the usual execution search for a Land Titles property. In addition to the usual search against the seller, you should also search for executions against the condominium corporation. If there is a judgment against the corporation, the unit owners may be liable for a portion of the judgment.

## Status Certificate

In addition to conducting the above searches, the buyer of a condominium unit must obtain a **status certificate** from the condominium corporation. A status certificate is prepared by the board of directors and provides a written report on the current state of the condominium corporation. It is the most important document in the purchase of a resale condominium. Offers to purchase a resale condominium are usually made conditional upon review of the status certificate by the buyer's lawyer.

The status certificate will contain the following information:

1. the amount of common expenses for the unit and whether or not the seller is in default of payment of common expenses;

2. whether the common expenses will be increased and, if so, the reason for the increase;

3. whether or not assessments have been levied against the unit and, if so, the reason for the assessments;

4. whether or not there are any judgments against the condominium corporation, including the status of any legal actions to which the condominium corporation is currently a party;

5. the address for service of the corporation, including the names and addresses for service of all directors and officers of the corporation; and

6. a copy of the current declaration (discussed in Chapter 11 under the heading "Declaration").

Pursuant to section 76(6) of the *Condominium Act, 1998*, the status certificate will bind the corporation "as of the date it is given or deemed to have been given, with respect to the information that it contains or is deemed to contain, as against a purchaser or mortgagee of a unit who relies on the certificate."

The condominium corporation must also provide a copy of the following documents:

- the last annual financial statements of the corporation;
- the corporation's current budget;
- the condominium's current declaration, bylaws, and rules;
- the property management agreement; and
- the current insurance certificates.

It is important that the lawyer in charge of the file review all of these documents with the client prior to closing. Collectively they are known as the status certificate package and will provide answers to questions that are very important to a buyer such as:

- Who manages the condominium?
- Will I own my parking space and locker?
- Can I have a pet?

**status certificate**
certificate from the condominium corporation that includes, among other things, financial information, the names and addresses for service of all directors and officers, and the declaration

- Can my guests use the swimming pool?
- Is there enough money in the reserve fund for future repairs or will a special assessment be needed?
- Are there any lawsuits against the corporation?

## Requisitions on Title

In addition to the requisitions that might arise on any residential property purchase, you may have requisitions that arise from your review of the status certificate and condominium documentation if the information provided differs from that in the agreement of purchase and sale.

## Statement of Adjustments

In addition to the usual adjustments, there will be an adjustment for the monthly common expense payment, which is generally payable on the 1st of the month and covers the month that follows.

**declarant**
upon registration, the person who owns the land described in the description and who registers the declaration and description that create the condominium plan

**proposed declarant**
prior to the registration of the declaration and description, the person who owns the land described in the description

**disclosure statement**
document given to every buyer of a condominium unit that includes details pertaining to the physical, legal, and financial aspects of the condominium corporation

**cooling-off period**
10-day period during which the buyer can back out of the purchase

# Purchase of a New Condominium

As in the case of other types of newly constructed homes, the agreement of purchase and sale for a new condominium is often signed before construction of the condominium has started. In fact, in many agreements, the builder is not even obligated to start construction of the condominium until a specified number of units are sold. This is because most banks will not provide financing for construction unless a specified number of units are presold. However, in the case of a new condominium, the agreement of purchase and sale is not binding on the buyer until the seller, referred to as the **declarant** (or as the **proposed declarant** until such time as the declaration and description are registered on title to create the condominium), delivers a **disclosure statement** to the buyer. This document, which must be given to every buyer of a new condominium unit, includes:

- a description of the property and its amenities;
- a copy of the declaration, bylaws, and rules;
- construction dates (if not completed);
- a description of contracts involving the corporation;
- a copy of the budget for the year of registration; and
- a copy of the insurance trust agreement.

The buyer has a 10-day **cooling-off period** from the later of (1) the receipt of the disclosure statement and (2) the receipt of an executed copy of the agreement of purchase and sale, during which time the buyer may cancel the agreement without having to give a reason. This very important protection is given to buyers of new condominiums only. In order to cancel the agreement, the buyer must give the proposed declarant written notice, which must be received by the proposed declarant within the 10-day cooling-off period. If there are subsequent material changes to the disclosure statement, the proposed declarant must give the buyer an amended disclosure statement, and the buyer then has another 10-day cooling-off period.

Section 74(2) of the *Condominium Act* defines what constitutes a material change. There is a lot of case law on what kinds of changes require the delivery of an amended disclosure statement, which will trigger the buyer's right to cancel. This is an important issue because buyers often try to get out of a deal in a falling market. The case of *Abdool v Somerset Place Developments of Georgetown Ltd* states that the test is one of materiality and the onus is on the buyer to

> establish objectively that had the information that was not disclosed, or that was inaccurately or insufficiently disclosed, been properly disclosed in the disclosure statement at the time it was delivered to the purchaser, a reasonable purchaser would have regarded the information as sufficiently important to the decision to purchase that he or she would not likely have gone ahead with the transaction but would instead have rescinded the agreement before the expiration of the ten-day cooling off period.

## Deposits

All deposits that a buyer pays must be held in trust by the proposed declarant's lawyer or a designated trustee until title is transferred to the buyer, unless the proposed declarant provides security for the deposits. The first $20,000 of a deposit is secured under the *Ontario New Home Warranties Plan Act*. The proposed declarant must pay interest on any deposits up to the interim occupancy date.

## Budget

The declarant must also give the buyer a copy of the budget for the year following registration of the description and declaration. If the budget proves to be too low, the declarant is liable to pay the deficiency to the condominium corporation. This discourages declarants from underestimating costs to attract buyers.

## Two-Stage Closing

Often a condominium is built and ready for occupancy before the description and declaration are registered. Title cannot be transferred to the buyer until these are registered and so the final closing is delayed. Most agreements of purchase and sale require the buyer to occupy the unit as soon as it is ready, even if the buyer cannot get title to the property at that time. The date of occupancy is called the **interim occupancy date**. The final closing date will occur when title can be transferred to the buyer.

**interim occupancy date**
date on which the buyer takes possession prior to final closing and transfer of title

Tarion has a delayed occupancy warranty for condominiums, based on both firm and tentative occupancy dates, that is similar to the delayed closing warranty (based on both firm and tentative closing dates) discussed in Chapter 25. The various dates and the warranty are discussed more fully below, under the heading "Statement of Critical Dates." For additional information, go to the Tarion website at <www.tarion.com>.

On the interim occupancy date, the buyer will have to pay any amounts required by the agreement of purchase and sale. The parties will enter into an interim occupancy agreement, which sets out the rights and obligations of the parties during the time between occupancy of the unit and the transfer of title to the buyer on the final closing date.

The *Condominium Act* allows the proposed declarant to charge monthly interim occupancy fees during the interim occupancy period. These fees can be no greater than the total of

- the monthly interest on any unpaid balance of the purchase price, the interest rate being based on the Bank of Canada rate for a one-year mortgage;
- a reasonable estimate of the unit's portion of municipal taxes, on a monthly basis; and
- the projected monthly common expenses for the unit.

Once the description and declaration have been registered, the declarant can provide the buyer with a transfer, and the final closing can take place. The buyer will have to pay the balance of the purchase price, subject to adjustments, at this time.

It is only on the final closing date that the buyer can obtain financing. That is another reason why the 10-day cooling-off period is very important. If a buyer is thinking about buying real estate because interest rates on mortgages are low, those low rates may not exist by the time of the final closing date. This is something that should be explained to a buyer during the 10-day cooling-off period.

## Statement of Critical Dates

The agreement of purchase and sale must contain a Tarion form, called the Statement of Critical Dates. This form is similar to the one discussed in Chapter 25 but is specific to condominiums. This document states the various occupancy dates, including a first tentative occupancy date, a final tentative occupancy date, and a firm occupancy date. If occupancy is not complete by each date, notice must be given to the buyer and the date by which notice must be given is stated in the Statement of Critical Dates. The statement goes on to say that if occupancy cannot be provided by the firm occupancy date, the buyer must be compensated. The compensation is $150 per day for living expenses, to a maximum of $7,500.

The statement also provides that the buyer can terminate the agreement if occupancy is not completed by the outside occupancy date (the latest date by which the seller agrees to provide occupancy).

Each agreement states the specific dates for the particular transaction.

These dates typically span a long period of time, usually about two years, so it is very important that the buyer's lawyer explain to him or her that buying a new condominium is very different from buying a resale condominium, because the actual move-in date is usually very vague. The 10-day cooling-off period gives a buyer time to meet with his or her lawyer in order to understand this unusual process.

## KEY TERMS

cooling-off period, 418

declarant, 418

disclosure statement, 418

interim occupancy date, 419

proposed declarant, 418

status certificate, 417

## REFERENCES

*Abdool v Somerset Place Developments of Georgetown Ltd*,
    1992 CanLII 7640 (Ont CA).

*Condominium Act, 1998*, SO 1998, c 19.

*Ontario New Home Warranties Plan Act*, RSO 1990, c O.31.

## REVIEW QUESTIONS

1. How do you conduct a title search of a condominium property?

2. How does an execution search for a condominium resale differ from the usual execution search for a Land Titles property?

3. What information is contained in the status certificate?

4. What is an interim occupancy agreement?

5. Sunita recently signed an agreement of purchase and sale for a new condominium. She now thinks that she made a huge mistake and wants to back out of the deal. She has not yet received any documents from the seller/builder. Can she withdraw from the agreement?

6. Betty signed an agreement of purchase and sale for a new condominium unit. The disclosure statement that she received two months ago indicated that the condominium was providing a games room and a health club. Betty has just been informed that these facilities will no longer be included in the condominium. What, if anything, can Betty do?

7. Last year, Sam signed an agreement of purchase and sale for a new condominium unit before construction of the building had even begun. Sam has just been told that although he won't get title to the property yet, his unit will be ready for occupancy next month.

   a. Is Sam obligated to occupy the unit before he gets title?

   b. What amount will Sam be required to pay to the seller/builder when he moves in?

**Figure 26.1 OREA Agreement of Purchase and Sale—Condominium Resale**

---

**OREA** Ontario Real Estate Association

**Agreement of Purchase and Sale**
**Condominium Resale**

**Form 101** for use in the Province of Ontario

This Agreement of Purchase and Sale dated this.................................. day of ...................................... 20........

**BUYER,**.................................................................................................................................., agrees to purchase from
(Full legal names of all Buyers)

**SELLER,**..................................................................................................................................., the following
(Full legal names of all Sellers)

**PROPERTY:**

a unit in the condominium property known as ................................................................................ No.....................
(Apartment/Townhouse/Suite/Unit)

located at ...........................................................................................................................................................................

in the ...................................................................................................................................................................................

being ........................................................................................ Condominium Plan No .................................................
(Legal Name of Condominium Corporation)

Unit Number .............................. Level No. .............................. Building No. ............................... together with ownership

or exclusive use of Parking Space(s) ....................................................................., together with ownership or exclusive use of
(Number(s), Level(s))

Locker(s) ..............................................................., together with Seller's proportionate undivided tenancy-in-common interest
(Number(s), Level(s))

in the common elements appurtenant to the Unit as described in the Declaration and Description including the exclusive right to use such other parts of the common elements appurtenant to the Unit as may be specified in the Declaration and Description: the Unit, the proportionate interest in the common elements appurtenant thereto, and the exclusive use portions of the common elements, being herein called the "Property".

**PURCHASE PRICE:**                                                        Dollars (CDN$).................................................

.................................................................................................................................................................Dollars

**DEPOSIT:** Buyer submits .............................................................................................................................................
(Herewith/Upon Acceptance/as otherwise described in this Agreement)

......................................................................................... Dollars (CDN$).................................................

by negotiable cheque payable to........................................................................................................ "Deposit Holder" to be held in trust pending completion or other termination of this Agreement and to be credited toward the Purchase Price on completion. For the purposes of this Agreement, "Upon Acceptance" shall mean that the Buyer is required to deliver the deposit to the Deposit Holder within 24 hours of the acceptance of this Agreement. The parties to this Agreement hereby acknowledge that, unless otherwise provided for in this Agreement, the Deposit Holder shall place the deposit in trust in the Deposit Holder's non-interest bearing Real Estate Trust Account and no interest shall be earned, received or paid on the deposit.

**Buyer agrees to pay the balance as more particularly set out in Schedule A attached.**

**SCHEDULE(S) A**..........................................................................**attached hereto form(s) part of this Agreement.**

1.  **IRREVOCABILITY:** This offer shall be irrevocable by ................................... until ........................ a.m./p.m. on
(Seller/Buyer)

    the .............................. day of .................................................... 20........., after which time, if not accepted, this offer shall be null and void and the deposit shall be returned to the Buyer in full without interest.

2.  **COMPLETION DATE:** This Agreement shall be completed by no later than 6:00 p.m. on the ............................... day

    of ................................., 20......... . Upon completion, vacant possession of the Property shall be given to the Buyer unless otherwise provided for in this Agreement.

**INITIALS OF BUYER(S):** ( )          **INITIALS OF SELLER(S):** ( )

**Form 101   Revised 2015   Page 1 of 6**

WEB*Forms*® Jun/2015

## Figure 26.1    Continued

3. **NOTICES:** The Seller hereby appoints the Listing Brokerage as agent for the Seller for the purpose of giving and receiving notices pursuant to this Agreement.  Where a Brokerage (Buyer's Brokerage) has entered into a representation agreement with the Buyer, the Buyer hereby appoints the Buyer's Brokerage as agent for the purpose of giving and receiving notices pursuant to this Agreement. **Where a Brokerage represents both the Seller and the Buyer (multiple representation), the Brokerage shall not be appointed or authorized to be agent for either the Buyer or the Seller for the purpose of giving and receiving notices.** Any notice relating hereto or provided for herein shall be in writing. In addition to any provision contained herein and in any Schedule hereto, this offer, any counter-offer, notice of acceptance thereof or any notice to be given or received pursuant to this Agreement or any Schedule hereto (any of them, "Document") shall be deemed given and received when delivered personally or hand delivered to the Address for Service provided in the Acknowledgement below, or where a facsimile number or email address is provided herein, when transmitted electronically to that facsimile number or email address, respectively, in which case, the signature(s) of the party (parties) shall be deemed to be original.

FAX No.: ............................................................
(For delivery of Documents to Seller)

FAX No.: ............................................................
(For delivery of Documents to Buyer)

Email Address: ...................................................
(For delivery of Documents to Seller)

Email Address: ...................................................
(For delivery of Documents to Buyer)

4. **CHATTELS INCLUDED:**




Unless otherwise stated in this Agreement or any Schedule hereto, Seller agrees to convey all fixtures and chattels included in the Purchase Price free from all liens, encumbrances or claims affecting the said fixtures and chattels.

5. **FIXTURES EXCLUDED:**




6. **RENTAL ITEMS (Including Lease, Lease to Own):** The following equipment is rented and **not** included in the Purchase Price. The Buyer agrees to assume the rental contract(s), if assumable:




The Buyer agrees to co-operate and execute such documentation as may be required to facilitate such assumption.

7. **COMMON EXPENSES:** Seller warrants to Buyer that the common expenses presently payable to the Condominium Corporation in respect of the Property are approximately $................................per month, which amount includes the following:.........................................................................................................................................................................
.........................................................................................................................................................................

8. **PARKING AND LOCKERS:** Parking and Lockers are as described above or assigned as follows:.............................
.............................................................. at an additional cost of:................................................................

9. **HST:** If the sale of the Property (Real Property as described above) is subject to Harmonized Sales Tax (HST), then such tax shall be ................................................. the Purchase Price. If the sale of the Property is not subject to HST,
(included in/in addition to)
Seller agrees to certify on or before closing, that the sale of the Property is not subject to HST. Any HST on chattels, if applicable, is not included in the Purchase Price.

INITIALS OF BUYER(S): ( )     INITIALS OF SELLER(S): ( )

Form 101    Revised 2015    **Page 2 of 6**
WEB*Forms*® Jun/2015

## Figure 26.1 Continued

10. **TITLE SEARCH:** Buyer shall be allowed until 6:00 p.m. on the ........................... day of.................................., 20......., (Requisition Date) to examine the title to the Property at Buyer's own expense and until the earlier of: (i) thirty days from the later of the Requisition Date or the date on which the conditions in this Agreement are fulfilled or otherwise waived or; (ii) five days prior to completion, to satisfy Buyer that there are no outstanding work orders or deficiency notices

    affecting the Property, and that its present use (...................................................................................................) may be lawfully continued. If within that time any valid objection to title or to any outstanding work order or deficiency notice, or to the fact the said present use may not lawfully be continued, is made in writing to Seller and which Seller is unable or unwilling to remove, remedy or satisfy or obtain insurance save and except against risk of fire (Title Insurance) in favour of the Buyer and any mortgagee, (with all related costs at the expense of the Seller), and which Buyer will not waive, this Agreement notwithstanding any intermediate acts or negotiations in respect of such objections, shall be at an end and all monies paid shall be returned without interest or deduction and Seller, Listing Brokerage and Co-operating Brokerage shall not be liable for any costs or damages. Save as to any valid objection so made by such day and except for any objection going to the root of the title, Buyer shall be conclusively deemed to have accepted Seller's title to the Property. Seller hereby consents to the municipality or other governmental agencies releasing to Buyer details of all outstanding work orders and deficiency notices affecting the Property, and Seller agrees to execute and deliver such further authorizations in this regard as Buyer may reasonably require.

11. **TITLE:** Buyer agrees to accept title to the Property subject to all rights and easements registered against title for the supply and installation of telephone services, electricity, gas, sewers, water, television cable facilities and other related services; provided that title to the Property is otherwise good and free from all encumbrances except: (a) as herein expressly provided; (b) any registered restrictions, conditions or covenants that run with the land provided such have been complied with; (c) the provisions of the Condominium Act and its Regulations and the terms, conditions and provisions of the Declaration, Description and By-laws, Occupancy Standards By-laws, including the Common Element Rules and other Rules and Regulations; and (d) any existing municipal agreements, zoning by-laws and/or regulations and utilities or service contracts.

12. **CLOSING ARRANGEMENTS:** Where each of the Seller and Buyer retain a lawyer to complete the Agreement of Purchase and Sale of the Property, and where the transaction will be completed by electronic registration pursuant to Part III of the Land Registration Reform Act, R.S.O. 1990, Chapter L4 and the Electronic Registration Act, S.O. 1991, Chapter 44, and any amendments thereto, the Seller and Buyer acknowledge and agree that the exchange of closing funds, non-registrable documents and other items (the "Requisite Deliveries") and the release thereof to the Seller and Buyer will (a) not occur at the same time as the registration of the transfer/deed (and any other documents intended to be registered in connection with the completion of this transaction) and (b) be subject to conditions whereby the lawyer(s) receiving any of the Requisite Deliveries will be required to hold same in trust and not release same except in accordance with the terms of a document registration agreement between the said lawyers. The Seller and Buyer irrevocably instruct the said lawyers to be bound by the document registration agreement which is recommended from time to time by the Law Society of Upper Canada. Unless otherwise agreed to by the lawyers, such exchange of the Requisite Deliveries will occur in the applicable Land Titles Office or such other location agreeable to both lawyers.

13. **STATUS CERTIFICATE AND MANAGEMENT OF CONDOMINIUM:** Seller represents and warrants to Buyer that there are no special assessments contemplated by the Condominium Corporation, and there are no legal actions pending by or against or contemplated by the Condominium Corporation. The Seller consents to a request by the Buyer or the Buyer's authorized representative for a Status Certificate from the Condominium Corporation. Buyer acknowledges that the Condominium Corporation may have entered into a Management Agreement for the management of the condominium property.

14. **DOCUMENTS AND DISCHARGE:** Buyer shall not call for the production of any title deed, abstract, survey or other evidence of title to the Property except such as are in the possession or control of Seller. Seller agrees to deliver to Buyer, if it is possible without incurring any costs in so doing, copies of all current condominium documentation of the Condominium Corporation, including the Declaration, Description, By-laws, Common Element Rules and Regulations and the most recent financial statements of the Condominium Corporation. If a discharge of any Charge/Mortgage held by a corporation incorporated pursuant to the Trust And Loan Companies Act (Canada), Chartered Bank, Trust Company, Credit Union, Caisse Populaire or Insurance Company and which is not to be assumed by Buyer on completion, is not available in registrable form on completion, Buyer agrees to accept Seller's lawyer's personal undertaking to obtain, out of the closing funds, a discharge in registrable form and to register same, or cause same to be registered, on title within a reasonable period of time after completion, provided that on or before completion Seller shall provide to Buyer a mortgage statement prepared by the mortgagee setting out the balance required to obtain the discharge, and, where a real-time electronic cleared funds transfer system is not being used, a direction executed by Seller directing payment to the mortgagee of the amount required to obtain the discharge out of the balance due on completion.

15. **MEETINGS:** Seller represents and warrants to Buyer that at the time of the acceptance of this Offer the Seller has not received a notice convening a special or general meeting of the Condominium Corporation respecting: (a) the termination of the government of the condominium property; (b) any substantial alteration in or substantial addition to the common elements or the renovation thereof; OR (c) any substantial change in the assets or liabilities of the Condominium Corporation; and Seller covenants that if Seller receives any such notice prior to the date of completion Seller shall forthwith notify Buyer in writing and Buyer may thereupon at Buyer's option declare this Agreement to be null and void and all monies paid by Buyer shall be refunded without interest or deduction.

**INITIALS OF BUYER(S):** ⬭  **INITIALS OF SELLER(S):** ⬭

## Figure 26.1   **Continued**

16. **INSPECTION:** Buyer acknowledges having had the opportunity to inspect the Property and understands that upon acceptance of this offer there shall be a binding agreement of purchase and sale between Buyer and Seller. **The Buyer acknowledges having the opportunity to include a requirement for a property inspection report in this Agreement and agrees that except as may be specifically provided for in this Agreement, the Buyer will not be obtaining a property inspection or property inspection report regarding the Property.**

17. **APPROVAL OF THE AGREEMENT:** In the event that consent to this sale is required to be given by the Condominium Corporation or the Board of Directors, the Seller will apply forthwith for the requisite consent, and if such consent is refused, then this Agreement shall be null and void and the deposit monies paid hereunder shall be refunded without interest or other penalty to the Buyer.

18. **INSURANCE:** The Unit and all other things being purchased shall be and remain at the risk of the Seller until completion. In the event of substantial damage to the Property Buyer may at Buyer's option either permit the proceeds of insurance to be used for repair of such damage in accordance with the provisions of the Insurance Trust Agreement, or terminate this Agreement and all deposit monies paid by Buyer hereunder shall be refunded without interest or deduction. If Seller is taking back a Charge/Mortgage, or Buyer is assuming a Charge/Mortgage, Buyer shall supply Seller with reasonable evidence of adequate insurance to protect Seller's or other mortgagee's interest on completion.

19. **DOCUMENT PREPARATION:** The Transfer/Deed shall, save for the Land Transfer Tax Affidavit, be prepared in registrable form at the expense of Seller, and any Charge/Mortgage to be given back by the Buyer to Seller at the expense of the Buyer.

20. **RESIDENCY:** (a) Subject to (b) below, the Seller represents and warrants that the Seller is not and on completion will not be a non-resident under the non-residency provisions of the Income Tax Act which representation and warranty shall survive and not merge upon the completion of this transaction and the Seller shall deliver to the Buyer a statutory declaration that Seller is not then a non-resident of Canada;
(b) provided that if the Seller is a non-resident under the non-residency provisions of the Income Tax Act, the Buyer shall be credited towards the Purchase Price with the amount, if any, necessary for Buyer to pay to the Minister of National Revenue to satisfy Buyer's liability in respect of tax payable by Seller under the non-residency provisions of the Income Tax Act by reason of this sale. Buyer shall not claim such credit if Seller delivers on completion the prescribed certificate.

21. **ADJUSTMENTS:** Common Expenses; realty taxes, including local improvement rates; mortgage interest; rentals; unmetered public or private utilities and fuel where billed to the Unit and not the Condominium Corporation; are to be apportioned and allowed to the day of completion, the day of completion itself to be apportioned to the Buyer. There shall be no adjustment for the Seller's share of any assets or liabilities of the Condominium Corporation including any reserve or contingency fund to which Seller may have contributed prior to the date of completion.

22. **PROPERTY ASSESSMENT:** The Buyer and Seller hereby acknowledge that the Province of Ontario has implemented current value assessment and properties may be re-assessed on an annual basis. The Buyer and Seller agree that no claim will be made against the Buyer or Seller, or any Brokerage, Broker or Salesperson, for any changes in property tax as a result of a re-assessment of the Property, save and except any property taxes that accrued prior to the completion of this transaction.

23. **TIME LIMITS:** Time shall in all respects be of the essence hereof provided that the time for doing or completing of any matter provided for herein may be extended or abridged by an agreement in writing signed by Seller and Buyer or by their respective lawyers who may be specifically authorized in that regard.

24. **TENDER:** Any tender of documents or money hereunder may be made upon Seller or Buyer or their respective lawyers on the day set for completion. Money shall be tendered with funds drawn on a lawyer's trust account in the form of a bank draft, certified cheque or wire transfer using the Large Value Transfer System.

25. **FAMILY LAW ACT:** Seller warrants that spousal consent is not necessary to this transaction under the provisions of the Family Law Act, R.S.O. 1990 unless Seller's spouse has executed the consent hereinafter provided.

26. **UFFI:** Seller represents and warrants to Buyer that during the time Seller has owned the Property, Seller has not caused any building on the Property to be insulated with insulation containing ureaformaldehyde, and that to the best of Seller's knowledge no building on the Property contains or has ever contained insulation containing ureaformaldehyde. This warranty shall survive and not merge on the completion of this transaction, and if the building is part of a multiple unit building, this warranty shall only apply to that part of the building which is the subject of this transaction.

27. **LEGAL, ACCOUNTING AND ENVIRONMENTAL ADVICE:** The parties acknowledge that any information provided by the brokerage is not legal, tax or environmental advice.

28. **CONSUMER REPORTS: The Buyer is hereby notified that a consumer report containing credit and/or personal information may be referred to in connection with this transaction.**

29. **AGREEMENT IN WRITING:** If there is conflict or discrepancy between any provision added to this Agreement (including any Schedule attached hereto) and any provision in the standard pre-set portion hereof, the added provision shall supersede the standard pre-set provision to the extent of such conflict or discrepancy. This Agreement including any Schedule attached hereto, shall constitute the entire Agreement between Buyer and Seller. There is no representation, warranty, collateral agreement or condition, which affects this Agreement other than as expressed herein. For the purposes of this Agreement, Seller means vendor and Buyer means purchaser. This Agreement shall be read with all changes of gender or number required by the context.

**INITIALS OF BUYER(S):** ( )        **INITIALS OF SELLER(S):** ( )

## Figure 26.1    Continued

30. **TIME AND DATE:** Any reference to a time and date in this Agreement shall mean the time and date where the Property is located.

31. **SUCCESSORS AND ASSIGNS:** The heirs, executors, administrators, successors and assigns of the undersigned are bound by the terms herein.

SIGNED, SEALED AND DELIVERED in the presence of:    IN WITNESS whereof I have hereunto set my hand and seal:

.......................................    .......................................    ● DATE...............
(Witness)    (Buyer)    (Seal)

.......................................    .......................................    ● DATE...............
(Witness)    (Buyer)    (Seal)

I, the Undersigned Seller, agree to the above offer. I hereby irrevocably instruct my lawyer to pay directly to the brokerage(s) with whom I have agreed to pay commission, the unpaid balance of the commission together with applicable Harmonized Sales Tax (and any other taxes as may hereafter be applicable), from the proceeds of the sale prior to any payment to the undersigned on completion, as advised by the brokerage(s) to my lawyer.

SIGNED, SEALED AND DELIVERED in the presence of:    IN WITNESS whereof I have hereunto set my hand and seal:

.......................................    .......................................    ● DATE...............
(Witness)    (Seller)    (Seal)

.......................................    .......................................    ● DATE...............
(Witness)    (Seller)    (Seal)

**SPOUSAL CONSENT:** The Undersigned Spouse of the Seller hereby consents to the disposition evidenced herein pursuant to the provisions of the Family Law Act, R.S.O.1990, and hereby agrees with the Buyer that he/she will execute all necessary or incidental documents to give full force and effect to the sale evidenced herein.

.......................................    .......................................    ● DATE...............
(Witness)    (Spouse)    (Seal)

**CONFIRMATION OF ACCEPTANCE:** Notwithstanding anything contained herein to the contrary, I confirm this Agreement with all changes both typed and written was finally accepted by all parties at.................a.m./p.m. this...........................day

of................................................, 20........... .    .......................................
(Signature of Seller or Buyer)

### INFORMATION ON BROKERAGE(S)

Listing Brokerage........................................................    Tel.No. ...............

.......................................
(Salesperson / Broker Name)

Co-op/Buyer Brokerage........................................    Tel.No. ...............

.......................................
(Salesperson / Broker Name)

### ACKNOWLEDGEMENT

I acknowledge receipt of my signed copy of this accepted Agreement of Purchase and Sale and I authorize the Brokerage to forward a copy to my lawyer.    I acknowledge receipt of my signed copy of this accepted Agreement of Purchase and Sale and I authorize the Brokerage to forward a copy to my lawyer.

.................... DATE...............    .................... DATE...............
(Seller)    (Buyer)

.................... DATE...............    .................... DATE...............
(Seller)    (Buyer)

Address for Service................................    Address for Service................................

.................... Tel.No. ...............    .................... Tel.No. ...............

Seller's Lawyer................................    Buyer's Lawyer................................

Address................................    Address................................

Email................................    Email................................

.......................................    .......................................
Tel.No.    FAX No.    Tel.No.    FAX No.

Property Manager:................................................
(Name)    (Address)    (Tel No.,FAX No.)

FOR OFFICE USE ONLY    **COMMISSION TRUST AGREEMENT**

To: Co-operating Brokerage shown on the foregoing Agreement of Purchase and Sale:
In consideration for the Co-operating Brokerage procuring the foregoing Agreement of Purchase and Sale, I hereby declare that all moneys received or receivable by me in connection with the Transaction as contemplated in the MLS® Rules and Regulations of my Real Estate Board shall be receivable and held in trust. This agreement shall constitute a Commission Trust Agreement as defined in the MLS® Rules and shall be subject to and governed by the MLS® Rules pertaining to Commission Trust.

DATED as of the date and time of the acceptance of the foregoing Agreement of Purchase and Sale.    Acknowledged by:

.......................................    .......................................
(Authorized to bind the Listing Brokerage)    (Authorized to bind the Co-operating Brokerage)

**Form 101**    Revised 2015    **Page 5 of 6**
WEB*Forms*® Jun/2015

**Figure 26.1    Concluded**

**OREA** Ontario Real Estate Association

## Schedule A
**Agreement of Purchase and Sale – Condominium Resale**

**Form 101** for use in the Province of Ontario

This Schedule is attached to and forms part of the Agreement of Purchase and Sale between:

**BUYER,**................................................................................................................................................, and

**SELLER,**.................................................................................................................................................

for the purchase and sale of ...........................................................................................................................

..................................................... dated the ........................................ day of .................................., 20......... .

Buyer agrees to pay the balance as follows:

This form must be initialed by all parties to the Agreement of Purchase and Sale.

**INITIALS OF BUYER(S):** ( )    **INITIALS OF SELLER(S):** ( )

**Form 101**    Revised 2015    **Page 6 of 6**

WEB*Forms*® Jun/2015

# Purchase of a Rural Property

# 27

## LEARNING OUTCOMES

After reading this chapter, you will understand the additional issues that may arise in the purchase of a rural property, including:

- Water supply and sewage systems

- Access, whether by road, water, or right of way

- Unopened road allowances

- Waterfront properties

- Zoning

# Introduction

If the client is buying a rural property such as a cottage or farm property, the steps and procedures to complete the transaction are largely the same as those for the purchase of an urban residential property. There are, however, a number of additional concerns. This chapter highlights only some of those concerns. It is not intended to be an exhaustive study of rural conveyancing.

Some of these matters may be covered by title insurance. However, even if title insurance is being obtained, you should verify that the policy covers them. If not, the appropriate searches may have to be conducted.

# Water

Most rural properties are not connected to municipal water systems. They obtain their water from wells located on the property, and their waste water is discarded by way of septic systems.

If the property has a well, it is important to verify that the water is potable. Often the agreement of purchase and sale is conditional on the buyer obtaining proof that the water is potable. The buyer (or the agent for the listing broker) can obtain proof by getting a sample of the water and sending it to the local health unit to be tested.

If the property has a septic system, you may write to the local health unit to find out whether it was installed according to the regulations in effect at the time of installation. If it was not, the buyer's lawyer should submit a requisition that the system be reinstalled pursuant to the regulations. If it is an older system, the health unit may not have any record of the installation. Most agreements of purchase and sale for rural properties contain a warranty by the seller that to the best of his or her knowledge the septic system was properly installed and has operated satisfactorily during his or her occupancy. The buyer will have to rely on that warranty if no records are available.

Both of the above matters may be dealt with by title insurance, if you are able to obtain a policy containing endorsements that deal with water potability and septic systems. In that case, no inquiries are necessary.

# Access

A number of issues may arise with respect to access to rural properties.

## Property Fronting on a Provincial Highway

If the property fronts on a provincial highway, you will want to ensure that there is proper access to the property. This can sometimes be determined by looking at any reference plans on Teraview that show the property and the highway. If not, you may have to write to the Ministry of Transportation to make sure that the entrance to the road from the property has been approved.

In addition, there are restrictions on what can be built or placed near a highway without a permit, so you must check section 34(2) of the *Public Transportation and Highway Improvement Act* to determine when a permit is required. If the property fronts on a controlled access highway, you may have to write to the Ministry of Transportation to find out whether or not a permit is required and, if so, whether or not one has been issued pursuant to section 38 of the Act.

## Property Abutting an Unopened Road Allowance

Some properties abut **unopened road allowances**, which do not look any different from the rest of the property. On occasion, owners of rural property assume possession of the road allowance property and build on it. If that is the case, the municipality (which still owns the road allowance) can insist that any buildings be demolished.

If you have a plan of survey, you should check it to make sure that there are no structures located on an unopened road allowance. If structures have been built on the road allowance, you should requisition the seller's lawyer to apply to the municipality to have the road allowance conveyed to the seller prior to closing.

Title insurance covers many problems that a survey might have disclosed, so if you do not have a survey, and your client is getting title insurance, it is important to check to see whether the policy covers the above situation, before you take further steps.

**unopened road allowance**
a strip of Crown land originally designated for use as a road allowance, which has never been used

## Access by Right of Way

If access to the property is by right of way over other private or government property, the client should be aware that the right of way is not maintained by the municipality and maintenance of it will be an added expense to the client. Often there are cottage associations that attend to the maintenance of rights of way through membership fees.

## Access by Water

If there is no road access to the property and access is only by water, the buyer should make inquiries as to what boat launching and mooring and parking facilities are available, and what costs are associated with these.

# Waterfront Properties

Other than issues of access as noted above, there are a number of other issues that may arise with respect to waterfront properties.

## 66-Foot Reservation

Some rural waterfront properties do not go right to the waterline. There may be a 66-foot strip between the lot line and the waterline that is owned by the Crown or the local municipality. The landowner has the right to cross over the strip, but not to build on it or pipe water across it without municipal permission. You should use Teraview to find the property identifier number for the 66-foot strip to determine who owns it.

### Shoreline Ownership

Buyers of shoreline property should be aware that they cannot alter the shoreline in any way or build anything over the water, such as a dock or a boathouse, without obtaining permits from the Ministry of Natural Resources and Forestry and the Ministry of Transportation.

### Conservation Authority

Properties near or on a watercourse may be governed by the *Conservation Authorities Act*. Section 28 of the Act gives a conservation authority the right to require its approval before any building is erected or fill is placed on land within its jurisdiction. Thus, a buyer may be restricted in what can be done with the property.

## Zoning

If the client intends to use the property year-round, he or she should make sure that the property is not zoned "seasonal," because municipal services may not be provided year-round to properties with this zoning.

## KEY TERMS

unopened road allowance, 431

## REFERENCES

*Conservation Authorities Act*, RSO 1990, c C.27, as amended.

*Public Transportation and Highway Improvement Act*, RSO 1990, c P.50, as amended.

## REVIEW QUESTIONS

1. How are most rural properties supplied with water, and how do they dispose of waste water?

2. If there is a well on the property, how can a buyer be sure that the water is potable?

3. What rights does the owner of a waterfront property have over the 66-foot strip between the lot line and the waterline?

## DISCUSSION QUESTIONS

1. Frank has just purchased a cottage on a lot that extends to the shoreline of Lake Simcoe. As soon as the deal closes, he plans on building a boathouse. What should Frank be aware of before he goes ahead with his plan?

2. Alice loves the outdoors and wants to purchase a rural property that she can use year-round. She has found a property that is close to both a beautiful lake and a ski resort. She thinks it's perfect and wants to make an offer. What should Alice do before she makes an offer?

# Purchase of a Property Under Power of Sale

# 28

## LEARNING OUTCOMES

After reading this chapter, you will understand:

- What constitutes default under a charge/mortgage
- How to purchase a property under power of sale
- What a notice of sale under charge is
- Who has the right to sell a property under power of sale
- The legal requirements of buying a property under power of sale

# Introduction

In Chapter 6, Charges/Mortgages, we discussed mortgages from the perspective of the mortgagor. As stated in that chapter, a charge or mortgage is a loan secured against land. If the chargor or mortgagor (the borrower) defaults under the mortgage, usually by failing to make payments on the loan when due (or, less commonly, by failing to pay taxes or a prior mortgage, not having insurance, or not maintaining the property), the chargee or mortgagee (the lender) has the right to realize on the security of the land by seizing and selling it. This chapter discusses mortgages from the perspective of a buyer purchasing the land from a mortgagee selling under the power of sale contained in the mortgage and examines the special conveyancing concerns that arise on such a purchase.

# The Power of Sale

As discussed in Chapter 6, virtually every mortgage contains power of sale provisions that allow the mortgagee to sell the mortgaged property and use the proceeds from the sale for payment of the mortgage debt. A mortgagee can take steps to sell the mortgaged property if the mortgagor is in default for at least 15 days. As a practical matter, mortgagees rarely act this quickly and instead provide warnings, usually in the form of a demand letter, before taking such action. The first step in a sale is the service of a notice of sale under charge. The notice of sale is served on the mortgagor and on any other parties having an interest in the property, such as the mortgagor's spouse and any **subsequent encumbrancers**. The notice gives the mortgagor at least 35 days to redeem the property by paying the amount due under the mortgage. It is only after that redemption period has expired that the mortgagee is permitted to sell the property. Figure 28.1, at the end of the chapter, is an example of a notice of sale under charge.

**subsequent encumbrancer**
the holder of an interest in the mortgaged property; registered on title after the mortgage

Pursuant to sections 35 and 36 of the *Mortgages Act*, the buyer of a property under power of sale will obtain good title to the mortgaged property, free and clear of the mortgagor's interest in the property, provided that the notice of sale was proper and was given in "professed compliance" with the Act. If the notice of sale is defective, however, the sale may be declared invalid and the buyer's title will be tainted. Accordingly, it is essential for the lawyer acting for the buyer to ensure that the mortgagee has fully complied with the notice of sale provisions contained in the Act.

Although the mortgagor or any other person who suffers as a result of the sale may have a remedy against the person who exercised the power of sale, pursuant to section 36, a notice given in "professed compliance" with the Act cannot be challenged on the basis that the provisions of the Act were not, in fact, complied with. As a result, even a defective notice of sale may be enough to give good title to the buyer if it was given in professed compliance with the Act. The courts have interpreted "professed compliance" to mean that the notice

> must be such as to enable the parties to whom the notice is required to be given to protect their interests. It must, in other words, identify the mortgage, stipulate the amount due thereon for principal, interest and costs and state that

unless the sum is paid by the specified date the property will be sold. (*Re Bot-iuk and Collison et al*)

As long as the notice provides this required information, it will not be struck out if it contains a minor omission or typographical error.

# Conveyancing Considerations

The lawyer acting for the buyer in a power of sale transaction must take steps to ensure that the provisions of section 35 of the *Mortgages Act* have been complied with.

## The Agreement of Purchase and Sale

Ordinarily, the agreement of purchase and sale will include an acknowledgment by the buyer that the property is being sold by the mortgagee under power of sale.

## The Title Search

In addition to the usual searches and inquiries, the lawyer for the buyer should review the mortgage under which the property is being sold to ensure that its power of sale provisions have been complied with.

## Closing Documentation

The documentation differs depending on whether the property is registered in the Registry system or the Land Titles system.

### Property in the Land Titles System

There is a specific type of transfer used for properties that are sold under power of sale in the Land Titles system. See Figure 28.2. To create the transfer, in Teraview, select "Instrument," "Create New," "Transfer," and then "Transfer: Power of Sale." See Figure 28.3.

The chargee's solicitor will include in the electronic transfer the following compliance with law statements:

- that the document is authorized under the charge and the *Mortgages Act*;
- that money was advanced under the charge;
- that the charge was in default when the notice of sale was given and continues to be in default;
- that the sale complies with the charge and the *Mortgages Act* (and other acts, where applicable);
- identification and particulars of instruments registered after the charge;
- identification and particulars of writs of execution filed subsequent to the charge; and
- identification of spousal status for each person whose interest may be deleted upon registration of the transfer and whose spouse was not served with a notice of sale.

Because the statements are considered "compliance with law" statements, they can be electronically signed only by a lawyer, not by a law clerk. See Figure 28.4 for a list of all statements generated in Teraview. The lawyer must choose and complete the appropriate statement.

### Property in the Registry System

In the unlikely event that the property is in the Registry system, the lawyer for the seller (mortgagee) proves compliance with the notice of sale provisions in the *Mortgages Act* by delivering the following statutory declarations at the time of registration of the transfer:

- a statutory declaration confirming default under the mortgage;
- a statutory declaration proving service of the notice of sale, together with copies of the post office registration receipts, if any; and
- a statutory declaration that the sale complies with the Act.

Examples of these three declarations are provided in Figures 28.5, 28.6, and 28.7.

These declarations are deposited on title prior to registering the transfer, by registration of a document general to which the declarations are attached. Figure 28.8 is an example of the document general. In addition, the transfer will include recitals that refer to the registration of the mortgage, the power of sale provisions in the mortgage, details of the notice given, and the mortgagor's continued default. Figure 28.9 is an example of the transfer.

Prior to closing, the buyer's lawyer must carefully review the declarations, including the notice of sale and registration receipts, to ensure that the sale, in fact, complies with the Act.

### General Concerns

Whether the property is registered in the Land Titles system or the Registry system, the lawyer for the buyer must do the following:

- review the charge/mortgage to ensure that it contains a power of sale clause;
- review the declarations or statements to make sure that the registration particulars of the charge/mortgage are stated correctly; and
- review the declarations or statements to confirm that the charge/mortgage was in default for the appropriate period of time before the notice of sale was served and that the property was sold only after the expiry of the required notice period.

These steps are required notwithstanding the fact that section 36 of the *Mortgages Act* protects the buyer's title, because the buyer will lose the protection if it can be shown that there was notice of the invalidity of the notice of sale.

It should be noted that the transfer is signed not by the owner, but by the chargee.

# Effect of a Power of Sale

When the sale is completed, the chargee/mortgagee will have no further interest in the property. The sale will also extinguish the interests of the chargor/mortgagor, and of any subsequent encumbrancers, who must satisfy their claims from any surplus remaining after the chargee's/mortgagee's loan and related expenses have been paid out of the sale proceeds. The buyer's title will be subject only to any prior registered encumbrances.

## KEY TERMS

subsequent encumbrancer, 436

## REFERENCES

*Botiuk and Collison et al, Re* (1979), 26 OR (2d) 580, 103 DLR (3d) 322 (CA).

*Mortgages Act*, RSO 1990, c M.40.

## REVIEW QUESTIONS

1. Does the buyer of a property under power of sale get good title to the mortgaged property, free and clear of the mortgagor's interest in the property?

2. When searching title to property being purchased under power of sale, what steps, in addition to the usual searches and inquiries, should the buyer's lawyer take?

3. If the property being sold under power of sale is registered in the Land Titles system, what is required in order to transfer good title to the buyer?

4. A property is being sold under power of sale by the second mortgagee, DEF Bank Inc. The mortgagor is Bethany Borrower. There is also a first mortgage in favour of ABC Bank Inc. and a third mortgage in favour of GHI Bank Inc. When the property is sold, will the sale extinguish the interests of ABC Bank Inc. and GHI Bank Inc.? Explain.

5. In the above question, will ABC Bank Inc. still have an interest in the property? Will Bethany Borrower still have an interest in the property?

6. Rona is buying a property under power of sale from Best Bank Inc. The owner of the property is Owen Owner. Will Owen need to sign the transfer?

## Figure 28.1    Notice of Sale Under Charge

**Notice of Sale Under Charge**

TO:                   The Parties shown on Schedule "A" attached hereto.

TAKE NOTICE that default has been made in payment of the moneys due under a certain charge dated the 1st day of February, (*year*) made

BETWEEN:

DAVID DEFAULTER & DONNA DEFAULTER

Chargor

- and -

SECURE TRUST COMPANY
a trust company incorporated under
the laws of the Province of Ontario,

Chargee

on the security of ALL AND SINGULAR that certain parcel or tract of land and premises situate, lying and being in the city of Toronto and being composed of the whole of Lot 26, according to Registered Plan 329 registered in the Land Registry Office for the Registry Division for Metropolitan Toronto (No. 64) which charge was registered on the 3rd day of February, (*year*) in the Land Registry Office for the Registry Division for Metropolitan Toronto (No. 64) as instrument number 987654 (the "Charge").

AND Secure Trust Company hereby gives you notice that the amounts now due on the Charge for principal money, interest and costs, respectively, are as follows:

| | |
|---|---:|
| Principal money | $65,000.00 |
| Interest as of April 1, (*year*) | 5,250.00 |
| Cost of these proceedings | 1,000.00 |
| TOTAL | $71,250.00 |

AND UNLESS the said sums, together with interest thereon at the rate of 12% per annum calculated half-yearly, not in advance and any further costs and disbursements incurred in these proceedings, are paid on or before the 6th day of May (*year*), Secure Trust Company shall sell the property covered by the said Charge under the provisions contained in it.

THIS NOTICE is given to you as you appear to have an interest in the charged property and may be entitled to redeem the same.

DATED at Toronto, Ontario, this 1st day of April, (*year*)

SECURE TRUST COMPANY

By its solicitor and authorized agent,
Susan Smart, Barrister & Solicitor
456 Bay Street
Toronto, Ontario, M5G 8D3

per:_____
                    S. Smart

**Figure 28.1 Concluded**

**SCHEDULE "A"**

DAVID DEFAULTER
123 Picket Fence Drive
Toronto, Ontario
M2B 4L7

SPOUSE OF DONNA DEFAULTER
123 Picket Fence Drive
Toronto, Ontario
M2B 4L7

DONNA DEFAULTER
123 Picket Fence Drive
Toronto, Ontario
M2B 4L7

SPOUSE OF DAVID DEFAULTER
123 Picket Fence Drive
Toronto, Ontario
M2B 4L7

## Figure 28.2 Transfer: Power of Sale

---

LRO # 61    **Transfer: Power Of Sale**                            **In preparation** on 2015 11 24        a.: 17:52

*This document has not been submitted and may be incomplete.*                              yyyy mm dd    Page 1 of 1

### Source Instruments

| Registration No. | Date | Type of Instrument |
|---|---|---|
| YR456127 | 2014 02 21 | Charge/Mortgage |

### Consideration

Consideration          $350,000.00

### Transferor(s)

The transferor(s) hereby transfers the land to the transferee(s).

| | |
|---|---|
| Name | ANYBANK |
| | Acting as a company |
| Address for Service | 111 Any Street |
| | Nowhere, Ontario |
| | L0L 1M0 |

I, John Bank have the authority to bind the corporation.

This document is not authorized under Power of Attorney by this party.

### Transferee(s)                                    Capacity                Share

| | |
|---|---|
| *Name* | PURCHASER, PATTY |
| | Acting as an individual |
| *Date of Birth* | JANUARY 1, 1970 |
| *Address for Service* | 222 Other Road |
| | Nowhere, Ontario |
| | L0L 1D0 |

### Statements

The document is authorized under the charge and the Mortgages Act.

The sale proceeds and transfer comply with the charge, the Mortgages Act, and if applicable the Bankruptcy and Insolvency Act (Canada), the Condominium Act, the Construction Lien Act and the Farm Debt Mediation Act (Canada).

The charge was in default at the time notice of sale was given and continues to be in default and the money has been advanced under the charge.

Notice of the transfer of charge and the address for the new chargee, was served on the registered owner(s) as well as all the parties having any interest in the land and the charge was in default when the chargee entered into an agreement of purchase and sale of the charge and continues to remain in default.

The spouse(s) was not served.

There are no encumbrances to be deleted.

This transaction is not subject to any writs of execution.

The owner was not a spouse within the meaning of the Family Law Act at the time notice was served.

### Calculated Taxes

Provincial Land Transfer Tax        $3,725.00

**Figure 28.3    Creating a Transfer: Power of Sale**

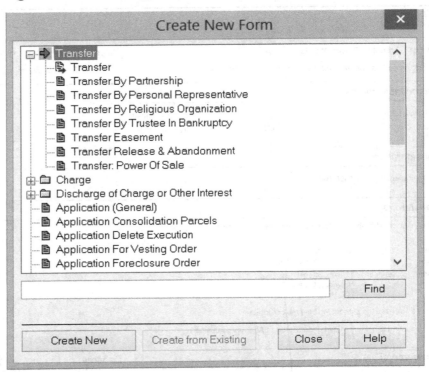

## Figure 28.4 Compliance with Law Statements

☐ 4048   The NAME has consented to the severance herein. IMPORT IMAGE

☐ **3301**   The document is authorized under the charge and the Mortgages Act.

☐ **3308**   The sale proceedings and transfer comply with the charge, the Mortgages Act , and if applicable the Bankruptcy and Insolvency Act (Canada), the Condominium Act, the Construction Lien Act and the Farm Debt Mediation Act (Canada).

☐ **3305**   The charge was in default at the time notice of sale was given and continues to be in default and the money has been advanced under the charge.

☐ 3309   Notice of the transfer of charge and the address for the new chargee, was served on the registered owner(s) as well as all the parties having any interest in the land and the charge was in default when the chargee entered into an agreement of purchase and sale of the charge and continues to remain in default.

☐ 3311   The spouse(s) NAME(S) was not served.

☐ **902**   The encumbrance(s) listed in the related deletions field is/are subsequent in priority to the charge and is/are to be deleted

☐ **904**   There are no encumbrances to be deleted

☐ **903**   This transaction is being made subject to the following writ(s) of execution NAME & WRIT NO.

☐ **908**   This transaction is not subject to any writs of execution

☐ **905**   Title to the land is not subject to spousal rights under the Family Law Act

☐ 906   Title to the land is subject to  spousal rights of the spouse of NAME

☐ 36   The owner was not a spouse within the meaning of the Family Law Act at the time notice was

☐ 37   The owner is a spouse who is not separated from their spouse and the property was not ordinarily occupied by the spouses as their family residence

☐ 38   The owner is a spouse who is separated from their spouse and the property was not ordinarily occupied by the spouses, at the time of their separation, as their family residence

☐ 39   The property is not designated by both spouses as a matrimonial home and that another property is designated as a matrimonial home by both spouses and that such designation is registered and not cancelled.

☐ 40   The spouse of the owner has released all rights under Part II of the Family Law Act by a separation agreement

☐ 41   The owners were spouses of one another at the time notices were served.

☐ 1606   The party executing this document is one and the same as NAME and the document evidencing the change of name was registered as number INSTRUMENT NUMBER AND DATE.

☐ 61   Schedule:  TEXT

☐ 92   This document is supported by evidence which is indexed at the Land Registry Office as index number INDEX NO..

☐ 34   The statutory covenants are to be amended as follows TEXT

☐ 3730   This document relates to registration no.(s)INSTRUMENT NOS.

☐ **3726**   NAME(S), has consented to the registration of this document, subject to the continuance of registration no. INSTRUMENT NO.

☐ **3733**   Registration of this document is not prohibited by registration number INSTRUMENT NO., which prevents dealings against charge number INSTRUMENT NO..

☐ **3756**   The registration of this document is not prohibited by registration INSTRUMENT NO..

☐ 3757   In accordance with registration INSTRUMENT NO., NAME(S) has consented to the registration of this document. IMPORT CONSENT

☐ 4046   The land is being acquired or disposed of by the Crown in Right of Ontario or the Crown in Right of Canada, including any Crown corporation, or any agency, board or commission of the Crown; or a municipal corporation.

**Figure 28.5    Declaration Regarding Default**

### Declaration Regarding Default (Registry)

| | |
|---|---|
| PROVINCE OF ONTARIO | ) IN THE MATTER OF TITLE to<br>) Lot 26, Plan 329, in the City of |
| JUDICIAL DISTRICT OF TORONTO | ) Toronto |

) AND IN THE MATTER of a sale
) thereof contained in a mortgage
) dated February 1, (*year*), made by
) David Defaulter and Donna
) Defaulter, as mortgagor, and Secure
) Trust Company, as mortgagee, and
) registered in the Land Registry
) Office for the Registry Division of
) the City of Toronto (No. 64) as
) instrument number 987654

) AND IN THE MATTER of a sale of
) of the above-noted lands and
) premises by Secure Trust Company

TO WIT:

I, ALVIN ADMINISTRATOR, of the City of Toronto, do solemnly declare that:

1.  I am the Chief Financial Officer of Secure Trust Company, and as such have personal knowledge of the matters herein deposed to.

2.  Pursuant to the mortgage dated February 1, (*year*), and registered in the Land Registry Office for the Registry Division for the City of Toronto (No. 64) on the 3rd day of February, (*year*) as instrument number 987654 (the "Mortgage"), David Defaulter and Donna Defaulter mortgaged the above-noted lands and premises to the mortgagee.

3.  The Mortgage has been in default since the 5th day of October, (*year*), and has remained in default to the date hereof.

4.  The Mortgage remained in default at the time when the mortgagee entered into the agreement of purchase and sale of the above-noted lands and premises to Peter Purchaser.

## Figure 28.5   Concluded

5. There is presently owing on the Mortgage for the principal money, interest, taxes, insurance premiums, appraisal fees and costs in excess of the sum of $71,250.00 and the costs and expenses of the above-noted sale.

6. The mortgagee has not, nor has any other person or persons on its behalf or as agent, received the moneys referred to in paragraph 5 hereof, or any security for the same, other than the Mortgage.

7. So far as I am aware, the mortgagee has not received any written notice of any statutory lien against the above-noted lands and premises in favour of the Crown or any other public authority, and, so far as I am aware, the mortgagee has not received actual notice in writing of any other interest in the above-noted lands and premises other than those served with the notice of sale herein.

8. No action for foreclosure of the mortgagor has been commenced by the mortgagee.

AND I MAKE this solemn declaration conscientiously believing it to be true and knowing that it is of the same force and effect as if made under oath.

DECLARED BEFORE ME at the City of Toronto,          )
In the Province of Ontario                          )   _____

                                                    )   Alvin Administrator
this          day of          , (year)              )
_____              )
A Commissioner, etc.                                )

**Figure 28.6 Declaration of Service**

**Declaration as to Service (Registry)**

PROVINCE OF ONTARIO ) IN THE MATTER OF TITLE to
) Lot 26, Plan 329, in the City of
JUDICIAL DISTRICT OF TORONTO ) Toronto

) AND IN THE MATTER of a sale
) thereof contained in a mortgage
) dated February 1, (*year*), made by
) David Defaulter and Donna
) Defaulter, as mortgagor, and Secure
) Trust Company, as mortgagee, and
) registered in the Land Registry
) Office for the Registry Division of
) the City of Toronto (No. 64) as
) instrument number 987654

) AND IN THE MATTER of a sale of
) of the above-noted lands and
) premises by Secure Trust Company

TO WIT:

I, CAROL CLERK, of the City of Toronto, do solemnly declare that:

1. I am a law clerk at the law firm of Susan Smart, solicitor for Secure Trust Company, and as such have knowledge of the matters herein deposed to.

2. I did on the 1st day of April, (*year*), serve by prepaid registered mail David Defaulter, Donna Defaulter, the Spouse of David Defaulter, and the Spouse of Donna Defaulter, with a notice of sale under mortgage, a true copy of which is attached hereto and marked as Exhibit "A" to this declaration, in accordance with the *Mortgages Act*.

3. The original certificate of post office registration in support is attached and marked as Exhibit "B" to the declaration.

AND I MAKE this solemn declaration conscientiously believing it to be true and knowing that it is of the same force and effect as if made under oath.

DECLARED BEFORE ME at the City of Toronto, )
In the Province of Ontario )
) _____
) Carol Clerk
this          day of          , (*year*) )
_____ )
A Commissioner, etc. )

**Figure 28.6   Continued**

EXHIBIT "A"

### Notice of Sale Under Charge

TO:                    The Parties shown on Schedule "A" attached hereto.

TAKE NOTICE that default has been made in payment of the moneys due under a certain charge dated the 1st day of February, (*year*) made

BETWEEN:

DAVID DEFAULTER & DONNA DEFAULTER

Chargor

- and -

SECURE TRUST COMPANY<br>a trust company incorporated under<br>the laws of the Province of Ontario,

Chargee

on the security of ALL AND SINGULAR that certain parcel or tract of land and premises situate, lying and being in the city of Toronto and being composed of the whole of Lot 26, according to Registered Plan 329 registered in the Land Registry Office for the Registry Division for Metropolitan Toronto (No. 64) which charge was registered on the 3rd day of February, (*year*) in the Land Registry Office for the Registry Division for Metropolitan Toronto (No. 64) as instrument number 987654 (the "Charge").

AND Secure Trust Company hereby gives you notice that the amounts now due on the Charge for principal money, interest and costs, respectively, are as follows:

| | |
|---|---:|
| Principal money | $65,000.00 |
| Interest as of April 1, (*year*) | 5,250.00 |
| Cost of these proceedings | 1,000.00 |
| TOTAL | $71,250.00 |

AND UNLESS the said sums, together with interest thereon at the rate of 12% per annum calculated half-yearly, not in advance and any further costs and disbursements incurred in these proceedings, are paid on or before the 6th day of May (*year*), Secure Trust Company shall sell the property covered by the said Charge under the provisions contained in it.

THIS NOTICE is given to you as you appear to have an interest in the charged property and may be entitled to redeem the same.

DATED at Toronto, Ontario, this 1st day of April, (*year*)

SECURE TRUST COMPANY

By its solicitor and authorized agent,
Susan Smart, Barrister & Solicitor
456 Bay Street
Toronto, Ontario, M5G 8D3

per:_____
                    S. Smart

**Figure 28.6 Concluded**

### SCHEDULE "A"

DAVID DEFAULTER
123 Picket Fence Drive
Toronto, Ontario
M2B 4L7

DONNA DEFAULTER
123 Picket Fence Drive
Toronto, Ontario
M2B 4L7

SPOUSE OF DONNA DEFAULTER
123 Picket Fence Drive
Toronto, Ontario
M2B 4L7

SPOUSE OF DAVID DEFAULTER
123 Picket Fence Drive
Toronto, Ontario
M2B 4L7

**Figure 28.7   Declaration of Compliance with the Mortgages Act**

---

### Declaration of Compliance with the *Mortgages Act* (Registry)

| | |
|---|---|
| PROVINCE OF ONTARIO | )   IN THE MATTER OF TITLE to <br> )   Lot 26, Plan 329, in the City of |
| JUDICIAL DISTRICT OF TORONTO | )   Toronto |

)  AND IN THE MATTER of a sale
)  thereof contained in a mortgage
)  dated February 1, (*year*), made by
)  David Defaulter and Donna
)  Defaulter, as mortgagor, and Secure
)  Trust Company, as mortgagee, and
)  registered in the Land Registry
)  Office for the Registry Division of
)  the City of Toronto (No. 64) as
)  instrument number 987654

)  AND IN THE MATTER of a sale of
)  of the above-noted lands and
)  premises by Secure Trust Company

TO WIT:

I, SUSAN SMART, of the City of Toronto, do solemnly declare that:

1. I am the solicitor for Secure Trust Company, and as such have knowledge of the matters herein deposed to.

2. Pursuant to a mortgage dated the 1st day of February, (*year*) and registered in the Land Registry Office for the Registry Division for the City of Toronto (No. 64) on the 3rd day of February, (*year*) as instrument number 987654 (the "Mortgage"), David Defaulter and Donna Defaulter mortgaged the above-noted lands and premises to Secure Trust Company.

3. I have read over the material in connection with the sale of the above-noted lands and premises under the power of sale contained in the Mortgage, and I am of the opinion that it complies with Part III of the *Mortgages Act*, and this statutory declaration is delivered pursuant to section 35 of the said Act.

AND I MAKE this solemn declaration conscientiously believing it to be true and knowing that it is of the same force and effect as if made under oath.

| | |
|---|---|
| DECLARED BEFORE ME at the City of Toronto, <br> In the Province of Ontario | ) <br> ) <br> )   _____ |
| | )   Susan Smart |
| this    day of    , (*year*) | ) |
| _____ | ) |
| A Commissioner, etc. | ) |

**Figure 28.8 Document General for Declarations**

---

DYE & DURHAM CO. INC.—Form No. 985
Amended NOV. 1992

Province
of
Ontario

## Document General
Form 4 — Land Registration Reform Act

**D**

| | |
|---|---|
| (1) Registry ☒ Land Titles ☐ | (2) Page 1 of 5 pages |

**(3) Property Identifier(s)**

Block     Property
12345-6789

Additional: See Schedule ☐

**(4) Nature of Document**
DEPOSIT under s. 106(1) of the Registry Act

**(5) Consideration**

Dollars $

**(6) Description**

Lot 26,
Plan 329
City of Toronto

Registry Division for the City of Toronto
(No. 64)

New Property Identifiers

Additional: See Schedule ☐

Executions

Additional: See Schedule ☐

**(7) This Document Contains:**

(a) Redescription New Easement Plan/Sketch ☐

(b) Schedule for: Description ☐ Additional Parties ☐ Other ☐

FOR OFFICE USE ONLY

**(8) This Document provides as follows:**

I, Susan Smart, of the City of Toronto here deposit with and require you to take into your Custody, pursuant to Part II of the Registry Act, the following documents:

| Description of Documents | Names of all Parties | Any Other Particulars or Subject of Certificate, Affidavit, Etc. |
|---|---|---|
| Statutory Declaration | Carol Clerk | Re: service of notice of sale |
| Statutory Declaration | Alvin Administrator | Re: default under mortgage |
| Statutory Declaration | Susan Smart | Re: compliance with Mortgages Act |

Continued on Schedule ☐

**(9) This Document relates to instrument number(s)**

**(10) Party(ies) (Set out Status or Interest)**

| Name(s) | Signature(s) | Date of Signature Y M D |
|---|---|---|
| SMART, Susan, Solicitor | Per:    Susan Smart, Solicitor | |
| 456 Bay Street | | |
| Toronto, Ontario M5G 8D3 | | |

**(11) Address for Service**   456 Bay Street, Toronto, Ontario M5G 8D3

**(12) Party(ies) (Set out Status or Interest)**

| Name(s) | Signature(s) | Date of Signature Y M D |
|---|---|---|
| | | |

**(13) Address for Service**

**(14) Municipal Address of Property**

123 Picket Fence Drive
Toronto, Ontario
M2B 4L7

**(15) Document Prepared by:**

Susan Smart
Barrister and Solicitor
456 Bay Street
Toronto, Ontario
M5G 8D3

**Fees and Tax**

| | |
|---|---|
| Registration Fee | |
| | |
| | |
| | |
| Total | |

FOR OFFICE USE ONLY

## Figure 28.9   Registry System Transfer Under Power of Sale

| | |
|---|---|
| Province of Ontario | **Transfer/Deed of Land** |
| | Form 1 — Land Registration Reform Act |
| | DYE & DURHAM CO. INC.—Form No. 970 |
| | Amended NOV. 1992 |

**A**

(1) Registry ☒   Land Titles ☐   (2) Page 1 of 2 pages

(3) Property Identifier(s)   Block   Property
12345-6789   Additional: See Schedule ☐

(4) Consideration
Three Hundred Thousand   Dollars $ 300,000.00

(5) Description   This is a:   Property Division ☐   Property Consolidation ☐

Lot 26
Plan 329
City of Toronto

New Property Identifiers   Additional: See Schedule ☐

Executions   Additional: See Schedule ☐

(6) This Document Contains   (a) Redescription New Easement Plan/Sketch ☐   (b) Schedule for: Description ☐   Additional Parties ☐   Other ☒   (7) Interest/Estate Transferred   Fee Simple

(8) Transferor(s) The transferor hereby transfers the land to the transferee and certifies that the transferor is at least eighteen years old and that

Name(s)   SECURE TRUST COMPANY
Signature(s)   Per:
Alvin Administrator
Chief Financial Officer
Date of Signature Y M D

(9) Spouse(s) of Transferor(s) I hereby consent to this transaction
Name(s)   Signature(s)   Date of Signature Y M D

(10) Transferor(s) Address for Service   86 King Street West, Toronto, Ontario, M4H 5D2

(11) Transferee(s)
PURCHASER, Peter   Date of Birth Y M D   1965 06 24

(12) Transferee(s) Address for Service   123 Picket Fence Drive, Toronto, Ontario M2B 4L7

(13) Transferor(s) The transferor verifies that to the best of the transferor's knowledge and belief, this transfer does not contravene section 50 of the Planning Act.
Date of Signature Y M D   Signature...................
Solicitor for Transferor(s) I have explained the effect of section 50 of the Planning Act to the transferor and I have made inquiries of the transferor to determine that this transfer does not contravene that section and based on the information supplied by the transferor, to the best of my knowledge and belief, this transfer does not contravene that section. I am an Ontario solicitor in good standing.
Name and Address of Solicitor   Signature...................   Date of Signature Y M D

(14) Solicitor for Transferee(s) I have investigated the title to this land and to abutting land where relevant and I am satisfied that the title records reveal no contravention as set out in subclause 50 (22) (c) (ii) of the Planning Act and that to the best of my knowledge and belief this transfer does not contravene section 50 of the Planning Act. I act independently of the solicitor for the transferor(s) and I am an Ontario solicitor in good standing.
Name and Address of Solicitor   Signature...................   Date of Signature Y M D

(15) Assessment Roll Number of Property   Cty. 01   Mun. 25   Map 023   Sub. 076   Par. 00024   Fees and Tax

Registration Fee

Land Transfer Tax

(16) Municipal Address of Property
123 Picket Fence Drive
Toronto, Ontario
M2B 4L7

(17) Document Prepared by:
Susan Smart
Barrister and Solicitor
456 Bay Street
Toronto, Ontario
M5G 8D3

Total

**Figure 28.9 Concluded**

Province
of
Ontario

DYE & DURHAM CO. INC.—Form No. 286
Amended NOV. 1992

**Schedule**
Land Registration Reform Act
**Recitals for Deed Under Power of Sale (Registry)**
*(Attach to Form 1)*

Page 2 of 2

**S**

**WHEREAS:**

1.  By a Mortgage dated the 1st day of February (year) and registered in the Land Registry Office

    for the Registry Division for the City of Toronto (No. 64)

    as Instrument No. 987654 on the 3rd day of February (year) ,

    David Defaulter and Donna Defaulter

    as Mortgagor

    did mortgage the lands herein to

    Secure Trust Company

    as Mortgagee

    for securing payment of the sum of SIXTY THOUSAND----------------------------------

    --------------------------($60,000.00)--------------------------------- DOLLARS

    and interest as therein mentioned.

2.  The Mortgagee, on default of payment under the said Mortgage for fifteen days

    is entitled on thirty-five days' notice to sell the said lands.

3.  Such default has been made in payment of the principal and interest secured by the said Mortgage and notice of

    exercising the power to sell the said lands has been duly given by the Mortgagee to all persons entitled thereto.

4.  Such default has not been remedied and the time set forth in the notice of sale has expired.

5.  Statutory Declarations setting forth the particulars of such default, the service of notice of sale and the sale pro-

    ceedings have been deposited and registered in the said Land Registry Office as Instrument No. 987654

    AND THEREFORE under and by virtue of the powers of sale contained in the said Mortgage, the said lands were sold

    to the Transferee.

In construing this document, the words "Mortgagor", "Mortgagee" and "Transferee" and all personal pronouns shall be read as the number and
gender of the party or parties referred to herein requires and all necessary grammatical changes, as the context requires, shall be deemed to be made.

FOR OFFICE USE ONLY

# Acting for the Mortgagee

# 29

## LEARNING OUTCOMES

After reading this chapter, you will understand:

- How to prepare both paper and electronic charge/mortgage documents

- The requirements for a new charge/mortgage

- The requirements for refinancing a property by way of a charge/mortgage when your firm acted on the purchase of the property

- The requirements for refinancing a property by way of charge/mortgage when your firm did not act on the purchase of the property

- What amounts may be deducted from the mortgage proceeds

# Introduction

There are several situations in which your firm will act for the mortgagee. The most common one is when your client is financing a purchase by way of a third-party mortgage, and your firm is representing both the buyer and the mortgagee.

You may also act for the mortgagee when your client is refinancing his or her property. The owner may be getting a new first mortgage to replace an existing one or a second mortgage, perhaps as a line of credit or perhaps to finance an unrelated purchase (a car, for example).

If you act on a purchase transaction involving a vendor-take-back mortgage, your firm may prepare the mortgage document even though the seller's lawyer is representing the seller/mortgagee.

In all cases, the preparation of the documents is the same.

# An Overview of the Process

The mortgagee sends instructions to your firm, setting out the terms of the mortgage and the mortgagee's specific requirements. Mortgagees usually require title insurance or

- a statement by the lawyer that he or she has verified that the owner has good and marketable title;
- proof of adequate insurance on the property;
- a direction to the mortgagee as to how the mortgage funds are to be paid; and
- completion and registration of the charge/mortgage of land.

In addition, mortgagees may require

- life and/or disability insurance (or the mortgagor's waiver of same); and
- a sample cheque on the mortgagor's account (to allow for automatic withdrawal of mortgage payments).

Some mortgagees want to receive an interim report from your firm stating that these requirements have been met before releasing the funds under the mortgage. Many do not require an interim report, but rely on the lawyer to follow their instructions. The mortgagee will then release the funds, either by sending your firm a cheque in the amount your client is entitled to receive under the mortgage, or by directly depositing this amount into your firm's trust account. In a purchase, you will use this money as part of the balance due on closing. If your client is getting a new first mortgage to replace an existing one, the money will be used to discharge the existing mortgage. When the transaction is completed, the mortgagee will want to receive a final report.

# Preliminary Matters

You must take certain steps before you can ask the mortgagee to release the funds.

## Title Searches

If the mortgage is part of a purchase transaction, you can rely on the searches you are already conducting for the buyer. In the case of a refinancing, if you acted for the owners on their purchase of the property, you can rely on the searches that you conducted at that time. However, you must conduct a subsearch from the last time you registered a document to make sure there have been no new registrations. If it is a refinancing, and you did *not* act for the owners on their purchase, you will have to do a full search to ensure that the owners have good title to the property, and to verify that the mortgagee's security is protected. For example, if it is to be a second mortgage, you must make sure there is only one mortgage already on title. If it is to be a first mortgage to replace an existing one, you must make sure that there is only one mortgage on title.

## Other Inquiries

If your client is refinancing to replace an existing first mortgage, you will have to contact the existing first mortgagee to find out how much money is required to get a discharge of the mortgage, so that the new mortgagee will have a valid and secure first mortgage.

## Title Insurance

Most mortgagees will require that the client have title insurance. See Chapter 17 for a discussion of title insurance.

## Proof of Insurance

The mortgagee is taking an interest in the property as security for its loan. If the buildings on the property are damaged or destroyed, the value of its security will decrease. Accordingly, the mortgagee wants to make sure that the property is insured to its full insurable value and that the insurance proceeds will be paid to the mortgagee.

You must advise the buyer to obtain insurance on the property. Get the name, address, and telephone number of the insurance agent. Call the insurance agent to provide the name and address of the mortgagee and ask for an **insurance binder** confirming

- the name of the insurance company;
- the policy number;
- the amount of the coverage; and
- the inclusion of a standard mortgage clause providing for payment to the mortgagee.

**insurance binder**
documented confirmation that a property has been insured and that, in the event of a claim, insurance proceeds will be paid to the mortgagee

# Document Preparation

There are a number of documents that you have to prepare.

## Mortgage Preparation

The form of the document used depends on whether the property is in the Registry system or, far more likely, the Land Titles system.

### Registry Properties

If the property you are dealing with is in the Registry system, the form used is the standard POLARIS paper form used for mortgages under the *Land Registration Reform Act*. It is called a charge/mortgage of land and contains numbered boxes that you must fill in. A blank copy of the form is reproduced as Figure 29.1, at the end of the chapter.

- Boxes 1, 3, and 5 deal with the legal description of the property. Copy the information from the corresponding boxes in the draft transfer (if the mortgage is part of a purchase transaction). If it is a refinancing, have the client bring in his or her original transfer/deed of land.

- Box 4 contains the principal amount of the mortgage. Get the amount from the mortgage instructions and insert it first in words and then in numbers (like a cheque).

- Box 8 is entitled Standard Charge Terms. All institutional lenders use certain mortgage terms in all of their mortgages. Under the *Land Registration Reform Act*, these commonly used terms are not included in each mortgage document that is registered on title. Instead, each lender drafts a set of its own **standard charge terms** and files it with the government, which then assigns a number to it. The actual mortgage document includes only the principal amount; the interest rate; payment amounts and due dates; and special additional provisions, such as prepayment privileges. The standard charge terms are incorporated into the document by reference to the assigned number. The mortgagor must be given a copy of the standard charge terms, which will be included with your instructions from the mortgagee. To complete box 8, insert the number found on the standard charge terms provided.

- Box 9 sets out the payment provisions of the mortgage. Some mortgagees require that the interest rate and calculation period be set out in a schedule attached to the mortgage rather than in box 9. In that case, the principal amount of the mortgage is inserted in box 9(a) but the rest of box 9 is completed by reference to the schedule. Other mortgagees require that box 9 be completed in full, according to their instructions. In that case, box 9 is completed as follows:

  (a) *Principal Amount.* Insert this amount in numbers only.

  (b) *Interest Rate.* Insert the rate in numbers only, or insert "See Schedule 1."

  (c) *Calculation Period.* This is the period over which interest is calculated under the mortgage. The calculation period may be inserted here or on an attached schedule.

  (d) *Interest Adjustment Date.* This is the date from which interest starts to accumulate and, assuming that the mortgage is paid monthly, will be one month before the date of the first payment, or, if a schedule is used, will be left blank.

**standard charge terms** mortgage terms that are used in all mortgages issued by an institutional lender, which are filed with the government and are then assigned a file number

(e) *Payment Date and Period.* This specifies when payments are to be made under the mortgage. For example, if the payments are to be made on the 1st day of every month, insert "1st—monthly," or if the mortgage is payable on demand, insert "On demand."

(f) *First Payment Date.* Insert the date on which the first mortgage payment is to be made, or, if payable on demand, leave it blank.

(g) *Last Payment Date.* Insert the date on which the last payment under the mortgage is to be made, or, if payable on demand, leave it blank.

(h) *Amount of Each Payment.* Insert the amount in words and numbers, or, if payable on demand, leave it blank.

(i) *Balance Due Date.* This is usually the same date as the last payment date, or, if the mortgage is payable on demand, is left blank. If the mortgage has not been paid in full, the balance of the principal must be paid on this day. Usually the mortgagor will have to renew the mortgage or arrange a new one.

(j) *Insurance.* The common practice is to insert the words "Full insurable value" or "See Standard Charge Terms."

- Box 10 sets out any additional provisions not included in the standard charge terms, such as prepayment privileges. If there are any additional provisions, the exact wording is usually provided in the mortgagee's letter of instructions. If the provisions do not fit in the box, insert the words "See attached schedule" and set out the provisions on the schedule. In box 6(b), check "Other."

- Box 11 requires a statement of age and spousal status. You will have to obtain this information from the buyer. See Chapter 21 for a discussion of the wording of this statement. You must also insert the name of the mortgagor in exactly the same form used in box 11 of the transfer/deed of land.

- Box 12 provides a place for spousal consent, if required. This box must be completed only if box 11 states, "I am a spouse. The person consenting below is my spouse."

- Box 13 sets out the mortgagor's address for service. It should be the same address as set out in box 12 of the transfer/deed of land.

- Boxes 14 and 15 set out the name and address of the mortgagee.

- Boxes 16 and 17 should be the same as boxes 15 and 16 of the transfer/deed of land.

## Land Titles Properties

If the property is in the Land Titles system (as most will be), the charge is prepared electronically. The document is completed, according to the mortgagee's instructions, in much the same way as the electronic transfer, discussed in Chapters 7 and 21. The information that goes into an electronic charge is the same as that in the paper charge, but it is formatted differently, as you can see from Figure 29.2. Teraview creates a separate acknowledgment and direction for the charge/mortgage, which must be signed by the mortgagor to evidence consent and authorization to use e-reg. See Figure 21.18 in Chapter 21 for a sample. Print a paper copy of the mortgage document from e-reg to give to the mortgagor together with a copy of any schedules that are attached to the registered document. This is to comply with section 4 of the *Mortgages Act*, which requires that a copy of the mortgage be delivered to the mortgagor.

## Direction Regarding Funds

Your law firm will usually want the mortgage proceeds to be made payable to your firm in trust. The buyer will have to give the mortgagee a written direction to that effect. A sample direction regarding funds is shown in Figure 21.14 in Chapter 21. Make sure that the direction is addressed to the mortgagee and not to the buyer, and is signed by the mortgagor (the buyer) and not the seller.

## Other Forms and Matters

Mortgagees often offer life and/or disability insurance policies to mortgagors. Under these policies, the mortgage will be paid if the mortgagor dies or becomes disabled. The policies are optional, but most mortgagees will want the mortgagor to sign a waiver if the insurance is not desired.

If the mortgage payments will be taken automatically from the mortgagor's bank account, the mortgagee will require a sample cheque. Obtain a cheque from the client with the word "VOID" written across it in large letters.

## Interim Report to Mortgagee

Once you have prepared the mortgage documents, depending on the mortgagee's instructions, you may have to complete the mortgagee's standard-form interim report on title and enclose all of the required documents. Interim reports are usually faxed or sent electronically to the mortgagee.

# Preparation for Registration

A number of steps are necessary before you are ready to register the mortgage documents.

## Review and Execution of Documents

You must arrange to have the mortgagor attend at your office to sign the charge/ mortgage, the direction regarding the mortgage funds, and the acknowledgment and direction, as well as other documents such as declarations regarding construction liens, a statement as to spousal status, and sometimes a statement regarding the state of the property as shown on a survey. If the mortgage is part of a purchase, this can usually be done at the same time that the client is signing the purchase documents. You or the lawyer handling the file will also have to review the terms of the charge/mortgage and the standard charge terms with the client, to make sure that the client understands the terms and that the terms match the **mortgage commit-ment** (the client's agreement with the institutional lender when the mortgage was arranged). If you are reviewing the documents with the client and any questions or problems arise, you should turn the matter over to the lawyer handling the file.

mortgage commitment
the mortgagor's agreement
with the mortgagee when
the mortgage is arranged

## The Mortgage Funds

You should tell the client how much money the mortgagee will be advancing under the mortgage. Sometimes that amount will be less than the principal of the mortgage because the mortgagee will make deductions for the following:

- *Appraisal fees.* The mortgagee may have required the property to be appraised and may charge the mortgagor a fee for the appraisal.
- *An interest adjustment.* Monthly mortgage payments are sometimes paid on the 1st or the 15th of each month, or on a weekly or bi-weekly basis. If the transaction is closing on another day of the month, the mortgagee will sometimes deduct an amount to cover the interest from the closing date to the date of the next payment, which is the interest adjustment date.
- *Mortgage insurance fees.* If the mortgage is for more than 80 percent of the purchase price, the mortgagee will require the mortgagor to pay for mortgage insurance through the Canada Mortgage and Housing Corporation. In that case, the mortgagor will have to pay an insurance application fee and a one-time premium for the mortgage insurance.

The mortgagee will give your law firm the mortgage funds, usually by way of a cheque payable to your law firm in trust, in accordance with your client's direction regarding funds. You will have to make arrangements to have the cheque picked up from the mortgagee. Sometimes the mortgagee will arrange to transfer the funds directly into your law firm's trust account. The mortgage funds are payable to the law firm in trust on the understanding that your law firm will not release the money to the seller until the mortgage has been registered (during the closing of the transaction).

## Payments out of the Mortgage Funds

If the mortgage that you registered is being used to replace an existing mortgage, or to pay a property owner's other debts, you may be required to provide the mortgagee with proof that the necessary payments were made. In the case of a replacement mortgage, you may have to provide the mortgagee with the registration particulars of the discharge of the original mortgage.

# Final Report to Mortgagee

When the mortgage has been registered, you must complete the mortgagee's standard-form final report, which confirms that all its requirements have been met, the charge/mortgage of land has been registered on title, and the mortgagee has a good and valid first (or second, as the case may be) mortgage on the property. You enclose

- the duplicate registered charge/mortgage of land (or a copy of the electronic charge if the document was registered electronically);
- the insurance binder;
- the mortgagor's direction regarding funds (if not previously forwarded); and
- in the case of a refinancing, proof of any payments that you made, or particulars of a discharge registered, as required by the mortgagee.

## KEY TERMS

insurance binder, 457

mortgage commitment, 461

standard charge terms, 458

## REFERENCES

*Income Tax Act*, RSC 1985, c 1 (5th Supp), as amended.

*Land Registration Reform Act*, RSO 1990, c L.4.

*Mortgages Act*, RSO 1990, c M.40.

## REVIEW QUESTIONS

1. Bora is buying a house with a closing date of April 15th. He is financing with a mortgage. The mortgagee wants the payments to be made on the first of each month. What would be the interest adjustment date and the first payment date?

2. Why might a mortgagee require an interim report?

3. What is an insurance binder?

4. What is the purpose of standard charge terms?

5. Sandeep is getting a mortgage on his property, which is in the Land Titles system. What document will he have to sign with his lawyer in order to authorize his lawyer to register the mortgage electronically on his behalf?

6. Why is the amount that the mortgagee advances sometimes less than the principal amount of the mortgage?

# Figure 29.1 Charge/Mortgage of Land

Province of Ontario

## Charge/Mortgage of Land

Form 2 — Land Registration Reform Act

DYE & DURHAM CFS POLARIS 1995

**B**

FOR OFFICE USE ONLY

New Property Identifiers — Additional: See Schedule ☐

Executions — Additional: See Schedule ☐

**(1) Registry** ☐ **Land Titles** ☐

**(2) Page 1 of** pages

**(3) Property Identifier(s)** Block Property — Additional: See Schedule ☐

**(4) Principal Amount** Dollars $

**(5) Description**

**(6) This Document Contains** (a) Redescription New Easement Plan/Sketch ☐ (b) Schedule for: Description ☐ Additional Parties ☐ Other ☐

**(7) Interest/Estate Charged**

**(8) Standard Charge Terms** — The parties agree to be bound by the provisions in Standard Charge Terms filed as number and the Chargor(s) hereby acknowledge(s) receipt of a copy of these terms.

**(9) Payment Provisions**

| | | | |
|---|---|---|---|
| (a) Principal Amount $ | (b) Interest Rate % per annum | (c) Calculation Period | |
| (d) Interest Adjustment Date Y M D | (e) Payment Date and Period | (f) First Payment Date Y M D | |
| (g) Last Payment Date | (h) Amount of Each Payment | Dollars $ | |
| (i) Balance Due Date | (j) Insurance | Dollars $ | |

**(10) Additional Provisions**

Continued on Schedule ☐

**(11) Chargor(s)** The chargor hereby charges the land to the chargee and certifies that the chargor is at least eighteen years old and that

The chargor(s) acknowledge(s) receipt of a true copy of this charge.

Name(s) Signature(s) Date of Signature Y M D

**(12) Spouse(s) of Chargor(s)** I hereby consent to this transaction.

Name(s) Signature(s) Date of Signature Y M D

**(13) Chargor(s) Address for Service**

**(14) Chargee(s)**

**(15) Chargee(s) Address for Service**

**(16) Assessment Roll Number of Property** Cty. Mun. Map Sub. Par.

**(17) Municipal Address of Property**

**(18) Document Prepared by:**

FOR OFFICE USE ONLY

| Fees | |
|---|---|
| Registration Fee | |
| | |
| | |
| | |
| Total | |

# Figure 29.2   Charge Created Electronically

LRO # 65   **Charge/Mortgage**                              **In preparation**  on  2015 07 02      at  10:26

*This document has not been submitted and may be incomplete.*                    yyyy mm dd      Page 1 of 2

## Properties

*PIN*   12345-6789            *LT*          *Interest/Estate*     Fee Simple

*Description*   Parcel 170-1, Section 65M-1234

*Address*      166 Valley Road
               Newmarket, Ontario

## Chargor(s)

The chargor(s) hereby charges the land to the chargee(s). The chargor(s) acknowledges the receipt of the charge and the standard charge terms, if any.

*Name*              GRANT, HENRY ALBERT
                    Acting as an individual

*Address for Service*   166 Valley Road
                        Newmarket, Ontario
                        L3H 1V2

I am at least 18 years of age.

I am not a spouse

This document is not authorized  under Power of Attorney by this party.

*Name*              GRANT, WILMA HEATHER
                    Acting as an individual

*Address for Service*   166 Valley Road
                        Newmarket, Ontario
                        L3H 1V2

I am at least 18 years of age.

I am not a spouse

This document is not authorized  under Power of Attorney by this party.

## Chargee(s)                                    *Capacity*              *Share*

*Name*              DATA BANK OF CANADA
                    Acting as a company

*Address for Service*   111 Richmond Street
                        Toronto, Ontario
                        M1B 1B1

## Figure 29.2 Concluded

LRO # 65 **Charge/Mortgage**                                                In preparation  on  2015 07 02      at  10:26

*This document has not been submitted and may be incomplete.*                                        yyyy mm dd     Page 2 of 2

| **Provisions** |
| --- |

|  |  | | |
| --- | --- | --- | --- |
| *Principal* | $ 350,000.00 | *Currency* | CDN |
| *Calculation Period* | semi annually, not in advance | | |
| *Balance Due Date* | 2020/12/31 | | |
| *Interest Rate* | 3.0% | | |
| *Payments* | $740.00 (monthly) | | |
| *Interest Adjustment Date* | 2015 12 31 | | |
| *Payment Date* | first day of each month | | |
| *First Payment Date* | 2016 01 31 | | |
| *Last Payment Date* | 2020 12 31 | | |
| *Standard Charge Terms* | 202020 | | |
| *Insurance Amount* | full insurable value | | |
| *Guarantor* | | | |

# Glossary

**abstract:** record of all registrations affecting a parcel of land

**abstract book:** book in the Registry system that records registered interests in land

**abstracting:** process of examining and summarizing into search notes the contents of all registered documents that affect title

**accelerate:** demand immediate payment

**acceleration clause:** clause permitting the chargee to demand immediate payment of the full amount of the loan in the event of default

**acknowledgment and direction:** document signed by a party to a real estate transaction authorizing his or her lawyer to sign and release a document electronically on his or her behalf

**adjoining land:** property that shares a common boundary with the property being searched

**advanced:** given or provided

**adverse possession:** valid title to land through open, visible, and uninterrupted possession of that property, without the owner's permission, for a period of at least 10 years

**adversely:** without the owner's permission

**affidavit of spousal status:** affidavit attached to a deed (in use after 1978 until the *Land Registration Reform Act* came into force) that provided evidence of the marital status of the grantors or transferors

**agreement of purchase and sale:** contract created once an offer of purchase and sale has been accepted

**amortization period:** length of time it takes to repay a loan in full following the schedule of monthly payments in the charge

**amortization schedule:** schedule setting out the breakdown of each monthly blended payment between principal and interest, and the remaining principal balance after each payment

**annexation:** attachment

**arrears of rent:** unpaid rent that is owed to a landlord

**assignment:** arrangement whereby a tenant transfers tenancy to another person for the remainder of the tenancy's term

**assumed charge:** existing charge taken over by the buyer, who pays the seller the purchase price of the property minus the outstanding balance of the charge

**balance due on closing:** exact amount the buyer pays to the seller when the real estate deal closes

**balloon payment:** final payment for the amount of principal that remains unpaid at the end of the term of a charge

**binder letter:** a letter from an insurance company confirming that the property will be insured as of a specific date, and showing the amount of coverage, and the names of the mortgagees

**blanket mortgage:** a mortgage creating a lien against more than one property; developers use blanket mortgages when subdividing large parcels of land into many separate lots; a blanket mortgage is spread over the entire parcel of land, rather than applied to each individual lot

**blended payment:** charge payment combining principal and interest into equal monthly payments

**block:** area of land created during the mapping of property under POLARIS

**block number:** five-digit number assigned to a block; the first part of the PIN

**bona fide purchaser for value:** buyer of property who gives valuable consideration for the property and is acting in good faith

**building permit:** document that grants legal permission to start construction of a building, as defined by the *Building Code Act, 1992*

**buyer:** purchaser of the property

**bylaw:** law that is passed by a municipality

**bylaws (condominium):** rules governing the internal operation of the condominium corporation

**capital gains tax:** federal tax levied on the profit realized when capital property, other than a principal residence, is sold

*caveat emptor:* Latin term meaning "let the buyer beware"

**certificate of action:** certificate of the court verifying that a statement of claim has been filed in a construction lien action

**certify title:** describe the state of the owner's title, including any limitations

**chain of title:** list of all owners within the search period

**chargee:** lender

**chargee in possession:** chargee who takes possession of the charged property after default by the chargor

**chargor:** borrower and owner

**chattels:** movable possessions not attached to the real property

**Children's Lawyer:** government official charged with protecting the best interests of children in the province

**closed charge:** charge that prohibits repayment of the loan before the expiry of the term

**closing date:** day on which a real estate transaction is completed and title is transferred

**commencement date:** starting date of the title search period

**commit waste:** destroy, abuse, or make permanent undesirable changes to a property

**committee of adjustment:** independent body appointed by a municipality with the authority to grant consent to conveyances that result in a severance

**common elements:** areas of the condominium development owned by all of the individual unit owners as tenants in common

**common-elements condominium (CEC):** a condominium composed solely of common elements

**common expenses:** monthly fees paid by unit owners to cover the condominium corporation's obligations

**compliance with law statement:** a lawyer's statement that the applicable legal requirements have been met

**compounding interest:** adding interest to the principal and then calculating future interest on that amount

**concession:** large parcel of land created during the original division of land in Ontario resulting from the creation of east–west road allowances in a township

**condominium corporation:** corporation that comes into existence upon registration of the condominium plan and whose role is to manage and administer the condominium property

**condominium unit:** unit that is part of a condominium development

**consent to variance:** committee of adjustment approval of a building or use of a property when it does not conform to a current bylaw and is not a legal non-conforming use

**construction lien:** lien against land that may be claimed by a person providing labour, services, or materials to a construction project

**construction pyramid:** illustration of the contractual relationships between parties in a typical large construction project

**cooling-off period:** 10-day period during which the buyer can back out of the purchase

**counteroffer:** offer tendered by the original offeree as an alternative to the original offer; also known as a sign-back

**covenant:** promise

**Crown patent:** grant of land by the Crown (the government) to the first owner

**damages:** financial compensation for losses arising out of a breach of contract

**declarant:** upon registration, the person who owns the land described in the description and who registers the declaration and description that create the condominium plan

**declaration:** document that describes the units, setting out their boundaries, the percentage of common elements associated with each unit, and the percentage of common expenses that each unit owner will be required to pay

**deed:** document that transfers ownership of land

**deemed:** accepted as conclusive of a certain state or condition in the absence of evidence or facts usually required to prove that state or condition

**default:** breach of one or more of the obligations contained in the charge; most commonly, the failure to remit principal and interest payments when due

**deposit:** (1) part of the purchase price prepaid when the contract is entered into and applied against the purchase price; (2) document registered on title that verifies or clarifies facts related to the title

**description:** document that includes a survey showing the boundaries of the units, common elements, and exclusive-use common elements

**diarize:** record on a calendar the dates by which work must be completed

**digital signatures:** unique digital identifiers used by lawyers when documents are registered electronically, comparable to a password or bank PIN

**disbursements:** a lawyer's out-of-pocket expenses

**discharge of charge:** a document given by the chargee to the chargor confirming that the loan has been paid in full and extinguishing the chargee's interest in the property

**discharge of lien:** document registered on title that discharges a construction lien

**disclosure statement:** document given to every buyer of a condominium unit that includes details pertaining to the physical, legal, and financial aspects of the condominium corporation

**distress:** the right of a commercial landlord to seize and dispose of a tenant's property

**docket:** file in which all documents pertaining to a particular transaction are located

**document registration agreement (DRA):** agreement entered into by the lawyers for the parties in a purchase and sale transaction that deals with the procedures for electronic registration and the escrow closing arrangement

**dominant tenement:** land that benefits from an easement

**dower:** entitlement of a widow to a one-third life interest in the total value of any land that her husband owned during their marriage

**due-on-sale clause:** provision in a charge permitting the chargee to accelerate full payment of the loan in the event that the chargor sells the property and the chargee does not approve the buyer

**e-reg:** an electronic registration system under POLARIS

**easement:** right to use a portion of someone else's land for a specific purpose, without requiring the owner's permission

**easement implied by law:** easement that is created when the only way to gain access to a property is by crossing over another property

**encroachment:** building or structure intruding upon someone else's land

**encumbrances:** charges, claims, liens, or liabilities attached to a property

**environmental audit clause:** clause in the agreement of purchase and sale that provides the buyer with the right to obtain an environmental audit or soil test of the property, and that, if the audit discloses the existence of contamination on the property, gives the buyer the right to either terminate the transaction or insist that the seller clean up the contamination

**escheat:** reversion of property to the Crown

**escrow closing:** exchange and holding of documents, keys, and money by the lawyers pending registration of the electronic documents

**estate:** interest in land that provides the right to exclusive possession

**exclusive possession:** sole possession of the land; denial of possession to all others

**exclusive-use common elements:** areas of the condominium development owned by all unit owners but used only by designated unit owners

**execution:** signing of a document; also a short name for a writ of execution or a writ of seizure and sale

**express grant:** creation of an easement by written document from the owner of the servient tenement to the owner of the dominant tenement

**expropriation:** reacquisition of land, with compensation, by the Crown for public purposes

**extinguish:** bring to an end

**fault grounds:** grounds for termination based on the conduct or behaviour of the tenant or a guest of the tenant

**fee simple (or freehold) estate:** the right to exclusive possession and the right to dispose of the land for an indefinite period of time

**first charge:** charge registered first and thus taking priority over subsequently registered charges

**fixed interest rate:** rate of interest that remains the same for the term of the charge

**fixed-term tenancy:** tenancy that has a specified beginning and end date; can be for any period of time, from months to years

**fixtures:** immovable possessions attached to the real property, or chattels that have become attached or affixed to the real property

**flip:** resale of property before the closing of the original purchase

**foreclosure:** court action whereby the chargee obtains legal title to the property after default by the chargor

**forfeit:** lose the right

**grant:** document that transfers ownership of land

**grantee:** person who receives title to real property

**grantor:** person who transfers title to real property

**harmonized sales tax (HST):** blended federal and provincial sales tax

**high ratio mortgage:** a mortgage for more than 80 percent of the value of the property

**holdback:** sum of money required to be deducted by the payer and held for a specified period of time from the amount owing to a payee in a construction contract

**improvement:** changes made to real property, including construction, alteration, repair, installation, erection, and demolition

**in escrow:** holding of funds or documents by a third party to be released only on certain specified conditions

**institutional lender:** lender other than an individual, including a bank, trust company, credit union, or insurance company

**insurance binder:** documented confirmation that a property has been insured and that, in the event of a claim, insurance proceeds will be paid to the mortgagee

**interest:** amount added to the principal amount of the loan in return for the right to obtain and use the money advanced

**interest adjustment date:** date on which an adjustment is made for interest that accumulates between the date the loan was advanced and the charge payment date for the following month; assuming that charge payments are being made monthly, this date will be one month before the date of the first regular payment

**interest differential:** difference between the lender's current interest rate and the interest rate of the charge

**interest rate:** rate charged for the use of borrowed money, calculated as a percentage of the amount of the loan

**interests:** rights to land that are not estates and do not confer a right to exclusive possession of the land

**interim occupancy date:** date on which the buyer takes possession prior to final closing and transfer of title

**joint tenants:** two or more people owning property where on the death of one, the survivors inherit the deceased's share

**judgment creditor:** party to whom a court awards the payment of money

**judgment debtor:** party against whom a court awards the payment of money

**judicial sale:** sale of charged property ordered and administered by a court

**Land Titles Absolute (LT Absolute):** properties originally in the Land Titles system; corporate existence and *Planning Act* compliance are not guaranteed

**Land Titles Assurance Fund:** fund established under the *Land Titles Act* to compensate a person wrongfully deprived of an estate or interest in land as a result of an error regarding title

**Land Titles Conversion Qualified (LTCQ):** properties originally in the Registry system and converted to the Land Titles system as a result of POLARIS; *Planning Act* compliance and corporate existence are guaranteed for the period prior to the date of conversion; properties remain subject to any pre-existing mature claims for adverse possession, prescription, or misdescription

**Land Titles Plus (LT Plus):** properties upgraded from LTCQ with the additional guarantee against any mature claims for adverse possession

**Land Titles system:** land registration system in Ontario governed by the *Land Titles Act*

**land transfer tax:** provincial (and possibly municipal) tax on the purchase of land

**Large Value Transfer System:** electronic wire payment system which allows for the transfer of large sums between financial institutions

**latent defect:** defect of which the seller of a property was aware but which the buyer did not know about and could not have discovered upon reasonable inspection of the property

**Law Society of Upper Canada (LSUC):** professional body governing the activities of lawyers in Ontario

**Lawyers' Professional Indemnity Company (LAWPRO):** insurance company controlled by the Law Society of Upper Canada that insures lawyers against errors and omissions and administers TitlePLUS, a title insurance product

**leasehold estate:** right to exclusive possession of property for a specified period of time in return for the payment of rent

**legal description:** description of land that is used in documents creating an interest in land; describes the land with reference to recorded maps, surveys, or plans

**legal non-conforming use:** status of a building or use of a property that does not conform to the current municipal bylaw but is acceptable because the building or use existed before the passing of the bylaw and has not subsequently been altered or discontinued

**lien:** charge for payment of a debt that allows the land to be sold to satisfy the debt

**life estate:** right to exclusive possession of the property for the length of a particular lifetime

**lot:** 200-acre parcel of land created during the original division of land into concessions; also, a parcel of land created by a plan of subdivision

**matrimonial home:** defined under the *Family Law Act* to include every property in which a person has an interest and that is (if the parties are still married), or was (if the parties have separated) at the time of separation, occupied by the spouses as their family residence

**maturity date:** date on which any outstanding balance of a charge is to be paid

**metes and bounds description:** written description of the boundaries and dimensions of a parcel of land in relation to lot lines; enables a sketch of the parcel to provide a picture of the area of land

**monthly tenancy:** a periodic tenancy that renews automatically at the end of each month until terminated by the landlord or the tenant

**mortgage commitment:** the mortgagor's agreement with the mortgagee when the mortgage is arranged

**mortgagee:** lender

**mortgagor:** borrower and owner

**municipality:** form of urban organization including cities, towns, and villages

**natural environment:** air, land, and water, or any combination or part thereof

**new charge:** arrangement by the buyer for a new loan by way of a charge for the purchase of property

**no-fault grounds:** grounds for termination unrelated to the conduct or behaviour of the tenant or a guest of the tenant

**non-blended payment:** charge payment that does not blend or combine principal and interest into equal payments; the amount of principal repaid each month is a fixed amount and the amount of interest is calculated on the outstanding principal at the time

**notice of sale under mortgage:** document used in a power of sale setting out the particulars of the default and the amounts owing under the charge

**offer:** proposal from one person to another that, when accepted, becomes a contract

**offeree:** person to whom an offer is made

**offeror:** person who makes an offer

**official plan:** statement of planning principles prepared for a municipality by the local planning board

**off-title documents:** documents that are required for closing but are not registered on title

**open a file:** start a file

**open charge:** charge that permits repayment of the loan before the expiry of the term

**parcel register:** book in the Land Titles system that records all registered interests in land

**parcels of tied land (POTLs):** parcels of land whose owners have consented to their property being permanently tied to a common-elements condominium

**part lot control:** government control over transactions involving part of a subdivision lot

**per diem:** per day; for each day; daily

**perfect:** ensure that a preserved lien does not expire by commencing an action to enforce the lien and registering a certificate of action against title to the property

**periodic tenancy:** a tenancy that renews automatically at the end of the relevant period until terminated by either the tenant or the landlord, the period being defined by the frequency of rental payments

**personal property:** chattels; property that is not real property

**personal undertaking:** a written promise given by a lawyer that is binding on the lawyer personally

**phase I environmental assessment:** assessment of property conducted to determine the likelihood that one or more contaminants have affected all or part of the property

**phase II environmental assessment:** assessment of property conducted to determine the location and concentration of contaminants on the property; follows completion of a phase I environmental assessment

**plan of subdivision:** registered plan illustrating the measurements and boundaries of all lots and streets created by the division of concession lots into many smaller lots

**plan of survey:** schematic sketch showing the boundaries of a property and the location of all fences, structures, and rights of way

**POLARIS:** Province of Ontario Land Registration Information System; computerized land information system

**possession:** control or occupancy of land regardless of ownership

**power of attorney:** document authorizing someone to deal with land or other property on the owner's behalf

**power of sale:** power to exercise the remedy of sale in case of default under a charge

**prepayment penalty:** penalty charged by the lender if the borrower pays off the charge before the end of the term

**pre-population:** electronic process of copying information from a database into a document

**prescription:** means by which an interest is acquired in another's land after a period of 20 years of open and uninterrupted use

**preserve:** ensure that lien rights are protected and do not expire by registering a claim for lien against title to the property on which work was performed within 45 days of completion of the work

**prime lending rate:** interest rate, based on the Bank of Canada rate, at which banks lend to most credit-worthy customers

**principal:** amount of money borrowed under a loan

**priority:** rank or status of a registered interest in land as determined by the date of registration of that interest

**privity of contract:** doctrine of contract law that prevents a person from seeking enforcement of a contract unless he or she is a party to the contract

**profit à prendre:** interest created when mineral rights are acquired in the land of another person

**property:** term used to describe area of land created by the division of blocks during the mapping of land under POLARIS

**property identifier number (PIN):** unique nine-digit number for each property created by combining the block number and property number for that property

**property number:** four-digit number assigned to a property; the second part of the PIN

**proposed declarant:** prior to the registration of the declaration and description, the person who owns the land described in the description

**public utility:** system that provides to the public water, sewage, fuel (including natural gas), energy (excluding electricity), heating, cooling, or telephone supplies or services

**real property:** land, including everything that is attached to it

**realize on the security:** seize and/or sell the charged property

**recital:** statement that sets out facts on which a document is based

**redeem:** release or free land from a claim against it by paying the amount owing under the charge

**redemption period:** period of 35 days, after the chargor is in default, during which (1) the chargor has the opportunity to put the charge back into good standing and redeem the property and (2) the chargee cannot take steps to sell the property

**reference plan:** registered survey prepared to illustrate the boundaries of a parcel of land

**Registry system:** land registration system in Ontario governed by the *Registry Act*

**reporting letter:** letter signed by the lawyer, outlining what was done in the transaction

**requisition:** request made to the seller to clear up problems revealed by the title search and other inquiries

**requisition date:** deadline by which the buyer must submit any title requisitions to the seller

**requisition going to the root of title:** requisition based on a defect that calls into question the legal enforceability/validity of the title

**requisition on conveyance:** requisition that requires the seller to produce an effective conveyance, assuming that the seller has the ability to do so

**requisition on matters of contract:** requisition for specific things that the buyer is entitled to receive under the contract

**requisition on title:** query of directives made by the buyer that asks the seller to remedy problems with title

**reserve fund:** fund that covers costs of major repairs to and replacement of common elements

**restrictive covenant:** promise by an owner of land to refrain from doing something on the property

**right of survivorship:** automatic vesting of an interest in the surviving joint tenant or tenants when one joint tenant dies

**right of way:** right to use a portion of another's land for access purposes

**riparian rights:** rights to the use of a watercourse running through or adjacent to the property

**root of title (root deed):** first conveyance of the fee simple estate (a deed or transfer) registered after the commencement date of a title search

**search notes:** summary of the contents of all registered documents affecting title; reveals the state of the title including any encumbrances

**search the title:** conduct an investigation into the status and history of title to land

**second charge:** charge registered after the first charge and thus having subsequent priority to the first

**seller:** vendor of the property

**servient tenement:** land over which an easement runs

**severance:** division of land into smaller parcels

**sign-back:** offer whereby the original offeree changes some of the terms in the original offer, initials the changes, and then submits it to the original offeror

**simultaneous conveyance:** two abutting parcels of land conveyed at the same time to two different people

**specific performance:** court order requiring a transaction to be completed; a type of remedy for breach of contract

**spousal consent:** consent of the spouse of the owner on title to the transfer or mortgage of a matrimonial home, required under the *Family Law Act*

**standard charge terms:** mortgage terms that are used in all mortgages issued by an institutional lender, which are filed with the government and are then assigned a file number

**statement of adjustments:** statement that outlines the various credits and debits against the purchase price and specifies the exact amount to be paid on closing

**status certificate:** certificate from the condominium corporation that includes, among other things, financial information, the names and addresses for service of all directors and officers, and the declaration

**statutory declaration:** sworn statement given by a person that attests to a given set of facts

**subdivision agreement:** agreement between a municipality and a builder setting out the terms under which the builder is allowed to subdivide the land

**subdivision control:** government control over the division of land into smaller parcels

**sublet:** arrangement whereby a tenant moves out of a rental unit for a period of time and allows another person to reside in the unit until the tenant returns at a specified future date

GLOSSARY

**subsearch:** brief examination of title records, undertaken on closing, that covers the period from the date of the title search up to the date of closing, to make sure that nothing has been registered on title since the title search was done

**subsequent encumbrancer:** the holder of an interest in the mortgaged property; registered on title after the mortgage

**tenancy agreement:** written, oral, or implied agreement between a landlord and a tenant that creates the tenancy

**tenants in common:** two or more people owning property where on the death of one, the deceased person's share passes to his or her heirs rather than the other owners; no right of survivorship

**tender:** presentation of executed copies of all closing documents or funds to the other party in a real estate transaction

**Teraview:** software used to access the Electronic Land Registration System in Ontario

**term:** length of time that the borrower and lender are bound by the charge contract

**termination for cause:** termination by the landlord on fault grounds

**title:** legal right to the ownership and possession of property; evidence showing such a right

**title opinion:** lawyer's statement as to whether or not the buyer has good title to the property

**title requisition:** request made to the seller to clear up a problem found during the search of title

**transfer:** document that transfers ownership of land

**transmission application:** document that is registered on title in order to enable an estate trustee to transfer property

**UFFI:** urea formaldehyde foam insulation

**unopened road allowance:** a strip of Crown land originally designated for use as a road allowance, which has never been used

**vacant possession:** free or empty of all people and chattels

**vacated:** removed from title by registration of a court order that vacates or annuls the certificate of action

**variable interest rate:** rate of interest that fluctuates with changing market conditions during the term of the loan

**vendor-take-back charge (or charge taken back):** charge created when the seller of a property agrees to lend the buyer money toward the purchase price and the buyer gives the seller a charge on the property as security for the loan

**vest:** provide an immediate right to present or future ownership or possession

**whiteprint:** copy of the plan of survey of a plan of subdivision that shows the dimensions of individual building lots

**will:** document stating how a person's property will be dealt with upon the person's death

**writ of execution:** judicial order addressed to the sheriff requiring the enforcement of a judgment

**writ of possession:** court order giving the chargee the right to take possession of the property

**zoning:** classification of permitted land use that includes categories such as residential, commercial, industrial, and agricultural

**zoning bylaws:** bylaws enacted by a municipality to regulate the use of land

# Index

# Credits